Language, the Singer and the Song

The Sociolinguistics of Folk Performance

The relationship between language and music has much in common – rhythm, structure, sound, metaphor. Exploring the phenomena of song and performance, this book presents a sociolinguistic model for analysing them. Based on ethnomusicologist John Blacking's contention that any song performed communally is a 'folk song' regardless of its generic origins, it argues that folk song to a far greater extent than other song genres displays 'communal' or 'inclusive' types of performance. The defining feature of folk song as a multimodal instantiation of music and language is its participatory nature, making it ideal for sociolinguistic analysis. In this sense, a folk song is the product of specific types of developing social interaction whose major purpose is the construction of a temporally and locally based community. Through repeated instantiations this can lead to disparate communities of practice, which, over time, develop socio-cultural registers and a communal stance towards aspects of meaningful events in everyday lives that become typical of a discourse community. Additional resources for this publication are available at www.cambridge.org/watts

RICHARD J. WATTS is emeritus professor of Modern English Linguistics, retired from the chair in that discipline at the University of Bern since 2008. He is one of the world's leading experts in linguistic politeness research and is author of five books including *Politeness* (2003) and *Language Myths and the History of English* (2011).

FRANZ ANDRES MORRISSEY is a lecturer in Modern English Linguistics at the University of Bern, Switzerland and a regular performer. He has a background in TEFL, and has published language textbooks and several papers on teaching materials and language practice through games, music and creative writing, and sociolinguistics and the sociology of language.

Language, the Singer and the Song

The Sociolinguistics of Folk Performance

Richard J. Watts
University of Bern, Switzerland

Franz Andres Morrissey
University of Bern, Switzerland

CAMBRIDGE
UNIVERSITY PRESS

CAMBRIDGE
UNIVERSITY PRESS

University Printing House, Cambridge CB2 8BS, United Kingdom

One Liberty Plaza, 20th Floor, New York, NY 10006, USA

477 Williamstown Road, Port Melbourne, VIC 3207, Australia

314-321, 3rd Floor, Plot 3, Splendor Forum, Jasola District Centre, New Delhi - 110025, India

103 Penang Road, #05-06/07, Visioncrest Commercial, Singapore 238467

Cambridge University Press is part of the University of Cambridge.

It furthers the University's mission by disseminating knowledge in the pursuit of education, learning and research at the highest international levels of excellence.

www.cambridge.org
Information on this title: www.cambridge.org/9781107533042
DOI: 10.1017/9781316285657

First published 2019
First paperback edition 2021

A catalogue record for this publication is available from the British Library

Library of Congress Cataloging in Publication data
Names: Watts, Richard J. author. | Morrissey, Franz Andres, author.
Title: Language, the singer and the song : the sociolinguistics of folk performance / Richard J. Watts, Franz Andres Morrissey.
Description: Cambridge, United Kingdom ; New York, NY: Cambridge University Press, 2019. | Includes bibliographical references and index.
Identifiers: LCCN 2017054707 | ISBN 9781107112711 (alk. paper)
Subjects: LCSH: Music – Performance – Social aspects. | Music and language. | Folk songs – History and criticism.
Classification: LCC ML3916 .W37 2018 | DDC 306.4/842213–dc23
LC record available at http://lccn.loc.gov/2017054707

ISBN 978-1-107-11271-1 Hardback
ISBN 978-1-107-53304-2 Paperback

Additional resources for this publication are available at www.cambridge.org/watts

Contents

Images

Figures

Tables

Preface

R.J.W.

The idea of writing *Language, the Singer and the Song* reaches back at least as far as the final year of my career as full professor of Modern English Linguistics at the Institute for English Languages and Literatures at the University of Bern before my retirement in the summer of 2008. I knew I was going to miss the students and the wonderful times, academic and social, that both staff and students had enjoyed during my twenty-four years at Bern. So what was I going to do with the years of retirement ahead of me?

I had a number of ideas up my sleeve, of course, and in point of fact, two writing projects have already come to fruition. Both of these provided input into what I had been dreaming of writing for years, a fusion of my great active love of the folk song of the English-speaking world with my passion for pulling down hegemonically constructed assumptions about the English language. The first (*Language Myths and the History of English*) was a deconstruction of the potent myths surrounding the history of English from a discursive, sociolinguistic perspective. The second (*Letter Writing and Language Change*) was an editorial collaboration with Anita Auer and Daniel Schreier in investigating the historical need to readjust the focus of historical study by a sociolinguistic analysis of letter writing 'from below', i.e. socially 'below', from those who rarely get a look in when it comes to reconstructing how people used and use language socially. How much do we perform when we use language? And how do we shift our identities and our social relationships when we perform consciously for others and with others? That was it! It just had to be an investigation into the performing of songs from a sociolinguistic perspective. But I could hardly do this on my own.

F.A.M.

In hindsight, meeting Richard Watts in 1974 at what was then the biggest folk festival in Switzerland at Lenzburg was nothing short of fateful. I was seventeen, a wide-eyed, wildly enthusiastic folkie, and he was a prominent figure on the Swiss folk scene. He has never let me forget how I, obviously star-struck, opened up what was to be the first of our many exchanges about the passion we shared, folk song and folk music. We ended up working together, on the stages of Swiss folk clubs and at venues that promoted acoustic music, but I also became first his student, then his assistant and finally his colleague at Bern University. It took some persuasion on his part to get me on board this project, as I was not at all sure what I could contribute to it, but, as it turned out, the different areas of linguistics we had explored over the years complemented each other well. In short, I am deeply grateful that he kept up the pressure and that I became part of this study, a culmination of a lifelong love for this kind of music in a scholarly exploration that draws richly on the practice of performing these songs in a variety of settings. Writing this book together with Richard was probably the most pleasurable foray into academic research I have ever been involved in.

As a Duet

At this point we would like to thank the people who helped us in the exploration of the topic and of the songs. Looking back, after the mention of the 1974 Lenzburg Folk Festival, we realise that what we do and think today, including this book project, is built on contacts, friendships and experiences with people, in academia and the folk music world, made over the long course of the years.

Many of those to whom we dedicate our thanks will not even be aware that we have written this book, and we have lost contact with many of them. Some of them, alas, are no longer with us. But without them, the book would have been impossible. Andy Irvine, who at the time was playing with Planxty, and R.J.W. were trying a few musical things out under a wall in the gardens of Lenzburg Castle on that 'fateful' day in 1974 when F.A.M. joined us. Andy's singing and playing has been a source of inspiration to us ever since. R.J.W.'s folk 'mentor' at Leicester University, Roy Bailey, was instrumental in triggering his commitment to folk music, and it was Roy and Leon Rosselson who were the guests at the first festival. We would like to thank them for their support and enthusiasm.

The members of the High Level Ranters during the 1970s, Colin Ross (and his wife Ray Fisher, now, sadly, no longer with us), Ali Anderson, Tom Gilfellon and Johnny Handle, were regular visitors to Switzerland. What Roy began in terms of commitment, Johnny completed for R.J.W. with an unforgettable guest evening at the Leicester University Folk Song Club early in 1962. It was Johnny who sparked off R.J.W.'s love of the Northumbrian smallpipes and who gave him his first lessons in playing his own set. And it was Colin who made him a new chanter to give him a greater musical range. Tom invited Seamus Ennis to Switzerland for a tour after R.J.W. had first met

Seamus at his caravan home of 'Easter Snow' at Naul north of Dublin in 1971, and Tom also arranged for a cittern to be made for R.J.W. Both cittern and pipes are now in the capable hands of F.A.M. It was Ali who came to Switzerland for a breathtaking set of concerts with the English concertina and the smallpipes in the early 1970s. A heartfelt vote of thanks to all of you, in particular, bless his soul, to Seamus, who died in 1983.

As far as present musicians and friends go, a big thank you to the doyenne of folk song, Maddy Prior, for hosting such fascinating, inspirational workshops at Stones Barn – in particular the 2014 workshop on Child Ballads – which fundamentally rekindled F.A.M.'s interest, for being so generous with her time and her insights in allowing him to interview her at length, but also for having given so much great singing to the entire community. Without her work our musical tastes might have gone in a very different direction forty-five years ago. Thanks also to her daughter Rose Kemp and Rose's father Rick for their insights into song-writing and performing when F.A.M. met them at the Stones Barn workshops, as well as for acting as sounding boards for some of our ideas.

No expression of thanks would be complete without mentioning Martin Carthy, guest at one of the Lenzburg festivals in the early 1970s and co-presenter at the Child Ballad workshop, but, most importantly, a wonderful person. He has been an inspiration since F.A.M.'s teenage years and R.J.W.'s late twenties, in making us realise how as performers, without having to follow the 'tradition' slavishly, we can be true to the spirit of a song and keep the music alive. F.A.M. also owes a debt of gratitude to 'The Barn Stoners', alumni of the Stones Barn workshops; in particular, Suze, Ella-Joy Hunton and Kevin Wilkins, sadly missed, for songs and friendship; Siobhan and Chris Nelson for great music, great songs and discussions about how we stylise our singing; to Peter Little for his company and his ability to galvanise an audience with his voice and his repertoire; and Lynn Goulborn for organising song gatherings and forays to clubs that have proved so useful for our understanding of current folk practices.

Will Kaufman has been a great help to us with his perceptive work on the American folk scene, in particular his way of bringing the music of Woody Guthrie to life. Thanks are also due to Norman Blake for his generosity in letting us use his song 'Billy Grey' and to Scott O'Malley for establishing contacts with Norman and answering so many of our questions. Eric Bogle was very generous in allowing us to present and discuss 'No Man's Land' just as long as we used his first printed version of the song. We hope the interpretation of the genesis of the song is along the right lines. Thanks to Alexandra Burton, a librarian in the Vaughan Williams Memorial Library at Cecil Sharp House, who was kind enough to send us her own photographs of the entrance to Cecil Sharp House and Kennedy Hall, the venue of the Maddy Prior performance.

On the academic side of the fence, it is not often that one encounters colleagues who are also 'into' folk music, but one such, for whom we have an abiding affection, is Paul Simpson of Queen's University, Belfast. Thank you, Paul, for supporting us and thank you for an absolutely unforgettable Poetics and Linguistics Association meeting at the Åbo Akademi in Finland many many years ago, which we turned into a succession of three folk gigs reaching far into the small hours of the morning. Back in Bern, this work could not have been undertaken without the support and encouragement of F.A.M.'s old colleagues Simon Hicks, Dewi Williams and Margaret Mace-Tessler, and his new colleagues, Dave Britain and Crispin Thurlow, who all gave him the feeling that this work mattered. Thanks also go to Britta Sweers for conversations about folk music and folk singing that left F.A.M. buzzing with enthusiasm.

F.A.M. thanks the University of Bern for giving him a sabbatical in the spring term of 2015 to concentrate fully on this undertaking. And of course his thanks go to all those students whose feedback in related seminars and discussions helped set him straight on more than one occasion. We thank all those at Cambridge University Press for even being interested in this project, and in particular Helen Barton for showing the professional patience to get us to redo it and broaden its scope in the wake of justified criticism from the reviewers. With a vote of deep thanks and love for putting up with us over the period of writing, we now give two short a cappella performances for our families.

F.A.M. a cappella

As far as family is concerned, I am deeply grateful to this day to my mother Irène, whose love of music was the wellspring of musical enthusiasm in my childhood and in my family. She would have loved to see this book, a testimony to all the 'old' songs she had been so fond of all her life. Thanks also to my sister Suzanne, my partner in singing, talented multi-instrumentalist, arranger and vocalist performer, the other harmony voice in the polyphonic singing of our youth, and to my Dad and my brother Peter, lusty singers both. But the most profound gratitude is due to my wife and best friend Caroline Morrissey for her encouragement and her patience, especially when songs, in the interest of research, of course, were played over and over again. She was always there to support our work, and just as importantly during gigs, she was always that friendly face in the crowd that takes so much pressure off a performer.

I am also grateful to my daughters Corrina, Astrid and Frances for being such avid singers and musicians and making us realise how much the practice of singing in the family is to be valued. And lastly thanks to my son Andri, apparently a classic chip-off-the-old-block, who insisted – against his teachers' advice – in his college finals on tackling the power of sung protest as his independent study project. Many ideas were tossed back and forth in our discussions, helping to shape his work and some of my concepts.

R.J.W. a cappella

When discussing new ideas with my wife, Anne-Marie, I immediately detect her registering the ominous fact that I might be thinking of writing another book, and imagining all the hours spent behind the computer, reading up new material and getting more than a little frustrated. She is, of course, absolutely right in thinking, 'Oh no! Here we go again!' But this time she has been not only thoroughly cooperative; I think she has also secretly enjoyed seeing me do what I always wanted to do.

We have had lots of discussions about this book, from which I have profited immensely. My heart goes out to her for setting me right most of the time and, in particular, for being so patient with me. She also likes having Franz round at our place and lets us get on with our discussions. It's probably a case of 'Well, if I can't set him right, Franz will.' My daughter-in-law trained to be an opera singer, so it was great fun to explain to her (and my not particularly musical son) what the book was all about. We do not see one another all that often now as they live abroad. But my son, when he was a boy, thoroughly enjoyed coming to the Lenzburg festivals and having folk musicians staying at our flat through the 1970s. We also had a dachshund called Lotti, who insisted on barking right in the middle of Planxty's rendering of the Donegal reel 'The Dogs among the Bushes' at Lenzburg. Imagine the keying-out comments from the band! Our granddaughter, Jenny, has also shown a keen interest in England and its music. My love goes out to them all and my thanks for being so understanding about my passion. It goes without saying that none of those mentioned in this preface bears any responsibility for the errors of judgment and interpretation that readers might find in the book.

Introduction

Many, if not all, of music's essential processes may be found in the constitution of the human body and in patterns of interaction of human bodies in society. Thus all music is structurally, as well as functionally, folk music.

(Blacking 1973: xi)

Essentials of Folk Performance

At the legendary Woodstock Festival in 1969, Joan Baez, a few songs into her set, introduces the Stones' song 'No Expectations' ('one of my husband David's favourite songs'). She tells how the federal marshals picked him up from their home for resisting the draft. After singing the song, she picks up the story by relating how David had managed, after 'two and a half weeks', to convince forty-two other federal prisoners to join in what she refers to as a 'very, very good hunger strike'. She links this to her introduction to what she calls an 'organising song', i.e. Phil Ochs's 'Joe Hill'. The introductions to the two songs in front of an audience of thousands could best be characterised as a chat, in which she tells them that she and her unborn baby are doing well, that David has been transferred from county to federal jail, how the four marshals were hours late because they were too proud to ask for directions to her remote home and how one of the activist anti-draft girls at the farewell party had stuck a 'Resist the Draft' sticker onto their bumper as the Feds drove off 'on the wrong side of the road'. The combined account, punctuated by audience responses in the form of laughter and applause, is approximately two and a half minutes long.

The song 'Joe Hill' is an ode to a Swedish-American union organiser and writer of rabble-rousing labour movement songs (born Joel Emanuel Häglund, also known as Joel Hillström). Hillström was executed on a highly dubious murder charge in 1915, probably rigged by the 'copper bosses' (as they are referred to in the song) because of his political activities. In the song, which represents a dream, the narrative 'I' asks how it is possible for Joe Hill to be 'alive as you and me'. It contains the central notion expressed by Joe Hill that 'what they can never kill / went on to organize / went on to organize', in

1

keeping with Hill's final exhortation on the eve of his execution: 'Don't mourn, organize.'[1] The song repeats the last line of every stanza and is thus suited for an audience to join in, although it is impossible to tell with certainty from the Woodstock recording whether they did.

In spite of singing at a festival remembered primarily for its size, the way Baez performs the set is more in keeping with the intimacy of a club or a coffee house. She uses her platform not only to revive the memory of a labour activist in the decade after the McCarthy anti-communist witch-hunts in her choice of song (without mentioning the songwriter), but also links it, through the introduction, to the anti-Vietnam War protest movement of the period, thus taking on the US establishment of 1969 on two quite different levels. By that time, she had been involved in the folk scene for a good ten years and had a track record as a folk artist and an activist, the latter of which she has occasionally emphasised as being more important for her.

The audience, as far as can be heard on the recording, seems to go along with her story and her stance, as if they felt they were in a more intimate setting than a huge field on Max Yasgur's farm in upstate New York. They give the impression that they are in agreement with her criticism of the draft and her outlook on the necessity to 'organise'. In other words, despite the unlikely setting, this can be described as a genuine folk performance in the sense that

- it is *embedded in a tradition and complies with a practice* in terms of Baez's interaction with the audience, her detailed and personal introduction to the song, having adopted it as a piece of commonly owned music, not as the work of an author
- it adopts a *critical stance*, being *socially and politically* in opposition to established points of view and responding to contemporary anti-communist and pro-Vietnam War positions
- it creates a *rapport with an audience* through the interaction in the introduction and the potential for creating a community by joining in with the song and clearly by the mutually established theme of 'organising'
- it relies for all these aspects on the *singer's sincerity and credibility*, for which Baez was known even then
- it goes *beyond entertainment*, in the sense (a) that it calls to mind historical injustice and the related historical figure of Joe Hill and (b) that it contains at least a suggestion if not a plea for activism.

Our interest in the subject of folk song performance, which we have actively pursued since our student days, arises out of all these points, admittedly present in other kinds of music, but arguably not to this degree. The points listed above have motivated us to write this book, and they represent a thread that runs through our account. Aspects of folk performance give us insights into the

---

[1] See at: www.iww.org/content/dont-mourn-organize, accessed 29 May 2015.

workings of communities of practice, discourse communities, constructions of tradition, authenticity and identity, and they can be analysed using terms such as *indexicality, style* and *stylisation, 'text'* and *entextualisation, enregisterment,* etc. But things would be slightly one-sided if our discussion did not include other aspects that play into the topic. Song performances always involve performers and audiences in multimodal communication. Even though songs are primarily made manifest in sound, we cannot ignore the relationship between performance and phonological requirements arising out of this fact. Nor is it wise, as far as 'text' and entextualisation in the form of song lyrics are concerned, to ignore certain aspects of stylistics.

The Structure of the Book

We use this introductory chapter to explain how the book is structured, why we have decided to set up a website accompanying the book and how the reader might most efficiently make use of the website. The website also contains video clips of a concert given at Cecil Sharp House, the home of the English Folk Dance and Song Society, by Maddy Prior in October 2008, as an iconic example of what we define in Chapter 2 as a 'representational performance', and to which we refer in greater detail in several chapters throughout the book. We also include in the Introduction our own sociolinguistic definition of what we consider a 'folk song' to be, which differs radically from all other attempts at a definition that we have found in the literature, and we discuss in detail one example, the traditional ballad 'The Unquiet Grave'.

The book contains the present introduction and twelve chapters. We have chosen to consider Chapter 1 as the Prologue to the book since it opens the scene on language and song performance by focusing on the necessity to consider both language and music as socially emergent in instances of interaction. It stresses the ritual significance of combining language and music in song, thus satisfying, we hope, one of the assumed synonyms for 'prologue' defined in the Merriam-Webster online dictionary as a 'warm-up'. It is an important 'warm-up' in that it deals with the place of music and language in the phylogenetic development of the human species from a socio-cognitive perspective. Analogous to the Prologue, we have elected to call Chapter 12 the 'Epilogue', i.e. what Merriam-Webster defines as 'a concluding section that rounds out the design of a literary work'. The book is certainly not 'literary', but it *is* intended to be a 'work'. Hence Chapter 12 'rounds' the contents 'out' by providing an assessment of what our focus on the performance of folk song has achieved and what insights have been gained with respect to further research on more 'classical' areas of sociolinguistic research (e.g. different forms of verbal interaction, language contact situations, identity construction, etc.) from a performance perspective.

Chapters 2, 3 and 4 constitute Part I, entitled 'Creating Community and Identity through Song', in which we set up a sociolinguistic model of song performance and, within that model, demonstrate that the emergent social process of performing song as a means to construct, affirm and transform communities is what justifies the term 'folk song'. 'Folk song' cannot therefore be seen as a song 'genre', but rather as any song that helps to create a 'folk', or a community. It is also important to differentiate between types of performance, and one useful categorisation is to distinguish between 'relational performances', whose main focus is to create a community through joint performance, and 'representational performances', where performers and audiences are more clearly separated (see Chapter 2) and have the ritual functions of re-presenting and receiving and evaluating significant social issues. A central element in both performance types is the function of 'answering back' socially (cf. Chapter 4).

Part II, 'Variation in Language and Folk Song', consists of Chapters 5 to 7, in which the theoretical and methodological focus is on variation and change through time in the performance of songs. Recent work in historical sociolinguistics is invaluable here, but Chapter 7 presents a set of possible counterarguments to the argument that a performance is an emergent social process, arising from the urge to perpetuate songs by transcribing and recording them, i.e. by treating them like 'insects caught in amber'. In Part III, 'Folk Song Performance and Linguistics', which consists of Chapters 8 to 11, we discuss such issues as voicing, text and entextualisation, stylisation, indexicality and enregisterment through the social process of song performance geared towards the construction, reconstruction, affirmation and transformation of communities.

A Reference Performance

In Chapter 10, we argue that it is difficult if not impossible to work with videotaped examples of relational performances (see Chapter 2), yet it was also relatively difficult until a few years ago to access entire performances online, as restrictions on the lengths of video clips resulted in a tendency to break down representational folk performances, i.e. concerts and staged sets in festivals, into individual short snippets. The practical impact of this procedure is that many can only be viewed, to all intents and purposes, out of the context of the overall performance. Nevertheless, by way of a reference performance for the duration of this book, we are lucky to have obtained all the clips made from a concert given in Kennedy Hall, Cecil Sharp House, on 23 October 2008, by Maddy Prior and the two musicians she was working with at that time, Giles Lewin on the fiddle and the Arabic oud and Kit Haigh on the guitar.[2] She also invited John Kirkpatrick (accordion and concertina) and Barney Maze-Brown

---

[2] The title of the concert was 'Back to the Tradition'.

(cello) to play along in certain pieces, and her daughter Rose Kemp and singers June Tabor and Tim Hart to sing a number of songs with her.

The BBC originally made a video recording of the whole concert, but afterwards cut it down to a twenty-minute clip, omitting some of the songs and, unfortunately for our purposes, virtually all of the crucially important verbal insets typical of folk performance, in which the singer keys the audience into the performance mode of the song. As we show in Chapter 11, such keyings-in and keyings-out are an important part of the register common among the discourse community of folk music. Apparently, the original video recording is now no longer available, but most of it can be viewed on individual clips, with the majority of the keyings-in and keyings-out retained, making it a unique, and for our purposes central, document. In fact, most of the concert can be reconstructed from these clips, except for the keying-in of 'Dives and Lazarus' in the first half of the set and that of 'The Trooper's Nag' at the beginning of the second. There is thus enough material to be able to use this concert as a good example of a staged representational folk performance.

As we explain through Chapters 1 and 2, venues for both relational and representational performances are important as they define physically or metaphorically the nature of the symbolic container in which the performance is distinguished from other activities in the everyday world beyond the performance itself. The fact that Maddy Prior's concert took place in Cecil Sharp House (see page 6) is significant in that Cecil Sharp House in the London Borough of Camden has become what it set out to be in the 1930s, viz. the focal point of the folk music community in England, with its extensive collections of songs, broadsheets, dances, etc., available for public consultation (e.g. The Vaughan Williams Memorial Library, The Full English Digital Archive), and with facilities for performances and dances in Kennedy Hall.

The seating capacity in Kennedy Hall (See page 7) is around 400, and it is ideal for dancing purposes as it has a low stage along the back wall on which the players can stand (or sit), with the rest of the hall given over to the dancers. Singers, players, dancers and audience enter via the two doors on the right in Image Intro. 2. Singers are suitably close to their audiences, less so than they would be in a pub venue but far more so than on a stage at a festival. It is this proximity to the audience within an enclosed space that creates the most salient characteristic feature of a folk performance, distinguishing it from most other forms of music performance, i.e. the singer's/musician's will to communicate with the audience, to involve the audience in the singing and to bond with the audience in creating a community of practice for the duration of the performance.

Figure Intro. 1. *Musical notation*

Image Intro.1. *The entrance to Cecil Sharp House, photo by courtesy of Alexandra Burton, Assistant Librarian (Maternity Cover), The Vaughan Williams Memorial Library, English Folk Dance and Song Society*

The only differences between Kennedy Hall and the snug at the Eel's Foot pub in Eastbridge, Suffolk, shown in Image 3.2 in Chapter 3 are that of size and the fact that Maddy Prior and the other musicians are professionals. The social bonding function is common to both venues.

The Website

Image Intro. 2. *Kennedy Hall in Cecil Sharp House, photo by courtesy of Alexandra Burton, Assistant Librarian (Maternity Cover), The Vaughan Williams Memorial Library, English Folk Dance and Song Society*

From time to time throughout the book we refer to the Cecil Sharp House concert by Maddy Prior, and we have put the links to the video clips onto a website prepared in conjunction with this book. Readers who wish to acquire a feel for the whole performance are unfortunately constrained to view each clip separately, since it is not possible to recombine them into the total performance, but we have also prepared a transcript of each clip in the order in which the songs were performed, giving at least a written impression of the whole concert. Our suggestion to the reader is to look at the clips prior to tackling Chapter 1. However, readers who are keen to plunge straight into the business of reading the book will still have other opportunities to consult the Cecil Sharp House concert, notably in Chapter 2, where we discuss 'Who's the Fool Now?', in Chapter 5, where we take a look at 'The Four Loom Weaver', sung a cappella by June Tabor and Maddy Prior, and in Chapter 11 where we use the concert to provide evidence of a folk performance register that is enregistered with every performance, albeit in different ways by different artists.

The website also contains links to other significant video clips, our own renderings of some of the songs mentioned within the book with their lyrics and tunes as far as copyright restrictions have not presented a problem. Where we did not succeed in obtaining permission, links to websites that present versions of the lyrics for public access are provided there too.

Conventions

This is an opportune moment to present a few conventions followed in the book. Whenever an element referred to in the text is included on the website, we note the cross-reference to the website with the symbol ☙ together with a number, making it relatively easy to identify on the website. For example, the discussion of the ballad 'The Unquiet Grave' towards the end of this introduction is given as ☙1 both in the text and on the website.

The *tunes* are presented as simple melodies, and, as such, they represent a melodic 'skeleton', i.e. the tune without the variations or embellishments that singers usually introduce in emergent performances, an issue we will discuss in more detail in Chapter 7, and without instrumental arrangements, apart from chord symbols where they are helpful. However, the chords are to be seen as suggestions only and individual performers may use different chords altogether.

The *lyrics* are presented as lines in stanzas corresponding to segments of the music; the end of a stanzaic line is marked either with a breath symbol (') in the musical notation if it is in the middle of a line of music, or we split the bar to have a new line of the song correspond to a new line in notation. Where the focus is on the relation between stress patterns and musical notation (cf. Figure Intro 1), the beginning of each line of the lyrics, as in Bronson (1959), follows a breath symbol (cf. bars 2 and 6 in Figure Intro 1). The lyrics contain no punctuation at all since they represent not a written text, but the act of languaging[3] in a song. Our only concession to the conventions of graphology has been to begin the names of people and places with a capital letter.

The *transcription conventions* for the segments of conversation and discussion (and also for the keyings-in and -out of the Cecil Sharp House concert) are as follows:

---

[3] For the definition of the terms 'languaging' and 'musicking', see Chapter 1.

.	a tone unit ending with falling intonation
?	a tone unit ending with falling (*wh*-question) or rising (*yes/no*-question) intonation
,	a tone unit ending with rising intonation
(0.8)	a pause measured in fractions of a second
(.)	a pause of less than (0.5) seconds in length
(..)	a pause of between (1.0) second and (2.0) seconds in length
(…)	a pause of longer than (2.0) seconds in length
<@@>	laughter
<@abc@>	speech accompanied by laughter
?	a short utterance with a rise–fall intonation pattern
[/]	overlapping speech
[/]	
<???>	an uninterpretable utterance
to- to	stuttering
I/ what time is it?	self-interruption and restart
—	unfinished speech
:er: :erm:	filled pauses
^	rise-fall intonation pattern
\	end of tone unit

A Functional Definition of Folk Song

This book is about 'folk song', not the modern style of music and singing that is usually referred to as 'folk music' to distinguish it from other styles of music such as rock, pop, jazz, rap, country and western, classical and so on, but simply song that helps to create a 'folk'. We are not trained musicians, although we have played and sung most of the songs we discuss throughout this book for the greater part of our lives – and have thoroughly enjoyed doing so. So we claim a right to investigate the social activity of singing from our own academic perspective – that of socio-linguists studying the social and linguistic significance of performing 'folk song'.

A project of this kind is heterogeneous in the subject matter on which it draws. It thus needs to be inclusive with respect to the fields of study it relies on. Genres are notoriously difficult to delimit and define, and we choose to provide a functional rather than an essentialist definition of 'folk song'. The expression 'folk song' has given rise to so much controversy over precisely what kind of music it refers to that we are constrained to define it very clearly in our own terms. Since we intend to retain the expression 'folk song' throughout this book, the decision calls for a justification before we continue. 'Folk song' is not a monolithic kind of music in terms of either its provenance or its age. Songs might at some stage in their history have had an author or authors whose identity has been lost in the mists of time. New songwriters cherish the directness of the folk lyric, its unashamed appeal to the emotions of the audience and the apparent artlessness of acoustic instruments in preference to polished production.

If 'folk song' were taken to be a translation of Herder's expression *Volkslied*, it would mean something like 'national song' since *Volk* in German is translatable into English as 'people'.[4] But the lexeme 'folk' in modern English no longer refers to a people or a nation. In Britain, it has also been used to refer to the lower orders of the social class hierarchy, particularly to the rural labouring class, or what Cecil Sharp often referred to as the 'peasantry',[5] and it was the indigenous music of the rural areas of Britain that came to be referred to as 'folk music'. In North America, the term was used in a similar way, but it was extended to refer to the indigenous music of the working classes, rural or urban, in the 1930s before this became an accepted reference in Britain in the 1950s. After the Second World War, the International Folk Music Council struggled in their efforts to find an adequate all-embracing definition of 'folk music', and they finally came up with the following version in 1955:

Folk music is the product of a musical tradition that has been evolved *through the process of oral transmission*. The factors that shape the tradition are: (i) continuity which links the present with the past; (ii) variation which springs from the creative impulse of the individual or the group; and (iii) selection by the community, which determines the form or forms in which the music survives.

The term can be applied to music that has been evolved from rudimentary beginnings by a community uninfluenced by popular or art music and it can likewise be applied to music which has originated with an individual composer and has subsequently been absorbed into the unwritten living tradition of a community.

The term does not cover composed popular music that has been taken over ready-made by a community and remains unchanged, for it is the refashioning and re-creation of the music that gives it its folk character.[6] [our italics]

The first impression given by this definition of folk music is that it attempts to 'create', by definition, a genre of music on a level with but nevertheless distinct from 'popular music' or 'art music'. The first limitation of 'folk music'

---

[4] Herder first introduced the term in 1773, at the beginning of the German Romantic movement, anticipating the emergence of a German nation-state, which did not come about till after the Franco-Prussian War in 1871.

[5] For example, consider the following extract from Sharp's *English Folk Song, Some Conclusions* (1907): 'The English peasant still exists, although the peasantry, as a class, is extinct. Reformers would dispel the gloom which has settled upon the country side, and revive the social life of the villages. Do what they will, however, it will not be the old life that they will restore. That has gone past recall. It will be of a new order, and one that will bear but little resemblance to the old social life of the "Merrie England" of history' (p. 119).

[6] *Journal of the International Folk Music Council* 7 (1955), p. 23.

is that it is defined as having evolved 'through the process of oral transmission'. However, in the next paragraph, the definition contradicts itself by suggesting that it may also include 'music which has originated with an individual composer and has subsequently been absorbed into the unwritten living tradition of a community'. The definition suggests that it is a form of music that 'has been evolved from rudimentary beginnings by a community uninfluenced by popular or art music'. The expression 'rudimentary beginnings' locates it socially within the lower, less educated sectors of the social spectrum and also assumes, quite apart from the need to define what 'popular' or 'art' music is, that it is possible for any community not to be so influenced in the modern world.

The definition of 'folk music' includes a definition of 'folk song': so we need to locate the major problems here. Firstly, we reject the notion of a musical genre 'folk music' because we focus not on music so much as on 'musicking', on the activity, not the object or the genre.[7] Secondly, and more importantly, we need to consider how and when we use the expression 'folk' in instances of languaging in modern English. It is hardly, if ever, used to refer to a people, a nation. Nor do we currently use it to refer to a social class. But we do use it to refer to social groups, e.g. 'intellectual folk', 'the folks at home', 'folk like you and me', 'some folk agree and some don't'. It can be used exclusively (e.g. 'intellectual folk'), inclusively (e.g. 'folk like you and me', 'the folks at home') or used emergently to create a group of people on the spot. Any singing activity used originally to create, constitute and construct a group of people, a 'folk', to bond them together for a space of time and in a specific location, to allow individuals, however transiently, to construct identities with others does this through 'folk song', as we show in Chapter 3. If a song is created as a consumer commodity, not to be performed live in the construction of a 'folk', it is less of a 'folk song', but it is not necessarily not a 'folk song'. Some of the problems that arise here are dealt with in Chapter 7. So if a song can be used in the active construction of a community, it is used with no necessary reference to social class, musical ability or musical genre, and it is open in one form or another to communal participation, passive or active.

Bonding People Together through Song

How can a song, in the social process of a performance, exert the power to bond people together? We answer this question by briefly discussing a 'traditional' ballad, 'The Unquiet Grave'.[8] Our principal question is this: In what ways

---

[7] In any case, no crystal clear distinctions can be made between genres of any kind.
[8] Ballad no. 78 in Francis James Child's *The English and Scottish Popular Ballads*, 1965, Vol. II, p. 236.

could a performance of 'The Unquiet Grave' help to construct a 'folk'? The version of the ballad presented on the website was collected from Jane Hann in Stoke Abbot, Dorset in 1906 ⊛1.[9]

Imagine a social gathering in someone's kitchen or in an inn on a dark night. Talk might turn to matters related to hauntings and ghostly encounters, or to conversational conjecture about what prevents souls of the dead from finding their rest. Language used in this situation ranges over a large number of activity types, with references to sayings and beliefs including number magic, reporting the sightings of ghosts, debating taboos about physical contacts with spirits of the departed, perhaps even recounting popular visions and perceptions of limbo and hell. All this can take place in a variety of forms, with a short succession of turns at talk during which various beliefs and superstitions may be exchanged.

There might also be longer, largely uninterrupted turns of talk in the form of narratives where a storyteller recounts well-known stories of ghostly encounters with some form of authentication, e.g. by situating a story in a location familiar to the audience or relating it to a person of more or less distant acquaintance or even a relative. Shorter and longer turns might be freely exchanged and interlocutors might participate in the various performance activities by making comments, laughing, encouraging the storyteller, and so on. We can also imagine that someone might tell a story in which excessive mourning on the grave of a loved one led to an encounter with the loved one's ghost. In the telling of a story 'each tone is used where it is linguistically appropriate and there is no sense in which some are more stable or central than others' (Patel 2008: 183). It is possible, however, for such storytelling to use formulaic framing familiar to the audience, and there might be a certain number of folk-poetic elements not used in everyday conversation in keeping with the setting and the topic of superstition. On the whole, however, the conversational mode would probably result in less adorned language than if it had been in the form of a ballad. So what makes the song performance different from oral storytelling?

To begin with, ritualisation occurs on the level of the context in which the song is performed. Singing not only requires consent from the non-singers; it also requires the listeners, the audience, to listen carefully and to appreciate the singer's art. Secondly, the song itself is not likely to be new to every individual present. For this reason, members of the audience may all have certain expectations as to how the song progresses and how it should be sung. There is also ritualisation on the level of the interaction between the song and the singer. With the exception of two lines of a 'disembodied'

---

[9] The reader is reminded that ⊛ refers to the website, on which can be found the full text of the version discussed and a second version of the ballad played and sung by the authors.

narrative voice, i.e. 'the twelve-month and one day being up / the ghost began to speak' at the beginning of the third stanza (or second verse),[10] the entire ballad consists of a dialogue between the dead and the living lover. It is clear to all concerned that the singer her/himself is not an actual character in the song. In fact, s/he locates her/himself, in an 'I', the mourner (in this version a woman) as well as in the part of the dead beloved. The audience must then evaluate the superstition from within the two characters as presented in the (dramatic) dialogue between the two, as well as from their own perspective. The appearance of the loved one, the ghost, constitutes a warning against overdoing the mourning. Indeed, the ghost warns the 'I' that to do so would make it almost impossible to carry on living. This is the message that the singing instils ritually into the listeners, and in song it is much more effective than in a narrative or a tale. The song ritually enacts the conversation between the two in direct speech as well as the problem that a lament has gone too far: in both the dialogue and the message inherent in the exchange, we have here a social drama (see Chapter 2) that must be corrected.

Songs of this kind are structured on a progression of notes 'built around a stable set of pitch intervals' (Patel 2008: 183) and this song is no exception (for an explanation of the musical terminology, see Appendix). The melody follows a set of three parts A1, A2 and B, in which A1 and A2 do not form a musically simple repetition but an eight-bar period based on an overriding frame of 4 bars + 4 bars, A1 ending on the subtonic (C) in the Am chord and thus remaining open, followed by A2 closing on the tonic D in the Dm chord. Part B also ends in the dominant Am chord, and the second set of four bars in the frame come to rest on the tonic in the second occurrence of A2 (A2'). The overall melodic mode is Aeolian, although part B introduces aspects of the Ionian major mode. The two points of rest and/or dramatic emphasis at the end of A2 correspond with ends of speaking turns in the dialogue, which occasionally take place at the end of an even line or, more frequently, at the end of a stanza, thus heightening the drama through the change in musical texture.

---

[10] We shall use *stanza* when discussing the poetics of the lyrics and *verse* to refer to the repeated musical units that make up a song. In 'The Unquiet Grave' (see the transcript), a stanza consists of four lines whereas the verse consists of sixteen bars running over two stanzas.

The Unquiet Grave

adapted from Hammond D. 483, Jane Hann, Stoke Abbot, Dorset, June 1906

1. how pleasant is the wind tonight
   I feel some drops of rain
   I never had but one true love
   and in greenwood he is slain

2. I'll do so much for my true love
   as any young man may
   I'll sit and mourn all on his grave
   for a twelve month and a day

3. the twelve month and one day being up
   the ghost began to speak
   why sit you here and mourn for me
   and will not let me speak

4. what do you want of me sweetheart
   or what is it you crave
   I want one kiss of your lily-white lips
   and that is all I crave

5. my lips they are as cold as clay
   my breath be heavy and strong
   if you have one kiss of my lily-white lips
   your life will not be long

6. my life be't long or short sweetheart
   but that is all I crave
   then I shall be along with you
   a-lying in my grave

7. 'twas down in Cupid's Garden
   where you and I would walk
   the finest flower that ever was there
   is withered to a stalk

8. is withered to a stalk sweetheart
   the flower will never return
   and since I lost my own sweetheart
   what can I do but mourn

9. oh don't you see the fire sweetheart
   the fire that burns so blue
   where my poor soul tormented is
   while I stay here with you

10. mourn not for me my dearest dear
    mourn not for me I crave
    I must leave you and all the world
    and turn into my grave

One musical verse of sixteen bars covers two textual stanzas that are closely linked in their narrative content. Stanzas 1 and 2 focus on the bereaved lover and what she has promised to do; stanzas 3 and 4 focus on the dead lover's query as to why she mourns on his grave and the response by the bereaved lover; stanzas 5 and 6 are the dead lover's warning and the bereaved lover's response; stanzas 7 and 8 give the bereaved lover's reasons for making her request; stanzas 9 and 10 give the dead lover's reasons for giving his warning.

Typically the prosodic structure of the ballad has four stressed syllables in odd lines and three stressed syllables in even lines, with any number of unstressed syllables in between, and this is the case here. Unstressed syllables are realised with shorter notes (quavers or perhaps triplet quavers). They often account for the variations in prosody of different stanzas, but they also correspond to the stress timing of English. The combination of melody and lyrics makes a song fundamentally different from a conversation in a 'social gathering'. 'The Unquiet Grave' engenders 'a much richer set of perceptual relations' in the listener than if its contents had simply been talked about in a community or recounted as a story. It certainly triggers the generation of a wide range of meta-relations in both the performer and the listener.

'All Music is Folk Music'

In Chapter 1, we outline the path we have chosen to hack through the jungle of ideas, materials and literature at our disposal. Of the scholarly literature on music and language that has put our minds straight about making this choice, John Blacking's work *How Musical is Man?* (1973) is germane to the way in which we conceptualise 'folk song', and quotations from this work head each individual chapter. If we agree with the quotation from Blacking heading this introduction, that 'all music is folk music', then the 'folk music' of any culture is surely a valid object of study. However, our own active experience is with the 'folk song' of the English-speaking world, and, as a result, we have focused largely on material from this geographical origin. This is not as limiting as it might seem. Many songs from the British Isles travelled with emigrants to their new homes, and many songs, traditional or new, are recorded, sometimes in even greater variation, e.g. in the United States and Canada (see Bronson 1959–72).

With the growth in popularity of the folk music of the British Isles and the interest in 'things Celtic' since the 1970s, there has been a further diffusion of Anglophone 'folk song' beyond its geographical and even linguistic origins, with active interest spreading all over the European continent. Given the fact that songs may well have been collected in geographically narrowly defined areas but still show signs of having their origins elsewhere, we propose that one focus of this study, viz. the process of adoption, adaptation and transmission of folk songs (see the chapters in Part II), even though it uses the British Isles as its starting point, is applicable to other contexts as well.

The field of study is heterogeneous, as are the methods and approaches considered in our analysis. Interdisciplinarity brings with it certain difficulties. We are both linguists whose education has included literary studies. We are both keen amateur performers and have had to work our way into disciplines with which we were initially a little unfamiliar, such as palaeoanthropology, social anthropology, ethnomusicology, neurobiology, psychology and folklore studies. We have also had to acquire new skills, e.g. how to write music. It has been a steep learning curve, one supported by several musical friends. So we crave a little indulgence from experts in the fields into which we have ventured. Learning those new skills and discovering (and rediscovering) songs in the writing of this book has been a truly exciting experience. Books always force their writers into making choices. Due to space limitations, we have had to make some painful choices, but the songs we have encountered in the process will stay with us.

Prologue

1   Language and Music

There is so much music in the world that it is reasonable to suppose that music, like language and possibly religion, is a species-specific trait of man.

(Blacking 1973: 7)

Language and Music as Communication Systems

In the final chapter of *The Singing Neanderthals: The Origins of Music, Language, Mind, and Body* (2006 ([2005]),[1] Steven Mithen classifies human language and music as communication systems and maintains that once '[a] language had evolved as the principal communication system of modern humans, people were left with the question of who to communicate with through music' (2006: 272). We extend this question as follows: 'Who do we communicate with through song and who do we perform for?' Our starting point is the communication systems themselves. Communication, understood as the exchange of information among human beings and getting others to do things, is infinitely more effective through language than through music. But 'communication' also refers to expressing oneself to others and, more generally, to collaborating with others in carrying out some activity together, whether goal-directed or not. In these two senses, it involves other communication systems in addition to language, one of these being gesture and movement and the other being music.

Languaging and Musicking

Our primary focus is on song performance rather than songs as 'objects', and we thus conceptualise language as a social activity rather than simply as a semiotic system, although the signifiers and signifieds do not simply disappear when language becomes song. In fact, quite the contrary is the case. The emotive force of music lends a more potent set of possible meanings to the constructions of the language system in emergent instances of performance in

---

[1] In what follows we refer to the title of Mithen's book as *SN*.

the listener than if what is sung were simply spoken or recited. We refer to language as it is used emergently in social practice as 'languaging',[2] and, through the activity of 'languaging', we enact identities and construct, reconstruct and transform the social worlds in which we perform. Children are born into a 'languaging world' and are literally unable to avoid language. As Blacking once put it, '[w]e are born social. Our species is not human, but *human-and-fellow-human*' (Blacking 1987: 25; our italics). Infants must acquire human language in order to survive, and, in the first few years of life, surviving is dependent on becoming a ratified member of a nuclear social group, the family. In becoming a member of a social group, i.e. in the social part of the socio-cognitive process of acquiring the language faculty, the infant is totally 'dependent on her/his interaction with the immediate physical and social world' (Watts 2012a: 107). The vast majority of his/her early life is spent in intensive social interaction with others. In that environment, a child quickly perceives languaging to be the most important mode of collaborating in some activity, i.e. of communicating.

Since the musical structures produced in the analogous activity of 'musicking' do not have denotations or connotations outside the system of music itself, it is not a truly semiotic system, and indeed Benveniste (1974: 2, 54–56) explicitly excluded it from his theory of semiotics.[3] But we are not only born into a languaging world; we are also born into a 'musicking'[4] world. In that world, 'musicking' is an activity, 'something that people do. The apparent thing "music" is a figment, an abstraction of the action, whose reality vanishes as soon as we examine it at all closely' (Small 1998: 2). From a socio-cognitive point of view, therefore, we need to ask whether there is also a human music faculty from which the activity of 'musicking' is derived analogous to the human language faculty from which 'languaging' is derived. If this is so, is it generated from other cognitive abilities and from a human need for social integration, or put differently, can we also communicate by means of musicking?

The language faculty allows us to generate meanings with others and to negotiate how those meanings can be used in emergent instances of languaging. In the same way the music faculty allows us to generate meanings with others and to negotiate how those meanings could be used in instances of musicking. But music does not *have* meanings; it allows us to *derive* meanings. From a semiotic perspective, music systems, like language systems, have what van Leeuwen (1999: 8) calls 'semiotic resources', which offer those involved in languaging or musicking 'choices' with different semiotic values in different contexts. For van Leeuwen (1999: 196), sound 'connects, and it requires

---

[2] We have taken the term from Scannell (2002: 62).   [3] See Thomas (1995: 13).

[4] We follow Small (1998) in spelling the gerundive/participial form 'musicking' from the neo-verb 'music' with the grapheme <ck> to retain the sound of the phoneme /k/.

surrendering oneself to, and immersing oneself in, participatory experience'. Immersing oneself in music may be an individual or a communal activity, but the meanings negotiated by playing, singing, listening to or participating in musicking are primarily within the singer, player, listener or participant and are only definable by creating what Bateson (1979) calls *meta-messages* (i.e. second-order meanings) relating to the context of musicking itself. When those meta-messages relate to communal ritual of any kind, then regardless of whether or not they are expressible by language, they generate social meanings. Cook (2007: 223) takes a similar line to van Leeuwen when he argues that meaning is *not in music* but is 'created through the act of performance. And it is this emergent quality, together with the idea of a bundle or cluster of semiotic potential' that Cook takes as his starting point in the analysis of 'musical meaning'.

Missing Links

There are, however, some missing links in the relation between musicking and languaging. There are significant differences in the acquisition and universality of the language faculty and the music faculty. Despite Pinker's dismissive comment that music is nothing but entertainment, 'auditory cheesecake' and 'the making of plinking noises' (Pinker 1997: 528) and that it is 'useless' and 'quite different from language' (ibid.: 529, 539),[5] the evidence, as we shall see later in this chapter, suggests that the music faculty precedes the language faculty in the phylogenetic development of humankind. Music turns out to have been anything but useless in the evolutionary history of hominins.

There is an apparent difference in acquisition between the ontogenetic development of both faculties. Children seem to learn how to 'language' before they learn how to 'music', but only if we focus on 'music-making' rather than 'music-taking'. Infants participate *receptively* both in the world of language and the world of music. Neo-natal infants are responsive to music from birth, and there is also solid evidence to show that they are receptive to music at the pre-natal stage (Zentner and Kagan 1998; Deliège and Sloboda 1996). If we take the beginning of the acquisition of the music faculty to be instrumental music production, music may indeed be just auditory cheesecake. If we take the production of instrumental music as an indication of the universality of the music faculty, perhaps it is, after all, a 'useless' acquisition. Relative to the overall population, comparatively few children learn to play a musical instrument. But musical instruments are artificial extensions of the human body, and learning to play them requires complex motor skills. On the other hand,

---

[5] See Levitin's refutation of Pinker's arguments in Levitin (2008 ([2006]) and Mithen's (2006) book-length refutation of Pinker's comments.

everyone can sing simply by using her/his own body. Languaging and singing require both productive and receptive skills; we can all speak and hear[6] what is said, and we can all sing – for better or for worse. As Mithen (2006: 1) points out, '[t]he appreciation of music is a universal feature of mankind'. A child does not have to be 'musically minded' to be able to sing, but the manipulation of musical instruments requires complex motor skills. Not everyone needs to develop productive musical skills to be able to participate in musicking.

What, then, are the missing links? The interest in comparing and seeing connections and overlaps between languaging and musicking is not new. It goes back at least to the time of Plato. During the Age of the Enlightenment, a considerable amount of philosophical enquiry was devoted to the origins of language and music, particularly by the French 'philosophes' (see Thomas 1995). Thomas' discussion of Rousseau's *Essai sur l'origine des langues* (1781) suggests that Rousseau was more interested in languaging and musicking than in language and music. At one point in the second 'Discours', Thomas interprets Rousseau as suggesting that 'vocal sounds are not so much expressions of ideas as they are *moments of identification and social bonding*' (1995: 105; our italics). For Rousseau, 'language requires not simply a private subjectivity that experiences passion, but rather relies on the sympathy of a "public" to constitute that passion as a relation' (ibid.). One reason why music is said to have no real meaning is because meaning is looked for outside the activity of musicking, as if the structures of a musical system somehow relate to meanings in the outside world beyond the music (cf. Feld and Fox 1994), the activity of musicking and those involved in the musicking. Small (1998: 5) suggests that '[w]hatever meaning art may have is thought to reside in the object, persisting independently of what the perceiver may bring to it', and he roundly condemns that position.

Thomas (1995: 54–55) argues that '[t]hose writers who sought a specifically anthropological origin of music and language, despite their many differences, adopted a common narrative'. The common narrative was that music and language developed concurrently and that, for this reason, if 'melody and *parole* were one … true music was always, and must always have been, vocal or operatic'. The French philosophes of the eighteenth century, however, were not in possession of the most important missing link – Darwin's theory of evolution.

'Hmmmmm' and Human Language

The major missing link in philosophical speculations on the origin of music and language was the principle of natural selection and the acceptance of

---

[6] Obviously, those with specific physical disabilities may not fully acquire the faculty of language.

genetic mutation over millions of years from less evolved species of primates. Mithen's solution to the complex relationship between the two communication systems of language and music is to suggest, on the basis of the wealth of information gathered over the last 150 years in palaeoanthropology, that the ability to vocalise has been present in hominid species since the australopithecines of 5 to 2 million years ago. Recent advances in palaeoanthropology and other related disciplines provide strong evidence for the present hypothesis that the music faculty in the evolutionary development of all hominid species preceded the language faculty.

A second missing link in those speculations was the realisation that an increase in the size of hominid brains was in some way responsible for the evolution of the species, although the human brain remained a mysterious black box until well into the twentieth century. Human genetics and neuroscience have expanded enormously within the last sixty years to provide – at least partially – that missing link. For the study of the language and music faculties we now have a wealth of empirical evidence from various aspects of brain-lesion and brain-imaging studies showing that these two cognitive faculties only partially share common processing areas of the brain. The third missing link was research into the language and music acquisition of infants, which has been provided – again at least partially – by studies related to IDS (Infant-Directed Speech). Research shows that, in terms of ontogenetic development, the music faculty precedes the language faculty but takes second place to it during and after a child's language acquisition.

Mithen's Hypothesis

Throughout *SN*, Mithen offers convincing evidence from a range of research sources to support the hypothesis that the cognitive faculty concerned with music precedes the cognitive faculty of language in the phylogenetic history of hominid species. In the first seven chapters he amasses a wide range of evidence from brain-lesion and brain-imaging studies, research into so-called 'musical savants' and subjects with innate tone-deafness, or amusia, research into the receptivity towards music of neo-natal, pre-linguistic infants and Infant-Directed Speech (IDS) to support the argument that in ontogenetic development the music capacity precedes the acquisition of language.

The most convincing evidence for the evolutionary priority of the music faculty is amassed in chapters 8 to 16 in the second part of *SN*. Mithen suggests that the ability to vocalise was present very early on in the evolution of hominid species so that by the time we reach *Homo ergaster* at around 2 million years ago, a rudimentary vocal communication system, which Mithen calls 'Hmmmm', could have developed displaying the following characteristics:

(1) It was a **h**olistic system, by which Mithen means that vocalisations were either single utterances or a series of utterances that could not be taken apart and used in creating new utterances. Each utterance had one and only one denotation and had to be committed to memory as one unit.

(2) It was a **m**anipulative system in that it was used to induce 'emotional states and physical movement by entrainment' (Mithen 2006 [2005]: 25) and not to refer to things in the world.

(3) It was a **m**ulti**m**odal system in that it relied not just on vocalisation but also on gesture and physical expression.

(4) It was a **m**usical system in that it used melodic pitch variation and rhythm and had the property of recursion in allowing the embedding of certain musical structures within themselves. This is a property it shared with human language, which may have facilitated the shift to language once compositional structure took over from holistic structure.

Mithen calls this communication system 'Hmmmm' (**h**olistic, **m**anipulative, **m**ulti**m**odal, **m**usical), and he is careful to link the extended vocalising faculty of *Homo ergaster*, the first truly bipedal hominid species, to a slightly increased brain size when compared with the australopithecines and to the increased pressure for communication for hunting that arose from bipedalism. At the same time, he is quick to point out that '*Homo ergaster* certainly lacked the anatomical adaptations for fine breathing control that are necessary for the intricate vocalizations of modern human speech and song' (2006: 158). He sees *Homo ergaster* as being only the beginning of an evolutionary process that was followed by 'about one million years of effective stasis in brain expansion' until the 'immense and rapid growth of the human brain that began after 600,000 years ago'.

This second increase in brain size is best explained 'by selective pressures for enhanced communication' (ibid.). But what were those pressures? Why did encephalisation (increase in brain size) take place at around 1 million to 0.6 million years ago? Since the turn of the twentieth century, evidence has come to light of the presence of *Homo habilis*, *Homo erectus*, *Homo heidelbergensis*, *Homo floresiensis* and, eventually, *Homo neanderthalensis* in different locations in Asia and Europe. These were all evolutionary developments from *Homo ergaster*, and the finds indicate that at some time between 1.7 million and 0.6 million years ago, there was a dispersal, or dispersals, of Early Humans from Africa. The dispersals were not just of hominins; several other animal species resident in Africa – lions, elephants, gazelles, rhinos, and so on – on whom hominins were dependent in the delicate environmental balance of food sources and climatic living conditions, also dispersed out of Africa. In addition, hominid dispersals would hardly have been of individuals but of groups, in all likelihood some of them relatively large.

Mithen's hypothesis is that encephalisation was due to evolutionary pressures on survival that necessitated the cognitive development of 'Hmmmm'. As he points out,

dispersal means entering unfamiliar landscapes, in which new types of animals would have been encountered, and where new distributions of fresh water, firewood, stone and other resources would have had to be found and the information transmitted to others. Such communication would have been essential regardless of whether we think of Early Human dispersal as more similar to that of other large mammals or to that of modern human explorers. Whichever is the case, Early Humans were dependent for their survival and reproduction on working cooperatively as part of a group. (ibid.: 166)

Mithen's suggestion is that 'Hmmmm' was expanded and refined through the inclusion of the function of 'mimesis' (cf. Donald 1991). According to Donald (1991: 168; quoted in Mithen 2006: 167), mimesis is 'the ability to produce conscious, self-initiated, representational acts that are intentional but not linguistic'. This implies that gesture, movement, facial expression, etc., all became part of 'Hmmmm' – which is logical if we remember that 'Hmmmm' was in any case a multimodal system – and it implied that animal vocalisations could also be imitated by the human voice. If these additions to the vocalisation system are accepted, 'Hmmmm' can be extended by adding a fifth 'm' (for 'mimetic') to give 'Hmmmmm'. This would have been a very powerful communication system, but it would still have been holistic and not compositional. The fundamental point, however, is the strong social significance of 'Hmmmmm'.

What Happened to 'Hmmmmm'?

Survival of *Homo heidelbergensis* in Europe must have been exceedingly precarious between 475,000 and 450,000 years ago, with a very high volume of ice in the glacial that peaked around 450,000 years ago. So even with increased brain size and the 'Hmmmmm' communication system, it is probable that *Homo heidelbergensis* became extinct – at least in Europe. In Africa, however, two strains of the hominid species that evolved from *Homo heidelbergensis* were *Homo neanderthalensis* and *Homo sapiens*.[7] We find traces of *Homo neanderthalensis* in Europe at around 250,000 years ago. First traces of *Homo sapiens* are to be found in Africa at around 200,000 years ago, and there are indications of a dispersal of *Homo neanderthalensis* into Europe at around that period. So it is reasonable to talk, as Mithen does, of a European *Homo* lineage and an African *Homo* lineage. Both species had a very high

---

[7] As Mithen points out, Cambridge anthropologists Robert Foley and Martha Lahr suggest an intermediate species in Africa that they call *Homo helmei*, but nothing in the current discussion hinges on the plausibility of this hypothesis.

encephalisation quotient (EQ: brain size as a ratio of body size), *Homo nean-derthalensis* 4.8 and *Homo sapiens* 5.3. And yet, after the dispersal of *Homo sapiens* into Europe after around 40,000 years ago, the latter survived and the former became extinct around 30,000 years ago.

The difference lies in the strong assumption that *Homo neanderthalensis*, even with a highly advanced 'Hmmmmm' system of communication, which was a system of holistic vocalisation, could not compete for resources with *Homo sapiens*, who by this time had acquired a fully operative system of human language. That system allowed for what Mithen calls 'cognitive fluidity', i.e. the ability to use language in coordination with the technological faculty and with detailed knowledge of the natural environment. Human language was, and still is, a compositional system, ideal for transferring and working fluidly with information. 'Hmmmmm' was a highly developed holistic system, specialised in the expression of emotion, which was restricted by its 'domain-specific' nature.

The genetic origin of *Homo sapiens* is dated at around 200,000 years ago, and there were two migratory dispersals out of Africa, one at around 100,000 years ago, the other at around 60,000 years ago. Fossil remains of the first dispersal from caves in Israel are similar to those left by Neanderthals before and after the presence of *Homo sapiens* in the same area, and Mithen interprets this similarity to indicate that, if they had been fully in possession of human language at that time, they 'had not attained full cognitive fluidity'. The second dispersal, however, ended in *Homo sapiens* spreading across the whole globe by around 20,000 years ago. This could only have been achieved with the language faculty, which must therefore have become a genetic attribute of *Homo sapiens* at some time between 100,000 and 50–60,000 years ago. *Homo sapiens*, however, had evolved with 'Hmmmmm' before supplanting it with language, and there was still a need to express emotion through the musical, mimetic and gestural aspects of 'Hmmmmm'. Mithen thus suggests that rather than language supplanting the 'Hmmmmm' system, the latter formed the basis of the music faculty, music being a communication system 'specialising in the expression of emotion'. In his final chapter, Mithen illustrates this development with Figure 1.1, which we have modified for the purposes of our argument.[8]

Ontogenetic Evidence for the Priority of 'Hmmmmm'

Pinker is not by any means the only scholar to consider music as a mere cultural addition to language, as 'cheesecake', the dessert with no real

---

[8] Our thanks go to the Orion Publishing Group for permission to use the original figure by Mithen from *SN* with our own modifications.

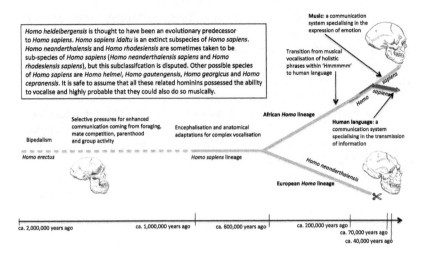

Figure 1.1. *The evolution of music and language as communication systems, adapted from Mithen with permission from Orion, (2006: 267)*

nutritional value to follow and complement the main course of the language faculty. Others have argued similarly, although from different points of view (see Barrow 1995; Sperber 1996; G. Miller 1997; Kogan 1997), that music is an exaptive ability rather than an adaptive and genetically transferred mental faculty. However, as Cross (2001: 50) points out, for these researchers 'the effects of music are at the level of the individual, whether in terms of affording hedonic experience or exhibiting protean attributes'. They are not at the level of the social group. Musicking involves not just individual singers and musicians but all those who participate in musical events. Cross and Morley (2008: 63) quote Brown (2000), who reflects on 'the notion of music as reinforcing "groupishness", which [Brown] defines as a "suite of traits that favour the formation of coalitions, promote cooperative behaviour towards group members and create the potential for hostility towards those outside the group"'.[9]

From this perspective, music is vital to the survival of the group as a collective of 'humans and fellow-humans' (Blacking 1987: 25). For Cross and Morley, music is an essential cognitive faculty in the human brain that offers opportunities 'for the maintenance of group identity, for the conduct of collective thinking (as in the transmission of group history and planning for action), for group synchronization ... and for group catharsis, the collective

---

[9] A perfect example is the Maori 'haka'.

expression and experience of emotion' (Cross and Morley 2008: 63). Fitch (2006), in a comparative study of approaches to the biology and evolution of music, is more cautious than Cross and Morley and restricts the evolutionary perspective to the consideration of possible adaptive functions of song, rather than music in general. His major point is that adaptive mutation is more likely to occur in evolutionary processes than group mutation, but he sees an advantage in the adaptive use of song in kinship groups since the individual would thereby be at an advantage. He suggests that 'many of the hypotheses arguing for group function in the evolution of music may be recast in terms of kin selection ' (Fitch 2006: 202).

The evidence amassed and reviewed by Mithen in the first part of *SN* to argue for the priority of music over language in the ontogenetic development of the individual is of five kinds:

1. cases of aphasia in which the language faculty is impaired but not the music faculty, and with so-called 'musical savants' (L. Miller 1989), i.e. those who from birth on show astounding musical abilities but have great difficulty in acquiring language;
2. cases of acquired and congenital amusia, i.e. damage to the music faculty through brain lesions (Peretz 1993) or as the result of a congenital inability to use the music faculty (e.g. tone-deaf subjects, see Peretz *et al.* 2002);
3. the neural networks of music and language processing (see Peretz 1993, 2003) in which each module has some degree of independence from the other and where subjects may display 'double dissociation', i.e. one of the faculties is lost or never developed without the other being impaired;
4. the phenomenon of Infant-Directed Speech (Fernald 1991, 1992; Saffran *et al.* 1999; Saffran 2003; Pelucchi, Hay and Saffran 2009) and singing to infants (Trehub and Trainor 1998; Trehub 2001; Trehub and Schellenberg 1995), which appears to be universal across all cultures, and for which Mithen claims that 'IDS is not primarily about language' (2006: 72) since 'the infants were listening to nothing more than melody' (2006: 73);
5. the power of music to evoke emotions (see Krumhansl 1997; Scherer and Zentner 2001), precisely because it has no obvious denotational meaning, and its resultant therapeutic power to arouse or soothe listeners.

In the course of his argument, Mithen is concerned to demonstrate that the music faculty and the language faculty, although they share some areas of the brain, are nevertheless independent of one another in terms of which neural circuits in the brain are active in languaging and musicking. He suggests that 'the neural networks for music processing evidently extend beyond the cerebral cortex and into parts of the brain that have had a much longer evolutionary history' (Mithen 2006: 67), and like Cross (2001) he maintains that this is the case because it is the social world that provides the greatest cognitive challenge to human beings. Indeed, it is coping with the demands of living in large social groups that provides the most likely explanation for the origin of human intelligence. And so it is not surprising that our more complex emotions relate directly to our social relationships. Without such emotions we would be socially inept; in fact we would be unaware of the complexities and subtleties of the social world around us, and would fail entirely in our social relationships. (Mithen 2006: 87)

Without the neural adaptation of the music faculty, we would be unable to deal with complex emotions and living in large social groups.

If we look at the research evidence on language and music as communication systems both from an ontogenetic and a phylogenetic point of view, we see a clear distinction between the communicative functions of language (largely the transfer and processing of information) and music (the holistic evocation of emotions and the creation of social bonding in groups of humans). We also note the priority of the acquisition of music as 'a communication system specialising in the expression of emotion' over the acquisition of language as 'a communication system specialising in the transmission of information'. Having said that, however, evolutionary priority nevertheless goes to the acquisition of language. The precursor of both language and instrumental music can only have been song. In the following section, therefore, we devote our attention to making a distinction between pre-linguistic 'song' and song as we know it today.

Song₁ and Song₂: Distinguishing Hominins from Other Species

All the evidence thus speaks in favour of the hypothesis that the music faculty, in the form of song, preceded the language faculty in terms of human evolution. For this reason, a clear distinction needs to be made between pre-linguistic, *language-less song* and *song that is a synthesis of music and language*. We are specifically interested in the latter type, and more specifically, in what is commonly labelled 'folk song', a decision that has much to do with the social, communal and bonding significance of song that Mithen, Cross and, to a lesser extent, Fitch (2005, 2006) attribute to pre-linguistic song (see also Foley 2012; Morley 2012; Dunbar 2012b).

Bird Song and Hominid Song

We begin by focusing on the discussion in Merker (2012) of vocal learning in avian species as an analogue to the vocal learning of *Homo erectus*. Merker begins by noting a striking comparison between the 'sources contributing to the mockingbird's song repertoire and those contributing to the forms of human spoken language' (ibid.: 218). He claims that this resemblance has not so far been mentioned in the literature, and it concerns the recognition of *ritual* rather than *instrumental culture* as the determining factor in the cultural transmission of song. As the central factor in determining a group's identity, ritual culture insists on the correct form and sequence of performance in ritual events. However, as Merker points out, the 'obligatory particulars of this form are *arbitrary* to the ritual's purpose ... in the sense that a hypothetical pattern substitution ... does not on those grounds alone allow one to predict that such a sequence would in principle be less fit to preserve the ritual purpose than the canonical version' (ibid.: 219). Two apparently contradictory points are important here: firstly, ritual vocal behaviour requires 'fidelity of copying by imitation'. This, in turn, implies that 'the carriers of a ritual tradition are possessed of a *conformal motive* which ensures that the practice and rehearsal that is needed to achieve fidelity converges in the end on actual duplication of the transmitted model ' (ibid.: 220). The goal of creating patterned forms of behaviour for cultural transmission is thus strong in imitative learning. However, this does not prevent individuals from improvising on already learnt behaviour by embellishing song sequences and inventing new sequences or parts of sequences. We have here a form of open-ended innovative behaviour that is remarkably similar to the actuation of language change in historical sociolinguistic theory (cf. Chapter 5), except that in the present case we are not yet dealing with language.

As Merker points out, '[o]pen-ended vocal learning and invention imply emancipation of vocal production from innate constraints that limit the outcome of song-learning to variations on a structural schematism or schematisms common to the species' (ibid.: 220), and 'emancipated' learners will tend to become 'extravagant and lavish' in their song productions. But why would those extravagant learners waste so much time and energy in their song displays? Or, as Merker puts it: 'Why prolong the song display beyond the boredom threshold, thus incurring the additional cost of acquiring the means to produce elaborate song?' (ibid.: 223). The answer is that it will eventually produce advantages for the singer in terms of mating and social significance within the group. 'Squandering', says Merker, 'becomes an asset' (cf. also Levitin 2008 [2006]), in that the singer shows s/he has reserves of energy, stamina and innovative talent. Over the course of time, this kind of singing, released as it now is from ritual events, will create an adaptive process that will improve the gene pool, encourage encephalisation and also lead to more socially stable monogamous relationships. After roughly 1 million years of song, it eventually led to a learning bottleneck in *Homo sapiens*, where more generalised vocal sequences were bound to survive and purely holistic imitation became stuck in the bottle. It is at this point that the transition to human language begins to occur, and Mithen mentions work by Wray (1998, 2000, 2002b), Kirby (2000, 2001, 2002a, b) and Saffran et al. (2006) that discusses how compositional language developed from holistic sequences of vocalisation. In other words, *Homo sapiens* was already a masterful singer before language came on the scene. What could be more natural than a combination of language and song during and after the evolutionary bottleneck?

Hominid Song as an Exaptive Ability or an Adaptive Faculty: Song₁?

In *Music, Language, and the Brain*,[10] Patel (2008) contradicts Mithen and argues that music has always been an exaptive ability and not an adaptive faculty. He reasons that 'the key question from an evolutionary standpoint is whether [musically relevant abilities] reflect mechanisms shaped by selection for music, or whether they are a by-product of mechanisms used in language comprehension or in auditory processing' (Patel 2008: 385). His principal argument for rejecting the innateness theory for the music faculty is that, if it were true, we would not be able to explain the existence of congenitally tone-deaf individuals who are nevertheless perfectly competent in language.

His argument, however, is based more on the productive side of the music faculty than the receptive side. The counter-argument runs as follows: Assume that in events involving song, ritual or otherwise, participants were expected to participate in communal singing. In that case, they must have had the ability to imitate everything they heard, and their music faculty, as at present, was receptive rather than productive. Tone-deaf members of a group may have had the ability to vocalise but not to do so musically, but it is highly unlikely that this excluded them from social participation in the event. We argued above that those few who were actively involved in extending and innovating sequences of song were the 'extravagant and lavish' singers. Once the step had been taken from holistic imitation to combinatorial vocalisation, quite different forms of pitch control and rhythmic organisation developed for human language than were already present for music, such that even the tone-deaf, like everyone else (musically receptive and musically productive individuals), were genetically subject to language adaptation. In all probability, tone-deaf group members existed before and after the bottleneck, but their inability to distinguish between forms of pitch control and rhythmic organisation in music did not prevent them from acquiring the different forms of pitch control and/or rhythmic control necessary to produce human language.[11]

From the sociolinguistic point of view adopted in this book, language change is initiated through a large number of linguistic innovations, the vast majority of which fizzle out without being adopted and diffused by

---

[10] We refer hereafter to *MLB*, rather than repeat the full title.

[11] The tone-deaf are still able to recognise rhythm and pitch changes. They can recreate or repeat rhythmic patterns but they cannot recreate exact pitches in pitch changes. Tone-deafness does not preclude intonation in speech, nor does it interfere with stress timing.

others through a population. Not everyone innovates in using language, but of those who do, it is highly likely that the language equivalents of the 'extravagant and lavish singers' will be amongst them. From a theoretical point of view, therefore, we support the hypothesis that the music faculty was an adaptive natural mutation driven by musical innovations to satisfy the need for social bonding and social grouping. For different reasons and from different academic perspectives, scholars like Cross (2003a, 2003b, 2012), Dunbar (2012a, 2012b), Morley (2002, 2003, 2012), Gamble (2012), Fitch (2006), Foley (2012), S. Brown (2000) and many others have argued that pre-linguistic song is an important factor in the evolution of humankind.

The Emergence of Song₂

What happens when we combine language and song$_1$ to produce examples of song$_2$? Patel focuses on this issue in chapter 4 of *MLB*, entitled 'Melody'. At the beginning of the chapter he asks whether it is possible to give a definition that 'encompasses both music and speech', and he concludes the following:

One possibility is 'an organized sequence of pitches that conveys a rich variety of information to a listener.' This definition emphasizes two points. First, melodies are tone sequences that pack a large informational punch. For example, speech melody can convey affective, syntactic, pragmatic, and emphatic information ... Musical melody can also convey a broad variety of information ... The second point is that a tone sequence qualifies as a melody by virtue of the rich mental patterns it engenders in a listener. That is, melody perception is a constructive process by which the mind converts a sequence of tones into a network of meaningful relationships. (Patel 2008: 182)

The problem at this point is that the two kinds of constructive process have very different purposes. In languaging, the purpose is to convey to the listener enough information with enough pragmatic and affective import to allow him/her to generate meanings and to activate some form of response, such that whatever the activity the participants are engaged in, it may be completed – satisfactorily or not. In musicking, as Patel points out, the purpose is 'to engender a much richer set of perceptual relations' in the listener and 'to provoke the generation of a wide range of meta-relations' (ibid.: 205). In languaging, the onus of accomplishing the activity is shared, since meaning making is constrained by the structures of the language, including prosody and intonation; in musicking, the listener is left free to interpret as s/he wishes. Meaning making is certainly constrained by melody, rhythm, tempo and timbre, but the activity is different. In musicking, it is the performance before and with an audience that is central; in languaging the principal concern is achieving something together. However, performance events may still be part of the activity of languaging, and it is this that creates the possibility of a fusion between language and music in song$_2$.

A Footnote on the Development of Instrumental Music

Fitch (2006: 196–97) observes that '[t]he oldest uncontested bone flutes are a pair, made from wing bones of a swan, from Geissenklösterle in Germany, dated to 36,800 ± 1000 years ago', which allows us to take 40,000 years, possibly more, as the minimum age for instrumental music. In other words, around the time when *Homo sapiens* dispersed into Europe – and possibly well before this, since *Homo sapiens* arrived in Australia 50–60,000 years ago – the completion of the transfer from 'Hmmmmm' to language allowed enough cognitive fluidity between vocalisation with language and *Homo sapiens'* technological abilities to create extensions of the human body that would also produce sound – musical instruments. This could only have been possible if 'Hmmmmm' had already been diverted into a communication system that specialised in the expression of emotion in ritual events and if song$_2$ were already in use at those events. Rituals involving religious rites, marriages, deaths, initiations, protest and social drama, seasonal festivities, the supplication of help from the natural world, the generational transference of cultural memory, preparations for war or defence would all, undoubtedly, have been accompanied with song and dance, and it is quite natural that any new means of making music beyond the use of the human voice would have been integrated into this system.

Hence, like song, musical instruments were a consequence of *Homo sapiens'* newly acquired cognitive fluidity and of the use of music in ritual events. Those events would have been communal and would have involved groups of hominins. In addition, it is likely that the events would have been celebrated apart from the normal procedures of everyday life and that special places would have been set aside in which to celebrate them. In the following section we will develop this idea further from the research of Clive Gamble.

Containing Ritual

The cognitive fluidity of combining experiences from one cognitive faculty with those of another allows human beings to perceive abstract concepts in terms of concrete physical experiences in or on their own bodies. Lakoff and Johnson (1980, 1999) argue that our mental abilities are derived from basic bodily knowledge very early on in our lives by means of metaphorical processes. We learn, for example, that by exerting physical pressure from our own bodies against an object in our environment, we can move its position (movement and force). Hence exerting other kinds of non-physical pressure in other contexts may allow us to move other human beings in more abstract situations. We learn about horizontal (*to* and *from*) and vertical (*up* and *down*) relationships between our own bodies and objects in our immediate environment, and we can project that experience onto other less physical contexts by metaphorical projection. We also learn that if we turn our attention away from an object, this does not mean that the object ceases to exist. Part of this early bodily experience is that containment is a central physical relationship between objects enabling us to enter a position of safety from which we can also venture out. It is the metaphor of containment that we focus on here.

Symbolic Containers

Gamble argues that most modern archaeology is dominated by rationalist attempts to interpret social structure from the concrete evidence that 'stones and bones' provide. He criticises the essentialist tendencies of palaeoanthropologists in searching for artefacts in their efforts to establish their possible symbolic significance in hominin evolution and concludes that 'music has always been a part of hominin social life, but that during evolution it was co-opted to enhance positive emotions at hominin gatherings' (Gamble 2012: 96). For most modern humans 'performance ... unites the mundane with the extraordinary' (ibid.: 85), and he sees no reason to assume that this would not have been the case at earlier periods in human evolution.

For Gamble, 'the body provides the source for experience and that knowledge is translated into corporeal culture (rhythms, gestures, body techniques) and material culture (artifacts, locales, landscapes)' (ibid: 92). He focuses specifically on the containment metaphor for two reasons: (1) the human body is itself a 'material container (trunk and head)' and also 'a set of instruments (limbs)' (cf. the connection with music) and (2) by choosing a particular performance location for ritual performance, human beings construct 'a contained space ... created through attention and association and imbued with an emotional charge' (ibid.: 94).

His fieldwork at Makuri village in northern Namibia included the observation of ritual song and dance events inside the village. 'At Makuri,' he says, 'containers abound. The performance space is set within the village. The oval is a container and the actions of the men encircled the women. In their turn the women surrounded the container of the hearth' (ibid.: 95). Repeated dancing around a central hearth had worn an oval around it and at a suitable distance from it, which took on the symbolic significance of the location within which song and dance occurred. The oval had thus become a symbolic container of the ritual enacted through the song and dance. He suggests that the Makuri performance he attended 'was an example of an architecture without walls; a container without hard-edged material boundaries, although delimited by the actions of bodies and the emotions generated' (ibid.: 96). Hence, all ritual performances take place in contained spaces, contained materially or symbolically, and in the absence of a material container the activity of singing helps to construct containment and, through that containment, the assertion of a social group. Bonding takes place within social containment.

A singing (and dancing) event takes place within a spatial container, either provided/constructed for singing or symbolically created by the participants. Gamble's argument that ritual performance implies some form of symbolic or material container in which the social group can perform opens up two significant points. Firstly, singing involves singers *and* non-singers, which makes them both participants in the ritual event. Secondly, material containers may be present and used as a space for ritual, or containers may be constructed physically in the emergent event of the performance to function symbolically as the container.

The Symbolic Container of Ritual as the Source of Music

Our central hypothesis is that all forms of music, hence all song genres, ultimately derive from the symbolic container of ritual in whatever group of hominins we consider. In the final subsection of the previous section we listed a set of ritual functions that are of fundamental significance for any social group. We can extend that list as follows:

(1) religious rites (worshipping); (2) entertaining others; (3) healing others; (4) expressing and perpetuating superstitions; (5) protecting the group (war and defence); (6) celebrating seasonal activities; (7) protesting at injustice; (8) remembering the past and its significance for the present and the future; (9) supplicating help from the natural environment; (10) empowering others; (11) criticising others; (12) initiating others; (13) rejoicing; (14) lamenting; (15) soothing and entrancing others; (16) flyting (i.e. ritually insulting) others.

The list is not definitive, but we claim that a ritual event, i.e. in our terms a song performance, should represent any one of these categories and may often represent more than one. Songs are thus used communally[12] to take the individuals of the group 'out of themselves' (Frith 1996: 251) or to induce 'boundary loss' and thereby to bond the group socially. 'Boundary loss' is a term used by McNeill (1995), which Mithen defines as 'the manner in which group music-making leads to "a blurring of self-awareness and the heightening of fellow feeling for all those who share in a dance"' (2006: 209), or, in our

---

[12] Regardless of whether one person performs or the whole group is expected to join in the singing.

case, 'a song'. In Chapter 3 we argue that songs within the ritual container have the function, through social bonding in the group, of constructing or reconstructing a community of practice. In the modern world, not all songs still have such bonding functions, but those that do are central to bonding a community of practice and are those that we take to be 'folk' songs, *whatever their origins may be.*

Figure 1.2 represents Gamble's oval of performance, the symbolic container in which ritual events involving song and dance are played out. The arrows from outside the oval indicate pressures exerted on the group from outside the protective container, and the arrows inside the oval indicate the resistance to extra-group pressures that the ritual event intends to strengthen.

We propose that all music is derived phylogenetically from the 'oval of performance' with the possible exception of three song genres, lullaby, love song and work song, which would hardly be performed ritually before and with an audience. Nevertheless, they are still derivative of the symbolic performance oval. Of these three, the love song is the most difficult to fit into the oval, but

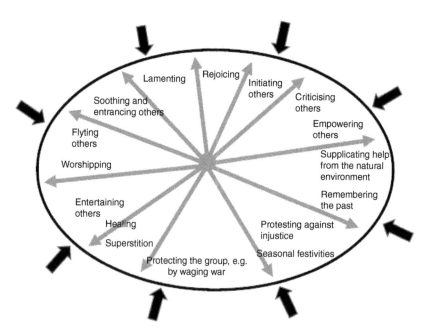

Figure 1.2. *The symbolic container of ritual as the oval of performance*

even here love songs may also protest, or lament the death of or abandonment by another, or be an occasion for rejoicing, or be simply intended to entrance a potential lover. They still derive their force from the performance oval, even though they are not meant to be performed primarily as part of a ritual. A declaration of love or the attempt to seduce someone would not, in any normal circumstances, entail song, but when song is in evidence in these two social activities, it represents their simulation before an audience.

The technological achievements of recording musical performances have revolutionised the relationship between performers and audience, and it is not always clear how recorded songs can be related back to the symbolic container of ritual. Problems involved in weakening the links between ritual and music in social bonding will be dealt with in Chapter 7, but in the western world the process had already begun with the beginnings of Western Art Music (WAM) at the time of the Renaissance. In the case of WAM, the symbolic container finally acquired the material solidity of the modern concert hall and, in the process, the function of the audience, the music-takers, has been reduced to that of passive appreciation of professional musical expertise rather than to the creation of group solidarity through participation (cf. Small 1998 on this topic).

The Sociolinguistics of Song Performance

Any song, modern or traditional, and without regard to the song genre it is normally assigned to, may evoke any of the bonding states significant in constructing the ritual container in which singers, musicians and participants construct a community. As we saw in the Introduction, if the performance of a song succeeds in contributing towards the construction or reaffirmation of a bonded social community, it has been used as a folk song, as Blacking understood the term. In the chapters to follow, we put this assumption to the test, and we do so by considering songs within a conceptualisation of performance as a social process. Our model of performance is sociolinguistic, and we use this section to define our own stance towards sociolinguistics before moving on to discuss the term 'performance' within the social sciences and to develop a sociolinguistic model of song performance in Chapter 2.

Sociolingistics focuses on the description and explanation of how interlocutors use language spontaneously and creatively in social interaction and social practice by varying the forms of language used in accordance with the perceived situational needs and exigencies of the emergent situation. Those varied forms of language thus help to construct (and reconstruct) social communities and to transform them where necessary. In languaging, they create cohesion (or dissension) among participants, they project a self or selves, and they position themselves within a social matrix. They may even shift from everyday interaction to what we call the *performance mode* of social practice, and when performance is embodied through both languaging and musicking, it takes on a ritualistic character, protecting and bonding the group. It is with the concept of song performance that we are centrally concerned in the present book.

Eckert (2008) has called attention to what she calls 'Third Wave Variation Studies' in sociolinguistics, in which a critical focus on the social meanings of linguistic variables as they occur in the speech of individual speakers in social practice has now moved to centre-stage. The consequence of this shift from language to languaging involves new sociolinguistic definitions of old concepts such as 'style' and 'stylisation' (Eckert and Rickford 2001; Coupland 2001, 2007), 'style-shifting' (Harper 2006; Rampton 2003), 'identity' (Bucholtz and Hall 2005; Bucholtz and Lopez 2011), and new concepts such as 'indexicality' (Silverstein 2003; Johnstone, Andrus and Danielson 2006) and 'enregisterment' (Johnstone 2011; Agha 2003, 2005), all of which will be defined in subsequent chapters and put to use in Part III. Third Wave approaches to language variation have shifted from a focus on whole speech communities to a focus on the social meanings generated and interpreted by individual speakers in the course of emergent social interaction. This shift from community to individual has created an increased awareness that all social practices are fundamentally 'emergent'. Through recurrent forms of social practice, a wide range of 'communities of practice' are constructed, reconstructed, modified and transformed (Wenger 1998; Eckert 2000; Eckert and McConnell-Ginet 1992), and through those communities participant identities are negotiated and renegotiated (Bucholtz 2004; Bucholtz and Hall 2005), as we shall see in the chapters comprising Part I. Within the framework of Third Wave approaches to language variation, we propose that a song performance is an instantiation of emergent social practice geared towards the construction or reaffirmation of a community of practice, a 'folk'.

A relatively new, but fast-growing, branch of sociolinguistics takes a historical perspective on the issues we have reviewed above, the interest here being in new approaches to looking at language change through the innovative mechanisms of language variation. We posit that performances involving languaging and musicking also display similar forms of mutation through time. The further back we go in history, the more scattered become the concrete data we have to go on, and, ultimately, we will never know exactly how things changed and developed in emergent social interaction, whether performative or not. However, Labov's Principle of Uniformity (1994, 2001) posits that the ways in which people communicate in oral social practice today are not likely to be fundamentally different from instances of social practice in the past. Close observation of social interaction in contemporary types of performance should allow us to speculate relatively securely about performances in the past, although we cannot escape from the territory of well-grounded speculation. The past will always be another country, even our own individual past. This fact can never be altered. These and many other similar issues will be dealt with in the chapters in Part II.

Part I

Creating Community and Identity through
Song

2   'Breaking through' into Performance

The effectiveness of the music depends on the context in which it is
both performed and heard.
(Blacking 1973: 44)

Singing, Languaging and Performing

In Chapter 1, we dealt with similarities and differences between languaging
and musicking from both a neuropsychological and a palaeoanthropological
perspective. Our theoretical take on the evolutionary development of human
language has been and will continue to be constructionist rather than
rationalist. Gamble's idea of the symbolic container in which song and
dance help to strengthen group ties through social bonding is a hypothetical
construct but is highly relevant given the mass of evidence at hand to support
the hypothesis that song preceded language in the phylogenetic development
of humankind. The theory of a symbolic container, as the locale in which
ritual events take place, including the performance of song, provides a robust
explanation for the evolution of the music faculty, in which a sociolinguistic
theory of performance can be grounded.

We use the term 'container' frequently throughout the book, so we need
to be explicit about how Gamble uses it. A physical container is a space
within which human beings are protected from inimical exterior forces
and are able to carry out in relative safety everyday ritual activities
(cooking and eating, sleeping, entertaining, working, etc.). A *symbolic
container* is a space, local or temporal or both, which metaphorically
projects everyday activities as having some protection from exterior
forces. It can be constructed at any time by co-participants within an
already existent physical space, as when a group of people at a committee
meeting come together in a corner of the room to discuss some issue.
In general, they form a circle or an oval to exclude others from participating. The song and dance performance witnessed by Gamble in Namibia
(see Chapter 1) took place in the open and around a fire, creating a visible
oval in the ground around it.

The container is also a space in which various forms of languaging can be expected to occur. Later in this chapter we show that within stretches of socio-communicative verbal interaction, participants may need to enter what we call the *performance mode* (PM). In fact, there are several genres of oral and written discourse which appear to be entirely devoted to performance and as such become ritualistic, e.g. speeches, lectures, discussions and interviews on radio and television, newspaper articles, etc. We postpone a discussion of performance in languaging till the final chapter of the book, since our major aim is to account for the performance of singing. In later chapters, we raise issues such as whether all linguistic interaction is performance, or only certain segments of interaction, whether an audience is always necessary for a stretch of interaction to be considered 'performance' and whether it can be said that the non-active participants in a conversation constitute an audience or simply a 'listenership'. Nevertheless, two theoretical concepts require a fuller definition in this chapter, viz. *breakthrough into performance* and *performance mode*. We begin by locating the first use of the term 'breakthrough into performance' in the work of Dell Hymes.

Hymes' Notion of Breaking through into Performance

Central to Hymes' conceptualisation of performance is the article entitled 'Breakthrough to performance', which first appeared in Ben-Amos and Goldstein (1975). In 1981 Hymes edited a set of his own articles with the title *'In Vain I Tried to Tell You': Essays in Native American Ethnopoetics*, in which his 1975 article is reprinted but much expanded with the addition of a postscript, two further articles that are pertinent to his concept of 'breakthrough to performance' and a final section entitled 'Breakthrough into performance revisited'. The expanded 1981 version is the one we refer to here. The title of the 1981 book indicates that two of Hymes' major interests, Native American languages (particularly of the Northwest coast) and ethnopoetics, are central to the 'Breakthrough' article. But at the same time Hymes was also concerned to underpin his notion of communicative competence and his redefinition of performance study as 'the ethnography of symbolic forms – the study of the variety of genres, narration, dance, drama, song, instrumental music, visual art, that interrelate with speech in the communicative life of a society, in terms of which the relative importance of speech and language must be assessed' (Hymes 1971: 284).

Hymes had returned to the data collected in the mid-1950s from his early fieldwork with the Wishram Chinook Indians. At the time of his fieldwork only a handful of people still spoke the language, so there were few opportunities to use it. He focuses on two informants, one of whom, Philip Kahclamet, was reluctant to tell narratives in either Wishram Chinook or English. The other,

Hiram Smith, was the son of a storyteller, but it took a long time for Hymes to win his trust and to coax him into telling some of the traditional stories of Coyote in Wishram Chinook. In 1975, three things puzzled Hymes: Why were the two informants so reluctant to tell stories in their native language? What factors caused them to break through into narrative performance? And what were the linguistic correlates of that breakthrough? Hymes, who knew Wishram Chinook but was a white American, felt that he was not an appropriate audience to listen to a story in anything but English. Kahclamet begins his story in English in the third person, but he ends it in Wishram Chinook in the first person. In Smith's case, Hymes had to persuade him that he, Hymes, *was* in fact an appropriate audience, and this could only be done through the close friendship he had built up with Smith.

Factors such as these led Hymes to ask what kind of communicative competence determines not only what people can do, but also, and more importantly, what they will do. He proposed that all adult members of a culture are able to interpret speech events, e.g. to say whether what they had heard was a proverb, a myth, a story and so on. But not all the members of a culture can report a speech event and not all speech events are reportable, both for reasons of *contextual or conventional appropriacy*. All members of a culture are able to repeat what they have witnessed, but only a small number have the power to repeat the same speech event (in different ways each time of course) and those who are able, or have a social warrant to do so, are narrators/storytellers, i.e. performers. But if the audience, or the setting, or the occasion is not culturally appropriate, performers also have the right *not* to perform. Hence, not only are there ratified performers, but there are also ratified audiences, and not everyone is a ratified performer or a member of a ratified audience. These are crucial factors in a sociolinguistic analysis of performance, and they will prove invaluable features of folk song performance in later chapters.

Because languaging is not inherently oriented towards or embedded within the performance mode (PM), i.e. is not inherently ritual, there must be ways of signalling to other participants the intention to perform rather than to inform, and there will always be ratified performers and ratified audiences. We use the term *keying in* to refer to the activity of attaining ratification for a breakthrough into performance. The following subsection gives an example from our data to illustrate how ratification may be obtained.

The Chip Shop: Keying-in and Keying-out

We illustrate the activity of 'breaking through' into performance with an extract from conversational data collected in the 1980s by R.J.W., which were at that time used for different research purposes. Assume that, during a conversation, one of the participants wants to tell a joke or give a personal narrative. In doing so, the participant exposes her/himself to evaluation as a ratified performer. On occasions such as these, the participant wishes to *present* rather than just *project a self*[1] and is thus dependent on the goodwill of the other participants in temporarily waiving their rights to contribute turns at talk. This is the juncture at which a shift from a conversation frame to the performance mode is imminent, and such a breakthrough needs to be signalled by conventionalised forms of linguistic behaviour. First, the request must be signalled beforehand. Second, if anyone objects, the performance may be cancelled. Third, if no one objects, the lack of a negative response can be taken as a sign to proceed. Such verbal procedures constitute the ritual of *keying in* a performance, and when they are effective, they constitute successful breakthroughs into the PM. They may also be accompanied by forms of non-verbal action. Examples of keying-in would be, 'Did you hear the one about …?', 'You'll never guess what happened to me today,' and so on. After a successful breakthrough into performance, the performer is obliged to return the conversational floor to the co-participants once s/he is finished. So there are also conventional, formulaic means to *key out* the 'performance'. An interesting feature of this kind of breakthrough into performance is that, once those who have given up the floor for the performer(s) are allowed back, they also have a right – perhaps even an obligation – to evaluate the performance in some way.

To illustrate the processes of *keying-in* and *keying-out*, consider the following example taken from Watts (1991: 114). The context is that of a family conversation consisting of four participants:

(1) → 01 R: <u>did I ever tell you when I was in Spain last year?</u> we were in this place called
              Nerja (0.8) which is[(0.9) a (.) very touristy place <???> around one of the
       02 B: [mm
       03   back streets in that town is a- (0.7) a shop called 'chish and fips'.
       04 B: <@@@ oh god @@@>
       05 S: is there?
       06 R: and it's [—
       07 D: ['chish and fi[ps'?
       08 R: [∧yeah
       09 B: 'chish and fi[ps'.
       10 D: [oh yeah. mm
       11 R: and it's run by an English woman, [(0.9] who'd gone out to Spain, and- and
       12 B: [yes. I was going to say, she must be of
       13 R: decided   ]that that might be a good idea to-[   ]to open up that fish and
       14 B: course. ∧mm]
       15 B: [yeah,]
       16 R: [chip shop. (1.2) where she knew that there were going to be lots of [(0.8)
       17 B: [yeah.   [∧mm
   → 18 R: British tourists. (1.1) <u>and apparently it's going like a bomb.</u>

---

[1] Presenting a self entails putting an already formed concept of the self before an audience for evaluation whereas projecting a self entails the construction of another self in the course of social interaction.

In extract (1) R intends to perform a story. To acquire the breakthrough, he keys into it with the very conventional and formulaic utterance underlined in line 01, and he keys out again in line 18 with a significant pause of 1.1 seconds followed by a less conventional but nevertheless significantly evaluative utterance (underlined). During the story, the other co-participants either utter requests for more information or give him verbal back-channel support. The 'performance' itself constitutes that stretch of speech between and including the keying-in and the keying-out.

The kinds of linguistic conventionalisation (cf. Pietsch 2015) used to key into and out of a performance can be called *performance bids* and *performance closures* since they are recognisable as requests to perform and indications that the performance is completed. If a participant in an interaction produces an utterance of the form 'Did I ever tell you ... ?', as does R in extract (1), it is immediately recognisable as a bid to enter the PM in order to create a performance frame in which some story will be told. At this point, the co-participants still have the option to prevent the breakthrough. The utterance is a *keying-in move*, a *performance bid* (see the first arrow in the transcript at the point where the keying-in utterance occurs), and the co-participants also know that the potential storyteller has implicitly promised completion through the utterance, although no information is given as to how long the performance will last. In this sense, performance bids can also be seen as instances of an *intent to complete*. And when the performer, after a significant pause, switches from the narrative past tense to an evaluation of the situation in the present tense (as does R in extract [1]: see the second arrow at the point where he keys out), it is immediately recognisable as a *performance* closure.

A bid to break through into performance places a responsibility on the shoulders of the would-be performer. If the bid to perform is granted, the performer(s) is/are then obliged to make it worth the others' while to waive their rights to the conversational floor and to present the experience in an interesting, significant, 'entertaining' way (see Watts 1982; Lakoff 2010). It also obliges the audience to acknowledge the efforts of the performer(s), i.e. to evaluate the performance and to register their evaluation of the presentation in some way. Figure 2.1 represents the process of 'breaking through' into performance during a languaging activity.

When one or more members of an emergent socio-communicative interaction bid successfully to perform to the others, such that the oval constituting the container is constructed within the frame of the ongoing interaction, we maintain that those present have gone into the *performance mode* (PM), the boundaries of which are constituted by the *keying-in* (the *performance bid*) and the *keying-out* (the *performance closure*), which necessitate different forms of languaging behaviour. The period of time during which the performance container is valid can be called the *performance frame*. Inasmuch as the communicative behaviour of the participants is demonstrably different during the time when the PM is

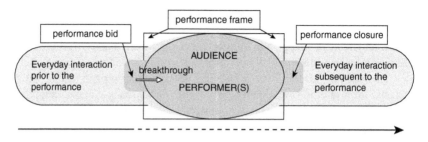

Figure 2.1. *The breakthrough into performance*

valid, i.e. they have now become 'the audience', the performance could be said to represent ritualised forms of behaviour, e.g. back-channel utterances, requests for clarification, explicit co-production of the narrative, etc. The following section outlines further work in the social sciences on the term 'performance' and focuses explicitly on the socio-anthropological work of Victor Turner. This is then followed by a section that develops a sociolinguistic model of performance as a ritual activity.

Performance in the Social Sciences since the 1950s

Performance has played a significant but disputed role in the social sciences since the 1950s. Turner (1982: 91) points out that '[t]he term *drama*' – which he was attempting, at the end of his life, to integrate with theatre studies – 'has been criticized ... as the imposition on observational data of a schema derived from *cultural* genres, hence "loaded" and not "neutral" enough for scientific use (Gluckman 1977: 227–43; Firth 1975: 1–2)'. Despite criticism of this kind from rationalist circles, *performance* has since appeared as a major concept in sociology (see Goffman 1959, 1974), anthropology (see Turner 1982, 1987), folklore (see Bauman [1975] 1977, 1986; Ben-Amos and Goldstein 1975; Glassie 1982), linguistic anthropology (Hymes 1964, 1974, 1981), cultural studies (see Diamond 1996) and, for obvious reasons, in areas of the performing arts such as theatre studies, dance and music (see Carlson 1994; Schechner 1985; Schechner and Appel 1990; Goldberg 1988; Royce 1984, 2004; Kallberg 1996).[2]

Languaging in the Performance Mode and Conceptualising
Performance in the Social Sciences

Because certain forms of activity involving languaging are specifically oriented to the PM, discourse types such as narrative, debate and speech-making have

---

[2] For an excellent introduction to ways in which the concept of 'performance' has been defined and used in all these disciplines, see Carlson (1996).

taken on a new lease of life as valid 'objects' of study in sociolinguistics. As a consequence, performance has re-emerged as a central concept in the social and cultural study of human language. As early as 1982, folklorist Henry Glassie declared that we should 'place the idea of performance in the middle of our thinking' (Glassie 1982: 155). In dealing with different ways of conceptualising 'performance' in the social sciences, some scholars have made a distinction between *staged performances* of various kinds and performances carried out in the cut-and-thrust of everyday instances of social practice, which we define later in this chapter as *relational/impromptu performances* (see also Bell and Gibson 2011: 557).[3]

In the writings of Mikhail Bakhtin, we find a focus on 'speech genres' rather than language structure, indicating that Bakhtin was more interested in languaging than in the language system. Bakhtin insists on the dialogic and heteroglossic nature of language in use (i.e. languaging). He was not himself a linguist, but his philosophical writings on language have been influential in developing notions such as variability, hybridity and heterogeneity (three notions subsumable under Bakhtin's *heteroglossia*), all of which have been central to sociolinguistics since its emergence in the late 1950s and in particular to recent developments in the field. In Bakhtin's work, the concept of 'performance' does not appear explicitly, but the anthropological, sociological and, above all, dialogic approach to language in his work strongly implicates the presence of performance as a major social activity in languaging.

From the 1950s, the work of Erving Goffman in the sociology of communicative interaction presaged a return of the term *performance* to sociolinguistics, although this did not occur till Third Wave Variation Studies emerged in the 1990s. Goffman's work is ambiguous with respect to the degree to which socio-communicative interaction, or languaging, can be taken to be inherently performative (cf. Chapter 12). If languaging is not inherently ritual, it needs forms of keying-in and keying-out to assure the breakthrough to performance. We argue that musicking (singing) is always inherently ritual and as such is more likely to occur in activities oriented to or located in performance.

Richard Bauman's work on performance began in the early 1970s, i.e. a little later than that of Hymes. It emerges from his first major interest, folklore. Bauman (1975: 291) contains a conceptualisation of performance as a synthesis of two things, 'the doing of folklore – the artistic *event* – and the performance situation, involving performer, art form, audience and setting – both of which

---

[3] We prefer the term 'relational or impromptu performance' to refer to 'a performer–audience situation ... created spontaneously in the midst of an otherwise everyday language situation' (Bell and Gibson 2011: 557) to Coupland's alternative 'mundane performance' (2007). 'Mundane' has a slightly pejorative overtone to it, which most everyday performances do not deserve. In Chapter 12 we develop the notion of 'relational performance' to refer to all instances of socio-communicative verbal interaction with the exception of 'representational performance'.

are central to the developing performance approach to folklore'. In his introduction to Bauman (1977), he expands this original definition by taking
performance to be a form of social process and seeing it as 'a unifying thread
tying together the marked, segregated esthetic genres and other spheres of
verbal behavior into a general unified conception of verbal art as a way of
speaking' (ibid.: 5). In accounting for forms of verbal art, Bauman is aware that
these frequently emerge out of day-to-day social practice and that they require
the setting-up of a specific performance frame ('frame' in the sense of Bateson
1972 [1955] and Goffman 1974).[4] This can only be achieved by using culture-
specific forms of *keying-in*, e.g. special codes, special formulae, figurative
language, formal stylistic devices (rhyme, alliteration, vowel harmony, other
forms of parallelism), special prosodic patterns, appeal to tradition, or even
disclaimers to performance, or any combination of these (Bauman 1975: 295).
An ethnography of performance – and also a sociolinguistics of performance –
must aim at discovering and making explicit 'the culture-specific constellations
of communicative means that serve to key performances in particular communities' (Bauman 1977: 22).

Bauman (1977: 43) also argues that part of the essence of performance is
'that it offers to the participants a special enhancement of experience, bringing
with it a heightened intensity of communicative interaction which binds the
audience to the performer in a way that is specific to performance as a mode of
communication'. It is precisely the expectation of 'a special enhancement of
experience' that characterises the performance frame, and the 'enhancement of
experience' is part of the ritual character of performance.

Charles Briggs' work is situated within the tradition of the ethnography of
speaking, and his particular field of research has been with a Mexicano community in northern New Mexico. Briggs (1988) gives a detailed ethnographic
analysis of different forms of verbal art practised by a Mexicano community in
and around Córdova, New Mexico. Most of the points we have made concerning the nature of performance are reiterated in this work, but his main interest is
to stress the relationship between text and context in performance. 'Text' for
Briggs is what is produced in a verbal performance. It consists not only of
words, but also of gestures, prosodic features and other visual and aural
semiotic forms of communication. It indexes what he calls the 'textual sphere'
(ibid.: 20). Like most other scholars, Briggs underscores the significance of

---

[4] In *Steps to an Ecology of Mind*, Gregory Bateson (1972) republished a set of his essays, one of
which, 'A theory of play and fantasy' (1956), contained the concept of 'frame', which pro-
foundly influenced Erving Goffman in *Frame Analysis* (1974). In Bauman's words, Bateson's
idea of a frame was 'a defined interpretive concept providing guidelines for discriminating
between orders of message', and it is exactly these different orders of message that occur when
a performer keys a change from non-performance to performance. If such a key is successful, the
performance mode (PM) is set up.

being able to delineate the stretch of discourse considered to be 'performance' from that which is 'non-performance', although the attempt to do this often results in what he calls 'fuzzy boundary problems'.

The 1990 article by Bauman and Briggs brings together these lines of thought and argues that the danger of an infinite regress in attempts to contextualise performances should alert us to a reconceptualisation of the term 'text' itself. Bauman's work on storytellers in Texas focuses on performance as an event and an interpretive frame, and his analysis of essentially the same 'texts' by professional storyteller Ed Bell reveals different 'entextualisations' in different types of performance context at different points in time. We can assume that Ed Bell's entextualisations spring from the same cognitive blueprint, fixed in the mind of the performer, and that the entextualisations are based on it and not some written document. In this sense, the blueprint can never be realised in exactly the same way from one telling to the next. Bauman and Briggs (1990) thus argue for a refocusing of attention on what it is about a blueprint that allows it to be decontextualised from an earlier context of performance and re-entextualised in a new context. Essentially, the blueprint is 'the same', but it may be shortened or lengthened, adapted sociolinguistically to suit an audience, adapted musically to suit changing cultural tastes, modified to allow different stylisations and much more besides. The 'text', understood as a blueprint, is malleable, flexible and adaptable to different conditions of performance.

In the following subsection, we look in some detail at an anthropological approach to 'performance' by Victor Turner that is often passed over by sociolinguists, unjustly, as we shall illustrate. It is in Turner's work that performance, particularly in musicking, dance and drama, is seen as ritual behaviour.

Performance as Ritualised Social Drama

A definition of 'ritual' taken from the Merriam-Webster online dictionary[5] – taken, as it happens, from the work of Victor Turner himself – runs as follows: 'a sequence of activities involving gestures, words, and objects, *performed in a sequestered place*, and performed according to set sequence' (our italics). Song is not mentioned here, but a large number of rituals in all societies make use of song, thus making a singing performance a form of ritual event. Rituals may be enacted by a social group to ward off danger, to enhance well-being, to ensure success, to retain and transfer the cultural traditions and beliefs of the group, to resolve social conflict, to lament the deaths of others or to initiate others into new stages of their lives (cf. Figure 1.2 in Chapter 1). At the

---

[5] www.merriam-webster.com/dictionary/ritual, accessed 13 June 2015.

crossroads of conflicting cultural, social and individual needs, there is a sense in which all forms of performance are sets of 'rituals' enacted to achieve such functions.

The study of ritual in cultural anthropology became significant in culturally enacted forms of performance in the work of Victor Turner (1920–1983), particularly in his collaboration with Richard Schechner at the end of the 1970s. Turner stressed the need to study ritual as a social process, and by doing so he presents us with a conceptualisation of performance that confirms what was said about the social activity of singing in Chapter 1. Much of what Turner has to say about performance was written towards the end of his life, so we restrict ourselves here to a collection of essays entitled *From Ritual to Theater* put together and published in 1982, and a posthumous collection edited by Richard Schechner, entitled *The Anthropology of Performance* and published in 1987, four years after his death.

The major influence on Turner's thinking was the French ethnographer Arnold van Gennep. But before reading van Gennep's *Les rites de passage* (1909),[6] Turner's extensive fieldwork on the Ndemba of Zambia during the 1950s had already convinced him that rituals were significant in helping to resolve what he termed 'social drama'. Turner conceptualised instances of social drama as '*crises* [arising] in the daily flow of social interaction' (1987: 76; italics in the original) or as 'eruption[s] from the level surface of ongoing social life' (ibid.: 90) that '[alter], in however miniscule a fashion, the structure ... of the relevant social field' (ibid.: 92). Social drama is 'the empirical unit of social process from which has been derived, and is constantly being derived, the various genres of cultural performance' (ibid.: 92–93). Importantly for our present purposes, he maintains that 'the major genres of cultural performance ... and narration ... not only originate in the social drama but also continue to draw meaning and force from the social drama' (ibid.: 94).

Social dramas can be divided into four stages: 'breach'–'crisis'–'redress'–'outcome'. By 'breach' Turner understands a rupture in 'regular, norm-governed social relations made publicly visible by the infraction of a rule ordinarily held to be binding' (ibid.: 34). A 'crisis' is a period of time 'when people take sides or ... are induced, seduced, cajoled, nudged or threatened to take sides' (ibid.). A 'redress' consists of the ways and means to effect the resolution of the crisis socially. It is therefore the most reflexive phase of the social drama. The 'outcome' is defined as 'either ... the reintegration of the disturbed social group, or ... the recognition and legitimation of irreparable schism between the contending parties' (ibid.: 35).

Turner adopts van Gennep's conclusion that a rite of passage is a *liminal* event. Public crises represent 'a threshold (*limen*) between more or less stable

---

[6] Translated into English in 1960 as *The Rites of Passage*.

phases of the social process' (Turner 1987: 74–75), and a rite of passage is performed in order to assist an individual or group of individuals to move from one cultural stage of life to the next. It is thus ritualised and conventionalised as a drama, or, in our own case, as song. Turner, however, distinguishes *liminal* events from what he calls *liminoid* events. He defines *liminality* as follows:

> The passage from one social status to another is often accompanied by a parallel passage in space, a geographical movement from one place to another. This may take the form of a mere opening of doors or the literal crossing of a threshold which separates two distinct areas, one associated with the subject's pre-ritual or preliminal status, and the other with his post-ritual or post-liminal status. (Turner 1982: 25)

A liminal area is that area (of ritual and transformation) in which an individual moves (or is moved) from one socio-cultural state of existence to another. It is an unavoidable aspect of what it means to be a member of a cultural group, and it can be located at the point of redress in a social drama. It is, in other words, an aspect of cultural reality. By *liminoid* Turner understands an event which '*resembles* without being identical with liminal' (from the Greek *-eidos*, a 'shape', a 'form'). *Liminoid* thus means 'in the shape of liminal, but not liminal' (ibid.: 32). The difference is significant because anything which is liminoid involves play, unreality, something that re-presents reality, something modelled on ritual or on social drama, some form of celebration. Hence, for Turner, all performances are *ritual liminoid* events, created and conventionalised as unreality in the shape of reality.

Defining 'Performance'

Dialogic social practice entails at least two (possibly more) participants; hence all communication involving human language also entails this fact. The social process consists of an *activity* (or set of activities) carried out by the participants to *achieve a calculated optimal effect*, and in the case of song this will be ritual bonding within a social group.[7] The active participants in a performance are the *performers*, and those observing and possibly also participating actively in the performance are the *audience*. The activity has been successful if the calculated optimal effect *is* actually achieved. The process is therefore oriented towards a goal, and the goal is to create something which did not exist (or at least not communally) before the performance began. So a 'performance' must display the following five fundamental characteristics:

---

[7] Singing is not an activity which explicitly needs to be a performance. In Chapter 3 we deal with work songs, in which singing takes on the function of bonding a group of workers but not primarily before an audience. In addition, we also frequently sing to ourselves to calm down in 'scary' situations, or even just because we love singing.

1. *Human agency*: A 'performance' is an action (or set of actions) initiated consciously by a human being or a group of human beings.
2. *Goal directionality*: The action (or set of actions) carried out by A in a performance must be intended and directed by the actor A towards the achievement of a goal.
3. *Human beneficiary*: The intended goal is oriented towards the benefit[8] of a person or group of persons who are co-interactants in the performance but have willingly, temporarily and partially waived their own rights to perform (i.e. the audience).
4. *Temporality*: The actions carried out by A are expected to take up a period of time which may have been agreed upon by the performers and the audience prior to the performance or may remain undefined.
5. *Process*: Since the actions are carried out by A through a space of time with an intended goal, they constitute a process, and since the process involves other co-participants, that process is always a *social process*.

The goal of influencing the audience in some way is congruent with Bauman's point that the intended goal of a performance is to offer a *special enhancement of experience* to the audience by creating 'a heightened intensity of communication' (Frith 1996: 208). Frith suggests that the goal of a musical performance is 'to be taken *out* of oneself (and one's society)' (ibid.: 251). Whatever the effect on the audience is intended to be, the assumption on both sides, performer(s) and audience, is that some affect will be experienced by the audience at the end of the performance. Points 2 and 3 above thus represent the ritual nature of performance most explicitly.

Constructing and Using the Container

In Chapter 1 we presented Gamble's argument that ritual performance implies some form of symbolic or material container in which the social group can perform. The argument opens up two significant points. Firstly, singing involves singers *and* non-singers, which makes them both members of the ritual event. Secondly, the kinds of ritual containers range from large spaciously constructed concert halls right the way down to outdoor gatherings of groups of people round campfires. From these two points we can derive an important distinction between *relational* (or *impromptu*) and *representational* (or *arranged*) *performances*. The former are events for which the participants construct the symbolic container during the course of the performance for the purpose of reconstructing and reaffirming *social relations* between the participants; the latter are events for which material containers are physically present

---

[8] By 'benefit' we mean that the audience have enjoyed the performance, have potentially learnt something from it or been emotionally affected by it.

prior to the event for the purpose of presenting and *representing* ritual functions – in this case through song.[9] Maddy Prior's Cecil Sharp House concert is an example of a *representational* (or arranged) performance. A practical example of a folk performance in which the participants constructed their own container as a means of establishing social relations leads us into a discussion of the distinction between a 'relational performance' and a 'representational performance'.

Constructing the Container in Emergent Social Practice

The following practical example of the construction of a symbolic container was, unfortunately, not recorded. However, R.J.W. took an active part in the event, and it etched itself into his memory. In 1972, R.J.W. was one of a team of folk music lovers who felt that the time was ripe to introduce a folk festival to Switzerland. The venue chosen was an idyllic castle on a hill next to the small town of Lenzburg in Canton Aargau, and the event became known as the Lenzburg Folk Festival.

At the very first festival in 1972, the organisers decided to institute a musicians' evening in the castle cellar on the evening before the first day of the festival, in which the organising committee and all the musicians who had been invited could enjoy a meal and a drink together. One of the co-organisers, Daniel Perret, also remembers this occasion, and he described it in an email as follows:

The organisational flexibility of the festival allowed us to introduce new ideas every year ... the first example was the introduction of the musicians' evening on the evening prior to the festival down in the huge vaults of the castle cellar. And so it happened that Roy Bailey and Leon Rosselson suddenly stood up in the middle of the meal and sang 'Martin Said to his Man', and everyone joined in the chorus. [translated from the German by R.J.W.][10]

It was indeed a memorable occasion. The everyday activity was eating a meal together, and apart from the fact that Bailey and Rosselson simply stood up, thus alerting those present to the fact that something was about to happen, there was no explicit keying-in. The fact that they were guests at the festival and well-known English folk singers in the early 1970s might have eased their entry into the PM, but the song was so well chosen that everyone joined in with the chorus, which was evidence of the audience's appreciation. After that, the meal continued, and a lot more beer and wine was consumed. The version of 'Who's the Fool Now?' that we sang can be found on the website as ☺2.

---

[9] We return to this distinction in Chapter 12 to argue that, unless there are clear, socio-culturally recognised keyings-in, all socio-communicative verbal interaction is relational performance.

[10] The song is more frequently known by the title 'Who's the Fool Now?'.

'Who's the Fool Now?' is a drinking song constructed to allow maximum participation from the audience in lines 2, 4, 7 and 8 of each stanza (cf. website ⊛2). Tim Hart leads the singers at the Maddy Prior concert in singing this song, which he keys in as a 'nonsense song', and he explicitly invites the audience to sing along with those on stage. It roughly follows the ballad structure of one line of four stressed syllables followed by a line of three stressed syllables, but not slavishly as we can see in lines 5, 6 and 7. The co-singers need no instruction about when to come in with the chorus. They do so automatically from the very beginning if they know the song, and pull in those who do not know the song from that point on. If no one in the audience knows the song, it is almost certain that they will be there at the latest in the second stanza.[11] In the symbolic container of ritual types in Chapter 1 (Figure 1.2), 'Who's the Fool Now?' belongs primarily to the category 'Entertaining others', but there is also a trace of social drama, of social criticism, which shifts it into the 'Protesting against injustice' category, belying Hart's assessment of it as a 'nonsense song'. The occasion is ritual, as pub singalongs tend to be, but this performance was lifted out of its conventional ritual container. In not keying-in the song linguistically, Bailey and Rosselson led the whole group into the construction of a symbolic container, the group defining itself through the song as a coherent bonded community, facilitated by the fact that the container of the overall social activity was the vaulted cellar of a medieval castle.

The social criticism is generated by the singer of stanza 1, the 'lead' singer, adopting Martin's voice and continuing the 'lead' in the following hallucinating stanzas, the chorus taking over the voice of Martin's man. In stanza 1, Martin addresses a servant, a 'man', who is instructed to fetch himself a cup from which to drink his ale and a can from which he, Martin, can drink his. The question 'Who's the fool now?' implies that whoever was calling someone else a fool before the 'now' of the performance has mutated into the fool in the current situation. From this, we can infer that Martin was in the habit of calling his servant a 'fool', but that the servant is now calling *him* a fool. So, although the song is a good rousing drinking song, still

---

[11] This is of course only the case if the audience is familiar with the practice that repeated parts are expected to lead to audience participation. In the interview data collected by F.A.M. from Maddy Prior and Martin Carthy, Carthy recounted that when singing Child ballad 104 'Prince Heathen', where repeated lines (5 and 6) occur in each stanza presenting what Prince Heathen does to humiliate and subjugate Lady May (e.g. 'oh bonny May winna greet now? / ye heathenish dog nae yet for you' or 'oh bonny May what do you now? / you heathenish dog dying for you'), he felt it necessary to ask audiences *not* to join in. In other words, what may look like a chorus was not meant to be taken as such, mainly because the lyrics of this ballad are too distressing to be taken as an opportunity for something as rousing as communal singing.

popular well over 400 years after it was first licensed to be printed,[12] there is a discernible trace in it of the social drama between master and servant.

The resounding success of this relational musical performance rested not just in the singers' indisputably high singing standards, nor in the fact that they were 'stars', but – and above all – in the perfect fit between the song, the performance and its contextualisation. The occasion was one of eating and drinking. The song evokes the past; the dinner was in the 'huge vaults of the castle cellar', a historic venue if ever there was one. But the container was not so much the castle vault as the relational closeness that the song created during the performance, a closeness constructed on the spot by Bailey, Rosselson and everyone else.

Relational and Representational Singing Performances and the Performance Continuum

The way in which Bailey and Rosselson shifted from the languaging of the social activity in progress at the time to musicking, i.e. to the construction of a community for the duration of the song, was different from the way in which R, in the story about the fish and chip shop, carefully keyed into the performance mode and keyed out of it when he was finished. The keying-in might have been the two singers both standing up unexpectedly, but there still seems to be a significant difference between a performance emerging from an instantiation of languaging and one carried out in singing, a ritual social event taking place in a temporal liminoid space set aside for the special social functions that it serves. The event takes place within a spatial container, either provided or constructed for the purpose or symbolically constructed by the participants (cf. the example from Gamble 2012 in Chapter 1). A breakthrough into performance in languaging may occur at any time in the social activity, and it simply puts on hold non-performative social practice until the completion of the performance. A singing performance is set aside from everyday social practice both temporally and spatially. We can represent this in Figure 2.2.

Figure 2.2 represents the process of creating a relational (impromptu) performance frame that is principally concerned to create and strengthen *relations* between those present. Participants in the symbolic oval container of performance consciously move out of the everyday interaction in which they are

---

[12] Simpson (1966: 776) gives the following succinct history of the song 'Who's the Fool Now', the first part of which refers to the song and the second part to the tune: '"Martyn said to his man, whoe is the fool now?" was licensed in 1588 to Thomas Orwin. Although no broadside copies have survived, the song was included among the "Freemens Songs of 4. Voices" in Thomas Ravenscroft's *Deuteromelia*, 1609, No. 16 (Fig. 518). It is also found in Forbes's *Cantus*, 1662 ed. only, and in *Pills*, 1699–1714, I, 47. An anonymous arrangement of the tune is in *The Fitzwilliam Virginal Book II*, 275.' For the record, the tune given by Simpson is almost exactly the same as the one we have given in the transcript of the Maddy Prior concert and the one Bailey and Rosselson used at the first Lenzburg Festival.

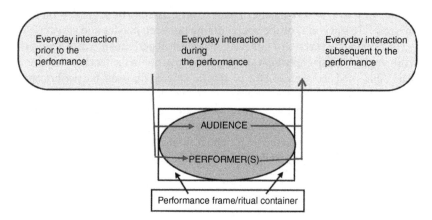

Figure 2.2. *Creation of an impromptu/relational performance frame for a ritual performance*

involved to take on the 'role' of performer or that of 'audience' in full recognition of the fact that these roles may change during the performance frame. When the performance event is over, each of the participants, performer and audience, moves out of the ritual container back into everyday interaction. The impromptu creation of a relational performance oval is more typical of folk performance, but less so for other genres of music, e.g. Western Art Music, rock, jazz, etc.

While relational performances occur spontaneously, it is more likely that a folk performance, like many other types of performance, is pre-arranged and also advertised before the event. The 'container', the venue, may vary from a living-room at home to a huge concert hall, and as it changes, so does the predisposition of the audience to participate actively in singing the songs. In the living-room, everyone may join in and participate in the event actively. In the concert hall, this will only be the case if the performer explicitly encourages participation (cf. Hart's keying-in to 'Who's the Fool Now?' in the Maddy Prior concert) or if the material is so iconic for the performer and well known to the audience that they join in spontaneously.[13] In a representational performance,

---

[13] During Crosby, Stills and Nash's 1991 'The Acoustic Concert', filmed in Warfield Theatre in San Francisco, the audience, on their feet by then, join in quite spontaneously at the lines 'Friday evening, Sunday in the afternoon' and then sing 'What have you got to lose' while the performers stop singing and playing before handing over to the audience entirely during 'Judy Blue Eyes'. The same happens in the encore during 'Teach Your Children' where the audience sing the final line of the chorus 'and know they love you' by themselves (https://www .youtube.com/watch?v=Mjbq6K2ziDQ; 1:05:39 and1:23:10, accessed 10 February 2014). Such spontaneous singing by the audience can also be seen in Paul McCartney's concert film *Back in the U.S.* 2002 with multiple shots of the audience singing along with all the Beatles songs unprompted.

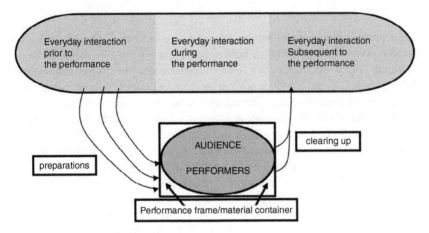

Figure 2.3. *Preparations for and clearing up of a representational/arranged frame for ritual performance*

a certain amount of work goes into its prior preparation, e.g. advertising, organising ticket sales, printing programmes (although this is rare in folk performances), organising the layout of the seating and playing area appropriately, collecting tickets at the door, clearing up after the closure of the performance, and so on. We thus have a continuum of performance types ranging from *relational* to *representational*, and as we move along this continuum, the importance of a 'stage' becomes more significant. 'Stages' are spaces reserved for the singers and musicians, and they create degrees of distance between them and the audience. As material locations, they raise the performers 'above' the audience, but even without their presence in the containers, performers often insist on a certain amount of distance between themselves and the audience. In folk performances the opposite is often the case,[14] as we shall see in Chapter 3. Figure 2.3 represents the situation of a representational/arranged performance.

There are two important distinctions between Figure 2.3 and Figure 2.2. In Figure 2.3 the performers do not set up the performance frame from scratch, and helpers (and possibly performers) are busy well before the ritual event in preparing, drumming up interest, etc. and clearing up immediately after the event.

---

[14] Bean (2014: 375) quotes several musicians' and singers' accounts of how in folk clubs the boundary between audience, floor singers (i.e. singers from the audience) and the invited talent was and is fluid. Richard Thompson, a founding member of Fairport Convention and highly respected songwriter and guitarist, sums it up as the 'sometimes rather brusque equality of the clubs. As a performer you were nobody special, rather one of the crowd who happened to sing.'

Representational Performances

The separation between performers and audience is not merely physical. It is also marked off by different kinds of behaviour on and off stage by the performers. Different types of music are often characterised by those behavioural differences (cf. Small 1998) as well as by the dress codes of those performing the music and those listening. The separation between performers and audience is least exclusive in folk, country and western, and local performances of rock and pop, a little more exclusive in jazz[15] and most exclusive in Western Art Music (WAM). The amount and type of audience participation are also markers distinguishing different types of representational performance in different types of musicking. In the staged performance of WAM, the audience is expected to remain absolutely quiet during the performance frame and to register its appreciation by applause at the end of each work performed. In staged performances of jazz, the audience is expected to applaud after solos, in rock/pop concerts the audience may even participate by dancing in the aisles[16] and in folk the audience is expected to participate actively in the singing when appropriate. The defining feature of a representational performance is the 'stage', which is designed as an area set off physically from the audience, on which the performance is held (cf. the stage in Kennedy Hall, Cecil Sharp House, in the Maddy Prior concert). A stage often has a backstage area in which those waiting for an entrance can do so without being observed by the audience, and where they can relax before, after and sometimes during the performance.

The social process of a representational performance is an activity distinct from everyday activities, and as such is highly ritualised. The relational performance of 'Who's the Fool Now?' took less than ten minutes to complete, whereas an organised concert or gig can last for several hours.[17] A staged representational performance constrains both performers and audience to take time out of their everyday activities to be present at the performance, so both need to prepare themselves well before the event. The venue of relational performance is that of everyday interaction. Keying-in processes in representational performances involve a large number of 'non-musical', more matter-of-fact activities well in advance of the performance itself by the performers and friends and supporters of the performers. Advertising the event must be arranged, a suitable venue must be organised, tickets need to be printed, someone must be responsible for ensuring that the costs of the performance do not exceed the takings, and so on. In her ethnographic

---

[15] Earlier forms of jazz up to the end of the 1920s were considerably less exclusive than swing, bebop and modern jazz.

[16] Levitin (2008: 257) claims that the separation of music and bodily movement is a relatively recent and largely Western phenomenon.

[17] The Beatles concert at the Shea Stadium lasted just 28 minutes 19 seconds. By way of contrast, Bruce Springsteen concerts have been known to last for three to four hours.

study of local music worlds in Milton Keynes in the early 1980s, Finnegan sums this up as follows: 'In all these contexts – and many many more – the act of performance represented the high point and validation of a whole series of both musical and back-up activities by performers and supporters before and after the event, something which, apart from its utilitarian purpose, also gave a special symbolic value to these *specially framed moments in time*' (Finnegan 2007 [1989]: 144; our italics).

Representational performances are thus 'specially framed moments in time', the culmination of long periods of unseen musical and other activity on the part of the performers, all focused on those 'moments'. We quote Finnegan again on the nature of musical performances:

Such performances, furthermore, are not just any ritual or any artistic experience, but specifically *musical* ones. They take place in public, characteristically through a co-operating group of enactors (in notable contrast to the relatively solitary acts of some other artistic experiences), and are made up of the joint participation of a number of people in the combined visual, kinaesthetic and acoustic experience which, in its various manifestations, is in our culture defined as live performance. (ibid.: 338; our italics)

The Performance Continuum and Hybrid Performance Types

In any type of singing and musicking[18] there may also be languaging activities that lie between the two poles of relational and representational performance, creating 'hybrid' varieties. The hybridity is a consequence of the freedom of the music to be used in different socio-cultural contextualisations. While a folk song (and, of course, other types of song, e.g. blues, music hall, certain pop songs, etc.) can be used in a relational performance, it is highly unlikely that an operatic aria or a jazz version of a song from the 'Great American Songbook' could be. A campfire sing-song, for example, is more relational, but the probability of a relational performance occurring increases for the jazz song in a jam session, although hardly for an aria. If there are get-togethers or family gatherings of jazz musicians or opera singers, the likelihood of a relational performance occurring in that socio-cultural context increases considerably. We pre-empt discussions in later chapters here by presenting ten situations as a demonstration of the range of hybrid performance types lying between impromptu relational performance and arranged representational performance. Some of these lie on the margins of definability with respect to performance, but if we assume that simply singing a song in front of, together with or for others involves us in the ritual nature of performance, we can see that co-participants, listening bystanders and others engaged in other activities within

---

[18] This is probably also the case for any type of performance.

range of the music may at any time constitute an audience. The performance contexts that we have chosen do not exhaust all the possible situational contexts within which folk songs can be sung, but many of them may be familiar, and they represent the continuum between relational and representational settings. The performance contexts are as follows:

1. *An impromptu song*: a situation in which one or more of the participants in the process of the current emergent social activity break(s) into song. An example of this is given with 'Who's the Fool Now?' in this chapter.

2. *A family gathering*: a stretch of time in the everyday life of a family when members assemble at one of their residences just to be together and enjoy one another's company, during which one or more members take it into their heads to play music and sing songs (a regular occurrence in F.A.M.'s household).

3. *A campfire sing-song*: an activity in which a group of people engaged in some outdoor activity relax around a fire and start telling stories and singing songs.

4. *A jam session*: an out-of-performance activity in which musicians get together (possibly after a concert or a gig) and start playing and singing together.

5. *A get-together (often referred to in folk music circles as a 'gathering')*: a get-together at a musician's house with the explicit purpose of enjoying one another's musical company and where an elevated standard of musicianship can be expected.

6. *A singers' night at a folk club*: a get-together at a folk club at which members are on their own and are sharing the evening's playing and singing between themselves.

7. *A guest night at a folk club*: a night at a folk club which is devoted to a guest player/singer. Most of the gig will be held by that person but there may also be songs from so-called 'floor singers', i.e. club members.

8. *A pub gig*: a concert (gig) arranged, generally by the player/singer/group themselves, to take place in a local pub.

9. *A staged performance* an official concert held at premises where there is a stage, in particular at festivals.

10. *A recording*: a session at a recording studio in which folk artists have arranged to record some of their repertoire with the purpose of producing a CD/DVD for public release.

Classifying Performance Contexts

Performance contexts 1 and 10 are at the two ends of the performance continuum, and all the other contexts lie somewhere in between, i.e. they are hybrid performance types, and are represented along the horizontal axis in Table 2.1.

Table 2.1. *A selection of hybrid performance types in the folk music world*

	impromptu song (1)	family gathering (2)	campfire sing-song (3)	jam session (4)	get-together/ gathering (5)	folk club (singers' night) (6)	folk club (guest night) (7)	pub gig (8)	staged performance (9)	recording (10)
a) pre-arranged	−	−	−	−	±	+	+	+	+	+
b) announced	−	−	±	±	±	+	+	+	+	±
c) programme	−	−	−	−	−	±	+	+	+	±
d) need for feedback	+			−	±	+	+	+	+	+
e) rehearsed	−	−	±	±	±	±	+	+	+	+
f) need for perfection	−	−	−	−	−(±)	−(±)	±	±	+	+
g) time-bound	±	−	±	±	±	+	+	+	+	±
h) audience/co-participant participation	±	+	+	+	±	+	+	±	±	−
i) listeners in addition to audience	−	±	−	−	+	−	−	+	+	±
j) accompanied by other activities	±	+	+	+	+	+	+	−	−	−

The features significant in characterising the performance types are listed along the vertical axis. They can be described by a set of questions which receive either a positive answer (+) or a negative answer (−). In some cases, either a positive or a negative answer may be appropriate (±). The ten questions are as follows: (1) Has the event been pre-arranged?; (2) Has the event been formally or semi-formally announced?; (3) Is there a programme for the event (even if only in the minds of the players/singers)?; (4) Does the performance context require feedback from the 'audience'/'listeners' or not?; (5) Has the music been rehearsed for this occasion?; (6) Do the players/singers need to present their offerings to a high degree of perfection?; (7) Is there a time-limit to the event?; (8) Is audience participation required or desired from the audience/co-participants?; (9) Are there any listeners present other than what we might see as the 'audience', e.g. the bar-keeper at a folk club, or a few people sitting at a table during a jam session who are not listening to the music?; (10) Are the participants in the events concurrently engaged in other activities than singing and playing, and moving around at whatever they are doing?[19]

Table 2.1 reveals that between the two poles of the impromptu song and the staged performance (cf. Maddy Prior's 2008 performance at Cecil Sharp House or a performance at one of the many annual festivals) the two folk club nights, the pub gig and the recording session are all closer to the representational end of the continuum. Apart from the recording session, all performance types involve a spatially and temporally present audience, and those further away from the staged representational performance also require audience participation. Types 6–10 require to be pre-arranged and to have at least an internal programme[20] (with the possible exception of the singers' night at the folk club). They are restricted to a specific period of time, again with the possible exception of the recording session. With the exception of the singers' night at a folk club, they require – and the audience will expect – the performers to perform to the best of their ability. The hybrid performance types closer to the impromptu relational performance are not bound by these conditions, and the most interesting case is the gathering, which seems to link the two ends of the continuum.

We can map these performance types onto two complementary performance spaces:
(1) Producing a performance with a ratified audience present, thus requiring rehearsal. The ultimate goal of the performance (or in spatial terms, the

[19] For example, at a family gathering, one of the participants might leave the room temporarily to put on the kettle for a cup of tea.

[20] By 'internal programme' we mean that the performers have probably organised the order of what they are to present from their repertoire, i.e. they have made a set-list, even if no concert programme is provided for the audience, a printed programme not being usual for a folk music performance in any case.

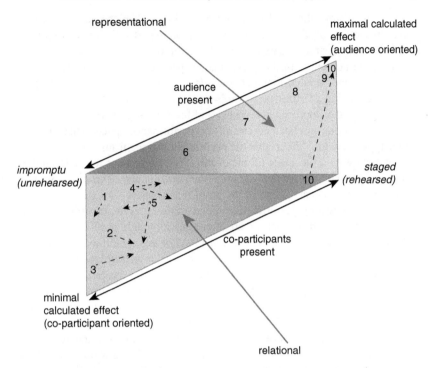

Figure 2.4. *Performance spaces and the location of performance types within them*[21]

outermost limit of the performance space) is to achieve the maximum calculated effect on the audience.

(2) Involvement of co-participants, who may or may not be musicians, rather than an audience. The maximum effort here is to enjoy oneself and the minimum effort needs to be expended in attaining an effect in the co-participants.

Mapping the performance types from Table 2.1 into a diagram representing these two performance spaces gives us Figure 2.4. The upper space represents a performance given *for* an audience, and its apotheosis is a fully staged concert at the top right-hand apex of the upper triangle. The lower space represents a performance given *before* co-participants so that little or no calculated effect on those co-participants is aimed at, the main aim being to enjoy the musicking.

Performance types 6–9 are arranged in ascending steps relatively close to the axis 'audience present'. Type 6 (the singers' night at the folk club) is placed

---

[21] We have decided to retain type 10, 'recording', in the figure, as much of Chapter 7 will deal with the relatively modern phenomenon of recording.

furthest away from the need to rehearse and lower than the achievement of a maximal effect on the audience. Type 9 (the staged folk concert) requires detailed planning and rehearsing, and the main aim is to achieve a maximal effect on the audience. In the performance space below the line, the performance types are bundled together towards the unrehearsed end of the space with the gathering (5) furthest towards the rehearsed end. Only the campfire sing-song (3), the impromptu song (1) and the family gathering (2) are relatively close to the unrehearsed end of the performance space. These performance types may all shift around the performance space from one event to the next or even within the space of one event. If the singers opt for material they and the co-participants are familiar with, the performance types move marginally closer to the rehearsed end of the performance space.

The most interesting performance type in Table 2.1 is the recording session which is not performed before an audience, although producer(s), sound technicians and others may be co-participants. For this reason we have located it at the very end of the lower space where rehearsal is an absolute necessity for the session to be successful. The musicians' aim is to produce a recording of their music with a higher quality even than a staged performance with an audience present so that it can be marketed, not to an audience, but to what we designate as 'listeners'. Performance type 10 thus needs to appear a second time in the upper performance space above performance type 9 and as close as possible to the maximal calculated effect aimed at by the performer(s). Taking the central element in the performance to be the performers themselves and the most natural kinds of performance to be those in the bottom part of the overall performance space, the performance concerns the co-participants in the event whether or not they are the singers and players and regardless of what other social activities they may be engaged in. We label these as the 'addressees'. If the performance moves away from the impromptu end of the spectrum and shifts across to the upper part of the overall performance space, the addressees become members of an audience. As these become too numerous for the kind of immediate feedback that addressees can give, the further towards the top right-hand apex we move, we label these the 'auditorium'. If the performance is carried out with a minimum number of co-participants with the aim of producing music of a very high quality suitable to be marketed, the performance is then aimed not at an audience but at an indefinite number of potential listeners. We label these as the 'listeners/viewers (public)'. This set of relationships between performers and others can be visualised as a set of embedded circles in Figure 2.5.[22]

---

[22] This figure is a development from Bell's concentric circle graphic 'Persons and roles in the speech situation' (Bell 1984: 159). It is developed further in Chapter 6.

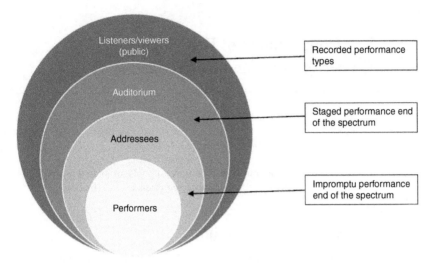

Figure 2.5. *Distance (spatial and social) from performers in performance types*

Performance type 10 (a recording session or a broadcast) is thus furthest away from the target group of the performance and, possibly for this very reason, requires the highest degree of perfection in the musical product. This will be the topic of Chapter 7.

After the detailed analysis of singing performance provided in this chapter, Chapter 3 continues with the underlying theoretical principle that folk song is song that helps to construct social communities and is situated within the symbolic container of ritual functions (cf. Figure 1.2). As such it lies deep in the minds of singers and listeners and deep in the evolutionary development of *Homo sapiens* during and after the development of the language faculty and the fusion of language and music in song$_2$ at around 60,000 years ago. Repeated performances aimed to create and strengthen communal bonding bear all the hallmarks of the sociolinguistic concept of 'community of practice', as we shall see in Chapter 3.

3   The Communality of Folk Song: Co-performance and Co-production

> The chief function of music is to involve people in shared experiences within the framework of their cultural experience.   (Blacking 1973: 48)

Singing to Create a Community

In the Introduction, we argued that a song has to be open to communal participation, passive or active, but we did not give an essentialist definition of what a folk song 'is'. Many have tried to provide such a definition, and many have failed. It is our view that if a song bonds a community together 'for a space of time and in a specific location, to allow individuals, however transiently, to construct identities with others', we are prepared to call it a 'folk song'. Any song composed in the past or the present for other purposes can be used to bond a community together, and if and when it does, it takes on the function of a 'folk song'.[1]

How can songs help to bond a community together? We begin our answer to this question with three examples from a performance 'container' that has been the cradle of community singing and the enactment of ritual and resultant social bonding for centuries: the pub. We first look at the historic recordings made by the BBC at the Eel's Foot pub at Eastbridge in Suffolk in 1939 and 1947. We then compare this with sessions of the University of Leicester Folk Song Club in the winter of 1962/63 at the Princess Charlotte pub in Leicester. Finally, we look at song sessions at the Monkseaton Arms at Monkseaton, Tyne and Wear, in 2014. The question we pose is the following: Would the sessions in the Princess Charlotte and the Monkseaton Arms have been similar enough to those at the Eel's Foot for a singer at the Eel's Foot sessions to relate empathetically to sessions in very different parts of the country and at very different points in time? What similarities can we discern in all three places and times that would have enabled the recognition of similar communities with a high chance of a member of one community being accepted into the others?

---

[1] This definition goes well beyond traditional definitions of folk song, giving rock and pop anthems that an audience might sing along with and fan chants at sports events an aspect of 'folkness'.

Image 3.1. *The Eel's Foot pub in the early twentieth century*

The Eel's Foot

To test this out, we compare performance features from a communal singing session recorded by the BBC at the Eel's Foot pub in Eastbridge, Suffolk, on two occasions, one immediately prior to World War II (13 March 1939) and the other two years after the end of World War II in 1947, to each of the other two pub sessions.[2] A selection from the two recorded broadcasts at the Eel's Foot, giving the listener a vivid aural impression of such an event, was later issued as a CD. No film was made, but photographs of the pub exist and some photographs were taken at the Saturday night sessions. To give the reader a visual impression of the venue, we present a photograph of the exterior of the Eel's Foot in the early twentieth century and one taken during a Saturday evening session in the 'snug' in the late 1930s (Images 3.1 and 3.2).

The pre-war recording at the Eel's Foot was made possible by one of the influential figures in the post-war Folk Revival in Britain, A. L. ('Bert') Lloyd. The programme was, as Young (2010: 124) puts it, 'the first time authentic traditional singers – not classically trained interpreters or arrangers – had been heard on national radio'. Young tells how Lloyd (born in 1908) had collected a large number of folk songs as a young man during his time in Australia from 1924 to 1930 and was hired by the BBC in 1938 to write a radio documentary about seafaring life. During the 1930s Lloyd had become a member of the

---

[2] As with the discussion of 'Who's the Fool Now?' in Chapter 2, we have only R.J.W.'s and F.A.M.'s vivid memories of these events with which to make these comparisons. The evidence, therefore, is conjectural rather than objective.

Image 3.2. *The snug at the Eel's Foot, where weekly singers' nights were held in the 1930s*

Communist Party of Great Britain and was an admirer and friend of Marxist historian A. L. Morton.

One Saturday evening in early 1939, while visiting Morton in Leiston, not far from Eastbridge, the two visited one of the singers' nights in the snug at the Eel's Foot. Lloyd was amazed at the vitality and ability of the singers he heard there and at the participatory nature of the performances. Young continues the story as follows: 'Lloyd . . . later persuaded a producer friend of his at the BBC, Francis Dillon, to record the lively jamboree. The pair turned up on the thirteenth of March in a car loaded with recording gear. The result of their labours was *Saturday Night at the Eel's Foot*'. The session recorded on 13 March and broadcast on 21 July is a landmark in the history of the Second Folk Revival in Britain, but, except in Young's book, it is often only mentioned in passing. E. J. Moeran also made recordings in the pub in 1947, and the BBC CD was put together from these two sessions.

Table 3.1. *Characteristics of sessions at the Eel's Foot*

	The Eel's Foot
Frequency and venue	(1) Sessions took place *on a regular basis*, every Saturday evening. (2) The 'container' for the ritual event was a small room called the 'snug', and it was always full (with enough room for about fifteen people). *Physical proximity thus helped to create an atmosphere of intimacy and exclusiveness*, making the venue (the 'container') the perfect place in which to construct social bonding.
Musicians, type of organisation, MC, musical contributions, performance aims, comments on performance	(3) *The participants were local musicians, who also performed at other pub sessions* in southeast Suffolk, and non-musicians who enjoyed the sessions and participated actively in them. (4) The performance event consisted of numerous songs by different singers, so that *those not performing became members of the audience*. (5) *Order was maintained by a master of ceremonies (MC)*, Philip Lumpkin, banging on a table with an old cribbage board. (6) *All the participants were expected to provide some input* or to provide a monetary contribution towards a round of drinks. (7) None of the singers and players were 'professional musicians', so *their intent was not to display musical proficiency, let alone virtuosity*. (8) *The purpose was to entertain and be entertained*, although individual songs aimed to take the audience 'out of themselves' (see Chapter 1).
Material	(9) *Song and dance* were valued more than instrumental performance. (10) Songs with choruses were not in the majority, but when they did occur, there was *enthusiastic overall participation* in them. Otherwise, comments, some witty and some encouraging, were allowed by non-performers during the performance of a song. (11) *Stretches of time between songs were filled with lively conversations* between groups of participants.
Style and accent	(12) *Conversation was carried out in the local dialect, but songs were sung not in the dialect nor in the standard*, but in an intermediate form of language typical of these singing occasions (cf. our discussion of this phenomenon in Chapter 7).

What are the significant performance features of the Eel's Foot sessions? We list these in Table 3.1, and use them as a basis for comparison with the sessions in the Princess Charlotte and the Monkseaton Arms. The first group of characteristics concerns the frequency of the sessions and the venue, the second the musicians, the organisation, musical performance and aims of the performance and comments on performances, the third the material (with or without audience participation and comments on the material) and the fourth the distinction between languaging as conversation and languaging as song.

The 1947 programme was introduced by a very RP BBC announcer in a rather patronising tone:

> There is in Suffolk in sound of the Trinity House foghorn *a remote hamlet* reached by narrow high-hedged lanes. Among its few cottages and farms is a single inn, the Eel's Foot. To the passer-by this beer house, for that is all it is, is like many another country pub. *It's small and undistinguished,* except for its curious name. But on Saturday evenings the Eel's Foot is *the scene of a dramatic rite, which after years of acquaintance is still exciting.* The bar, a room some 15 ft square with tables at either end, is full. Darts is impossible. And at the end of one of the tables sits Philip Lumpkin under an oil lamp and in his hand is a cribbage scoreboard one corner of which is strangely rounded. Near him is the fiddler with his concertina. He starts to play, and Mrs Howard climbs onto the table and begins to dance. . . . This is *the traditional overture to an evening of song* over which Philip rules with his cribboard, but its corner has been rounded by years of beating on the table to call for 'Good order! Good order! Ladies and gentlemen, please.' [our italics]

Italic print emphasises what we consider significant in the announcer's introduction. The pub containing the symbolic container (the snug) is in a remote rural district and is 'small and undistinguished', conveying the impression that this kind of communal singing event, in the eyes of the BBC, is hard to find, unusual and somewhat unremarkable, at least on the surface. This point will be significant in the following chapter and in Chapter 6. The scene is described as 'a dramatic rite, which after years of acquaintance is still exciting'. The announcer does not specify what the rite is, but we can infer that it has to do with the communal nature of the event. Secondly, he recognises that the members of the group have known one another for many years, stressing the resilience of the community that the singing sessions help to construct. Thirdly, despite the fact that the members know one another well and have frequently taken part in the proceedings, it remains 'exciting'. The participants are 'taken out of themselves' through the performance event, or they experience degrees of individual identity 'boundary loss' in the rite of reconstructing the group. The announcer's statement that '[t]his is the traditional overture to an evening of song' stresses the regularity and ritual nature of the event. Certain non-singing factors are important in the 'correct' re-enactment of the rite, e.g. the opening dance on the table by Mrs Howard, Philip Lumpkin's phrase 'Good order! Good order! Ladies and gentlemen, please' and his deformed cribbage scoreboard.

The Princess Charlotte

Moving twenty-four years into the future, we review whether the twelve features listed as characteristic of the Eel's Foot sessions were also characteristic for a university folk club held at a pub in Leicester called the Princess

Charlotte in the winter of 1962/63. What differences would have confronted a regular performer at the Eel's Foot if s/he had been able to participate in the weekly sessions held there? How easily might that person have 'felt at home' in the communal atmosphere created at the Princess Charlotte? Or would the differences have prevented a guest from the past and the 'remote countryside' from participating in the social bonding that went on during these sessions?

In R.J.W.'s first year at the University of Leicester in 1961/62, he became a member of the university Folk Song Club, which was held with singers' evenings and guest evenings in the Students' Union Building. The major figure in the club was folk singer Roy Bailey, who was then in his final year at Leicester. At the end of that academic year, after Bailey had left university, the club became defunct, and R.J.W. and others interested in folk music restarted it in the winter of 1962/63, choosing to move out of the university premises into the 'pub' atmosphere of the Princess Charlotte in the centre of the city.

The room in which the regular weekly meetings were held was small and on the first floor at the back of the pub. There was a bar in one corner of the room, and between the door and the bar an open coal fire. There was enough room for twenty to thirty participants, i.e. it was a little larger than the snug at the Eel's Foot. At most sessions, R.J.W. took on the role of MC and also joined in the singing. His attitude towards communal participation was that if anyone had something to sing, they were welcome to contribute to the proceedings. Potential singers were told not to worry about the musical quality of what they produced. Obviously, there were 'regulars', but the policy of 'anyone can get up and sing' worked, and there was never any hesitation about the audience joining in with the choruses. The instruments in vogue at the time were guitars and banjos, and from time to time someone played a fiddle or a concertina. The participants were all in their early twenties and the majority were students at the university and the nearby teacher training college. The songs were a mixture of American and British, with about 50 per cent of the songs written by songwriters at the time and the other 50 per cent 'traditional' songs. No ideologies about how to sing 'authentically' (cf. Chapters 4 and 6) were ever laid down. Roughly 70 per cent of the songs were self-accompanied; the remainder were sung a cappella or with someone accompanying the singer. Going through the checklist of features given earlier in this section, the situation emerges as in Table 3.2.

The most difficult aspects of the Princess Charlotte sessions for our time traveller would have been (a) the age difference in the participants at both venues and possibly also social class differences and (b) the 'strange' new instruments in use at the Princess Charlotte. In general, however, a member of the Eel's Foot sessions would have been able to adapt to the new conditions of the Princess Charlotte as they essentially represented the same type of social practice.

Table 3.2. *Characteristics of sessions at the Princess Charlotte*

	The Princess Charlotte
Frequency and venue	(1) The sessions were *weekly*, which would have been no different for the visitor from the Eel's Foot. (2) The ritual container would have *been quite similar to the snug at* the Eel's Foot, giving the visitor a very similar environment, although the Princess Charlotte was in the centre of Leicester whereas the Eel's Foot was on the rural Suffolk coast.
Musicians, type of organisation, MC, musical contributions, performance aims, comments on performance	(3) The singers/musicians were not local musicians, but *students from different parts of the country*. This might have disoriented the visitor, since the students singing in the Princess Charlotte were *not known as members of a local team of singers* moving from pub to pub. (4) *Numerous singers performed during the evening*, providing a similar procedure to the Eel's Foot. The visitor would have had little difficulty in adapting, except for the fact that the choice of songs (some traditional, some American and some self-penned) would have seemed somewhat strange. (5) *Some semblance of order was maintained by the MC*, but the absence of a reified tradition represented by Philip Lumpkin's cribbage board would have been noticeable to the visitor. (6) *Participants at the 'Princess Charlotte' were not required to 'sing or pay'*, but the degree of co-participation would have been very similar. (7) None of the singers at the Princess Charlotte were professional singers and *the focus was not on musical proficiency*. (8) As at the Eel's Foot *the purpose was to entertain and be entertained*, although, once again, the songs would have been somewhat different.
Material	(9) *There was no dancing at the Princess Charlotte sessions*, and the songs were more frequently accompanied by instruments unfamiliar to the visitor from the Eel's Foot. (10) As at the Eel's Foot, *chorus songs would not have been in the majority, but the degree of co-participation would have been very similar*. The student audience, however, did not usually make comments during the performance. (11) The intervals between songs were, as at the Eel's Foot, *filled with animated conversation in different varieties of English*.
Style and accent	(12) This feature would have been different. *The student population came from different parts of the country, leading to the production of several varieties of English* whereas the Eel's Foot sessions would have displayed a rural Suffolk dialect.

The Monkseaton Arms

The session in 'the Monkeys' (the Monkseaton Arms) discussed here took place on Sunday 7 September 2014. F.A.M. and his wife attended after an impromptu afternoon jam session with the folk duo Hicks & Gouldbourn in Beadnell, Northumberland, who are occasional participants in song meetings at 'the Monkeys'. The sessions take place in a small, L-shaped function room on the first floor of the pub, a fairly nondescript building on the main road running through Monkseaton to the coast. The room contains several tables, and a performance space is cleared in the corner, which is visible from all seats. The room can accommodate at most about thirty people; at the time there were about twenty of various ages, from students to old-age pensioners, with the average around fifty-plus. All were locals with the exception of Hicks and Gouldbourn, who perform in clubs in Britain and Germany, and F.A.M. and his wife. Drinks had to be bought individually downstairs in the bar and brought up, with a break in the proceedings for the recharging of glasses.

The MC first sang three songs, establishing the mode for the evening, but when it became clear that there might be a time problem due to the comparatively large number of contributors, he cut the contribution to two songs or tunes halfway through the evening. Some of the regulars were accompanied by partners or spouses, but these did not perform individually throughout the session.

June Tabor describes performing in clubs as 'an absolutely unique way of giving people the opportunity to perform in front of an audience and to *learn how to do it*' (Bean 2014: 373, emphasis added). This was evident as the atmosphere was one of communal support for each of the performers. The session provided several performers with a space to test self-penned songs that they were obviously still working on, and some younger contributors also seemed to have tried out the craft. But all were applauded generously, even when nerves prevented them from completing their performance. Similarly, musical prowess was not expected and competence varied accordingly. No comments were made apart from the MC evaluating professional musician and luthier Steve Hicks' stunning performance with the quip, 'The sound that you are hearing now is that of guitarists crying.'

The material, apart from a set of Northumbrian smallpipe tunes, was a mixture of traditional and songwriters' songs with a strong presence of local songs related to coal mining, but also classics like 'The Three Ravens' (Child 26) or 'Twa Corbies'. Many songs had what one of the performers described as 'joiny-inny-bits', which in some cases were formally introduced and briefly rehearsed, but most of the time the audience sang along spontaneously to repeated phrases or choruses. The two ballads were entirely a cappella solo performances, but the fact that they were sung in succession by two different singers demonstrated a communal experience, as the second was chosen specifically on the spur of the moment to complement the former.

Because of the relatively packed programme, there was little time for conversation between sets, but occasionally audience members directed a question at a performer. Conversation in the breaks demonstrated the mix of the performers present; most of them were Geordies, but some maintained their own dialect, e.g. a young Irish singer and a number of performers who spoke RP. The singing styles mostly reflected the origin of the songs, although in the case of songwriters there was a variety of regional accents and some indications of American reference features, depending mostly but not always on the provenance of the song.

Table 3.3 puts the above into the framework used in the previous accounts.

Table 3.3. *Characteristics of sessions at the Monkseaton Arms*

	The Monkseaton Arms
Frequency and venue	(1) Like the sessions at the Eel's Foot and the Princess Charlotte the get-togethers at 'the Monkeys' take place on *a relatively regular basis*, most Sunday evenings. (2) *The space is clearly separated* from the main pub, creating a 'container' for the practice of singing and playing.
Musicians, type of organisation, MC, musical contributions, performance aims, comments on performance	(3) As in the Eel's Foot, *the musicians and singers were mainly local*. The musicians came from different social backgrounds and ranged in age from early twenties to late seventies. (4) The MC maintained a *relatively tight order*, managing the number of songs sung to fit the time frame available. (5) The MC, who sang as well, then invited all those present to sing or play. Those *not performing became members of the audience*. (6) As at the Eel's Foot sessions, all participants were expected and/or encouraged *to provide some musical input*. However, drinks were not provided by non-performers as remuneration. (7) The musicians and singers were *all amateurs* with the exception of Hicks and Gouldbourn. (8) *Musical proficiency varied widely but was not commented upon*; all performers received respectful applause, even if they did not complete their turn.
Material	(9) *The majority of the performances were songs*, although a piper played a set of Northumbrian tunes. Much of the material, also the local traditional songs, had a clear political slant. American songs were rare. (10) For many songs *the audience would sing along spontaneously*, although not with 'Three Ravens' and 'Twa Corbies', which might have been well known but had no chorus or participatory elements.

Table 3.3. (*cont.*)

	The Monkseaton Arms
	(11) Due to time constraints between the songs, *there was little conversation.* Occasionally there were comments on the songs and sometimes questions to performers about their material and the meaning of some obscure phrases.
Style and accent	(12) *Conversation was mainly in the local (Geordie) dialect,* though some performers, in-migrants, maintained their own variety of English and/or spoke RP. The styles used in the songs tended to reflect their origins.

The accounts of the Princess Charlotte and 'the Monkeys' show that the format of the club session has not changed significantly in terms of the container, the attendant rituals and the feeling of community. In all cases, there is regularity of time and venue, of an MC structuring the performances, of attendees being both audience and performers, and the inclusivity of and support for the performers along with the absence of comment on musical prowess. However, the choice of material, which includes non-local songs as well as singer-songwriter material performed by the singers themselves, has changed over the years as has the choice of instrumentation (from fiddle and concertina to guitar). The demographic make-up of the clubs has shifted from relative homogeneity in terms of background and class to greater heterogeneity, and with it the style choices in the songs have shifted, which may still be different from a speaking style, but reflect a broader set of choices, origins and song types. One crucial change over the years, however, is that, compared with the late fifties, the sixties and seventies, the age group has shifted back to an older generation; there are young musicians but they often fail to bring their age group along as an audience.[3]

Community Concepts in Sociolinguistics

In her book on the vitality of local music-making in Milton Keynes, Finnegan puts the question 'Why do we have music?', and she offers the following answer:

This is a more puzzling question than it seems, and *one we seldom ask ourselves.* There is no utilitarian answer, for despite its profound social functions – of linking people, giving them identity and status, and making out and constituting the rituals of our time – music of itself has no essential use. Why after all should people engage in music? ... [M]usical enactment is not an essentially utilitarian practice at all but one form of celebratory and non-useful artistic action, one unparalleled mode to realise and create

---

[3] A comment made by Maddy Prior in an interview with F.A.M.

the age-old blend of fantasy and reality, ritual and ordinariness, sacred and profane of our human existence. *Musical practice is essentially of society, dependent on and expressed in all kinds of activities and settings described in this book*; but it is also perhaps a unique and distinctive mode through which people both realise and transcend their social existence. (Finnegan 2007 [1989]: 339; our italics)

The ritual functions of music are in the forefront of her explanation. But her recognition that 'musical practice is essentially of society' is significant in supporting our view that music, and more specifically song, helps to constitute communities.[4]

The Community of Practice

Sociolinguistics focuses on language and society, so it is natural that some definition of a social unit in relation to varieties of human language is necessary. In the first phase of Variational Sociolinguistics, that unit was assumed to be the *speech community*, but as variation in the language use of the individual speaker in emergent social practice became more important in identity construction than variation in whole communities in Third Wave Variation Studies, the term itself came under attack. Bucholtz (1999), for example, highlights six weaknesses in the concept of the speech community: (1) the focus was on *the community* rather than the individual; (2) the focus was on *social consensus* as 'the organizing principle of the community' rather than possible dissent; (3) the focus was on *central group members* rather than marginal members; (4) the focus was on *studying the group* rather than individual members; (5) the focus was on *a static* rather than a fluctuating emergent *conceptualisation of identity*; and (6) the focus was on *researchers' interpretations* rather than participants' understandings of what they were doing and why (1999: 203–7). These six points began to emerge as negatively critical assessments of the speech community concept throughout the 1990s when research on variation gradually came to be based on the theory of the 'community of practice'.[5]

In this subsection, we describe how audiences participating in repeated performance events of the same or a similar kind can develop a communal sense of the social practices constituting the wider singing community. For example, if a member of a singing community visits another community in the same kind of social and physical environment, we predict that s/he will have little difficulty in adjusting to the practices of that new group. Singers move

---

[4] American activist and folk singer Pete Seeger saw it as his mission to help create a singing workers' movement because he clearly felt that through singing it was possible to promote collective action, to demand political change and to lend power to such demands (Winkler 2009: 36).

[5] A further significant critique of the speech community concept is given in Rampton (1998).

from one *community of practice*[6] (CofP) to another and can compare the practices of the new group with those of the old. How, then, are we to understand a CofP?

Wenger (1998) uses the term 'community of practice' (CofP) to explain how people learn, through repeated communal events, to carry out activities or to gain knowledge about those activities through forms of social practice. We define *practice* as social behaviour resulting from the ways in which speakers situate themselves and others in interaction. Practice thus *emerges* from social interaction, and since performance is a social process, it must contain specific forms of behaviour in accordance with the ways in which performer(s) and audience situate themselves.

There are three structural features of a CofP: (1) the *domain*, specifying a common ground in which participants are motivated to participate in the social interaction (and thus uphold the social contract) and which gives meaning to their actions, e.g. the common ground for any folk performance is a ritual performance oval such as that in Kennedy Hall at Cecil Sharp House for the Maddy Prior concert; (2) the *community*, created by the social interaction, which shapes the set of social connections between the participants and facilitates their collaboration, e.g. the community (the 'folk') created through the Maddy Prior concert consists of the singers, musicians and audience, which accounts for the ways in which Prior consistently creates social links, through her keyings-in, between those on stage and the audience for the length of the concert; and (3) the *practice*, around and through which the social process evolves, enabling the participants to construct, share and maintain the community's core of knowledge, e.g. stories told and socio-historical information given by the performers and personal evaluations of the songs shared with the audience in the keyings-in of the Prior concert (see Chapter 11 for a more detailed discussion).

Within this structure, three features emerge from the social practice: (1) *mutual engagement*, in which those in the social interaction establish the norms of the performance and build collaborative relationships resulting in bonding and 'boundary loss', which is clearly in evidence in both the performers and the audience at the Cecil Sharp House concert; (2) a *joint enterprise*, in which members construct an understanding of what bonds them together, e.g. the frequent references to the audience in the keyings-in and the vocal responses given by the audience during the keyings-in and sometimes during the songs; and (3) a *shared repertoire*, constructed through repeated interaction among the participants and constituting their shared resources in achieving the joint enterprise. In the

---

[6] The term 'community of practice' is often written with capital letters. We prefer to use either lower-case first letters or the abbreviation CofP.

'Back to the Tradition' concert at Cecil Sharp House that shared repertoire is immediately in evidence and is strengthened for the benefit of the younger members of the audience throughout the evening's performance.

Four types of duality are involved in creating a CofP, the first term in each pair providing the premise for the second:

1. Through participation in the joint enterprise, symbolic objects or activities (including linguistic expressions and varieties) are *reified* (participation→ reification) (e.g. participation at the Maddy Prior concert reifies how Prior formulates linguistically what she says to the audience and the kinds of knowledge they share).

2. Through the *emergent* social practice, forms of behaviour may develop as a *design* that can be used in future occurrences (emergent→designed) (cf. the design of having guests to join the main performer on stage, of relating directly to the audience concerning the songs and the music and of offering the audience general participation in the singing in 'Who's the Fool Now?').

3. Through the *negotiation* of relationships in the social practice, individual and group *identities* are formed (negotiability→identification) (cf. Prior's need to shed the image of the 'star' during the concert in favour of that of the knowledgeable singer relating personally to what she is singing).

4. *Local* occurrences of social practice give rise to *global* forms (local→global).

A CofP can only develop through time by repeated engagements in the joint enterprise. In addition, a member of a CofP can easily participate in the instantia- tion of a CofP unknown to her/him just as long as s/he recognises the types of reification emerging from the social practice, the design of the social practice itself and the identities that are being formed. Once these conditions are fulfilled, there is no difficulty in moving from local to global forms of social practice.

In the social event of communal singing, the domain is the singing and appreciation of the songs. The community is the performer(s) and the audience. The practice is the construction of a bonded community in which members can transcend the boundaries defining their individual identities to achieve a group identity (*pace* Turner 1969, an existential and spontaneous *communitas*, see Chapter 4) through appreciation of and participation in the singing. In a communal song performance, the mutual engagement consists of efforts to achieve bonding, and the joint enterprise is the construction of a 'folk' through the shared repertoire of the songs that the performer(s) choose(s) to sing, their sociolinguistic bonding with the audience and the audience's sense of when and how to participate in the singing. In song performance, e.g. in the Cecil Sharp House concert given by Maddy Prior and her guests in October 2008, where the joint enterprise is to construct a 'folk', the use of certain singing styles, certain forms of instrumental accompaniment, certain song types and domain-relevant linguistic expressions are reified through participation and communally accepted for further performances.[7]

The Discourse Community

From locally bound song performances, participants may also align themselves with more *global* (less *local*) communities, and it is this duality (local→global) that provides the key to moving from a CofP, or different CofPs, to a *discourse community*. Strictly speaking, the concept of 'discourse community' belongs to the field of discourse analysis rather than to sociolinguistics proper. It was first proposed by Nystrand (1982) and then further developed by Swales (1990) in discourse genre analysis. Swales proposes the following six characteristics of a discourse community:

1. It has a broadly agreed set of *common public goals*.
2. It has *mechanisms of intercommunication* among its members.
3. It uses its *participatory mechanisms* primarily to provide information and feedback.
4. It utilises and hence possesses one or more genres *in the communicative furtherance of its aims*.
5. In addition to owning genres, it has also acquired some *specific lexis* of its own.
6. It has a *threshold level of members* with a suitable degree of relevant content and discoursal expertise.

The world of 'folk music' is characterised by all six features listed above; hence we can interpret it as a discourse community. Swales (1990: 9) states that a discourse community is a group whose members have a set of shared goals and who 'use communication to achieve these goals', which certainly describes the 'folk music' world. Originally, the concept of 'discourse community' was developed to explain the difference between text types. However, if a discourse is a body of statements that form part of a single system in the overall formation of statements (Foucault 1972: 127), it is a community whose members share those goals and communicate with one another to achieve them, whether they are contained in texts or not. A discourse community is not constrained historically or geographically, nor is it dependent on face-to-face contact in emergent practice as our discussion of the three settings in the first section of this chapter bears out.

In England and Wales, as in Scotland and in Ireland, there is a 'folk music community'. It is not spatio-temporally bounded, but it is dependent on face-to-face interaction in performance events of various kinds (see

---

[7] This does not mean that those reifications are historically factual, i.e. that they are 'a tradition' of singing. See the discussion in Chapters 4 and 6.

Chapter 2). The community has arisen through different types of song performance at different points in time and in different localities and through the historical institutions of song collecting and publication and competing discourses about folk music in general. The 'folk music' community has developed a specific lexis with respect to types of song (e.g. night visiting songs, broken token songs, ballads, shanties, miners' songs, etc.) and ways of singing (e.g. a cappella, harmony, chorus, traditional, etc.). It has mechanisms of intercommunication and participatory mechanisms through the institutionalisation of a network of folk clubs and folk festivals and the national information centre of the English Folk Dance and Song Society (EFDSS) based at Cecil Sharp House in London for England, the various local branches of the Comhaltas Ceoltóirí Éireann in Ireland and Traditional Arts and Culture Scotland in Edinburgh.[8] As Finnegan says of the 'folk music world' of Milton Keynes, '[f]or Milton Keynes dwellers their local clubs were what they were most regularly involved in, but they were also very aware of the country-wide "folk world" of which they were a part' (2007: 61).

The world of folk song in the English-speaking countries thus constitutes a discourse community.[9] It may differ from one country to another, even within Britain, but it has a history, or rather histories, in which different forms of discourse with different discourse values have been more dominant at various historical periods than others. The most grass-roots types of performance (family get-togethers, gatherings, impromptu breakthroughs into song, jam sessions, pub sessions and even folk club meetings) have changed little in their commitment to the communal participation of everyone present, i.e. musicians, singers and audience members. It is here that we see the bonding and 'boundary loss' which, following McNeill (1995), Mithen defines as 'the manner in which group music-making leads to "a blurring of self-awareness and the heightening of fellow feeling for all those who share in a dance"' (2006: 209).

Co-performance and the Co-production of a 'Folk'

Co-participation in a singing event need not require active participation in singing the songs performed. Participants may also remain passive in terms of singing or providing musical accompaniment, but this does not mean that they contribute nothing to the performance. Every performance needs an audience of some sort, even if it is an audience of one, and passive members of the

---

[8] There are similar institutions in other English-speaking countries, e.g. in the USA the Library of Congress, American Folklife Center in Washington, in Canada at Folk Music Canada/Musique Folk du Canada in Ottawa, in Australia at the Australian Music Centre in Canberra, in New Zealand at the Centre for New Zealand Music in Wellington.

[9] Due to the popularity of the 'Celtic' branch of English-speaking folk music, we might need to consider extending the discourse community to continental Europe.

community contribute just as much as active performers to the production of a CofP simply by turning up at performances more than once and, in this way, indexing their support.[10] The joint enterprise of regularly held singing sessions aims at achieving the type and amount of social bonding through which a 'folk' can be constructed, a 'folk' being a community of practice.

However, the co-performance and co-production of a 'folk' does not need to take place in instances of interaction in the performance mode (PM). Communal singing has been reified in the creation of other CofPs where the construction of a 'folk' is important and the notion of an audience is irrelevant. Certain types of heavy physical work that can only be achieved efficiently by the combined efforts of groups of workers rather than by individuals frequently have recourse to communal singing to lighten the labour by creating a group identity. In situations such as these, workers collaborate with each other in coordinating their physical labour as a group, and they do so by singing together. Communal singing is thus a central practice in the joint enterprise of welding a group together (i.e. constructing a 'folk') to accomplish the work efficiently and successfully.

Different kinds of work song fall into this category (e.g. shanties, waulking songs, weaving songs, rowing songs, work-gang songs, marching songs, steel-driving songs,[11] and so on). A group of sailors singing a shanty, a group of men rowing a boat and singing as they row, a group of soldiers on the march and singing to ease the boredom and fatigue, two steel-drivers hammering in the steel ties to hold the rails down firmly, or a chain gang singing and breaking stones to the rhythm of their song are not performing for an audience but for one another. They are using song to make the work easier for themselves and to accomplish it more efficiently. In each case, singing allows individuals to break down the boundaries of their own identities and to forge a group identity with which they become 'human-and-fellow-human'.

Shanties and Rowing Songs

The most well-known category of working song is, without any doubt, the shanty (or sea shanty), although it lost its significance as a working song after the disappearance of the great sailing vessels at the end of the nineteenth

[10] Similarly, in the container of a club with a minimal distance between performer and audience, a singer can detect when an audience member is affected by the contents of a song.

[11] Steel-driving songs were sung by 'two powerful men' employed in railway construction to drive in the steel clamps holding the rails in position before the invention of the steam drill: 'They struck the steel from each side and as they struck the steel they sang a song which they improvised as they worked' (from the introduction to the song 'John Hardy', related by the Hon. W. A. MacCorkle, in John Harrington Cox's *Folk-Songs of the South* (2013 [1925]: 224). See also the opening scene of the 2000 film *O Brother, Where Art Thou?*, where a group of prisoners are breaking stones to the rhythm of 'Po Lazarus'.

century. The fact that shanties are still performed reveals their ritual significance as a means of 'Remembering the past' (see Chapter 1, Figure 1.2), i.e. as
a way of asserting a significant section of Western cultural memory.

Shanties differed from sea songs. They were used to carry out physical work
aboard sailing ships that could only be done by groups of sailors rather than
individuals, whereas sea songs were songs about sailors, events at sea, ships,
etc. These might have been sung on board ship, but only in sailors' leisure time,
or in the pubs and bars of ports between which the ships plied. Shanties were
sung on merchant and passenger vessels but were not allowed on naval vessels.
To ease the work by providing a communal rhythm for work on naval vessels,
fiddlers or tin whistle and fife players were often used.

The heyday of the shanty was between the eighteenth and the end of the
nineteenth century, but there is a wealth of literature on the subject and an
even greater wealth of recorded material available.[12] In addition, shanties
were not restricted to English. German, Dutch and Norwegian ships also used
shanties, in their own languages, to aid physically demanding work on board
ship.

All shanties have a stanza, sometimes very short (as in 'Sally Brown') and
sometimes longer depending on the kind of work that needed to be done,
followed by a longer chorus in which the whole group of men put all their
energy together into the singing and the work itself. Stanzas were sung out by
a shantyman, who often created one stanza after another on the spot if the work
promised to be longer than usual. A good shantyman on board ship was worth
his weight in gold. See the website for the windlass shanty 'Sally Brown' ♪3.

So-called 'rowing songs' or 'boat songs' are not common in the English-
speaking world, so as an example we have chosen a song in Scots Gaelic. Songs
like 'Thoir mo shoraidh thar Gunaigh' ('Bear my Farewell across Gunna
Sound') (see website ♪4) are sung by oarsmen to ease the hard labour of
rowing large boats plying between the islands of the Inner and Outer Hebrides
and the mainland with passengers or cargo. As with shanties, rowing songs
consist of stanzas, sung by one person to the rhythm of the rowing, followed by
slightly longer choruses containing nonsense syllables interspersed with meaningful lines sung by the team of rowers. A few rowing songs from Gaelic
Scotland are also sung in English, e.g. 'The Mingulay Boat Song', but most are
atypical in not displaying the lead singer/communal chorus format. Since

---

[12] Two books are interesting here, G. E. Clark. 1867. *Seven Years of a Sailor's Life*. Boston: Adams
and Co., from the early days of the shanty in America, and the other from 1960s Britain, viz.
Stan Hugill. 1961. *Shanties from the Seven Seas: Shipboard Work-songs and Songs Used as
Work-songs from the Great Days of Sail*. London: Routledge & Kegan Paul. There are also some
compilation albums which include shanties, such as *Ballades et shanties des matelots anglais* in
several volumes or the Topic sampler no. 7 *Sea Songs and Shanties*.

'The Mingulay Boat Song' was composed to be sung by a choir, this is hardly surprising.[13]

Marching Songs

Three examples of marching songs are given here, the first, 'Over the Hills and Far Away', from the early eighteenth century ☺5, the second, 'Here We Are! Here We Are! Here We Are Again!' ☺6, and the third the rather grimmer 'The Old Battalion/Hanging on the Old Barbed Wire' ☺7[14] from the First World War. 'Over the Hills and Far Away' is in several singers' repertoire, but we have never heard 'Here We Are!' sung in a folk performance, probably because it was originally a music hall song and because of its militaristic gung-ho sentiment. All three songs have the regular rhythms characteristic of tunes used for marching. The first two were sung to drum up or maintain interest in recruiting men for wars, in the first instance for the War of the Spanish Succession and in the second for the First World War. Only the second and third songs are specifically aimed at boosting morale and creating comradeship and social bonding in addition to easing the physical exertion of marching. Several other marching songs at the time of the First World War were also derived from music hall songs, but although they fulfil the conditions we have set up to allow a song to be considered a folk song, even outside the performance frame, they are hardly ever sung in folk performance events.

In 'Here We Are! Here We Are! Here We Are Again!' and 'The Old Battalion', a lead singer (or lead singers), as in shanties, rowing songs and waulking songs, usually sang the stanzas and the marchers joined in the chorus. There are several other marching songs used by the troops in the First World War, e.g. 'Pack Up Your Troubles in Your Old Kit Bag' ☺8, 'It's a Long Way to Tipperary' ☺9, 'Hello, Hello! Who's Your Lady Friend?' ☺10, 'Lloyd George's Beer' ☺11, 'Fred Karno's Army'☺12, and yet, to our knowledge, none of these, even though they are sung to enable soldiers to bond socially as

---

[13] It is attributed to Hugh S. Roberton, founder of the Glasgow Orpheus Choir, although it is not clear whether he wrote the song or simply translated it into English.

[14] This song can be traced in a number of compilations, but Palmer (1990: 118–19) reprints a verse about 'Joe Driscoll ... [l]aying [sic] on the firing step / with half his head blown away' acknowledged to a singer (Gordon Hall), who was a friend of his mother's, suggesting that such additions were made on the spot. 'The Old Battalion' seems to be more popular, sung by Jon Boden, June Tabor, Chumbawamba and most recently by Show of Hands with a poem by Siegfried Sassoon (https://www.youtube.com/watch?v=x8yNYu1G-EI, accessed 8 January 2015), though it is hardly sung as a marching song. Palmer claims that the song was discouraged by the officers but proved unbelievably popular, no doubt because of its scathing attack on all authorities, to the point where it was taken over by American soldiers in World War I and even in World War II. The Canadian Princess Patricia's Light Infantry Regiment adopted the tune as a march past.

a group, are sung in folk performances. Like work songs they help to 'co-produce' the CofP and are thus, in this function, 'folk' songs.

Community in Song

What we have seen in the previous sections is that singing represents a powerful way of creating a community. In this section, we explore how this is achieved, in particular in terms of the songs that create such a community and in what contexts. To develop this idea, it is helpful to suggest a very general categorisation of songs of this kind.[15] Two questions are addressed here: what sort of songs are likely to be chosen because they create that communal mood so clearly part of sing-songs, and what features do those songs have in common, i.e. what makes a good community song?

Song Choices

Environments where such songs are prevalent relate mainly to categories 2 (*family gathering*) and 3 (*campfire sing-song*) in Chapter 2, although *impromptu singing* (1), the *jam session* (4), the *get-together* (5) and the *singers' evening* (6) can also provide opportunities for such communal singing. In the first two settings – more so than in settings 1, 4, 5 and 6 – it is possible for solo performances to occur, but the problem is that a singer taking the floor and performing on her/his own excludes all the other members of the group. The call for 'one that we all know' from the company may become quite insistent, which makes family gatherings and campfire sing-songs different from the other settings where such solo performances may be encouraged. In what follows, we concentrate on three settings where communal singing is prevalent.

We begin with the military. Soldiers' wet canteens in the first half of the twentieth century were spaces for lively sing-songs with rules that are reminiscent of the folk club settings mentioned above. Palmer (1990) quotes a conversation in 1976 with Tom Langley, a member of the Grenadier Guards, who describes the institution of the 'canteen king, an old soldier, often with a passable voice ... [who] would always oblige with a song and accept a pint', in other words, a master of ceremonies of some kind, informal but institutionalised. As far as audience involvement is concerned, Palmer quotes Royal Field Artillery man John Gregson, who recalled that he 'learnt many songs at "boozy singing sessions" held in wet canteens' and that 'those present were obliged, in the time-honoured formula, to "sing, say, pay or

---

[15] We explore this notion in more detail in Chapter 10 when we consider the repertoire of performers and the decisions that underlie the choices of both material and rendition.

show your arse"' (Palmer 1990: 13). So there would have been considerable pressure to contribute to the entertainment, as long as it involved the community.

An overview of popular soldiers' songs in the twentieth century reveals that three types were favoured. One obvious choice is popular music of the day or of the period. In World War I, this was music hall material; later, it was what was known from the radio.[16] The second type consisted of songs that were well known from other sing-song environments (family gatherings, pub evenings and, of course, school). Traditional drinking songs like 'Seven Nights Drunk' ☮13 (which goes back at least to the eighteenth century) were among the favourites here, possibly because of the sexual theme that becomes increasingly lewd towards the end. Others were well-known ditties such as 'My Bonnie Lies Over the Ocean' ☮14, whose familiar tune would resurface in the third group of songs originating from the army context, usually about the campaigns, serious incidents in the barracks or complaints concerning army life. They were usually based on the first two song types, certainly with respect to the tune but also to the linguistic structures, mainly prosody. For example, the hymn 'Holy Holy Holy' became the World War I song 'Raining Raining Raining' ☮15, or the prosodic pattern of 'What a Friend We Have in Jesus' was converted to 'When this Bloody War Is Over' ☮16. 'My Bonnie' partly represents another strategy in which only minimal changes are made to the original lyrics: 'last night as I lay on my pillow / last night as I lay on my bed / I dreamt that my Corporal was dying / [last night as I lay in my pillow] / I dreamt the old bugger [that my bonnie] was dead.'[17] In this context, it is interesting to note that one song often sung among the rank and file – and one for which singers could at times be punished – was 'McCafferty' ☮17. The narrative tells the story of an Irish soldier, who, in revenge for ill treatment, killed his captain and with the same bullet, accidentally, the colonel. He was hanged in 1862. Interestingly, it is sung to the tune of 'The Croppy Boy' ☮18, an Irish rebel song.

Another setting is a close circle of individuals who know each other well, an evening around the campfire, which typically involves several singers and some individuals accompanying the songs on musical instruments, usually guitars or ukuleles. The choice of songs here depends largely on the repertoire of the group members and to a certain extent on the musical dexterity of those playing an instrument. The songs are often found in semi-formal collections

---

[16] Bob Copper of the legendary folk singing Sussex family noted this with some disappointment about his service in the 1930s (Palmer 1990: 13).

[17] During World War I, music hall songs also provided a fertile ground for newly created soldier songs, but as the choruses were the main elements in performance in which the audience was meant to join in, such rewrites were overwhelmingly based on the chorus rather than the verses of the songs.

and reflect the situation found in military circles. Among them we find rock and pop classics, e.g. 'Yellow Submarine', 'Ob-la-di Ob-la-da' and 'Let It Be' by the Beatles, 'No Woman No Cry' by Bob Marley, Dylan's 'Knockin' on Heaven's Door' as well as more recent hits such as 'Wonderwall' by Oasis or REM's 'Losing My Religion'. Part of the repertoire also consists of familiar favourites like 'My Bonnie', 'What Shall We Do With the Drunken Sailor' ♪19, 'Banks of the Ohio' ♪20, 'Tom Dooley' ♪21 and 'Oh Susanna' ♪22, spirituals such as 'Let My People Go' ♪23 or 'When the Saints Go Marching In' ♪24 (often with members of the present company inserted for the 'saints'), 'folkie' songs like 'The Wild Rover' ♪25, 'Where Have All the Flowers Gone' ♪26, 'Five Hundred Miles' ♪27, 'Puff the Magic Dragon' ♪28 or more recent songs like 'Blowin' in the Wind' ♪29 and 'Streets of London' ♪30.[18]

The third setting is the family circle in which families still sing together. The repertoire is likely to include children's songs but also pop songs and 'folk' tunes of general currency, as borne out by *Sing as We Go*, a song collection of familiar material for singing on car journeys (hence the title). The choices in individual settings are determined by family experiences over a number of years, such that the repertoire of different families may be more varied and more idiosyncratic than in the other two settings. It is also subject to change as the children grow older and some songs are considered too childish. One influence on song choice is determined by whether the songs are accompanied, e.g. when singing takes place at home, but not on a car journey or a walk. With these considerations in mind, we now look at what characterises these community songs.

Characteristics of Communal Songs

The major characteristic of the songs discussed is that they are very familiar to the participants. They are either timeless classics, many frequently played on middle-of-the-road radio stations, or they are sung widely in several communal singing settings, the family, schools, clubs and pubs and, in the case of spirituals, choirs. If rock and pop classics are adopted by other artists for performance or recording, this often happens in the form of acts of tribute, i.e. the songs are almost exact copies of the originals. If recorded with artistic pretensions, the artists often go quite far to reinvent the songs (cf. Stevie Wonder's versions of 'Blowin' in the Wind' in 1966 and at Dylan's thirtieth anniversary concert in 1992). In other words, the covering artists' renditions range from faithful imitation to what could be described as *claiming the song* for themselves.[19] Familiar favourites are rarely if ever adopted by artists except

---

[18]   A survey of the classic Swiss Scouts songbook *Rondo*, although compiled by and for non-native speakers of English, includes all the songs mentioned. It is therefore fair to say that the campfire repertoire of English songs has considerable currency beyond the Anglophone world.

[19]   We return to this concept of claiming a song in Chapter 10.

in the case of special interest performances or recordings of children's songs or nursery rhymes.[20] With these songs, however, overly familiar songs may be taken up and reinvented, e.g. 'The Wild Rover' by Robin and Barry Dransfield on their 1971 album *Lord of All I Behold*, which departs from the iconic Dubliners version with the additional stanza after the landlady refuses drink on credit 'if I had all the money I left in your care / I would buy me a new house my family to rear / I would buy me a new house I would thatch me a barn / I would buy me a new coat to keep myself warm', giving the song a much more serious slant, but also one that would not be easily accepted in the jollity of a sing-song setting. Summing up, we can say that because of their general familiarity these songs are likely to be restricted to an informal gathering where audience and performers are indistinct from each other and where the goal is the enjoyment of communal singing. One contributing factor, almost a criterion, in their selection is that they are undemanding in terms of their chord changes, few having more than the simple major and some minor chords (cf. Appendix). This can be illustrated with Beatles songs taken up by the sing-song canon, where harmonically complex songs like 'Penny Lane' are completely absent.[21] In addition, songs with the vocal complexity of 'She's Leaving Home', whose choral arrangement appears to be too intricate for unrehearsed communal singing, are also absent from the sing-song canon.

Song lyrics can also be expected to play a role in the choice of songs. This is obvious in the context of soldiers' songs that express dissatisfaction with the status quo, or where lewd stanzas are an incentive for their choice. Depending on the type of campfire setting, songs with political impact and protest songs may also be a popular choice, in both cases creating a bond because of shared experiences. But the lyrically most consistent feature is a chorus that everyone present can sing if they do not know all the words of the song. Unsurprisingly, this tends to be the most confidently sung element in a communal song.

This leaves us with the following conclusion. In Chapter 2, we discussed the notion of relational (impromptu) vs representational (staged) performances. The songs discussed here and the settings in which they are produced do not readily fit into the latter type of performance. Thus, given their use as a means for bonding in and through communal singing, the function of the songs discussed here is *relational*, i.e. they are meant to create and maintain relationships in a community. The primary focus is on the shared experience, not on the ability of an individual performer. Whoever ventures a contribution to a circle

[20] Donovan's 1971 album *H.M.S. Donovan* and Tim Hart of Steeleye Span's *My Very Favourite Nursery Rhymes* of 1981 and *The Drunken Sailor and Other Kids' Songs*, all recorded at a time when the songs were relevant to the artists' children.
[21] Because the tune is as memorable as it is complex in terms of key changes, 'Penny Lane' lends itself to singing without accompaniment and was therefore sung on car journeys in F.A.M.'s family.

of this kind needs to balance the individual wish to shine, a *representational* function of performance, with the collective goal of the shared activity of singing together.

From Rubber Soul *to* Rubber Folk

The above discussion has demonstrated that it is problematic to think of a folk song as anything other than a song that creates a community in performance, a community that results from communal singing. It is not, in other words, a clearly delimited song genre. Pop songs, classic or more contemporary, can fulfil this function as well as any 'traditional' song, in some cases even more effectively because they have greater currency. If they are easy to learn, undemanding to accompany and if they stimulate communal singing, almost any song – country, world music, reggae, jazz ('Summertime'), possibly even a classical piece (usually in the form of carols) – can function as a folk song.

A fascinating illustration of how this works[22] is the 2006 album *Rubber Folk*, on which various artists including June Tabor, Ralph McTell, Waterson: Carthy, Cara Dillon, Show of Hands, etc., each interpret a song from the Beatles album *Rubber Soul* (1965). In some cases this works very convincingly; in others it seems more of a creative reinvention. Unsurprisingly, the translation from pop/rock to folk is most effortless where at least some of the criteria mentioned above apply, i.e. in songs that have relatively simple chord changes or are unaccompanied, that are not too demanding in terms of vocal arrangements and that have a memorable chorus. In many ways, however, *Rubber Folk* also represents the means by which a performer, in this case a folk singer, can 'claim a song' and, in this case, make it a folk song for *representational performance*. A remarkable characteristic of the album is that it presents many well-known songs from a very new perspective and endows some of the rather well-known lyrics with an unexpected poignancy, highlighting a conflict that may be present in the original but not with the same intensity. The ability of folk song to affect the community, not always at the forefront of the communal singing experience, is a central feature and will be discussed in the following chapter.

---

[22] Although the focus is more on how folk singers can claim a pop/rock song.

4   Answering Back: Rebels with and without a Cause

> Music can express social attitudes and cognitive processes, but it is useful and effective only when it is heard by the prepared and receptive ears of people who have shared, or can share in some way, the cultural and individual experiences of its creators.
>
> (Blacking 1973: 54)

A Social Conundrum

Finnegan's research into amateur music-making in Milton Keynes in the early 1980s ranged over a number of 'music worlds', and her ethnography links those music worlds to the family and class structures of the musicians. Western Art Music (WAM) turned out, as we might expect, to be a largely middle-class world, whereas brass-band music was working-class. Rock, and country and western, surprisingly, ranged across the whole social spectrum.

And the folk music world? To answer this question, Finnegan first outlines a 'folk' ideology and then discusses her findings. Here is her take on the ideology: 'It may be questionable whether there really ever was a distinctive corpus of music produced by a definable "folk" in the rural setting envisaged by the purists, but this belief, conjoined with socially recognised definitions and practices, provided an implicit authorisation for "folk music" as it was being performed and enjoyed in urban settings in the 1980s' (Finnegan 2007: 67). Here is her take on the social background of folk musicians in Milton Keynes:

When one looks at how 'folk music' was actually organised in Milton Keynes ... it is striking how far it was at variance with many of the tenets of this implicit ideology.

First, the social background of the local folk music participants was far from the rural unlettered 'folk' of the ideal model. ... Members of the folk music world liked to think of themselves as in some sense 'the folk' or at any rate as 'classless'. In a way they were justified: once within a folk club or band their jobs or education became irrelevant. They were thus themselves startled if made to notice the typical educational profile of folk enthusiasts. If any of the local music worlds could be regarded as 'middle class' it was that of folk music, for all that this ran so counter to the image its practitioners wished to hold of themselves. (Finnegan 2007 [1989]: 68)

MacKinnon's 1993 study of the English folk scene arrives at similar conclusions, but from a different angle:

My view is that the folk scene attracts those who have benefited materially from upward social mobility, but who have not chosen to identify with and refuse to aspire to the dominant competitive individualistic ethic. A pointer to this is to note that it is a specific sub-section of the middle class which is heavily over-represented in folk music, those in service occupations which are largely in the public sector, jobs such as teaching and social work. (MacKinnon 1993: 130)

How has it come about that present-day producers, performers, audiences and supporters of folk music are largely from the middle classes and not from the 'people'? This question arose implicitly in our comparative discussion of the sessions at the Eel's Foot, the Princess Charlotte and the Monkseaton Arms in Chapter 3. Whereas those at the Saturday evening sessions at the Eel's Foot were frequented by members of the rural labouring classes, those attending the folk club sessions in the Princess Charlotte were either middle-class students or, if not, students aspiring to gain an academic qualification that would enable them to access the middle classes socially. The sessions at 'the Monkeys' were a mixture of middle- and lower-middle-class people, with perhaps a few from the lower classes. So there does appear to be a shift from working- to middle-class people playing, singing and listening to folk music from the 1940s to the present. In the present chapter we attempt to explain this shift, and we argue that it is only significant if singing folk songs means using the voice of the people, rather than using a voice to create a folk.

Finding a Voice

We now wish to examine our definition of folk song in the Introduction in the light of Richard Middleton's search, in his book *Voicing the Popular* (2006), for the 'people' as the source (or goal) of 'popular music'. Folk music is often subsumed under the label 'popular music', presumably on the grounds that 'folk' is to be equated with 'people', and 'people' is to be equated with what Middleton calls 'the Low'. He begins his discussion with a Chartist song written by Ernest Jones in the 1840s entitled 'Song of the Lower Classes' and argues that the oppressed and disenfranchised sections of society from the late eighteenth century constructed themselves, in France, as 'the revolutionary citizenry of the *Marseillaise*' and elsewhere as 'an emergent working class, poised to smash the bourgeois system', or as 'representatives of long-suffering yet resilient plebeian forces' (Middleton 2006: 4). Middleton's comments on Jones's conversion to Chartism include a significant point, viz. that 'Jones's basic historical picture, *rooted in a vision of lost pastoral harmony, disrupted by industrialism and a ruling-class usurpation*, never left him. It was a mythic construction not untypical of the Chartist leadership' (ibid.: 5; italics ours).

The 'singing voice' constructed to represent the 'people' in the Chartist era was not, therefore, a proletarian voice but a voice from the middle classes, and the song was written specifically for 'political soirées (or "evenings for the people")' (ibid.: 1) rather than circulated orally and across generations among the 'people'. 'Song of the Lower Classes' was also put to music by composer John Lowry, so in the purist terms of the folk music movement in Britain in the late 1960s and 1970s it was not a folk song. It was a song *for* the people but not a song *of* the people.[1] Nevertheless, it appeared as a broadsheet in the second half of the nineteenth century, was revived in a Workers' Music Association pamphlet in the late 1930s and was recorded by folk singers Martin Carthy and Bob Davenport ☺31.

The Voice of Folk Song

Before going into Middleton's arguments in more detail in this section, however, we return briefly to our notion of folk song. A folk song is not 'a song *of* the people' if the term 'people' refers only to the working classes. A song *for* the people (working classes or not) may be called a folk song if it is sung to construct, reaffirm or transform a community of practice by strengthening social bonding mechanisms. In our terminology, a 'folk' refers to a group of people coordinated around a specific joint enterprise, whether this has to do with solidarity amongst workers, reaffirming local communities, strengthening kinship bonds or even promoting and furthering interest in song itself.

The term 'folk' in English has a more local sense than a social class or nation (see the quotation from MacKinnon above and points that we make on 'defining' the term 'folk song' in the Introduction). Turner (1969: 132) makes a distinction between three types of '*communitas*':

1. *existential* or *spontaneous communitas*, the transient personal experience of togetherness; e.g. that which occurs during a counter-culture happening;
2. *normative communitas*, transformed from its existential state into a permanent social system due to the need for social control;
3. *ideological communitas*, which can be applied to many utopian social models.

---

[1] In addition, as Middleton points out, the style of the tune was defined by János Maróthy as deriving 'from that of the bourgeois marches that developed out of song types typical of the vaudeville, comic opera, and pleasure garden repertoires of the late eighteenth century' (Middleton 2006: 4).

A 'folk' is simply an *existential* or *spontaneous communitas*, but folk music and folk song theorists have discursively created an *ideological communitas*, which, Turner says, is a 'utopian' move. Folk singers in the 1960s and 1970s also attempted to create a *normative communitas*.

The fundamental aim of folk music and folk song is to create different kinds of *existential* or *spontaneous forms of communitas* – and this is precisely the significance of folk song. It enables the performers and the members of an audience to construct a 'transient, personal experience of togetherness' (see the discussion of hybrid forms of folk song performance in Chapter 2). Folk song then refers to song that brings individuals together and moulds them into a *communitas*. Other types of song may also do this, but the purpose of a folk song is precisely the transient social construction of a 'folk' through the emergent performance event. For this very reason, songs from other musical genres may be used as folk song. And because folk song occurs in such a wide number of performance types, relational, representational and hybrid forms, it is the perfect medium to examine performance. Folk songs bond people together, transiently but over and over again. Posen, in his contribution to Rosenberg (1993), comes to the same conclusion:

> One of the conclusions I came to in my thesis was that any songs sung in such a close little group had to be folksongs. My argument was as follows: items are not intrinsically 'folk'; rather, their 'folkness' lies in the functions and processes and ultimately the contexts of which they are part. Camp exhibits all the qualities that have been tradition- ally associated with folk groups; its songs function as folksongs for the group; therefore campsongs, in fact any songs sung at camp (all things being equal), are folksongs. (Rosenberg 1993: 135)

Any song used to achieve any of these goals, and a host of other goals within a community, may thus be called a folk song. From this point of view, 'Song of the Lower Classes' can function as a folk song. In the following subsection we focus on Middleton's notion of 'answering back', which is one of the ritual functions not only of folk songs but also of several popular songs.

Answering Back

One of the rituals in the symbolic container from which all song performance emerges, 'Protesting against injustice' (cf. Figure 1.2, Chapter 1), can have problematic consequences. Singing about a social injustice perpetrated by members of the group also places a focus on a social drama within the group and may have the effect of creating a schism. Bonding can only be achieved amongst those against whom the injustice has been perpetrated and others who can be persuaded to accept this fact. If, on the other hand, the injustice has been perpetrated by someone from outside the group, singing about it can be used to strengthen the determination of others in the CofP to adopt, as part of the joint enterprise, forms of action to counteract the injustice.

Within the sociolinguistic framework of song performance presented in Chapter 2, the term 'protest' expresses the communal need to disagree with actions or states that impinge upon or are inimical to the interests of the group, or endanger the social bonding of the group. Such actions or states incur moral disapproval. Middleton uses the term 'answering back', so we first briefly present the social implications inherent to this term. 'Answering back' implicates a response to a speaker that represents a challenge to and thus a rejection of a set of taken-for-granted attitudes implied by what has been said or done by that speaker. However, the speaker and the challenger are always of unequal social status; the speaker is the superior and the challenger her/his inferior. The what-has-been-said or what-has-been-done by the superior lies within what s/he is allowed 'by right' to say or do and brooks no challenge. But by whose right? 'Answering back' in certain institutional frameworks, notably the school or the military, may also be punishable.

'Answering back' thus involves an unequal duality, in which the 'answerer back' is the 'subjugated' Other to the 'answered back'. The question that Middleton raises is whose voice carries out the answering back. He discusses John Gay's *Beggar's Opera* and Brecht and Weill's *Die Dreigroschenoper*[2] and has this to say, 'No doubt Brecht and Weill hoped that ... [the use of the *Verfremdungseffekt*] would enable their low-life characters to *answer back* to their betters. Similarly, Gay's work is of course a *beggar's* opera, voiced (it seems) from below. But where do these answers come from? From the "people"? Surely, it might be objected, ventriloquism is at work ...' (Middleton 2006: 20). We define ventriloquism as giving a voice to someone, the Other, who is otherwise silent. This is even extended to William Shield's attempt, in writing the music for *Omai, or a Trip Round the World* in 1785, to draw on vernacular songs from Tyneside collected orally by his friend Joseph Ritson from colliers and keelmen. But Shield's music 'is placed into contexts that would attract his bourgeois audiences: contemporary songs of industrial workers[3] could not yet be voiced on the London stage' (ibid.: 21).

Middleton is aware that the 'Low' did have their own voices in the eighteenth and early nineteenth centuries, but that those voices 'come to us through the screens of class and historical distance, and may often seem hard to hear' (ibid.: 22). The best that we have from those 'Low' voices is 'hybrids and

---

[2] Brecht and Weill's *Die Dreigroschenoper* is obviously a twentieth-century reworking of *The Beggar's Opera*.
[3] For example, 'The Collier's Rant' (♪32), 'The Keel Row' (♪33) and 'Bonny Keel Laddie' (see Chapter 11).

mediations'. He then sets up four principles according to which his 'search' for the voice of popular music is guided. Two of these principles concern us centrally in this chapter: firstly, he concludes that 'there is no pure popular music; rather the voice of the people is always plural, hybrid, compromised'; secondly, he concludes that the voice of the people is a 'counterbalance to modernity' (*pace* Paul Gilroy 1993), i.e. that it is 'constitutive of modernity itself'. The first point implies that there is likewise no 'pure' folk song, only and always plurality, hybridity and compromise. The second point will be dealt with in the following subsection: the voice of 'popular song' is 'constitutive of modernity itself'.

Folk Song and Modernity

'Modernity' is used to refer to the most recent period of time in the history of Western thought when human beings began to reach beyond superstition and blind faith in and submission to religious and secular rulers to develop rationalist explanations for phenomena in the natural world and for human cultural and social formations. Hence in European history – and in the history of nation-states that arose in the New World – its beginnings can be found in the Renaissance, at precisely that period of time when Europeans extended their range of trading and colonisation beyond Europe, the Near East and North Africa and began their exploration of the New World. Its high point is generally accepted to be the Age of Enlightenment in the eighteenth century. As Adorno says, '[e]nlightenment, understood in the widest sense as the advance of thought, has always aimed at liberating human beings from fear and installing them as masters' (Adorno 1973: 1), although he follows this immediately with the following comment on the 1960s: 'Yet the wholly enlightened earth radiates under the sign of disaster triumphant.'

In sociology, itself born from modernism, the term relates to social processes developing after the Age of Enlightenment. Hence Giddens defines 'modernism' as follows:

[Modernism is] a shorthand term for modern society, or industrial civilization. Portrayed in more detail, it is associated with (1) a certain set of attitudes towards the world, the idea of the world as open to transformation, by human intervention; (2) a complex of economic institutions, especially industrial production and a market economy; (3) a certain range of political institutions, including the nation-state and mass democracy. Largely as a result of these characteristics, modernity is vastly more dynamic than any previous type of social order. It is a society – more technically, a complex of institutions – which, unlike any preceding culture, lives in the future, rather than the past. (Giddens 1998: 94)

But neither Adorno nor Giddens admits that modernism can only exist by virtue of its construction of a wide range of dualisms, deriving from the assumed foundational dualism 'the enlightened vs the non-enlightened', i.e. the West has a mission to spread the achievements and 'benefits' of the Enlightenment to the unenlightened rest of the world (cf. also Said 1993). Modernism depends on the construction of *alterity*, i.e. for every positive value there is a negative value. For men, the Other is women; for the 'white race', the Other is any non-white human being; for the master, the Other is the slave; for the ruling class, the Other is all the lower classes; for the coloniser, the Other is the colonised; for democracy, the Other is dictatorship, autocracy, feudalism, clan systems; for the manufacturer, the Other is the worker; for the heterosexual, the Other is the bisexual or homosexual, and so on. Alterity even extends into the field of culture and the arts, e.g. for Western Art Music, the Other is popular music, folk music, arguably jazz, brass-band music, country and western, etc.; for literature, the Other is non-literary forms of writing. One element of each duality is positively valued and the other negatively valued, resulting in a need on the part of those on the negative side of the duality to answer back to those on the positive side.

The search for a voice with which to represent the negative values is the search for a means to upgrade the negative and downgrade the positive. But if there can be no 'pure' popular voice, must we then automatically assume that there is a 'pure' WAM voice, and if so, what would that be? In the age of recorded music, is it not the case that part of whatever voice we are searching for, popular, jazz, WAM, folk, etc., is the recording technicians, the managers, the agents, the CD producers, marketing teams, the media? Is not all modern music hybrid?

Because songs are performed, the voice in every song – WAM, popular music and folk alike – is that of the ventriloquist, the point of whose voice is 'to reveal what was always already there – a structure built around a lost object, which is in one form or another a human constant' (Middleton 2006: 51). The lost object can never be re-found. In the folk music movement in Britain in the late 1960s and early 1970s, the lost object was taken to be 'the people', the 'Low', 'the industrial and rural working classes', those without a voice. In trying to reconstitute what was felt to be lost, those in the vanguard of the folk song movement were led to set up stringent values on singing that were proclaimed 'traditional' and 'authentic', values that took on the ventriloquist's voice in answering back but at the same time strove to make that voice reproduce the lost original. What isolated folk music and also insulated it from productive cross-fertilisation from other forms of music was the attempt to answer back in the name of the 'folk', the people, rather than to use an unashamedly hybrid voice to answer back as a means of bonding a community in an ongoing performance event. As a result it almost stifled the ability of folk song to answer back at all.

Folk Song and Protest

Many folk songs 'answer back', and they are thus part of an anti-hegemonic discourse.[4] They thematise some kind of social or cultural friction, e.g. between women and men, between the forces of nature and humanity or between life and death. In pop and soul with a focus on personal relationships, and to a lesser degree in rock music (which, like rap, provides a medium suited to voicing and channelling anger and rebellion), answering back is not entirely absent, but, arguably, less prevalent,[5] and many musicians in the pop world would hardly take an explicit political stance. By contrast, folk musicians, particularly in the twentieth century, feel (and felt) the need to address injustice and are often linked to or rooted in left-wing politics.[6]

It would be naïve and counterfactual to say that all folk song lyrics thematise social friction and are thus instances of anti-hegemonic discourse; many drinking songs, tall tales, lullabies or children's songs do not. However, even here we find examples that deliver overt or implied social comment: 'All Through the Beer/Punch/Grog' ♪34 refers to the ending of a social gathering, but also to drink-related poverty; 'I was Born about Ten Thousand Years Ago' ♪35 depicts mythical, biblical and historical moments of import from a mischievous underdog's perspective; 'Highland Lullaby' ♪36 presents superstition and the fear that children may be taken by supernatural entities or by a higher power; and an apparently innocuous nursery rhyme like 'Ring-Around-the-Roses' describes symptoms of plague and, with the expression 'we all fall down', the ultimate outcome, death. Implied 'answering back', in metaphorical terms or explicitly, is clearly an important element in the lyrics of folk song.

The Nature of Protest in Song: Musical Aspects

Why is song an effective means of 'transporting' protest? And what strategies are used in folk song to present protest? In his biography of American folk singer and activist Pete Seeger, Winkler describes Seeger's focus on songs as

---

[4] We use the term 'hegemonic discourse' as Gramsci (1971) defines it, viz. a dominant discourse that has been changed such that those in power may remain in power. In this sense, hegemonic discourses are always under challenge by alternative anti-hegemonic discourses.

[5] When folk songs tell tales of love, they tend to do so in the third person or they use an introductory stanza in the third person suggesting that the following first-person account is filtered through the observer presented in the first stanza, which creates the distance of third-person comment rather than first-person immediacy.

[6] British folk musician John Tams' remark 'I've never been to a Tory folk club yet' (Bean 2014: 376) is evidence of this, as is American guitarist and singer Dave van Ronk's comment, in the 'Preface' to the 1992 *Collected Reprints from Sing Out!*, on the eclectic bunch of songs printed in the magazine between 1964 and 1973, described as 'an Aladdin's cave with something for everyone except perhaps tone-deaf Republicans' (in Silber *et al.* 1992: 2).

the insight that 'singing songs in unison could foster a common commitment to work for social and political change' (Winkler 2009: 40). There is a long history of how communal singing is used to create a sense of unity in a group (cf. also our arguments in Chapter 3). Tunes of songs that function in this way tend to be relatively simple and to have a limited, i.e. manageable, vocal range, a predictability in terms of their sequencing and harmonies, and often few if any accidentals (for a more detailed discussion, see Nettl 2005; Bronson 1959, 1962; Roud and Bishop 2012: xlii–lxi). The need for simplicity in accompaniment and harmonies is stressed in most twentieth-century introductions to folk song collections, as are the variations in the tunes from verse to verse (cf., e.g., Purslow 1965; Buchan and Hall 1973; Kennedy 1975; Lomax and Lomax 1975). They are easily passed on but will also be varied by different singers, a process we return to in Chapter 5. Given their limited tonal range, they are easy to accompany with guitar, banjo, accordion or piano, with little need for complex chord changes, which explains the lasting popularity of songs like Dylan's 'Blowin' in the Wind' with three major chords (and one optional minor in the chorus; cf. Appendix), Pete Seeger's 'We Shall Overcome' ♪37 or Woody Guthrie's 'This Land is Your Land' ♪38. In addition, all these examples have lyrics that are structurally and lexically simple. They are thus easy to pass on and easy to learn, which makes them an ideal vector for the sentiments they carry and also promotes their performance in a group, in a community.

As we saw in Chapter 1, communal singing fosters a 'sense of commitment' if we consider the way in which music – and in particular vocal music – has an impact on human beings who do not suffer from *amusia* in its purest form where music is perceived as unpleasant noise – which is a rare condition, rarer even than simple tone-deafness (see Sacks 2007: 100). Most of us can relate to vocal music better than to purely instrumental music, as a study by Weiss *et al.* (2012) shows. Folk tunes were more easily remembered or learnt if sung rather than played on musical instruments (piano, banjo and marimba) even if 'pitch, duration and amplitude' were 'perfectly matched' (Williamson 2014: 181). The conclusion is that 'vocal music may stimulate a higher arousal and attention engagement in listeners' and that '[these] factors, including our liking response and apparent attraction to vocal music, contribute to the eventual laying down of strong and long-lasting musical memories' (ibid.). Levitin observes that '[m]usic breathes, speeds up, and slows down just as the real world does and our cerebellum *finds pleasure* in adjusting itself *to stay synchronised*' (2008: 191, our emphasis). Song is therefore a powerful and mnemonically useful tool to transport a message – particularly if that message is one that the singer or singers can relate to affectively. How is representing social injustice – or, in a wider sense, 'answering back' – realised in folk songs given that they help to create or foster a community either through communal singing or when sung by an individual at and for a gathering? We posit that there are three principal ways of articulating the act of 'answering back'.

Strategies for 'Answering Back' in Song

Many songs performed in clubs and on larger stages are 'traditional' in the sense that they have been transmitted from generation to generation of singers, in some cases for centuries (see Chapter 6 for a discussion of the term 'traditional'). Singers tend to present such songs in performance with social comment, presenting a social issue as 'history' and linking the unresolved social friction of the song to a similar – and still unresolved – situation in the present. The song itself will thus *entail* social friction leaving it to the audience to *infer* the protest, and we assume that both the performer[7] and the audience will make a connection given the socio-cultural context of folk song performance as presented so far. A song like 'Poverty Knock' ☺39, about the plight of workers, particularly women, in the cotton mills of nineteenth-century England describing pressure to arrive at work on time, not being allowed to stop work to assist a colleague after an accident, the sexually predatory nature of males higher up in the hierarchy – the 'tacker' (the engineer) and the 'gaffer' (the boss) – is a critical comment on the topicality of the exploitation of – particularly female – workers in sweatshops the world over. This entailed protest is the first mode of answering back through song.

The second mode is to *encode* the subject of protest *allegorically* or *meta-phorically*. For instance, the Irish song 'Four Green Fields' ☺40 is ostensibly about a 'fine old woman' who owns the fields. In effect, it is a metaphorically veiled way of 'answering back' to the British occupation of Ireland. One of the 'four green fields' is still 'in bondage / in strangers' hands that tried to take it from me', but because her 'sons had sons as brave as were their fathers / [her] fourth green field will bloom once again' – a clear reference to the Irish Republican struggle to restore Ulster to Ireland, the 'fine old woman'. A similar strategy is at work in Buffy Sainte-Marie's 'Universal Soldier' ☺41, where a nameless 'he' represents all ages and nations, as well as creeds and ideologies for which wars can be waged. In this *encoded* mode, a similar cooperation between performer and audience is required as is the case in entailed protest.

The third and most straightforward mode of presenting social friction is by being *explicit*, by pointing an accusing finger at culprits. An interesting

---

[7] The term 'performer' here includes the songwriter, who may or may not be known to performer and audience, which avoids the thorny debate of ownership of songs, an issue tackled in Chapter 6.

example is the song 'Which Side Are You On?' ☮42, written in 1931 by Florence Reece, the wife of a Harlan County (Kentucky) miners' union leader, who had been arrested for first-degree murder in an attempt to cow 11,000 striking miners into submission (Seeger and Reiser 1985: 132–33). She does not mince words in naming Harlan County and the arresting sheriff: 'they say in Harlan County / there are no neutrals there / you'll either be a union man / or a thug for J. H. Blair'. The song was taken up by Billy Bragg (on the 1985 EP 'Between the Wars') in response to anti-union legislation by the Thatcher government and the way it dealt with the miners in the 1984/85 strike, and opened with the lines: 'this government had an idea / and parliament made it law / it seems like it's illegal / to fight for the union anymore'. Another example is Leon Rosselson's 'They're Going to Build a Motorway' ☮43 describing the impact of the A406 North Circular Road on the communities it crossed, best expressed in the closing lines 'they've built an eight lane motorway / they've ripped up all the trees / now lorries zoom where once I grew / my cabbages and peas' (Rosselson 1974: 10–11). All three songs address an issue *explicitly* and *directly*, union-bashing in the coal mines of Kentucky in the 1930s and in Thatcherite Britain in the mid-1980s, and road building to the detriment of the local community in the 1960s and 1970s.

Each of these strategies for 'answering back', *entailed*, *encoded* or *explicit*, has its advantages and drawbacks. *Entailed* or *implied* social comment is useful in terms of the rather general truths it carries. An experience such as that described in 'Poverty Knock' may refer to a historically remote reality, but its lessons are as applicable now as they were then. But the lesson is at one or several removes from the audience, requiring a conceptual effort on their part to make the connection. Entailed protest relies for its efficiency on the audience being prepared to make such an effort, which may diminish its effectiveness, particularly if the social issue is relatively particular and not interpreted as immediately significant by hearers.

An *encoded* or metaphorical form of answering back has the advantage that it can protect the author or performer from repression because of its obscurity. It is likely to be more general in its applicability because its encoding renders it more universally true, as the anti-war song 'Universal Soldier' illustrates. In 'Four Green Fields', the underlying struggle for the integrity of ownership, in itself a potentially significant issue regardless of the metaphor, also communicates universality. But there is a potential problem in such obscurity: few listeners, thinking that it is a slightly nonsensical nursery rhyme, would be aware of the metaphorical implica- tions of 'Mary Mary Quite Contrary' in its reference to Mary Queen of Scots. When encoding is used in the form of satire, as in 'Cam Ye o'er frae France' ☮44, with the passing of time the lyrics can only be under- stood with detailed explanations in footnotes or with a detailed introduction in a live performance.[8] Making the conceptual step to understand the references of *encoded* answering back is even more demanding than in the case of *entailed* answering back.

The *explicit* approach is thus the most obviously focused, the most direct expression of social comment. Little if any explanation or prior knowledge is needed; the issue in question is likely to be obvious and generally known, involving little conceptual work on the part of the audience. However, this comes at a price: the transference to a more general expression of a wider social criticism is not a given and requires greater conceptual effort. As a result, the impact of the answering back may not last. In addition, the details presented may quickly become dated and, in the worst case, begin to appear irrelevant. A best-case scenario for such protest is that it undergoes a metamorphosis into 'entailed answering back'.

Answering Back in English-speaking Folk Worlds

Answering back may have been less widespread or less foregrounded in the world of folk song before the twentieth century. In the British Isles, there were a variety of other concerns that took precedence. Sir Walter Scott saw the poetic and literary soul of the Scots, as it manifested itself in his song collection, as the prime object of his study, which explains his focus on lyrics and his neglect of tunes.[9] Collectors in the late nineteenth and early twentieth centuries like Cecil Sharp, Lucy Broadwood and Sabine Baring-Gould saw folk song as the basis of a 'national music', which in any case precludes the acceptance of answering back in folk song. 'Authentic' folk music for them was an exclusively rural phenomenon.

Given the encroachments of urbanisation characteristic of the industrial revolution, there was a widespread belief that conservation work was urgently needed to save the 'remnants' of English folk song, making the neglect of urban folk music and, more specifically, of folk music as a way of answering back a problematic issue in the twentieth-century discourse archive of folk music (see Chapter 6). In this section we present examples of various kinds of answering back through song in Scotland, Ireland and the USA. Much has already been said of 'protest' songs in England, and more will be said in Chapter 6 when we focus more explicitly on the notions of discourse, discourse archives, and hegemonic and anti-hegemonic discourse. In other areas of the

---

[8] June Tabor's keying-in of 'The Four Loom Weaver' during Maddy Prior's Cecil Sharp House concert is a good example of the need to provide a historical explanation for the song.

[9] He had a tendency to edit ballads to make them fit the prevalent understanding of the ballad form, changing 'Clerk Saunders' (♪)45 from a metre with four stressed syllables in each line of the stanza to the more widespread 'ballad metre' (four and three stressed syllables in alternation), thus rendering it unsingable.

English-speaking world, e.g. Canada, Australia, New Zealand, songs that answer back to the establishment are just as potent and significant as those in what we might call the 'core' areas of the Anglophone world, England and the USA, and their fringes. But an attempt to give equal historical coverage of those areas would deflect from the major theoretical thrust of this book, viz. the sociolinguistic analysis of folk song as performance.

Answering Back in Scotland and Ireland: A Historical Sketch

In the course of the last eighty years, folk song as a means of answering back has primarily addressed the concerns of the lower social classes. The scope of the present study does not allow us to explore this topic in great detail, but it may be indicative of a wider variety of assumptions about the 'essential' character of folk song and folk music. To consider folk song only in terms of a liberal and left-of-centre political orientation as a way of thematising social inequality or social friction may be acceptable in a British or American setting, but it ignores the fact that songs perceived as emerging from an old tradition or songs written to reflect that old tradition have been a powerful tool in the hands of right-wing activists.

Two examples suffice to illustrate the right-wing nationalistic appropriation of folk song and music. The first is the use of folk song material (and songs written in the folk idiom) from the *Wandervogel* movement in Germany in the early twentieth century. The introduction to the 1915 songbook *Zupfgeigenhansel*[10] is very clear about the need to see hiking and singing the songs collected in the book as a national characteristic in becoming 'more German'. Another more recent example for the promotion of nationalist feelings in folk music and song is the Serbian 'Neofolk' or 'Turbo-Folk' movement of the 1990s (cf. Grujić 2009; Archer 2012; Čvoro 2014), which had its origin in traditional rural music and song but developed this into something more contemporary while at the same time harking back to traditional (nationalist) values. It represented a rejection of Yugoslav multiculturalism. 'Turbo-Folk' is characterised by songs designed and adapted for the purpose of 'self-exoticising and anti-neoliberalism' (Čvoro 2014: 55).[11] It could be argued that both these examples demonstrate an alternative discourse that constitutes answering back to a progressive hegemonic discourse (see Chapter 6). Songs of (Serbian) nationalism at the end of the 1980s represented a rejection of Tito's supra-regionalism and a return to what could be constructed as traditional values in the form of Serbian folk song and the use of the *gusle*, the traditional bowed string instrument typical of Serbian epic singers (cf., e.g., Lord 2000 [1960]).

---

[10] The collection contained both traditional songs and works by known authors like Herman Löns.
[11] In this sense the genre also represents a form of 'answering back'.

Both these movements stand in contrast to the discourse emerging from the songs of Scotland and Ireland before the twentieth century, with a thrust that could be seen as anti-colonialist. In Scotland, we can distinguish two main types of anti-hegemonic discourse, one revolving around the Jacobite Rebellions and the other focusing on the Highland Clearances and subsequent exile. Although the Jacobite Rebellion is seen as an attempt at restoring the Catholic Stuarts to the throne, it was also an attempt to create a politically stronger Scottish voice. The struggles and eventual defeat of the Jacobite Scots gave rise to a range of songs criticising the political establishment in London, e.g. 'Cam' Ye o'er frae France', and taunting the enemy, e.g. 'Johnnie Cope' ♪46, which heaps ridicule on Lieutenant-General Sir John Cope, commander-in-chief of the government troops in Scotland, defeated at the Battle of Prestonpans.

However, there were also songs that depicted the loss of life in the uprisings, e.g. the 'Highland Widow's Lament' ♪47 or the deeply moving 'Flowers o' the Forest' ♪48, the tune of which is still played at military funerals. And there were songs criticising the Jacobite stance, e.g. Burns' 1791 rewrite of 'Ye Jacobites by Name' ♪49 that reflects war-weariness. 'Both Sides of the Tweed' ♪50, on the other hand, with its reference to the river iconised as the border between England and Scotland, tentatively attributed to James Hogg and adapted by Dick Gaughan, has lyrics to suggest a conciliatory note against the prevalent anti-English discourse, particularly in the chorus: 'let the love of our land's sacred rights / to the love of our people succeed / let friendship and honour unite / and flourish on both sides of the Tweed'.

The underdog 'answering back' is even more explicit in songs of exile, most of which are connected with the Highland Clearances and the collapse of the kelp industry in the Hebrides, which saw a predominantly Gaelic-speaking peasant population driven from their crofts and often shipped to the New World by the landowners. Many of these songs are understandably in Gaelic, and several were recorded in the 1930s in Nova Scotia and on Cape Breton Island by John Lorne Campbell and his wife Margaret Fay Shaw. Campbell (1990) collected and published them 'with an account of the causes of the Highland emigration', as the subtitle of his book *Songs Remembered in Exile* states. With the shrinking population of Gaelic-speakers, such songs tend to be sung relatively rarely and more in concert settings by musicians celebrating their Gaelic origins or connections. However, among the English-speaking majority, songs of Scottish independence are still very popular, alongside others that would fit into the left-of-centre interest in songs about working and living conditions of the lower classes, both rural and urban.[12]

---

[12] Cf. 'The Warld is Ill Divided' chapter of songs in Buchan and Hall 1973.

A similar picture emerges in Ireland, which has a sizeable number of songs about exile and the sorrow at having to leave one's home. Many are not politically focused overtly but are laments at having to leave family, friends and familiar places. They extol the beauty of the countryside (e.g. 'The Emigrant's Farewell' ☻51 with its references to 'native green clad hills', 'verdant banks of sweet Lough Neagh' and 'bogs of sweet Dromore'), and they often describe the loss of a lover (e.g. 'Leaving Limerick' ☻52). However, there is a more overt form of answering back in songs of exile when the reasons for emigration are unequivocally identified, most explicitly perhaps in the following passage in one version of 'The Green Fields of Canada' ☻53:

> for the landlords and bailiffs in vile combination
> have forced us from hearth stone and homestead away
> may the crowbar brigade all be doomed to damnation
> when we're on the green fields of Americay

It is remarkable that these lyrics, as in other songs of protest in Ireland, display a sophisticated style, suggesting seasoned literary authorship. Indeed, as Zimmermann explains, the sources were often broadsides with 'the more topical songs . . . written to order by some hack poets employed by the printers [of the broadsides]. Well known men of letters like Oliver Goldsmith . . . are said to have done this anonymously in their younger days' (1967: 21). Zimmermann points out that other authors might have been teachers in small towns, men with some degree of education, and he quotes an account by Johann Georg Kohl, a German visitor to the Kilkenny Races in 1842, about how the 'ballad-mongers' (Zimmermann (1967: 23) sell their songs. 'Ballad singers', Kohl claims, were 'in no country as numerous as here . . . literally twice as many as lamp-posts', and their 'principal employment' was 'the sale of these songs' which they did by walking up and down in the streets and singing the songs while '[c]rowds of poor people, beggars and rabble . . . follow them . . . and listen with . . . eagerness'. He attributes this to 'the great delight that the Irish take in music and singing'. Many of these broadsides, as in England, told stories of murder and crime, of gallant outlaws who allegedly redressed social inequality by stealing from the rich and giving to the poor and of peasants sheltering criminal fugitives from the widely mistrusted legal authorities.[13] Other themes included in these kinds of song are those of exile and the Irish struggle for independence from the British colonists, which was an effective way of spreading protest.

The 1798 rebellion is a rich source for songs whose anti-hegemonic discourse addressed the struggle against the British and the reprisals for failed rebellions, particularly those about the execution of the insurgents, e.g.

---

[13] Cf. also Synge's *Playboy of the Western World*.

'Dunlavin Green' ♪54 (actually naming the volunteers shot by a firing squad) or 'Roddy MacCorley' ♪55. The Easter Uprising in 1916 was extolled in 'The Foggy Dew', but the tradition of the 'rebel song' lasted well into the second half of the twentieth century. Christy Moore, in *The Christy Moore Songbook*, comments on 'The Belfast Brigade' ♪56, a song about clashes between the Black and Tans and the IRA during the War of Independence from 1919 to 1921 as follows: 'I suspect I learnt this song at a republican session in Shepherd's Bush [London] in 1966. In those days it was considered good fun to hear Paddy sing a rebel song; eighteen years later it could get you seven days at Her Majesty's pleasure.' At the time when they were written, such songs were obvious examples of *explicit* answering back, but over time they had become instances of *entailed* political comment of sufficient potency to warrant a custodial sentence by the 1980s.

This account would be one-sided if it ignored another form of answering back in the Irish tradition, that of the Orange discourse against Irish Republicanism and the fervent condemnation of Catholicism, in what Zimmermann calls 'songs of the "loyal" party' (1967: 295). This type of song was, not surprisingly, less prevalent than the classic rebel song in the twentieth century partly because of its 'pugnacity' (Zimmermann 1967: 300). Unsurprisingly, the only songs that were in the folk mainstream in the 1960s were 'The Sash My Father Wore' ♪57 and 'The Old Orange Flute' ♪58,[14] the latter even performed by iconic Irish singing groups such as The Dubliners and The Clancy Brothers, whose repertoire would more typically reflect the other side of the confessional divide. The striking aspect of these songs is that they are sung from a position of power and they extol the might of the Orange community intimidatingly. In view of the asymmetry of power in Northern Ireland, perhaps we should question whether Orange songs really represent an instance of anti-hegemonic discourse or not. On the other hand, their potency and that of the marching tunes forming part of the same tradition indicate that they have a strong function in shaping their 'folk'.

Answering Back in the USA: A Historical Sketch

The picture in the USA is not homogeneous, but in the first half of the twentieth century there is little doubt that folk music was politically the domain of the left. We can only focus on a few iconic figures in this context, so it makes sense to start with Stephen C. Foster (1826–1864), whose songs 'Oh! Susanna' ♪59, 'The Camptown Races' ♪60 or 'My Old Kentucky Home' ♪61 survive to

---

[14] Zimmermann claims that on 12 July (the day that commemorates the Battle of the Boyne when William of Orange established control over Ireland) there was 'a tendency to replace the most violent ballads with innocuous songs' such as these two.

this day. It is interesting that Foster assumes a 'black voice' in some of his songs, e.g. 'My Old Kentucky Home' (though he uses the term 'darkies', which required rewriting later in the second half of the twentieth century[15]) or in 'Old Black Joe' ☺62. One of his songs, recorded to this day by artists as such Bob Dylan, Kate and Anna McGarrigle, Iron and Wine and soul/rap singer Mary J. Blidge, 'Hard Times Come Again No More' ☺63, has him take sides unequivocally with the unfortunate as the lines from the chorus demonstrate: '' tis the song the sigh of the weary hard times / hard times come again no more'. His work was published in New York by a company that specialised in sheet music as well as selling musical instruments. The music can best be described as parlour music, but it transcended its original domain and has clearly remained popular with musicians to this day as well as featuring in many campfire songbooks. In fact, it represents an early example of the middle classes lending their voice to the lower classes, but interestingly, Foster's lyrics, e.g. in 'Old Black Joe', do not display even token elements of black speech style.

This trend proved a model for twentieth-century folk musicians, most notably Pete Seeger, a Harvard student from a family that Winkler (2009: 1) describes as having 'blood ... as blue as [that of his contemporaries at Harvard], bluer by far than the Irish [John F.] Kennedy's', who was one of Seeger's fellow students. In 1938, Seeger was politically active as a member of the Young Communist League and came to see himself as a preserver of folk music, a calling to which he was brought by song collector, archivist, ethnomusicologist and political activist Alan Lomax. Folk music for both of them was the music of the underprivileged, and Seeger's sympathies clearly lay with 'the working people of this country – women and men; old and young; people of various skin shades, various religions, languages and national background – [who ...] have tried to better their lives and work toward a world of peace, freedom, jobs and justice for all' (cf. the foreword to the activist song collection *Carry It On*, Seeger and Reiser 1985: 9).

It was hardly surprising that he collaborated, albeit relatively briefly, with another iconic figure of the American folk movement, Woody Guthrie, an activist like himself (cf. Lampell 1972). Guthrie came from Oklahoma and had 'drifted to California with many other Okies uprooted by the dust storms of the 1930s ... Radicals across the country embraced him as a true proletarian able to understand the troubles of working men and women' because for his audiences, especially among the New York intelligentsia, his 'songs ... were authentic, lively, and tuneful, telling of the problems that real people faced during the depression' (Winkler 2009: 18–19). An important feature of his

[15] www.wnyc.org/story/my-old-kentucky-home-a-song-with-a-checkered-past, accessed 28 November 2017.

songs was that they were memorable precisely because he often used tunes that came from traditional material.[16]

Guthrie and Seeger, with fellow activist and singer Lee Hays, combined forces in 1940 to form the Almanac Singers, who performed for the American Youth Congress and for radical gatherings around New York, although they were never members of any political party or association. On account of their anti-war stance – which they later changed as a result of their anti-fascist attitude – they were described as 'poison in our system' by the *Atlantic Monthly* (cf. Winkler 2009). Their 1941 song 'Talking Union' ♪67 became a hit among the organised workers and clearly cemented Seeger's, Hays' and Guthrie's reputations as left-wing activists. This continued after Seeger returned from active service and founded People's Songs, 'an informal association to encourage the creation and spread of radical protest songs' with Guthrie and Hays on the board of directors (Winkler 2009: 38). Neither their involvement in political music during the 1946 congressional elections, which swept the Republicans to power, nor their involvement in a concert with African American civil rights activist Paul Robeson, that occasioned the 'Peeskill riot', a carefully orchestrated backlash against the musicians and their audience (Kaufman 2015), did much to endear them to the ruling powers. Guthrie, whose mental health was deteriorating, moved to California and in 1952 was finally correctly diagnosed as suffering from Huntington's disease. Seeger and Hays in the meantime had started a new group called the Weavers (named after Hauptmann's play *Die Weber*), singing folk songs from all over the world. They were investigated by the House Un-American Activities Committee (HUAC) for communist sympathies and blacklisted, which meant that they were effectively barred from playing any larger venues. By 1957 the Weavers had made a comeback (e.g. filling Carnegie Hall), but Seeger departed to work in summer camps with schoolchildren and to teach young people to play the banjo. He also wrote some of his best-known songs in the 1960s, in particular 'Where Have All the Flowers Gone', taken up and popularised by the young Joan Baez.

Baez was one of many younger musicians, including Phil Ochs, Tom Paxton, Dave van Ronk and of course Bob Dylan, who all owe a debt to Pete Seeger and to Woody Guthrie. Guthrie had by that time become iconic, not just as a prolific songwriter and activist, but also in his delivery, and Dylan imitated his nasal singing style, his relatively unadorned guitar playing and the use of a mouth organ on a stand. As Guthrie had done, Dylan also made use of a time-honoured strategy for acquiring songs from other singers

---

[16] His 'Jesus Christ' ♪64 is obviously based on 'The Ballad of Jesse James' ♪65, in popular perception another folk hero who 'took from the rich and gave to the poor', a motive that resurfaces in Guthrie's 'Pretty Boy Floyd' ♪66 (cf. Lampell 1972: 12).

by writing new lyrics to traditional tunes. Some of these he adopted from American material, but on his first trip to the UK in 1962, after appearances at the London folk venue, the Troubadour, he adopted tunes from Martin Carthy and Bob Davenport. His 'Masters of War' ☉68 uses the tune of 'Nottamun Town' ☉69; 'Bob Dylan's Dream' ☉70 borrows liberally from the melody of 'Lord Franklin' ☉71 (Bean 2014). Dylan's protest songs and his emulation of the acoustic guitar-playing troubadour Guthrie came to an end in 1965 at the Newport Folk Festival after his appearance with the Band. This was seen by many as an act of treason, resulting in calls like the infamous 'Judas' heckling at a concert in Manchester on his 1965/66 world tour. Pete Seeger's famous (alleged) attempt to cut the power cable at the Newport Festival was potentially a physical reaction to Dylan abandoning the role of the answerer-back.

Concluding Issues

The debate in this chapter has shown that there is a strong underlying element to the singing of folk songs, that of a (political) stance in favour of the underdog, even if it is not always the underdog that voices it. However, whether the politics are overt or not, there is an anti-hegemonic focus in a very large number of folk songs, whether 'traditional' or purpose-written. 'Answering back' is thus a central element in folk lyrics.

At this point, we need to stress the following claim: folk song is not commercially motivated. In pop and rock music we talk about artists 'covering' other artists when they adopt someone else's material, but this is not a term used in folk music circles. If another person's authored work is taken up and adapted by a singer in performance, a source has simply been adapted. The adaptation may be minimal or it may be extensive, and in the course of time further singers may come to refer to versions arising from those adaptations as 'traditional' songs (cf. Chapter 6). The song, or versions of the song, has entered a performance tradition quite unique to the folk song world, in which royalty lawsuits effectively representing litigation over who 'owns' the song are a rare occurrence indeed.[17]

We give a brief example of this process here. The Irish song commonly called 'The Bantry Bay Girls' Lament' ☉72 has been recorded by a wide variety of singers, who all refer to the song in the liner notes as 'trad.' or 'trad.: arr. X'.[18] Yet some commentators on the song have claimed that it was originally a poem by Irish poet Patrick Kavanagh. But does this matter?

---

[17] The reason for this is likely to be that the financial stakes are simply too low to make litigation a viable option.

[18] Which means that the song is now taken to be traditional and may be adapted and changed as the performer sees fit. The 'arr. X' assures the arranger of the song, who is sometimes referred to

Would Kavanagh's heirs, if they knew this – and if they cared – insist that recordings of the song should be explicitly labelled as 'Kavanagh: trad. arr/arr. X'? In our readings of Patrick Kavanagh's work, we have never come across this poem, although Kavanagh is known to have written songs in the 'folk idiom' (cf. 'On Raglan Road' ☉73). 'The Bantry Bay Girls' Lament' has even appeared on a CD of Spanish Civil War songs, as the Irish contribution, and it fits very well into the answering-back concerns of that war (anti-fascist, anti-monarchy, pro-republican, etc.), whether or not it was written by Kavanagh. Others have argued that the lyrics of the song refer to the War of the Spanish Succession in the first decade of the eighteenth century, or that it refers to the Peninsular War during the period of the Napoleonic Wars. The second interpretation is a little more likely, but it is still vitiated by a mention of the 'peelers', the first police force introduced in Britain in 1829 by Home Secretary Robert Peel, which places it almost twenty years later than the Peninsular War. Once again, the modes of answering back are appropriate to that war, too, peelers or no peelers. Our point, however, is that there do not seem to be other versions of the song than the one sung today, an unusual fact if it is claimed to be 'traditional'. Whatever the supposed facts, the song tells of the failure of Irish recruits to return home, which is arguably its central form of answering back. So whether it is referred to as 'traditional' or not has more to do with its lyrics and the sense of an individual singer that it belongs to a singing tradition than to its assumed oral transference from singer to singer over a long period of time.[19]

Most folk song collectors and (traditional) singers have considered their work as a last-ditch effort to preserve the music of the 'people' before the 'people' lose an interest in preserving their heritage. However, if we look at the history of folk music, it becomes clear that it changes over time. New instrumentations and new ways of presenting the material come into fashion, mutate and are reinvented, but the songs, the tunes, even their words are amazingly resilient. Songs and their performance change, but, like language, they do not disappear completely. Adapting Mark Twain's famous response to the premature news of his own death, we can assert that reports of the death of folk music and song have always been greatly exaggerated.

Part of the resilience of folk song is due to the fact that, on the one hand, it regenerates itself through 'traditions' and recourse to tried formulae (as we shall discuss in greater detail in Chapters 5, 6 and 9) and by combining new material and messages to similarly tried and tested melodies, which makes 'new' songs easy to pass on and to pick up. On the other hand, it is also a result

---

explicitly, a small amount of royalties from the sales of the LP or CD and may represent a 'claim' on the song, a notion we shall discuss in Chapter 7.

[19] For a more detailed discussion cf. Chapters 6 and 7.

of the way in which folk songs can adopt musical interlopers from other fields, from parlour songs to pop classics.[20]

By way of contrast, purism and notions of the 'right way to do it' have on the whole been ineffective. In fact, if they have become overpowering, artists and audiences have simply looked elsewhere. Purism is a driving force to relegate anti-hegemonic discourse in folk song to a purely entailed or possibly encoded form of answering back; the conceptual leap necessary becomes obsolete if a new generation of musicians or new orientations of contemporary musicians decide to opt for explicit anti-hegemonic discourse. A classic case for this was the way in which folk was largely replaced in the mid-seventies by punk, which did precisely that. What is more, like folk, punk required no extremely expensive equipment and, like folk, its musical demands were also open towards the amateur end of the spectrum.

---

[20] We refer to this kind of creative cross-fertilisation in Chapter 12.

Part II

Variation in Language and Folk Song

5 'The Times They Are a-Changin'': Language Change and Song Change

Changes in musical style have generally been reflections of changes in society.   (Blacking 1973: 76)

The Longevity of Songs

In the Introduction and in Chapter 2, we discussed two songs that are still favourites with folk song audiences when performed today, 'The Unquiet Grave' and 'Who's the Fool Now?'. In the case of 'Who's the Fool Now?' we can trace both the lyrics and the melody back at least as far as the sixteenth century. There is no way of knowing how frequently it is, or was, performed, but we do know that, given the appropriate setting and singers, it still generates much lively audience participation today. 'The Unquiet Grave' is still listened to by audiences willing to meditate on and appreciate the eternal problem of life and death and the loss of love. Both songs display traces of archaic language, which in no way interferes with their continuing popularity. In neither case can the 'origins' of the songs be traced back unequivocally to single singers or authors, although Simpson (1966: 776) does mention that 'Who's the Fool Now?' 'was licensed in 1588 to Thomas Orwin'. Authorship, however, is immaterial and unimportant for audiences and performers to enjoy the songs, which exist by virtue of being sung and not as the products of individual songwriters and composers.

In Chapter 3, we discussed the capstan shanty 'Sally Brown', the Scots Gaelic rowing song 'Thoir mo shoraidh thar Gunnaigh' and the three marching songs 'Over the Hills and Far Away' (from the early eighteenth century), 'Here We Are! Here We Are! Here We Are Again!' and 'The Old Battalion' (from the First World War). We argued in that chapter that songs do not need an audience if they are sung communally to help carry out tedious physical group work. As long as they are useful in bonding a group of people together in the work situation, they remain in currency. As work songs, they are tied to the kind of work for and with which they were developed, but if those forms of work become redundant, the songs themselves may lose their currency unless they retain an ability to evoke audience participation and/or appreciation.

This leads us to consider the question of the longevity and variability of a song and whether its major theme is strong enough to maintain currency over time. In the course of history, songs come and go, rise to fame only to fall out of favour, slowly regain their popularity, are renewed and adapted in various ways or retain their currency over centuries. They may be resurrected because their entailed or encoded protest closely mirrors or reflects the problems of the modern world, or, in the case of explicit protest, they may be (re)written specifically to give a voice to those problems. Songs, as Gammon says, are 'little works of art, a complex combination of words and music, which work through the simultaneous articulation of different structures: musical, narrative, poetic, verbal and so on' (2008: 12). They are the products of the synthesis of music and the semiotic communication system of human language. But like human language systems, folk songs also change through time. In fact, they are far less stable than a language system and far more prone to adaptation in performance. In one point, however, the trigger of change is the same in language and song: *innovation* (*creation*), which leads to *adoption, adaptation, transmission* and finally *diffusion*.

The Actuation Process in Language Change and the Transmission Process in Song Change

The key to the heterogeneity of language and its propensity to change through time lies in the fact that individual speakers, consciously or unconsciously, may at any point within a stretch of emergent social practice – primarily for pragmatic reasons – introduce an element of language that is entirely new, yet comprehensible to the addressee. The overwhelming majority of *innovations* are simply passed over as quirks, mistakes, linguistic infelicities, etc., and go no further than the single utterance. But if an innovation helps interlocutors in a linguistically problematic situation, there is a chance that the addressee will *adopt* it and use it in another communicative interaction. This does not guarantee that it will spread any further than the original adopter, but if it does, and particularly if it spreads to another community of practice, there is an increased statistical probability that it will, in time, *diffuse* through the whole speech community, eventually replacing or displacing the structure that caused the original difficulty in the first place (see Bergs 2005; Watts 2012b). In historical sociolinguistics, *innovation, adoption* and *diffusion* are referred to as *the actuation process*, and because a language variety is a semiotic system, stability and homogeneity in that system are perceived to be temporarily re-established after a period of change.[1]

---

[1] The appearance of homogeneity, however, is only an illusion as there will, at any one time, be a large number of actuation processes taking place simultaneously.

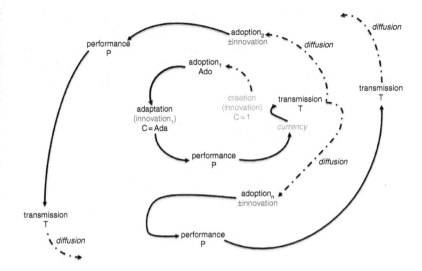

Figure 5.1. *The transmission process*

Can the actuation process or a similar type of mutation or hybridisation process be applied to variability in folk songs? Innovation is part of song making, song performance and song transmission, much more so than in language change. Adoption is also a crucial factor in song change, and, in the case of folk song, the primary (but not unique) means of adoption will be oral/ aural, i.e. someone hears a song performed and wants to add that song to his/her own repertoire. At this point, the hearer's powers of memorisation play a significant role. Palmer (1990: 15) maintains that '[t]he creation of song by one hand or many, and its adoption, variation and communal transmission, typify classic folk song', and the central motor in what we call the *transmission process* is transmission from one adopter to another. The transmission process can be visualised as in Figure 5.1.

The innovation of a novel linguistic construction in the actuation process is equivalent to two types of innovation in the song transmission process. The first of these is the original creation of the song itself ($C = I$); the second is adaptation as creation ($C = Ada$). After an 'original song' is adopted (Ado_1), it undergoes the process of adaptation by singers for their own use in performance (P), and if it gains enough currency, it will then be transmitted to other singers (T), who also adapt it ($Ada_{2 \ldots n}$). In this way, songs are transmitted to other singers in different spatio-temporal locations and in the process undergo even more adaptation. The ways in which songs are adapted for use by various singers through time and across space also constitute forms of innovation, and as in the actuation process, some of these may survive the test of time and others may not.

Various forms of *adaptation* may be made at any point in the transmission process by an adopter. The lyrics may be shortened or lengthened, extra material may be introduced, different wording chosen, or the language may be simplified or embellished. In some cases, as we shall see later in this chapter, an adopter may substitute the whole text with a new one that expresses the underlying theme of the original song. The music may be adapted in various ways, from small phrasing changes right the way through to the substitution of the melody heard by an alternative melody. In both the actuation process and the transmission process, diffusion of the change or the song from one community of practice to another is crucial for its acceptance and diffusion over considerable distances through time and space. In both cases, the wider community of speakers of a language and the wider community of folk singers and audiences constituting the discourse community of folk singing are derived from local CofPs.

Figure 5.1 resembles the shape of a Catherine wheel spinning out in all directions from a central point, but transmission may stop at one or more transmission points and a song may become extinct. On the other hand, it may suddenly come to life again through other forms of transmission than oral/aural. New creations may be constructed by giving an apparently extinct song a new tune or by fitting a new set of lyrics to a familiar tune at adoption points far away in time and place from the original creation. Adaptations are also innovations – albeit of a different kind from the original creation of a song – made by adopters prior to the transmission process (cf. Figure 5.1).

Whereas the researcher into language change usually starts at a particular linguistic point and plots the change through into the future, knowing, as s/he does, what linguistic constructions in the chosen 'present' are communicatively equivalent to those in the past, the researcher into folk song usually takes a song, or the several versions of a song, in the 'present' and plots it/them back into the past, occasionally arriving at a 'source' song, but very often not. As we see in Chapter 6, this can be a dangerous procedure as it may imply that there is an 'authentic' original song and increase the temptation to speculate on degrees of authenticity between versions, an intriguing but often inconclusive exercise.

In the study of ballads, three theories have been put forward to explain their emergence – and thus *mutatis mutandis* for the emergence of folk song itself. Child (1874) hypothesised that ballad-making should be placed within 'a medieval period "where the culture of the popular was produced by a singleness of faith, feeling and social class that was no longer possible"' (Bell 1988: 304), and this facilitates 'a ballad poetry of unalienated simplicity which modern poets aware of their individual creativity could no longer reproduce' (as quoted from Bendix 1997: 89). But as Bendix points out, having eradicated the need to distinguish between 'high' and 'low', Child still felt at ease to suggest that ballads were made by the *upper* sections of this 'classless' society and then filtered down into the lower sections. Naumann (1922) was more explicit than Child that folklore (including folk song) was simply 'gesunkenes Kulturgut' ('sunken cultural goods'), i.e. that the valuable products of the higher echelons of society sank down to and were taken up in primitive form by the lower classes.

The third explanation (adapted from the German Romantics) was offered by Gummere (1961 [1897]: 27) that folk song was the product of a group 'under conditions of communal exhilaration', e.g. in dance. His notion of communally improvised composition certainly has some merit, although not in the format he suggested, i.e. that it was an act at the time of composition. We can postulate that communal, at least partially improvised, composition of ballads considered as a *diachronic* process, i.e. in transmission and diffusion, is at work and shapes the ballad as we know it. Nevertheless, Gummere's suggestion is the least satisfying since it rejects individual creativity. If individual creativity lies at the heart of song composition, the weaker and stronger theories of 'sunken cultural goods' also deny creativity to all but the 'cultured', which is an equally unacceptable position.

Three Hypothetical Principles for Tracing the History of Folk Songs

We begin this subsection with a caveat: 'proving' that a song has great longevity is not the ultimate aim of studying folk songs, nor does it mean that great longevity is equivalent to 'authenticity'. If that were the case, we would need to discard all authored songs, old or new, as not being folk songs at all. Nevertheless, the premise that folk songs are created by individuals – or at most by very small groups – still confronts us with a difficulty. In some instances, the 'original' composer(s) of a song can be traced, and songs that can be shown to have changed little over time and space, either in their lyrics or in their tune, are more likely to be traceable to an identifiable songwriter/ composer than songs that turn up in a number of versions, differing in tune and lyrics. In the case of the ballad 'Barbara Allen' ♪74, however, the Roud index gives 54 versions, Child gives 84 and Bronson gives 198 versions and almost as many tunes. We thus propose the following hypothetical principle:

1. *The Principle of Increasing Variability*:
   a. The greater the number of existing versions of a song, the lower the probability of finding an 'original' version.
   b. The smaller the number of versions of a song, the greater the probability of finding an 'original' version, particularly in the case of more recent songs.

Songs that occur in several versions may have had the same song schema (see the following section), in which case they are, technically speaking, different instantiations of the same song. However, given a certain degree of variation between them, they may still be perceived by singers to be different songs. In such a situation, the song schema may help the singer to store two versions of the same song, but the lyrics and the tune may nevertheless differ to such an extent that the singer needs to apply two different cognitive blueprints to be able to store them. We therefore propose that there is a second principle concerning the extent and type of variability present, which often overrides Principle 1:

2. *The Principle of the Extent and Type of Variability*:

Given the same song schema, there is a point at which two versions differ from one another to such an extent that they require two different cognitive strategies to store each version. Beyond that point, the two versions are likely to be perceived by the singer (and the audience) as two different songs.

In a situation such as this, diffusion tends to set in at an early stage in the transmission process so that, although the versions may be technically the same song in the overall discourse community, the separation of the versions through time and space in transmission and diffusion leads to a secondary process of adaptation in local communities of practice. The examples we give of this phenomenon in the following section (and in more detail in Chapter 9) are the differences between 'Earl Richard', collected in the first decade of the twentieth century by Cecil Sharp in Somerset, and 'The Knight and the Shepherd's Daughter', collected in 1952 by Peter Kennedy in Herefordshire, in which, despite having the same song schema, the extent of variation is extensive.

In the third section of this chapter, we note a comparable degree of variation distinguishing the versions of 'A Sailor's Life', printed at least four times as a broadside throughout the nineteenth century and collected in the first decade of the twentieth century, on the one hand, and the three versions of 'Sweet William (The Sailor Boy)' collected in the second decade of the twentieth century in West Virginia (see Cox 1925), on the other.[2] But precisely because of the continuing currency of this song, as attested by those four nineteenth-century broadsides and because all the versions we have looked at (twelve in all) display a heavy focus on the narrative core of the song containing the complicating action (see the following section) that propels the narrative forward in most but not all the versions to the female protagonist's suicide (or death), it is highly likely to be seen as one song, rather than two (or even more).

The third principle concerns the diffusion of songs through time and space. In both Britain and the USA, songs, whether they can be traced back to an 'original' source or not, were likely to appear in cheap broadside or broadsheet versions[3] if they had reached some degree of currency or were deemed worthy of 'becoming'

---

[2] There were in fact nine versions, but Cox only gives three versions in full.

[3] To distinguish between 'broadside' and 'broadsheet' Shepard (1962) quotes from Evans' *American Bibliography* (1939): 'If the printed matter is on the recto, or face, of an unfolded sheet, only, it is, bibliographically, a broadside ... If the printed matter overruns the recto of an unfolded sheet, and the verso is also printed upon, it then becomes a broadsheet'.

popular. Since broadsides/broadsheets were sold on the streets of most towns and cities, their circulation also reached into rural areas,[4] increasing the likelihood of their being sung and, to a certain extent at least, reducing the degree of variability in different versions:

3. *The Principle of Currency*:

   Regardless of whether or not the source of a song can be traced, its appearance as a broadside, or part of a broadside/broadsheet, is an indicator of its currency (or popularity), a factor in the stabilisation of its variability and a significant reason for its increased diffusion, but not necessarily for its transmission from singer to singer.

With these three principles, given the large number of songs that are indexical of certain historical periods, e.g. the Napoleonic Wars or the era of early industrialisation, we are at least able to hypothesise that songs with a significant number of versions, including broadsides (e.g. those in both song complexes to be examined below), are unlikely to be traceable to an 'original' but are clearly current, whereas those that are still current (including the earlier appearance of a broadside) but exist in different localities with little variability are likely to be traceable to some 'original' source (e.g. 'Poverty Knock' in Chapter 4 or, in this chapter, 'The Four Loom Weaver'). But traceable or not, their survival into the present as folk songs indicates their ability to bond groups in performance.

A Song Schema

Our position on *song performance* is that it is a social process that can only be properly understood as an instantiation of emergent social practice combining music and language. This position entails that a *song* is what is produced in an emergent instantiation of performance. Bauman and Briggs (1990) maintain that every performance of a story – in our case, a song – is the *entextualisation* of a cognitively stored *text*. The text itself is a mental construct or blueprint, and a performance of it is an entextualisation, an enactment, of that text/blueprint. A song is therefore both text and entextualisation. Two or more singers may have slightly different blueprints, and performances by those singers may be perceived by audiences as being different and yet the same. This is particularly so in the case of song, since, even though two entextualisations may be similar to the point of being considered identical, the tunes used by the singers may differ. One singer may vary the lyrics by adding, changing or deleting certain elements. Another may sing the same lyrics, but to a different tune. A third singer may do both. Nevertheless, from the textual point of view (which includes the music to which the lyrics are sung), members of an audience are still able to perceive the versions as being the 'same song'.

---

[4] Cf. Vicinus (1974).

A song schema, the mental or cognitive blueprint of a song, exists on three (possibly more) structural levels:

(1) the musical level (i.e. the level at which the melody determines the song);
(2) the linguistic level (i.e. the level at which the lyrics determine the song);
(3) the narrative level (i.e. the level at which the song is determined by an identical set of character types and a sequence of events ordered in the same way).

On the narrative level, a song schema can be pared down to three major elements, *participants, events* and *sequence of events*, providing a mental scaffolding for the singer that forms part of her/his own personal blueprint of the song. Participants are characterised with respect to gender, age, social status, possibly also religion and ethnicity and, in addition, may be categorised as 'morally positive' or 'morally negative'. Events or states characterise whether or not the song is narrative, and if it is, the events occur in one unique sequence. However, the concept of a song schema relies first and foremost on whether or not all songs can be conceptualised as stories, potential stories or implied stories, and for this we first need a model of narrative discourse.

Songs as Narratives

Frith (1996) maintains that all songs, at their core, are narratives: 'Lyrics . . . let us into *songs as stories*. All songs are implied narratives. They have a central character, the singer; a character with an attitude, in a situation, talking to someone (if only to herself)' (1996: 169–70; our italics). At a first reading of Frith's position on songs, it might seem that he has somewhat overstated his case. After all, songs that accompany traditional occasions, e.g. wassailing and pace-egging, or songs that are of a cumulative nature, like 'The Herrin's Heid' �e75 or 'The Barley Mow' �e76, i.e. songs that are felt to have specific ritual functions, hardly tell or imply a story. Frith's point, however, is that the lyrics '*let us into* songs as stories', and we know that 'The Herrin's Heid' was sung by women gutting, salting and barrelling herrings every summer down the east coast of Scotland and the northeast coast of England. A description of this activity is offered as follows:

During the 19th century, women from fishing communities along the east coast of Scotland and England, the 'herring lassies' as they were known, would follow the herring fishing fleets down the coast to meet the catch at each port of call. With knives at the ready and strips of cloths tied around their thumbs and forefingers to protect [them] from the blades, they gutted, salted, and barrelled the 'silver darlings', the bountiful herring that were destined for markets across the world.[5]

---

[5] http://nrl.northumbria.ac.uk/23388/1/Follow%20The%20Herring%20brochure.pdf, accessed 27 November 2017.

'Letting us into' stories in the case of 'The Herrin's Heid' implies letting us into the endless stories those women could have told us of their lives. 'The Barley Mow' can be traced as far back as 1609, when it appeared in Ravenscroft's *Deuteromelia*, under the title 'Give Us Once a Drinke'.[6] It is a very popular drinking song, and it 'lets us into' the story of how each 'barley mow' or stack of barley was harvested. In point of fact, however, the overwhelming majority of songs *are* either overt or implied narratives; so we need a narrative model to assess the stories told or implied. For this purpose, Labov and Waletzky's high point analysis (1967) is still the most reliable and, with all the adjustments and additions to it over the years, the most detailed sociolinguistic model of narrative structure.[7]

Labov and Waletzky analyse natural 'narratives', or 'high point narratives' (cf. Peterson and McCabe 1983), which are understood to be fully developed oral narratives explicitly displaying all six functional categories posited by Labov and Waletzky. These categories are 1. *abstract* (a brief indication of what the story/narrative is about); 2. *orientation* (a section which allows the audience to locate itself in the time, place and circumstances of the story/ narrative); 3. *complicating action* or *complication* (an action or situation which disrupts a prior state of equilibrium and which needs to be resolved before the 'world' of the narrative can return to 'normal'; cf. Turner's notion of social drama resolved through performance); 4. *evaluation* (the subjective positioning of the narrator towards the characters of the story, the events which carry the narrative forward, the circumstances of those events and characters, etc. and the positioning of the characters themselves, *pace* the narrator, towards these elements); 5. *result* or *resolution* (which displays the solution offered in the narrative for the complication); and 6. *coda* (in which some comment is made on the whole narrative in an evaluative form). The abstract may also contain the keying-in of the performance of a narrative, and the coda may be seen as an explicit keying-out.

Songs as Blueprints

At the level of the singer's mental blueprint, learning a song is easier if it has a recognisable sequence of narrative events or states involving recognisable character types. Earlier in this chapter, we mentioned that 'The Knight and the Shepherd's Daughter' (TKATSD) and 'Earl Richard' (ER) have essentially the same song schema, which, at the structural level of the cognitive prototype,

---

[6] Incidentally, the *Deuteromelia* also contains a version of 'Who's the Fool Now?' under the title of 'Martin Said to His Man'.

[7] An excellent and very detailed article on the model and its modifications since Labov and Waletzky first published it in 1967 was written by Labov and published in the *Journal of Narrative and Life History* 7 (1997), 395–415.

indicates that they are two versions of the same song. If we compare one version of 'Earl Richard' (John Swain, Donyatt, Somerset, collected in 1904) and one version of 'The Knight and the Shepherd's Daughter' (Louise Holmes, Dinedor, Herefordshire, collected in 1952), the song schema is as follows:[8]

(A) *Character types*: a shepherd's/farmer's daughter (low social class, morally positive); a knight or a nobleman (upper social class, morally negative); a king or a queen (the apex of the secular social system)

(B) *Sequence of events*:
   (1) knight, while out riding, meets shepherd's/farmer's daughter;
   (2) knight seduces or rapes shepherd girl;
   (3) girl asks after knight's identity;
   (4) knight does not give a clear answer;
   (5) girl follows knight to the king's/queen's court;
   (6) girl accuses one of the king's/queen's knights of having had sexual intercourse with her;
   (7) king/queen calls up his/her knights and the culprit is revealed;
   (8) king/queen 'gives the knight's body' to the girl, i.e. orders him to marry her;
   (9) knight agrees to marry girl, or marries her, but is not pleased at the match he has made.

Earl Richard

1. it's of a brisk young shepherd maid
   kept sheep one summer's day
   and by there came a brisk young man
   who stole her heart away

Chorus: line twine the willow and the dew

2. you've stolen all my heart young sir
   yourself you are to blame
   but if your vows are made in truth
   pray tell to me your name

3. oh some do call me Jack fair maid
   and others call me John
   but when I'm in the King's own court
   they call me Sweet William

4. then I'll gang to the King she said
   he'll do a fair maid right
   to woo and mock a shepherd maid
   it ill becomes a knight

The Knight and the Shepherd's Daughter

1. 'tis of a shepherd's daughter
   keeping sheep on yonder hill
   a roving blade came riding by
   and vowed he'd have his will
   then if you have your will of me
   pray tell to me your name
   that when my baby it is born
   I may put it the same

2. oh some do call me Jack fair maid
   and some do call me John
   but when I'm in the king's fair court
   they call me sweet William
   then he mounted on his milk white steed
   and away from her did ride
   she picked her petticoats under her arm
   and she ran close by his side

3. she ran till she came to the riverside
   and she fell on her breast and swam

---

[8] The lyrics of both songs are presented below for reference.

5. the King's called up his merry men all
   by one by two by three
   Earl Richard used to lead them all
   but far behind came he

6. and he's brought up all fifty pounds
   brought up all in a glove
   take this take this my fair maid
   go and seek some other love

7. oh I want none of thy red gold
   nor any of thy fee
   but I will have thy body fair
   the King has given me

8. Earl Richard frowned Earl Richard sighed
   an angry man was he
   if I'm to wed a shepherd maid
   you'll rue it bitterly

9. the dog shall eat the wheat and flour
   and thou shalt eat the bran
   I'll make thee rue the very day
   and hour thou were born

10. I care not for thy threats my love
    nor all your words of ill
    you've vowed to wed the shepherd maid
    kept sheep upon the hill

she swam till she came to the other side
and she picked up her clothes and ran
she ran till she came to the king's fair court
and she loudly rang the ring
there was none so ready as the king himself
to let this fair maid in

4. what do you want of me fair maid
   what do you want of me
   there is a man in your fair court
   and he has robbed me
   what has he robbed you of fair maid
   of your gold or of your fee
   he's robbed me of my maidenhead
   the chief of my body

5. then if he be a married man
   oh hanged he shall be
   and if he be a single man
   his body I'll give to thee
   so the king he's called his merry merry men
   by one by two by three
   young William he came last of all
   when first he used to be

6. he pulled out a handful of gold
   and wrapped it in a glove
   take this take this my pretty fair maid
   and seek for another to love
   I neither want any of your gold
   nor any of your fee
   but I will have your body
   as the king has willed me

7. then he mounted on his milk white steed
   and she upon another
   they rode along the king's highway
   like a sister and a brother
   they rode till they came to the next fair town
   and he bought her a gay gold ring
   they rode till they came to the next fair
   and he gave her a gay wedding

8. oh I wish I'd been drinking barrel water
   while I've been drinking wine
   that ever a shepherd's daughter
   should have been a bride of mine
   I wish I'd been drinking of white wine
   when I've been drinking red
   that ever a shepherd's daughter
   should have brought me to my wedding bed

In TKATSD event (5) consists of (5a) – 'knight mounts horse and rides off' – (5b) – 'shepherd's daughter follows and swims across a river' – (5c) – 'shepherd's daughter rings the bell at court' – and (5d) – 'King/Queen lets shepherd's daughter in'. The sub-events, however, are simply an elaboration of event (5), so the fact that in this version of ER the details are left out does not change the song schema. Even the sixty-stanza E version of 'Earl Richard' presented in Child's *The English and Scottish Popular Ballads* has all nine steps plus an extra step in which the noble identity of the girl as the king of Scotland's daughter is finally revealed at the end.

If we invoke Principle 2, it is entirely reasonable to refer to ER and TKATSD, in both the context of a performance and that of an individual singer's mental conception of what to sing, as two songs since the extent/type of variability between the two is large. Similarly, if a singer has two blueprints for ER, each with a different melody, s/he may justifiably talk about two different songs. But looking at the songs with respect to their internal structure without considering the tune or the wording of the lyrics, it is also perfectly acceptable to refer to the song schema as indexing one 'song'. In this case ER and TKATSD are two versions of the same song. If we invoke Principle 1, however, the large number of versions of this song make it very improbable – and essentially unnecessary – that an 'original' version can ever be located.

Variable Song Schemata, but One Song

In this and the following section, we use the notion of the song schema to discuss issues of longevity, currency and variability in two song 'complexes', the 'Sailor's Life' complex and the 'Geordie' complex. By 'complex' we mean a cluster of song variants that often, but not always, have the same title and/or are readily recognisable as having the same creative origin. In the case of the 'Sailor's Life' complex, the variants, or versions, of the song are recognisable as belonging to the same complex even though there is, as one might expect, variation in the tunes used and variable endings to the overall narrative structure. The longevity of the song is less than that of 'Geordie', indexing, as it does, the age of British maritime power from the eighteenth to the nineteenth century. It was sung by Sandy Denny on the Fairport Convention album *Unhalfbricking* in 1969, and this version has since become iconic.[9] The tune and the lyrics used by Fairport Convention are as follows ♪77:

---

[9] Our own version uses roughly the same tune as Sandy Denny but with a few modifications in both the tune and the wording of the lyrics. We also add a stanza after stanza 4 to give seven stanzas in all.

A Sailor's Life

adapted from http://sniff.numachi.com/pages/tiSAILIFE;ttSAILIFE.html

1. a sailor's life is a merry life
   they rob young girls of their heart's delight
   leaving them alone to sorrow and mourn
   they never know when they will return

2. there's four and twenty all in a row
   my sweetheart he cuts the finest show
   he's proper tall genteel withal
   and if I don't have him I'll have no man at all

3. oh father build me a little boat
   that I might on the ocean float
   and every Queen's ship that we pass by
   I'll make enquire for my sailor boy

4. they had not been long all on the sea
   when a Queen's ship they chanced to see
   you sailors all come tell to me
   does my sweet William sail among your crew

5. what is the colour of our true lover's hair
   what kind of clothes does your true love wear
   he wears a coat of the navy blue
   and you would know him for his heart is true

6. oh no fair maid he is not here
   for he is dead we greatly fear
   on yon green island as we passed by
   there we lost sight of your sailor boy

7. she wrung her hands and she tore her hair
   much like a woman in deep despair
   her little boat 'gainst a rock did run
   how can I live now that my William is gone

Countless versions of this song have been collected and/or recorded in North America and in England, and we took on the task of collating twelve of those versions, nine from England and three published by Cox (2013 [1925]) from West Virginia. Four of the English versions are broadsides, two by Catnach, one by Pitts and one by Harkness, which attests to the currency of the song throughout the nineteenth and early twentieth centuries. Two further tunes from England in addition to the nine English versions presented have also been added, one from a version sung by Matthew Hunt from Sherborne in Dorset (collected by Hammond) and the other from a version sung by a Mrs Joiner (collected by Lucy Broadwood, in all probability from Sussex):[10]

---

[10] We have not included the lyrics of these two versions in the following analysis.

A Sailor's Life
(Matthew Hunt's tune, 1906, Sherborne, collected by Hammond)

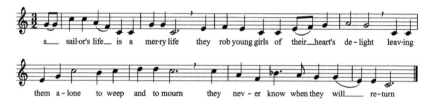

A Sailor's Life
(Mrs. Joiner Sep. 1914, collected by Lucy Broadwood)

Our goal was to locate the part of the song schema, the musical level, the linguistic level or the narrative level, which indicates that we are dealing with the same song despite the large number of variants. In the twelve versions that were examined there were in all ninety-one stanzas, the smallest number (five) in a version by Jake Toms from Bere Regis, Dorset, in 1905 and the largest number from a version by Matilda Heishman from Wardensville, West Virginia, noted down in 1901. The stanzas in all versions were assigned a narrative function in accordance with Labov and Waletzky's model. The language used in all versions was very varied indeed, which does not incline us to assume that the linguistic level of analysis was the cohesive element in the overall complex. For a start, only five of the twelve versions – and none of the American versions – have the title 'A Sailor's Life'. The musical level of analysis looks none too promising as a marker of cohesion, either.

Despite the difference in the story endings with two songs, notably broadsides, adding a two-stanza coda, the major feature suggesting a coherent song complex lies on the narrative level at the point where the narrative event leading to the complication and the narrative event containing the complication

Table 5.1a. *Narrative elements and contents in the 'Sailor's Life' complex*

Abstract	**1)** 3rd-person narrator/commentator, general statement on how sailors love and leave their sweethearts lamenting
	2) 3rd-person narrator tells of how a pretty girl is down by the riverside lamenting the fact that her lover has left her
Pre-orientation	**pO)** 1st person extols virtues of lover's beauty and depth of their love
Orientation	**1)** 1st person claims that lover would be finest in any group of sailors and vows she will have only him
	2) 1st person laments true love leaving to serve the king
Narrative Events	**1)** 1st person expresses the intention to build a boat to sail after him/requests her father to build a boat or: 3rd person states that she built a boat
	2) 3rd-person narrator>1st-person actor. Maid meets another ship and asks after her sailor boy
	2a) 2nd person (ship's crew/captain) asks her to describe her true love, colour of hair, what he was wearing, and 1st-person maid describes him
Complication	**C)** 2nd person (ship's crew/captain) tells her that he is dead and is buried on an island
Pre-resolution	**1)** 3rd-person narrator, maid sits down to write a song
	2) 3rd-person narrator>1st person. Maid dashes her boat against a rock avowing that she cannot live without her William
	3) 3rd-person narrator. William's body is washed ashore
Resolution	**1)** 3rd-person narrator>1st person. Maid dashes her boat against a rock avowing that she cannot live without her William
	2) 3rd-person narrator. Maid throws herself into the sea to be with her sailor in death
	3a) 1st person (maid) asks for her grave to be dug and a dove/rose to be placed on her breast
	3b) 1st person (maid) asks for a willow tree to be planted by her grave and a dove to be placed on her breast
	4) 3rd-person narrator, maid sits down to write a song
Coda	**1)** 3rd-person narrator. Narrator addresses other maids who have lost their true love
	2) 1st person (maid) consigns herself to mourning for her love

occur. All twelve versions refer to the same events (although with variations in the wording and lyrical and musical phrasing) (see Tables 5.1a and b).

A flow chart of the degree of linguistic variability in the lyrics of the stanza containing the narrative complication across all twelve versions is given in Figure 5.2.

If we look at the options for line 4 of this stanza in detail, the flow chart generates not only all the versions that have been analysed but also more potential options.[11]

[11] It also generates structurally impossible options.

Table 5.1b. *Organisation of narrative elements and contents into stanzas of the twelve variants of the 'Sailor's Life' complex*

Title	Abstract	Orientation	Narrative Events	Complication	Resolution	Coda
1) A Sailor's Life	1 Abstract1	2 Orient.1	3 Narr. Ev.1; 4 Narr. Ev.2	5 Comp.	6 pre-Resol. 1; 7 pre-Resol. 2; 8 Resol. 2	
2) A Sailor's Life	1 Abstract1		2 Narr. Ev.1; 3 Narr. Ev.2; 4 Narr. Ev.2a	5 Comp.	6 Resol. 2	
3) A Sailor's Life	1 Abstract1	2 Orient.1	3 Narr. Ev.1; 4 Narr. Ev.2	5 Comp.	6 pre-Resol.2; 7 pre-Resol. 2; 8 Resol.2	
4) Sweet William	1 Abstract1	2 Orient.1	3 Narr. Ev.2	4 Comp.	5 pre-Resol.1; 6 pre-Resol.2; 7 Resol.2	
5) A Sailor's Life	1 Abstract1	2 Orient.1	3 Narr. Ev.2	4 Comp.	5 Resol.1; 6 Resol.3a; 7 Resol.2	
6) The Sailor Boy and his Faithful Mary	1 Abstract1	2 Orient.1	3 Narr. Ev.1; 4 Narr. Ev.2	5 Comp.	6 pre-Resol.2; 7 pre-Resol.2; 8 Resol.2	
7) Sailor Boy	1 Abstract2		2 Narr. Ev.1; 3 Narr. Ev.2	4 Comp.	5 Resol.1	6 Coda1; 7 Coda2
8) A Sailor's Life	1 Abstract1	2 Orient.1	3 Narr. Ev.1; 4 Narr. Ev.2	5 Comp.	6 pre-Resol.2; 7 pre-Resol.1; 8 Resol.2	
9) The Maid's Lament for her Sailor Boy	1 Abstract2	2 Orient.1	3 Narr. Ev.1; 4 Narr. Ev.2	5 Comp.	6 Resol.1	7 Coda1; 8 Coda2
10) Moment's River Side	1 Abstract2	2 pre-Or.; 3 Orient.1	4 Narr. Ev.1; 5 Narr. Ev.2	6 Comp.	7 pre-Resol.3; 8 pre-Resol.1; 9 Resol.3a; 10 Resol.3b	
11) no local title	1 Abstract1	2 Orient.1	4 Narr. Ev.1; 5 Narr. Ev.2	6 Comp.	7 pre-Resol.1; 8 pre-Resol.3; 9 Resol.3a	
12) no local title	1 Abstract2	2 Orient.2	3 Narr. Ev.1; 4 Narr. Ev.2	5 Comp.	6 pre-Resol.1; 7 pre-Resol.2; 8 Resol.3b	

line 1

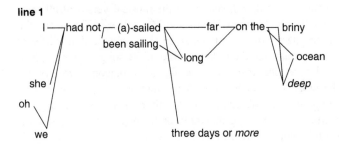

line 2

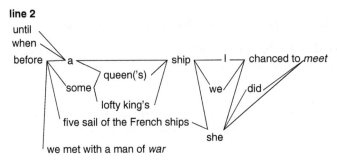

line 3

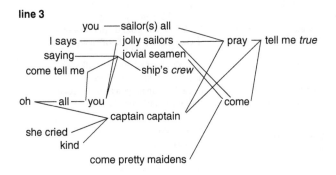

line 4

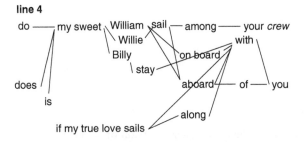

Figure 5.2. *Linguistic variability in the stanza containing the narrative complication in eleven of the twelve versions*

Each option, potential or real, will scan with the musical verses of all three tunes, Fairport Convention's, Matthew Hunt's and Mrs Joiner's. This is convincing evidence that, despite the different titles given to the song and the different endings of the versions analysed, the narrative core of the song – the complication that triggers the actions taken by the female protagonist to achieve a resolution in the story – is robust enough to warrant assigning all twelve versions to one song schema. We return to 'A Sailor's Life' in Chapter 8 to analyse the voice structure of the song, and move on to consider the song schema analysis of the second complex, which focuses on Child ballad 209, 'Geordie'.

Two Minimally Different Song Schemata and Two Songs

One song that has diffused throughout England, Scotland and North America in innumerable variants is commonly given the generic title 'Geordie', so henceforth we refer to it as the *'Geordie' complex*. An influential recording of one version was made by Joan Baez on her 1962 album *Joan Baez in Concert* ⊛78, which seems to have exercised a stabilising effect on the song schema of the ballad in subsequent recordings and performances. The lyrics of this version are as follows:

1. as I walked out over London Bridge
   one misty morning early
   I overheard a fair pretty maid
   lamenting for her Geordie

2. ah my Geordie will be hanged in a golden chain
   'tis not the chain of many
   he was born of king's royal breed
   and lost to a virtuous lady

3. go bridle me my milk white steed
   go bridle me my pony
   I will ride to London court
   to plead for the life of my Geordie

4. ah my Geordie never stole nor cow nor calf
   he never hurted any
   stole sixteen of the king's royal deer
   and he sold them in Bohenny

5. two pretty babies have I born
   the third lies in my body
   I'd freely part from them every one
   if you'd spare the life of Geordie

6. the judge looked over his left shoulder
   he said fair maid I'm sorry
   he said fair maid you must be gone
   for I cannot pardon Geordie

7. ah my Geordie will be hanged in a golden chain
   'tis not the chain of many
   stole sixteen of the king's royal deer
   and he sold them in Bohenny

The Song Schema of 'Geordie'

The narrative level of the song schema of Baez's version of 'Geordie' can be given as follows:

(A) *Character types*: third person narrator = the singer; a lady (major protagonist upper social class); a judge (secondary protagonist); Geordie, the
lady's husband/partner/lover (of royal blood)[12]

(B) *Sequence of events*:
(1) a woman who has borne children to a man learns that he has been
condemned to death;
(2) woman travels to the court/place of execution to plead for lover's/
partner's/husband's life;
(3) plea is refused.

Is this song schema of 'Geordie' valid in other versions of the song? To check
this out, we chose the version printed in *The New Penguin Book of English Folk
Songs* (taken from the singing of Mary Hayes of Hartlebury, Worcestershire, by
W. K. Clay in 1908) and the version taken from Joseph Taylor of Brigg,
Lincolnshire, collected by Percy Grainger in 1906:

Geordie

(Hayes)

as__ I crossed ov - er Lon - don Bridge 'twas__ on one morn - ing ear - ly

there__ I es - pied a fair la - dy la - ment - ing for her Georg - ie

1. as I crossed over London Bridge
'twas on one morning early
there I espied a fair lady
lamenting for her Georgie

2. come fetch to me some little boy
that can go on an errand quickly
that can run ten miles in an hour
with a letter for a lady

3. come saddle me my milk-white steed
and bridle it most rarely
that I may go to Newcastle gaol
and beg for the life of Georgie

4. when she got to Newcastle gaol
she bowed her head so lowly
three times on her bended knee did fall
and beg for the life of Georgie

6. the judge looked over his right shoulder
and seeming very sorry
he says my dear you are now too late
he is condemned already

7. oh six babies I have got with me
and I love them most dearly
I would freely part with them every one
if you spare me the life of Georgie

8. the judge looked over his left shoulder
and seeming very hard-hearted
he says my dear you are too late
there is no pardon granted

9. oh George shall be hanged in a chain of gold
which a few there not many
because he came by a noble bride
and beloved by a virtuous lady

---

[12] In Baez's version Geordie does not appear in person.

5. it is no murder George have done
   nor have he killed any
   but he stole sixteen of the king's fat deer
   and sold them in the army

Geordie

(sung by Joseph Taylor)

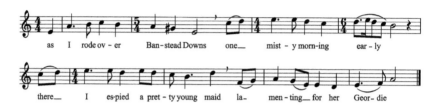

1. as I rode out over Banstead Downs
   one misty morning early
   there I espied a pretty fair maid
   lamenting for her Geordie

2. saying Geordie never stood on the king's
      highway
   he never robbed money
   but he stole fifteen of the king's fat deer
   and he sold them to Lord Newey

3. come bridle me my milk white steed
   come bridle me my pony
   that I that I might ride to fair London town
   to plead for my Geordie

4. and when she entered in the court
   there were lords and ladies plenty
   down on her bended knee she fell
   to plead for the life of Geordie

5. then Geordie looked around the court
   and saw his dearest Polly
   he said my dear you've come too late
   for I'm condemned already

6. then the judge he looked down on him and
      said
   I am sorry for thee
   'tis your confession hath hanged thee
   may the Lord have mercy on thee

7. Geordie shall be hanged in golden chains
   his crimes were never many
   because he came from the royal blood
   and courted a virtuous lady

8. I wish I was on yonder hill
   where times I have been many
   with sword and buckler by my side
   I'd fight for the life of Geordie

9. there's six pretty babes that I have got
   they belong to me and Geordie
   I'd freely give up every one
   but spare me the life of Geordie

As in Baez's version of 'Geordie', both Hayes' and Taylor's versions have four characters, the singer/narrator, the lady, the judge and Geordie/Georgie, but in both the older versions Geordie plays a more active part. In Hayes, he sends a messenger to inform his wife/partner of his predicament, and in Taylor

Geordie looks around the court, sees his 'dearest Polly' arrive and tells her she is too late. None of these narrative events in any way affects the outcome of the song. All three major events are present, except that London becomes Newcastle in Hayes, and London Bridge becomes Banstead Downs in Taylor. We conclude that the song schema in the English 'Geordie' complex is relatively stable but is also open to elements from other song schemata, elements that are freely transferable from song to song. But what about the Scottish ballads referred to generically as 'Geordie'?

'Geordie' in Child's The English and Scottish Popular Ballads

Child gives fourteen versions of 'Geordie' from Scotland, four of which are fragments, in two cases of only one stanza, and of the ten full versions A to J, E is very brief. In every full version, there is one major difference from the song schema of 'Geordie' collected in England and North America and that collected in Scotland; Geordie's lady is successful in getting Geordie freed on payment of a large sum of money. In none of the English or American versions is this so. Does this difference warrant the suggestion that we have two song schemata, one Scottish and the other English and North American? Roud and Bishop (2012: 500) suggest that '[t]here are sufficient similarities between the two national traditions to suggest either a common ancestor or a major influence one way or another'. They also suggest that 'on present evidence the English must take precedence', since 'Scottish versions were first recorded in the later eighteenth century, at least a hundred years after the earliest evidence south of the border' (ibid.). We submit that the question of which version has influenced the other is somewhat spurious. From the point of view of cross-fertilisation between song schemata, however, the Scottish ballads are a far richer source of historical evidence for how songs change and hybridise. To begin with, they are much longer with much clearer narrative storylines, and they provide a wealth of evidence for cross-fertilisation. We submit that we do indeed have two songs, one English/North American and one Scottish, the reason being the changes in the final event (3, 4 and 5):

(B) *Sequence of events*:
  (1) a woman who has borne children to a man learns that he has been condemned to death;
  (2) woman travels to the court/place of execution to plead for lover's/ partner's/husband's life;
  (3) *plea is granted on condition that woman pays a sum of money*;
  (4) *money is presented*;
  (5) *man is freed.*

In version J, from Buchan's *Ancient Songs and Ballads of the North of Scotland*, there is a further complication after Geordie has been freed. In stanza 32 of forty-one stanzas, Geordie turns on his lady saying 'a finger o Bignet's lady's hand / is worth a' your fair body', which is reminiscent of a song schema element to be found in other ballads (e.g. in 'Lord Thomas and Fair Eleanor' ☯79). Lady Anne tells him that she has made her marriage vows to him and that she wants no other, whereupon in stanza 39 'Geordie' pulls out a dagger and stabs her to death. In the final two stanzas, we learn that Geordie has fled, leaving his lands behind him, that he has not yet been found and that everyone living on Gight's lands is 'clad in black' for seven years in mourning for his lady.

The Scottish versions of the ballad constitute a different song from the English 'Geordie' versions, despite the occasional similarity in the wording. The motivating force behind version J is Geordie's illicit love affair with Bignet's wife, which makes his own wife simply a pawn in the game of getting his freedom at the cost of her life – which, as a consequence, transforms Geordie from a man unjustly or harshly condemned into a rather unsavoury character.

Two Seventeenth-Century 'Geordie' Broadsides

There are also two seventeenth-century English broadsides in the 'Geordie' complex, 'The Life and Death of George of Oxford' (in the Pepys collection of broadside ballads) and 'George Stoole', which we present in facsimile form as Images 5.1 and 5.2.

Contrary to what Roud and Bishop (2012: 500) maintain, these do not guarantee a greater longevity for the English versions of the song than for the Scottish versions. The complexity of the structural part of the song schema of the Scottish versions, the inescapable fact that they all end in a reprieve for Geordie and the fact that there are so many versions at the end of the eighteenth century equally indicate greater longevity. 'The Life and Death of George of Oxford' appears to have been concocted out of 'Geordie' versions circulating at the time in England to sell at the execution of 'George of Oxford', who, if the manipulation of the broadside is anything to go by, would appear to have been a common highwayman. The songwriter who was employed to create the broadside from the oral versions in circulation has effectively produced two songs from the material, the first presenting the situation from the lady's point of view, a song schema which is typical of the English oral versions, and an entirely new song called 'George's Confession'. Broadsides were often printed for sale at public executions for purely commercial reasons, which provides a feasible account for the adaptations made from the oral ballad to create 'George's Confession'.

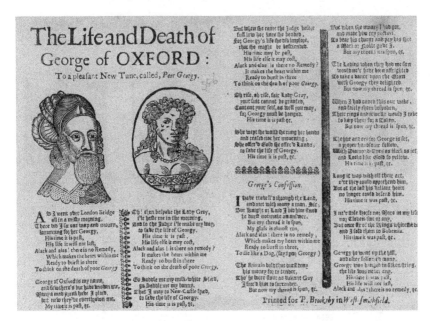

Image 5.1. *The Pepys broadsheet for 'The Life and Death of George of Oxford'*

The broadside is in the Pepys collection and is likely to have appeared some time after the Restoration of Charles II. Roud and Bishop (2012: 500) think it 'likely that the "George of Oxford" ballad in the Pepys collection was either based on or influenced by "George Stoole", and it is usually assumed that this is the case'. But if we look more closely at the two broadsides, another conclusion presents itself. In the earlier broadside 'George Stoole', the printer split the ballad into two parts, the first being a description of George's trial and the lament of his beloved, who, intriguingly, is 'his Lards wife / whom he lovd best of any' (see our discussion above of the J version in Child), the second part being a description of the execution, in which George is given an opportunity to confess his crime. George Stoole, the protagonist of the earlier broadside, also seems to have been a highwayman for whose execution the broadside was probably printed. If versions of 'Geordie', English or Scottish, had been used to put the text together, this would account for stanza 20 in 'George Stoole': 'I never stole no Ox nor Cow / nor never murdered any / but fifty Horse I did receive / of a Merchant's man of Gory', but this is the only stanza in which we can locate a cross-reference to 'George of Oxford' or to English or Scottish versions of 'Geordie'. 'George Stoole' is very different from versions of 'Geordie' collected at the beginning of the twentieth century (cf. Joseph

Image 5.2. *The broadsheet for 'George Stoole' from the British Library*

Taylor's version and Mary Hayes' version). It also contains the centrally important element of the J version in Child – that George's sweetheart is another man's wife – which occurs nowhere else in the English versions.

In conclusion, in the 'Geordie complex' we have two song schemata, similar in some respects but radically different in others, both with the title 'Geordie' or 'Georgie'. One of these is restricted to Scotland and may have provided the model for 'George Stoole', except that the resolution in the song schema for the Scottish 'Geordie' is that Geordie escapes the gallows, whereas in 'George Stoole' he does not. The other song schema is restricted to England and North America, and the final event is that Geordie does not escape the gallows. Whoever 'wrote' 'George Stoole' may have based the song on Scottish versions with the exception of George being hanged at the end. Whoever 'wrote' 'George of Oxford' based it on the English oral ballad and deliberately turned it into two different songs. The amount of adaptation in the original ballad is considerable and the hackneyed style of the songwriter is noticeable everywhere. However, the first stanza is almost a standard in singers' blueprints for 'Geordie' today (cf. Baez's version).

Songs with No Apparent Song Schema

'Earl Richard', 'The Knight and the Shepherd's Daughter', all the versions of
'A Sailor's Life' and all the 'Geordie' versions have a narrative persona distinct
from the protagonists of the song. In Chapter 8, we discuss the levels of
narrative persona to be found in folk songs and what those levels entail
stylistically in performing the songs. There are often whole stanzas or parts
of stanzas in which one protagonist or another is projected as speaking directly
to the audience, i.e. in which the narrative persona (the singer) steps into the
background leaving the communicative channel open to the protagonist(s). But
a very large number of songs have no clear narrative sequence and employ
a first-person/protagonist 'I'-narrator into which the singer needs to project her/
himself.

In Ewan MacColl's 'Shoals of Herring' ☺80, for example, if there is a story,
it is the life of a herring fisherman at sea, from his first job as a cabin boy to his
employment as a deckhand:

1. oh it was a fine and a pleasant day
   out of Yarmouth harbour I was faring
   as a cabin boy on a sailing lugger
   for to go and hunt the shoals of herring

2. oh the work was hard and the hours long
   and the treatment sure it took some bearing
   there was little kindness and the kicks were many
   as we hunted for the shoals of herring

3. oh we fished the Swarth and the Broken Bank
   I was cook and I'd a quarter sharing
   and I used to sleep standing on my feet
   and I'd dream about the shoals of herring

4. oh we left the home grounds in the month of June
   and to Canny Shields we soon were bearing
   with a hundred cran of the silver darlings
   that we'd taken from the shoals of herring

5. now you're up on deck you're a fisherman
   you can swear and show a manly bearing
   take your turn on watch with the other fellows
   while you're searching for the shoals of herring

6. in the stormy seas and the living gales
   just to earn your daily bread you're daring
   from the Dover Straits to the Faroe Islands
   as you're following the shoals of herring

7. oh I earned my keep and I paid my way
   and I earned the gear that I was wearing
   sailed a million miles caught ten million fishes
   we were sailing after shoals of herring

In his 'Go, Move, Shift' ☺81, the singer only uses the 'I'-form in the first
stanza ('born in the middle of an afternoon / in a horse-drawn wagon on the old
A5 / the big twelve-wheeler shook *my* bed / you can't stop here the policeman
said / you'd better get born in someplace else / so move along get along / move
along get along / move along get along / go move shift') and the third stanza
('the local people said to *me* / you'll lower the price of property') in which the
my/*me* appears to refer to the whole group of gypsies.[13] In the rest of the song

---

[13] The use of *my* and *me* in these two stanzas is way of committing the singer to an identification
with the gypsies, i.e. of bonding with them.

s/he sings of the hard lives of Romany gypsies ('the travelling people') and their social discrimination in British society in the 1960s:[14]

1. born in the middle of the afternoon
   in a horse drawn wagon on the old A5
   the big twelve-wheeler shook my bed
   you can't stay here the policeman said

   Chorus: you'd better get born in some place else
   so move along get along
   move along get along
   go move shift

2. born in the common by a building site
   where the ground was rutted by the trail of
   wheels
   the local Christian said to me
   you'll lower the price of our property

3. born at potato picking time
   in an old worn tent in a tattie field
   the farmer said the work's all done
   it's time that you was moving on

4. born at the back of a hawthorn hedge
   where the black hoar frost lay on the ground
   no eastern kings came bearing gifts
   instead the order came to shift

5. the eastern sky was full of stars
   and one shone brighter than the rest
   the wise men came so stern and strict
   and brought the orders to evict

6. waggon tent or trailer born
   last month last year or in far off days
   born here or a thousand miles away
   there's always men nearby who'll say

As in 'Shoals of Herring', each stanza represents a miniature implied narrative of its own, the totality adding up to a critical comment on the lives of herring fishermen or, in the case of 'Go, Move, Shift', Romany gypsies.

In songs of this kind, characterisation remains, but the sequence of events becomes almost arbitrary, each event indexing a wider social story that is frequently presented as a form of answering back. The song refers less to a unique story and more to a social state involving the life stories of the characters displayed. Since the indexing is from individuals to social groups, we refer to a *macro song schema* rather than merely a *song schema*. The macro-song schema of 'Shoals of Herring' would be something like the following:

(A) *Character types*: a herring fisherman (= first-person narrator) and those he works with.

(B) *Macro-narrative*:

(1) The life and work of herring fisherman in general.

That of 'Go, Move, Shift' would be:

(A) *Character types*: Romany gypsies and those who discriminate against them.

(B) *Macro-narrative*: Wherever gypsies are born, they are always moved on as undesirable citizens.

In the subsections below, we deal with songs with 'I'-narrators, into whose situation a singer has to place her/himself, and we present the macro-narratives of each song from a historical perspective.

---

[14] Christy Moore even adds two stanzas of his own to locate the song within an Irish context.

'The Four Loom Weaver' ☺82

Most song collectors in the nineteenth century were from the middle classes, and many of the songs they collected, which we now attribute to the peasantry and the labouring classes, were also collected from middle-class singers. Middle-class authors in the first half of the nineteenth century were often acutely aware of the songs created and sung by the industrial working classes. Both Wales (2006) and Watts (2011: 292–94) discuss Elizabeth Gaskell's inclusion of the entire song 'The Oldham Weaver' ☺82 (sung today as 'The Four Loom Weaver') in her novel *Mary Barton* (1849). Gaskell rendered the whole song in dialect, and Wales (2006) suggests that she did so politically to direct her middle-class readers' attention to the appalling conditions in the cotton mills of Lancashire at the time she was writing. Small though it is, this is an indication that members of the middle classes who were in contact with the labouring classes knew about and had heard songs created and performed by urban industrial workers well before the First Folk Song Revival in the last twenty years of the nineteenth century.

Elizabeth Gaskell's narrator in Chapter 4 of her novel *Mary Barton* (1849), in which Margaret sings 'The Oldham Weaver' for Mary Barton and Alice Wilson, takes the unusual step, for an omniscient narrator, of addressing the reader directly: 'Do you know "The Oldham Weaver"? Not unless you are Lancashire born and bred, for it is a complete Lancashire ditty. I will copy it for you.' She does this by giving the whole song in the Oldham dialect. She also comments that, aside from the humour in the lyrics of 'The Oldham Weaver', to those 'who have seen the distress it describes it is a powerfully pathetic song'. The macro-schema of 'The Oldham Weaver' is as follows:

(A) *Character types*: weaver (= first-person narrator) and his wife (low, poverty-stricken, morally positive); bailiffs (morally neutral); master/ employer (high, rich, morally negative)

(B) *Macro-narrative*:
  (1) weavers starving with no work and in debt;
  (2) landlord sends in bailiffs;
  (3) master claims workers are overpaid;
  (4) workers leave mills to work on the roads and to dig ditches

During the course of the nineteenth century the song had mutated into 'The Four Loom Weaver' protesting against the lay-offs and lockouts during the catastrophic slump in the cotton industry at the time of the American Civil War in the early 1860s.[15] The description of the bailiffs snatching their last

---

[15] June Tabor's information on the song at the Maddy Prior concert in October 2008 actually pushed the song further back into the nineteenth century to just after the Napoleonic Wars. Nothing much hinges on the difference between our explanation and Tabor's except to say that

piece of furniture, the master's claim that Jone of Grinfield was overpaid and the decision to look for alternative work breaking stones for road-making and digging ditches are dropped. The 'original' weaver, the lost or fictional voice, represents the whole workforce of Lancashire cotton weavers. Sung within a group of workmates, it bonds the group members perfectly in opposition to the masters and answers back on behalf of the whole group. Sung today, it serves to remind the audience of the defiant and often militant resistance against middle-class establishment oppression in the industrial regions of Britain, and it reminds present-day audiences of the need to resist in similar situations in the present or the future.

The history of the song is interesting and significant. It goes back to a poem for performance allegedly written by an Oldham schoolteacher by the name of Joseph Lees sometime in the late 1790s. Lees' poem/song was called 'Jone o' Grinfilt', and it told the humorous story of a naïve countryman from Greenfield just outside Manchester, who takes it into his head to enlist in the army at Oldham in the belief that French troops are just over the border between Lancashire and Yorkshire (see website ☺82). It was written in the Oldham dialect and was in print as a broadside shortly after Lees and a colleague, sitting under a hedge in the rain, had scribbled it down. Jone o' Grinfilt quickly became a folk hero and was used throughout the nineteenth century to protest about various aspects of working-class life in one broadside after another in the north of England. 'Jone o' Grinfield (Junior)'/'The Oldham Weaver' was widely circulated as a broadside (see the broadside 'Jone o' Grinfield' printed by Bebbington in Manchester around 1850 shown in Image 5.3) and underwent the usual process of change and mutation, finally becoming today's 'The Four Loom Weaver'.[16]

Although we can assume that the song must have been written by someone close to the workers or even by a worker her/himself, the fact that there is, in all probability, an author of the first 'Jone o' Grinfilt' poem, Joseph Lees, is strong evidence supporting the authorship of songs in broadsides. If we apply Principles 1 and 2 to Mary Gaskell's version in 1849, the Bebbington broadside (c. 1850) and 'The Four Loom Weaver', we find a restricted number of versions of the song and, apart from the cutting of stanzas, a narrow extent of variability within those versions, which increases the likelihood of ultimately identifiable authorship.

---

we are at least able to trace the development of the song from the original 'Jone o' Grinfilt' in the last decade of the eighteenth century right up to the 1860s, which indicates the immense currency the song must have enjoyed in the context of the Lancashire cotton industry.

[16] We apologise for the very poor quality of the printing in the final stanza. However, the website at ☺82 contains the version given by Elizabeth Gaskell in *Mary Barton*, which is almost the same as that in the Bebbington broadside, but with a slightly different written rendering of the dialect.

JONE O'GRINFIELD.

I'm a poor cotton weaver as many one knows,
I've nowt to eat i'th house an I've worn out my cloas,
You'd hardly give sixpence for all I have on,
My clugs they are brossen and stockings I've none,
You'd think it wur hard to be sent into th' world,
    To clem and do th' best ot you con.

Our church parson kept telling us long,
We should have better times if we'd hold our tongues,
I've houden my tongue till I can hardly draw breath,
I think i' my heart he means to clem me to death ;
I know he lives weel by backbiting the de'il,,
    But he never pickced o'er in his life.

I tarried six week an thought every day wur t' last,
I tarried and shifted till now I'm quite fast ;
I lived on nettles while nettles were good,
An Waterloo porridge were best of my food ;
I'm telling you true I can find folks enow,
    That are living no better than me.

Old Bill o' Dan's sent bailiffs one day,
For a shop score I owed him that I could not pay,
But he wur too late for d Bill o' Bent,
Had sent tit and cart and taen goods for rent,
We had nou bur a stoo, that wur a seat for two,
    And on it cowered Margit and me.

The bailiffs looked round assly as a mouse,
When they saw aw things were taen out ot house,
Says one to the other all's gone thou may see,
Aw sed lads never fret you're welcome to me ;
They made no more ado, but nipp'd up th' owd stoo,
    And we both went wack upoth flags.

I geet howd of Margit for hoo wur strucken sick,
Hoo sed hoo ne'er had such a bang sin hoo wur wick
The bailiffs scoured off with owd stoo on their backs,
They would not have cared had they brook our necks,
They're mad at owd Bent cos he's taen goods for rent,
    And wur ready to flee us alive.

I sed to our Margit as we lay upoth floor,
We shall never be lower in this world I'm sure,
But if wo alter I'm sure we mun mend ,
For I think in my heart we are both at far end,
For meat we have none nor looms to weave on.
    Egad they're as weel lost as found.

Then I geet up my piece and I took it em back
I scarcely dare speak mester looked so black,
He said you wur o'erpaid last time you coom,
I said if I wur 'twas for weaving bout loom ;
In a mind as I'm in I'll ne'er pick o'er again,
    For I've woven mysel toth' fur end.

Then aw coom out and left him to chew that,
When aw thought again aw wur vext till aw sweat,
To think that we mun work to keep them and awth set,
All the day o' my life and still be in their debt ;
So I'll give o'er trade an work with a spade,
    Or go and break stones upoth road,

Our Margt declared if hoo'd cloas to put on,
Hoo'd go up to Lundun an see the big mon
An if things didn't ████████████████
Hoo ████████ hoo'd ████████████
Hoo's ████████ again ████ but ████ a fair ████
    As hoo says hoo can tell when hoo's ████

Image 5.3. *The Bebbington broadsheet of 'Jone o' Grinfield'*

Creating New Songs from Old Material

One frequent method of creating new songs is to put new lyrics to an old and familiar tune. Some of the most familiar tunes in the nineteenth century were parlour songs and hymn tunes, particularly those of the Nonconformist confessions (Methodist, Baptist, Congregationalist, etc.). The late-nineteenth-century 'pitman poet' Tommy Armstrong from Durham, whose songs first appeared on broadsides and in chapbooks and are still sung today, originally set his song 'The Trimdon Grange Explosion' ☻83 to the Victorian parlour song 'Go and Leave Me If You Wish It' (or 'Once I Loved with Fond Affection'), and it has appeared in a number of variants (e.g. Percy Webb, Peta Webb, Norma Waterson, John Spiers and Jon Boden, Sarah and Rita Keane). The number of versions is indexical of the difficulty in finding 'Once I Loved with Fond Affection' and its songwriter, and, indeed, despite a long hunt we have been just as unsuccessful. Armstrong's song 'The Durham Lockout' ☻84 was set to a song by James Ballantine entitled 'Castles in the Air', which in its turn was based on the Scottish song 'Bonnie Jean of Aberdeen'. Tunes, in other words, appear to travel greater distances through time and space than lyrics.

The example we wish to discuss in a little more detail is the song 'A Stitch in Time' by Mike Waterson, using the tune of an older song 'The Press Gang' ☻85, which is as follows:

The lyrics that Ewan MacColl sings to this tune are the following:

1. as I walked out on London Street
    a press gang there I chanced to meet
    they asked me if I'd join the fleet
    on board of a man o' war boys

2. come brother shipmates tell me true
    what kind of treatment they give you
    that I may know before I go
    on board of a man o' war boys

3. when I got there to my surprise
    all they had told me was shocking lies
    there was a row and a jolly old row
    on board of a man o' war boys

4. the first thing they done they took me in hand
   they lashed me with a tarry strand
   they flogged me till I could not stand
   on board of a man o' war boys

5. now I was married and me wife's name was Grace
   'twas she that led the shocking delay
   'twas she that caused me to go away
   on board of a man o' war boys

6. when next I get one foot on shore
   to see them London girls once more
   I'll never go to sea no more
   on board of a man o' war boys

'The Press Gang' deals with conditions in the Royal Navy at some time in the late eighteenth and early nineteenth centuries, but it has remained popular right up to the present and is still sung today. It is a hard-hitting sea song sung by an 'I'-narrator, requiring the singer to stylise the voice of a seaman voicing his grievances. Once again we have a macro-schema dealing with the iniquitous institution of allowing able-bodied men to be pressed into military service on board of a man-of-war. The narrative voice is that of a sufferer of the iniquities described, but he indexes the sufferings of others. Any audience from the late eighteenth century on would have understood the protest.

In 'A Stitch in Time' ☻86, Mike Waterson took the ingenious step of evoking the protest of 'The Press Gang', a song about institutionalised violence, deflecting attention from the historical violence of pressing men into military service and focusing it on the modern violence of wife-beating husbands. The tune, followed by the lyrics as sung by Martin Carthy, is given below. It is not exactly the same as the tune for 'The Press Gang' given above, but quite clearly based on it:

A Stitch in Time

oh there was a woman who___ lived on her own she___

slaved on her own and she skivvied on her own she'd

two little girls and___ two little boys

and she lived on her own___ with her hus - band

1. oh there was a woman and she lived on her own
   she slaved on her own and she skivvied on
      her own
   she'd two little girls and two little boys
   and she lived all alone with her husband

2. for her husband he was a hunk of a man
   a chunk of a man and a drunk of a man
   he was a hunk of a drunk and skunk of a man
   such a boozing bruising husband

3. for he would come home drunk each night
   he thrashed her black and he thrashed her white
   he thrashed her to within an inch of her life
   then he slept like a log did her husband

4. one night she gathered her tears all round her
      shame
   she thought of the bruising and cried with the
      pain
   oh you'll not do that ever again
   I won't live with a drunken husband

5. but as he lay and snored in bed
   a strange old thought came into her head
   she went for the needle went for the thread
   and went straight in to her sleeping husband

6. and she started to stitch with a girlish thrill
   with a woman's heart and a seamstress' skill
   she bibbed and tucked with an iron will
   all around her sleeping husband

7. oh the top sheet the bottom sheet too
   the blanket stitched to the mattress through
   she stitched and stitched for the whole night
      through
   then she waited till dawn on her husband

8. and when he awoke with a pain in his head
   he found that he could not move in bed sweet
   Christ I've lost the use of me legs
   but this wife just smiled at her husband

9. for in her hand she held the frying pan
   with a flutter in her heart she gave him a lam
   he could not move but he cried God damn
   don't you swear she cries to her husband

10. then she thrashed him black she thrashed
       him blue
    with the frying pan and the colander too
    with the rolling pin just a stroke or two
    such a battered and bleeding husband

11. says if you ever come home drunk any more
    I'll stitch you in I'll thrash you more
    then I'll pack my bag and I'll be out the door
    I'll not live with a drunken husband

12. oh isn't it true what small can do
    with a thread and a thought and a stitch or two
    he's wiped his slate and his boozing's through
    it's goodbye to a drunken husband

Wife-beating is a burning social issue in Western societies, since the women sufferers are powerless unless they take legal action against their own husbands. The lyrics replace the 'I'-narrator of 'The Press Gang' with a third-person narrative persona, converting a macro-song schema into a narrative song schema. This allows a great deal of negative evaluation on the part of the singer, e.g. that the husband was 'a hunk and a chunk and a drunk of a man', or that the woman starts to stitch 'with a girlish thrill / with a woman's heart and a seamstress' skill', or that 'with a flutter in her heart she gave him a lam'. The song is almost twice the length of 'The Press Gang', and it provides a narrative of how the woman got her revenge on her husband. With slight changes, the song fits the tune. It is a new song based on an old tune, but it focuses on and indeed heightens the timeless theme of unnecessary violence.

In this chapter, we have discussed a variety of ways in which songs are open to adaptation, both in their lyrics and their tunes, as they are adopted, changed, transmitted from singer to singer and diffused through time and space. Just as language needs the flexibility of its users in social interaction to alter the constructions of language varieties as the need arises, so too do songs need to be constantly submitted to adaptation, modernisation, rebirth and revitalisation in the course of their histories. Songs that bond individuals into communities will always be a feature of human societies, but, as we see in the following chapter, there is a danger in insisting, for ideological reasons, on the 'authenticity' of a song or a mode of singing, i.e. a song tradition. Like human language, songs have to remain flexible and heterogeneous to be able to survive and recreate the links between the past and the present, and to offer those links to the future.

6   Ideologies, Authenticities and Traditions

Obviously the most deeply felt performance of any piece of music will be that which approaches most closely the feelings of its creator when he begins to capture the force of his individual experience with musical form.

(Blacking 1973: 110)

Tradition and Authenticity

The current chapter raises a set of thorny problems from the area of folk song performance that have arisen over the last 150 years or more as components of a constantly changing discourse archive of folk song and folk singing. We deal explicitly with the notions of 'discourse' and 'discourse archive' in the following section, and we use this opening section to set out in a practical way the issues that need to be dealt with.

We begin by reminding the reader of the title of Maddy Prior's concert in Kennedy Hall at Cecil Sharp House: 'Back to the Tradition'. The implicature derivable from this title is that the trajectory of folk song has departed from 'the tradition' and is now returning to it. But note that the noun phrase used is 'the tradition' and not simply 'tradition'. The determiner 'the' indexes one particular tradition and not simply tradition in general, so the inference that the title invites from members of the audience is that they will know what tradition is being referred to. As we shall see in this chapter, the inference cannot be made unless the addressee is thoroughly familiar with the British folk music register and the characterological stereotypes and stereotypical beliefs that it engenders in its enregisterment (cf. Agha 2003, 2005, 2007).

Folk song research is inextricably caught up in a web of cultural beliefs that can be understood both as lay and as theoretical concepts. One common assumption often made by folklorists, singers and audiences alike is that folk singing is the performance of 'traditional songs' in a 'traditional' way. In this sense, folk songs are considered to be 'authentic' productions by 'the people' handed down orally through generations of singers. Some songs are authentic, others inauthentic; some modes of singing and playing are authentic, others inauthentic. In accordance with hazy notions of how authenticity is connected to tradition, singers are often expected by audiences to display an authority in performance as the guardians and guarantors of a continuing tradition and as displaying knowledge, expertise, commitment to and involvement in this tradition.

We argue in this chapter that because discourse archives are continually open to change from a wide range of socio-cultural, socio-economic and socio-political influences, it is dangerous to try to restrict the flexibility and hybridity of folk song and its performance by demanding standards of authenticity and tradition which simply cannot be upheld in a rapidly changing world. We begin by looking at how the English lexemes {tradition} and {traditional} are currently understood (or misunderstood) with respect to folk song performance.

Tradition and 'Traditional' Songs

There is a tendency in recordings by several individual singers and groups to classify a song as 'trad.' ('traditional) even though there is an assumed or an identifiable creator (songwriter/composer) of that song. The tendency also extends to live performances of a song in representational performance settings. In relational performance settings, however, the singer is unlikely to make any comment on whether or not a song is 'traditional', although s/he may otherwise comment briefly on the content of the song, its assumed age or the need for the other participants to join in. One possible reason for this difference is that, in contrast to relational settings, recordings and representational performances are public events that may require payment for songs under copyright. But there are three good reasons for assuming that this explanation falls short of what is really going on in singers' minds when they label a song 'traditional'.

Firstly, our description of the transmission process in Chapter 5 includes the significant point that on the adoption of a song (from whatever source, written, oral or recorded), singers are free to adapt it as they wish. They may omit stanzas, change the wording of the lyrics, change the tune, etc., which is a time-honoured way of *re*presenting a song and shifting it into the wider process of transmission and diffusion. In doing so, they could be said to 'claim' a song in a version that is 'theirs'. Secondly, if singers sense that there must have been an original songwriter but cannot definitively identify that person, they will often make this point in representational performance settings or, in recordings, by labelling the song 'unknown', i.e. the songwriter is unknown to the singer. In Chapters 4 and 5, we mentioned the song 'Poverty Knock', which is often labelled in this way. Pete Coe, who recorded the song in 1989 on his LP *A Right to Dance*, made the following statement on a BBC Mike Harding show:

The probable writer of *Poverty Knock* was Tom Daniel, a weaver from [Batley]. I met him in about 1970, shortly before he died. He was born around 1890, left school at eleven and worked in various mills around Western Yorkshire and did other jobs too, outside of weaving. The story he apparently told was that he'd remembered bits of the song from his early years. However, the song bears striking resemblance to many of the poems that he did write. The collector of the song, Tony Green, reckons he wrote it too. I'm told there's no surviving relatives to claim royalties so as it's been designated a 'traditional' song for so long, that's how it's usually referred to.[1]

Thirdly – and, we believe, most significantly – singers often feel that a song sounds representative of a particular singing tradition, whether or not we can actually locate the originator, and they therefore feel no compunction about using the term 'traditional' to refer to it.

What, therefore, is 'traditional' about a particular song or performance of a song? To begin with, we take a tradition to be a mode of thought or behaviour passed down through time in a community, very often from generation to generation,[2] by means of specific social processes that may involve types of reification. Hence, the ways in which a tradition is enacted are imbued with ritual significance and form part of the way in which aspects of a culture are defined. The symbolic significance for a socio-cultural group is characterised by the fact that traditions change little across time. They seem to consolidate the impression of longevity and authentic value and are, no doubt for this reason, steeped in ceremony. However, many traditions, which we think of in terms of longevity, are relatively recent. In some cases their inception can even be dated quite precisely. In the introductory chapter to Hobsbawm and Ranger's book *The Invention of Tradition* (1983), Hobsbawm defines an 'invented tradition' as 'a set of practices, normally governed by overtly or tacitly accepted rules of a ritual or symbolic nature, which seek to inculcate certain values and norms of behaviour by repetition, which automatically implies continuity with the past' (Hobsbawm and Ranger 1983 [2003]: 1). The repetition of a tradition through time seeks to foster in the participants the feeling of temporal continuity, and the further back this longevity can be extended, the greater the value of the tradition for the cultural group. This may lead the supporters of the tradition to claim 'an ancient past beyond effective historical continuity' (ibid.: 7), by which Hobsbawm means that the available historical sources are not sufficient to warrant either the existence of the tradition itself or its temporal continuity. In this situation, Brocken (2003: 12) warns us that 'a tradition is obviously both real and imagined at one and the same time'.

---

[1] Cf. https://mainlynorfolk.info/folk/songs/povertyknock.html, accessed 4 March 2015.
[2] Some 'traditions' may even have a shorter life span.

'The Tradition'

Given these thoughts on the status of the term 'tradition', we now take a critical look at how folk musicians, critics and scholars researching 'folk music' use terms like 'the tradition', 'traditional songs', 'traditional singing styles', 'traditional instruments', etc. Songs, singing styles and musical instruments cannot in themselves *be* traditions but only their carriers. What, then, is 'the tradition' and how is it linked to authenticity? Picking up on the point made at the end of the previous subsection, Brocken posits with respect to Lloyd's notion of 'tradition' that 'there is a paradox at the core of [it]. It looks back to a long lost past and, in doing so, transforms and reconstructs that past as the image is being realised' (Brocken 2003: 29). But not even the principal proponents of 'the tradition', MacColl and Lloyd, have actually stated exactly what they understand by the term.

Some songs were part of traditional customs, e.g. wassailing songs, carols, laments, but they were never in themselves 'traditions'. Obviously, songs accompanying seasonal and religious traditions only constituted a small part of what MacColl and Lloyd conceptualised as songs of 'the tradition'. There were very many others, making up an extremely heterogeneous group – ballads, sea songs, protest songs, laments, love songs, erotic songs, drinking songs, humorous songs, and so on. The very heterogeneity of the songs and the impossibility of categorising them as the carriers of tradition indicated that '*the* tradition' could only mean the transmission of songs on the occasion of performances from one singer to the next and the perpetuation of the songs from generation to generation and over wide geographical distances, e.g. from the British Isles to the US or the Antipodes. The songs and the singing of songs, in other words, constituted 'the tradition'. Songs travelled with the singers, evolving, sometimes quite differently and sometimes with remarkably little change, in their new environments.[3] The need for the songs to be 'revived' and transmitted to a further generation of musicians was logical, and, as we saw in Chapter 5, it entailed their adaptation to suit the changed circumstances of late modernity.

Within the discourse of the Second Folk Revival, singers were therefore considered to be authenticators of 'the tradition', but so were the musicians themselves, audiences in folk clubs and at more representational venues (concerts and festivals), music critics in the media, recording companies and, most important of all, in the 1960s and 1970s, Ewan MacColl and A. L. Lloyd. But to insist, as did MacColl and Lloyd, that there was an

---

[3] Cf. Sharp's and the Lomaxes' work on Appalachian versions of ballads from the British Isles and Bronson's versions of Child ballads on both sides of the Atlantic. Cf. also Pound's (1913) discussion of cowboy songs as an answer to Kittredge's and Gummere's theory of communal improvisation as the poetic origin of the ballad.

authentic, traditional way of performing those songs, which they, and only they, could define and teach to others, denied singers the freedom to authenticate them in their own ways. In addition, the claim to know what traditional songs were and how they should be sung was grossly overstated. There is little beyond occasional remarks on singing styles that would give anyone the right to say how people sang before the invention of recording technology. The rise of electric folk and modern means of instrumentation outside the scope of the folk clubs was ample evidence that songs that had been sung for centuries could, and indeed should, be performed in novel ways to suit the tastes of late modernist audiences. As Brocken says, '[the tradition] became an encapsulating get-out clause for any debate about the future social role of the revival, and the whiff of snobbery on the part of the initiates towards the uninitiated knew few bounds' (Brocken 2003: 113–14).

Hobsbawm suggests that invented traditions are still traditions, in that they fill a niche in 'establishing or symbolizing social cohesion or the membership of groups, real or artificial communities' (Hobsbawm and Ranger 1983 [2003]: 9). They help to reconstitute communities whose older values have been eroded away by late modernist globalisation and may help to re-establish new forms of 'social cohesion' for a community. Invented traditions thus have a significant function in creating new authenticity values through performance in the modern world.

The Discourse on Folk Song in Britain: The First Folk Song Revival

The discourse on folk music in Britain has mutated considerably over the past 150–200 years, moving from the status of a sub-discourse within the dominant early-nineteenth-century socio-political discourse in Britain to an alternative discourse in the post-Second World War era. Since the 1990s it has struggled to free itself from an association with the dominant hegemonic discourse, and this struggle is still in process today. It involves the formation of alignments with forms of popular music in accepting the commercial vitality of folk music whilst retaining and strengthening its commitment to live performances of various kinds (see Chapter 7). The uncertainty at the beginning of this century as to whether folk music was able to break away from its commitment to the alternative discourse that had formed in the early 1970s caused Brocken to write his book on the post-war British folk revival. We thus open this section by outlining the ideological mutations contained within discourses on folk song.

Discourses and Discourse Archives

We understand discourse as a body of statements that form part of 'a single system in the overall formation of statements' (Watts 2011: 17), a conceptualisation derived from Foucault's work. According to Foucault, the statements of a discourse have been uttered, written and printed in the past, and they thus constitute 'events' situated in historical time. Each of us has been socialised through discourses into believing that the statements we are exposed to are 'true', not in the strictly logical sense but by virtue of the fact that they are shared and believed by others. The systems of statements that we refer to as 'discourses' are certainly bodies of statements, but they are also ways of organising our social worlds.

Foucault argues that, although we often think of a body of statements as being 'true' and internally consistent, there are always discontinuities, i.e. points at which the discourse is challenged and in danger of rupture. A significant rupture in a discourse is not in the interests of those controlling it; hence, discontinuities challenge the perceived coherence of the hegemonic discourse, and changes need to be made to it to assure that it stays under the control of those in power.

Foucault uses the term 'archive' in *The Archaeology of Knowledge* to refer to 'the law of what can be said, the system that governs the appearance of statements as unique events' (Foucault [1969] 1972: 129). Blommaert defines the 'archive' as 'the macro-sociological forces and formations that define and determine what can be said, expressed, heard, and understood in particular societies, particular milieux, particular historical periods' (2005: 102). Blommaert's 'macro-sociological forces and formations' are equivalent to the hegemonic discourse ideologies exerting control over what the members of a society feel they can say/express and hear/understand. Hegemonic discourse ideologies tend to be socio-political, but if we take 'ideology' to refer more generally to systems of ideas and beliefs, any discourse in any area of social practice must be ideological. Our aim in this section is to identify the discourse archives within which the folk song collectors of the nineteenth and early twentieth centuries went about their work.

History and Nostalgia

Brocken opens his book on *The British Folk Revival 1944–2002* with the following statement: 'History reveals our (often confused) sense of identity, and the notion of nostalgia is a foundation for much of this historically appraised identity' (2003: 1). Nostalgia, according to Brocken, 'insulates us from criticism' so that what we believe is history is too often determined by what we see through the rose-coloured spectacles of nostalgia, a longing for something that was never *then* what we would like it to have been *now*. There can, of course, never be a true history, and certainly not a complete history, but the 'facts' of history are ultimately only interpretable as 'facts' within the context of a hegemonic discourse archive, and relying on nostalgia is equivalent to substituting the facts of history with a mythical past.

The second half of the nineteenth century was a golden age of nostalgia and myth-making in Victorian Britain, particularly in history, but it was also the age of inventing traditions (see Hobsbawm and Ranger 1983 [2003]). Brocken posits that '[t]he writing of history is actually a corporate, politicised activity and what appear to be absolute standards usually have roots in compartmentalised ideologies, preferences and metaphors' (2003: 1). For the expression 'compartmentalised ideologies, preferences and metaphors' we substitute the term 'discourse archive', the 'what-we-can-say' and the 'what-is-true' of our own worlds.

We focus first on the work of the major figure in the First Folk Song Revival, Cecil James Sharp,[4] and, before continuing, we briefly exemplify his escape into a nostalgic view of history. Sharp has been severely criticised for his methods of collecting songs, his habit of editing and arranging them with a piano-forte accompaniment and also for his insensitive, often arrogant treatment of those he considered to be his rivals, particularly if they were women (see Boyes 1993; Harker 1985). Sharp's most influential work during the First Revival was not so much his compendious collection of folk songs from Somerset, collected after 1903 with the help of his friend the Reverend Charles Marson, but rather his book *English Folk Song, Some Conclusions* (1907). There are many flights of fancy into history in this work, evidencing a strain in Sharp's thinking which bears traces of an alternative late Victorian discourse evident in much of the literature of the period (e.g. in Tennyson, Browning, Rossetti and in the works of William Morris). The discourse is embodied in forms of fantasy literature (cf. Morris' novel *News from Nowhere*), and its themes are escapist. One major theme is the dream of transforming capitalist industrialised Britain into a model of pastoralism and common ownership (cf. Young 2010). The reality of grimy cities full of poverty-stricken slums and half-starved labouring denizens is transformed into idealised visions of harmonious country life in picturesque villages. The transformation is often projected into the future, as in *News from Nowhere*, but when projected back into the past, it reveals a history steeped in and constructed through nostalgia, in an attempt to find some 'lost object' (cf. Middleton 2006). In Sharp's writing this becomes evident in the following statement:

---

[4] It was to honour the memory of Sharp that the centre of the English Folk Dance and Song Society (EFDSS) in London was named 'Cecil Sharp House'.

Folk-songs and folk dances, *in days gone by*, played an important part in the social life of the English village. *That life is now waning*, and with it are passing away the old traditions and customs. It is, happily, still possible here and there, and in out-of-the-way nooks and corners, to come upon peasant men and women old enough to remember *the village life of sixty, seventy, or even eighty years ago*, and they will sing to you the songs and explain to you the dances that, in their young days, and *on summer evenings, were sung and danced on the village green*. The folk-singers of today ... are the last of a long line that stretches back into the mists of far off days. (Sharp 1907: 106; our italics)

Had Sharp been able to go back sixty to eighty years prior to 1907, he would have found himself in the period of the Tolpuddle Martyrs, a group of agricultural labourers in Tolpuddle, Dorset, tried for swearing oaths and founding a friendly society to protest against the lowering of agricultural wages, found guilty and duly transported to Australia for seven years. Or he would have found himself in the brief era of Chartism from 1838 to 1848, a period of serious social and political unrest that was in no way restricted to the urban industrial areas of Britain, i.e. the world in which Ernest Jones wrote his 'Song of the Lower Classes' (cf. Chapter 4). Villagers may indeed have sung and danced on some village greens on summer evenings in the 1820s–40s, but not all villages had village greens. Boyes (1993) shows in her discussion of the study of folklore in the nineteenth century that in many of the rural village celebrations

... customs were organised jointly by *'gentleman amateurs' and local publicans* – each, however, keeping to 'separate spheres' of sociability and 'business'. Perhaps the most telling description of this earlier form of 'communal' participation is Mary Russell Mitford's comments on the May festival in Three Mile Cross in Hampshire: 'the band struck up in the May-house, and the dance, after a little demur, was fairly set afloat – an honest English country dance ... with ladies and gentlemen at the top, and country lads and lasses at the bottom; a happy mixture of cordial kindness on the one hand, and pleased respect on the other'. (Boyes 1993: 32, our italics)

But such village jollities had a clear socio-political purpose promoting the economic interests of the '"gentlemen amateurs" and local publicans' and creating a feeling of *communitas* in the face of the threat to the status quo from Chartism.

Participants from all social classes 'knew their places' in the social order and acted accordingly. With respect to organised historical pageants and community drama in the nineteenth century, Boyes states that '[a]lthough relatively comprehensive ... both types of performance reflected the hierarchical structure of local society' (ibid.: 33–34), and her final ironic comment on such May Day celebrations is that in Three Mile Cross and elsewhere 'Mayday in Merrie England was then enthusiastically celebrated' (ibid.: 34).

Sharp's 'lost object' was an idealised, pre-industrial England in which there was assumed harmonious existence between country and town. The non-educated country-dwellers, the non-literate 'peasantry', were defined as the 'common people', the 'folk', whose musical expression was in the form of folk music, folk dance and folk song. Conveniently for Sharp and others, the 'peasantry', the 'folk', the 'common people' had left behind them traces of a 'national music' that was in need of revival.

The Discursive Expropriation of Folk Songs[5]

By the end of the nineteenth century, song hunters like Sharp, Sabine Baring-Gould and Lucy Broadwood had convinced themselves that the 'peasantry' was a fast declining sector of English society, to be found only in remote country backwaters,[6] in grave danger of being engulfed by the Moloch of industrialisation and urban development. All of them lamented the impending loss of rural culture (songs, dances, customs) in the age of industrial capitalism and British imperialism,[7] but it was Sharp who most unequivocally equated vernacular songs, or what he and Baring-Gould called 'folk songs', with 'national music' in the spirit of Herder.[8]

The discourse of the major figures in the late-nineteenth-century and early-twentieth-century folk song revival is in effect rather puzzling. On the one hand, it sees itself as an alternative to the hegemonic discourse archive of imperialism and industrial progress espoused by the late Victorian and Edwardian period in Britain by wishing to preserve folk songs from the destruction, through the expansion of capitalist industrialisation and urbanisation, of an idealised and largely hypothesised rural way of life. Folk songs, in other words, were to be preserved as the relics of a lost rural world. On the other hand, preserving them did not ensure that they would continue to be sung by the rural population. Amazingly, Sharp and others had not realised that the lost world was not lost at all, just rather different from the way they had idealised it.

---

[5] We return to the issue of 'expropriating songs' in the final chapter in which we develop the argument that singing any songs collected in the past need not be taken as an act of 'expropriation' but rather one of performative creativity.

[6] Cf. the remarks by the announcer of *Saturday Night at the Eel's Foot* discussed in Chapter 3.

[7] There is an uncanny similarity here between pre-sociolinguistic dialect studies that focused on NORMs (non-mobile, old, rural, male speakers), on the (mistaken) assumption that researchers were likely to gain the most authentic forms of dialect from such informants, and what we might call NORFs (non-mobile, old, rural folk singers) sought after by the song hunters of the First Folk Song Revival as the 'true' carriers of 'folk song', passing their songs on orally to younger generations of singers. Like NORMs, NORFs were older singers who could only be found in rural areas far from the 'taint' of an urban background.

[8] A critical appraisal of the discourse of the English Folk Dance and Song Society, which also centres on Sharp, is given in Georgina Boyes' book *The Imagined Village: Culture, Ideology and the English Folk Revival* (1993).

Collecting folk songs was not motivated by a revitalisation of rural communities, but by the urge to preserve for the nation what the collectors believed was a repository of 'national music' that could then be fostered in schools as the national musical heritage and used as an inspiration for new forms of art music. Sharp's motives were thus directed at the support and aggrandisement of the British nation-state and were therefore within the scope of the hegemonic discourse archive of the time.

Once the song hunters had acquired the texts, they felt free to edit and publish them in whatever form they wished.[9] Regardless of whether the singers were or were not, legally speaking, 'in possession' of the songs, the fact that they were not the original songwriters gave Sharp and others the liberty to treat the songs as 'theirs'. Expropriating songs meant that the collectors were able to adjust the tunes to the assumed musical tastes of a middle-class audience and to ignore any notion of how they should be performed other than as a performance that suited the middle class. So folk songs were taken out of pubs, family gatherings, ceilidhs, i.e. the hybrid forms of performance, and placed into the drawing rooms, concert halls and schools of the middle classes. However, unbeknown to the middle-class folk song and dance enthusiasts of the inter-war period and deliberately ignored by Sharp, folk songs continued to be made and played in all of the hybrid performance venues discussed in Chapter 2, and more[10] – as they always had been (cf. the argument in Chapter 12)![11]

Searching for Authenticity: The Second Folk Song Revival

Authenticity of performance entails making songs speak meaningfully and emotionally in the emergent event of performance to contemporary audiences. If they are authentic today, then they always were authentic. But why were the song hunters, and the antiquarians before them from the seventeenth to the mid-nineteenth century, so intent on collecting songs? Harker (1985) argues that their motivation was commercial rather than cultural; it was quite simply 'mediation', i.e. acquiring a commodity that was sellable in a market. From the latter two decades of the eighteenth century on there was a market in songs

---

[9] See E. David Gregory's assessment of Sabine Baring-Gould's editorial practices in his book *The Late Victorian Folksong Revival: The Persistence of English Melody, 1878–1903* (Lanham, MD: Scarecrow Press, 418–19). See also our discussion of Baring-Gould in Chapter 7.

[10] In working men's clubs, at political rallies, at weddings, christenings, get-togethers and barn dances.

[11] Evidence that Sharp knew this was the case is contained in *English Folk Song, Some Conclusions* (1907: 55) when he quite openly tells the reader the following: 'Only last winter ... I sat one day from noon till four o'clock in the parlour of a primitive way-side inn on the peat moors of Somerset. The company numbered on the average some twelve or fourteen men, and song followed song in quick succession ...'. In other words, Sharp knew only too well that folk songs were still being sung communally. He simply did not have any means of recording the session.

that could be freely taken from one publication and used in another, all the more so if they were labelled as 'traditional' or 'anonymous'. The market in antiquarian language products from around 1780 on, such as songs and anonymous poems, was healthy enough to guarantee a pecuniary profit. Even at the beginning of the twentieth century, Sharp's reason for using the songs in schools was motivated by a large ready-made market in folk song books if the education authorities could only be persuaded to accept the 'national' significance of folk song and dance.

Bonding the 'Nation'

A detailed critical description of the Second Folk Revival after the Second World War can be gleaned from various publications, with varying degrees of critical appraisal and various foci of attention (see Lloyd 1967; Pegg 1976; D. Harker 1985; MacKinnon 1993; Boyes 1993; Rosenberg 1993; Brocken 2003; Sweers 2005; B. Harker 2007; Gammon 2008; Young 2010). After the war had begun, and particularly after the evacuation at Dunkirk in 1940, it became important to create a common feeling of national solidarity in the face of the threat of invasion by German forces, in particular solidarity between the social classes. The Depression years had created an acute sense that something needed to be done to alleviate social distress and to close the huge social gap between the middle classes and the labouring classes. In 1936 John Grierson's GPO Film Unit produced the documentary *Night Mail*, which was first shown in cinemas in 1936. This was followed by a radio programme, entitled *Coal*, for the BBC North Region in 1938, produced by John Bridson assisted by Joan Littlewood. The programme was a huge success. Boyes notes that '*Coal* provoked a wave of sympathy throughout the country and Bridson arranged for money donated as a result to be divided among unemployed miners and those on short time' (Boyes 1993: 137–38). She goes on to point out that '[b]ourgeois culture had to be replaced by new forms relevant to the workers, and culture itself reconstituted as a direct instrument of class struggle, rather than a life-enhancing means of superseding class differences' (ibid.: 138).

To help close social ranks during the wartime period, the BBC launched the weekly programme *Country Magazine* in 1942, in which a selection of folk songs sung by traditional singers was a regular feature. The programme was very popular, and figured among its folk singers those recorded at the Eel's Foot and at the Ship in Blaxhall, Suffolk. The important point about presenting folk songs in all these programmes was to stress national solidarity, but the idea of 'urban' folk song was still not on the agenda.

Redefining the 'Folk'

As the generation of children born during the war and in the last five years of the 1940s passed through their childhood and entered their teens, past imperial glory and a longing to restore pre-war values and social structures in the grey reality of late 1940s and early 1950s Britain ran counter to their hopes for a brighter, different future. American influence was dominant in cinema, popular music, magazines, food habits and fashions and obvious too in the popularity of hire purchase. American films had been very popular in the inter-war years, but American dance music, jazz, Tin Pan Alley pop, blues and folk music, which boomed in the post-Depression years in the USA, were largely unavailable to the British, who, although they had radio, were generally not equipped with the technology to play 78 rpm shellac records.[12] During the war and in the post-war period, Britain became an open market for American music, and the number of record players and radiograms steadily increased.

The cultural generation gap in Britain in the late 1950s and 1960s helps to explain the unprecedented rise of folk music during that time. The new generation were beginning to answer back to their elders as rock 'n' roll shook the cultural foundations of the older generation to the core on both sides of the Atlantic. Lloyd's efforts to release folk music from its apparent insignificance in the 1930s had influenced Francis Dillon to produce the programme *Saturday Night at the Eel's Foot* (cf. Chapter 3), and it was Dillon who produced *Country Magazine*. Peter Kennedy, son of the president of the English Folk Dance and Song Society, also collaborated with Lloyd in persuading the BBC that this rich store of songs should be recorded. This led to the hiring of the Irish uilleann piper Seamus Ennis with the specific purpose of collecting songs throughout Britain and Ireland using a tape recorder and presenting what had been collected in a programme entitled *As I Roved Out*, produced and presented by Ennis and Kennedy with the collaboration of Hamish Henderson in Scotland and Bob Copper (of the famous singing Copper family of Rottingdean, Sussex).[13] The programme was immensely popular and ran till 1958, extending to fifty-three episodes.

---

[12] This was not helped by the official policy of the BBC in the pre-war years, which made sure that American music was not given an airing in BBC broadcasting. During the war, however, when a large number of American troops were stationed in Britain, they were forced to drop these restrictions.

[13] That the collecting was focused on singers performing just as much as on the songs themselves is evident from an anecdote told to R.J.W. by Seamus Ennis (personal communication). Seamus was collecting in Pembrokeshire and had recorded a song from a farmer. When the farmer was asked whether he would like to hear the song, Seamus played it back to him and the farmer started singing harmony with his own voice. Seamus then stopped the recorder and using the excuse that something was wrong with it, dashed out to the car, fetched in his second recorder, switched the tape to that one, placed a new tape in the first recorder, cunningly switched the first tape on to 'record' and then played the recording from the second tape recorder. The result was a beautiful two-part harmony recorded on the first tape recorder!

Americans were also in the forefront of the Second Folk Revival in Britain, first and foremost Alan Lomax. He and his father John had been active folk song collectors in post-Depression America, and Alan made no secret of their left-wing sympathies. McCarthy's anti-communist witch-hunt in the USA, which also temporarily forced Pete Seeger into obscurity because of being blacklisted, set its sights on Alan Lomax, who was not afraid to 'answer back' at the American political establishment. Lomax moved to England in the early 1950s. Without him the folk revival would probably have continued at its own pace, but Lomax injected energy and drive into recording folk singers in Britain and attracting young musicians to what was fast becoming a new taste in music. In 1953 he was offered an eight-part television show *Song Hunter: Alan Lomax* 'in which he presented a mixture of traditional singers and musicians such as Harry Cox, Jeannie Robertson, Charlie Wills, Michael Gorman and Margaret Barry, and the likes of Ewan MacColl,[14] Isla Cameron and Seamus Ennis, as well as showing Kennedy's Padstow footage.[15] Kennedy researched and co-presented the show, which was produced by the young David Attenborough (Young 2010: 131). It was Lomax, more than anyone else, who recognised the significance of folk song for the common people and its significant role in leftist politics. Without Lloyd, MacColl and Lomax the 1950s and 1960s music scene would have been very different.

The link between communism or left-wing activism and folk song was characteristic of the Second Folk Revival as it was in the US. Looking at the further development in folk music from the 1970s to the present, it has created a number of misconceptions in public opinion as to the nature of folk music in general. In a nutshell, MacColl, Peggy Seeger[16] (MacColl's partner and twenty years his junior) and Lloyd saw the major goal of the Folk Revival as being to give back to the working classes the oral patterns of culture that, as they saw things, had been taken away from them by the industrial revolution.

For MacColl, 'the tradition' – 'both a body of songs created or adapted by the people *and* a manner of singing those songs' (B. Harker 2007: 186) – was a part of the workers' culture in need of protection from the bourgeoisie. According to MacColl, the 'folk' in 'folk music' and 'folk song' was made up solely of the working classes, both rural and urban industrial. In the early 1950s, both Lloyd and MacColl collected a large number of songs from industrial workers, giving

---

[14] MacColl was one of the major figures in the Second Revival, so it is important to note that his real name was James (Jimmie) Miller. During the Second World War he deserted and went into hiding from the military police. Shortly after the war he assumed the name Ewan MacColl in place of Jimmie Miller.

[15] Kennedy filmed folk events such as the Padstow hobby-horse festivities in the 1940s, but it was only with the arrival of television that film footage could be shown in the intimacy of the home context rather than in the cinema.

[16] Peggy Seeger was the younger half-sister of the late Pete Seeger from their father Charles Seeger's, the ethnomusicologist's, second marriage to composer Ruth Porter Crawford.

the lie to Sharp's focus on the 'peasantry' as the repository of folk song. But MacColl's conception of a unified tradition of folk song comprising both the urban and the rural working classes was a political idealisation. Most of the songs recorded by MacColl and Lloyd were sung by the working classes, but the latter also sang other kinds of popular song, notably from the music hall. To state that folk songs were the property of the working classes representing a tradition of songs circulating only amongst those classes and, in addition, to imagine that there was one 'traditional' way of singing them, was a gross exaggeration and an unnecessary idealisation.[17]

However, despite the polarisation in the British folk music world that this insistence caused, MacColl and Lloyd's contribution to the revival of interest in singing songs of and for the people – whomever we take the people to be – was monumental. MacColl's contribution to the Second Folk Revival was massive, and many of his own songs have become part of the repertoires of singers today. But MacColl also amassed what Gammon (2008: 1–2) calls 'negative ideological baggage' connected to the term 'folk'. For Gammon, 'vernacular' refers to something handed down by tradition and learnt by example. It does not automatically mean that the subject matter and structures of the songs have a great age. Lloyd and MacColl's term 'the tradition', propagated as it was among the folk clubs of Britain, was 'the negative ideological baggage' referred to by Gammon, the search for the 'lost object' of the people that could never be found through the ventriloquist voices of middle-class singers, a search that began to paralyse 'folk' song in the 1970s.

During the 1960s and 1970s MacColl and Seeger regularly toured the length and breadth of Britain making use of the extensive folk club network, and it was MacColl's avowed policy in his elitist Critics Group to train singers to carry 'the message' to the folk clubs. The 'message' was socio-political rather than socio-cultural, and MacKinnon's research of the folk club scene, or what remained of it, at the end of the 1980s, attests to the depth to which MacColl's 'traditionalist', purist credo had been accepted and put into practice by a large number of clubs. Despite the closure of the majority of folk clubs since the 1980s, singing folk songs has persisted and found itself other performance niches, e.g. festivals, concerts, recording studios, and has re-strengthened the hybrid forms of performance discussed in Chapter 2, including those folk clubs that have survived. If folk song helps in constructing an existential or spontaneous *communitas*, it can, like other popular songs, still answer back. It does so not because it is the voice of the people but because it helps to construct a 'folk' and to link that 'folk' up with other 'folks' in

---

[17] This criticism, however, does not detract from the recognition of his untiring dedication to the vernacular culture of the industrial working classes.

answering back as a community. Why, then, was so much stress put on the notion of 'authenticity'?

The Authenticity Trope in Sociolinguistics and Music Performance

We begin this section with a brief but pithy quotation from the introduction to musicologist Richard Taruskin's book *Text and Act: Essays on Music and Performance* (1995), a collection of his essays from 1981 to 1994 on '[wrecking] the whole idea of authenticity' (ibid.: 3). In distinguishing performance from scholarship, he has the following to say about both areas of activity: 'The purpose of scholarship, including scholarly criticism, is to instruct. That of performance is to delight. Instruction can be delightful. Delight can be instructive. But instruction can require actions that are not always conducive to delight, and delight can merely "divert"' (ibid.: 30). Throughout the book, his position on *authentic performance* in WAM is driven by the conviction that whatever authenticity 'is', within the context of musical performance it can only be seen as the most complete experience of delight possible for an audience. The idea of authenticity as something derived entirely from the momentary process of performance is different from ways in which it is usually conceptualised – particularly ways in which it is conceptualised in the folk music world.

   In sociolinguistics, scholars have steered clear of grappling with the notion of 'authenticity' until relatively recently, when the issue was raised first by Coupland, then by Eckert (2001) and picked up again by Coupland (2003, 2010). In her 2004 article for the *Journal of Sociolinguistics* Eckert argues that 'authenticity implies stasis', and she discusses a number of limitations on implicit assumptions made by sociolinguists that the members of a group under study are all equally 'authentic members' (Eckert 2004: 393). Coupland (2010: 99) picks up on Eckert's arguments concerning those limitations but argues that if we are interested in engaging with communities-as-values, e.g. in studying communities of practice, we are automatically within the domain of authenticity since 'authenticity points above all to a value system' (ibid.: 104). The values that Coupland associates with authenticity are (a) *ontology*, by which he means 'authentic things being felt to have a particular depth of reality'; (b) *historicity*, i.e. 'authentic things being perceived to be durable and sometimes timeless', which clearly links up with the notion of 'tradition' (see the first section of this chapter); (c) *systemic coherence*, by which he means 'authenticity as a matter of "making sense" and imposing order'; and (d) *consensus*, i.e. 'authenticity resulting from some social process of authentication accepted by a group'. Objects and practices are deemed by a group to be 'authentic' by virtue of the group's authentication practices. An authenticity value is thus the result of discursive processes. Any change in the shared repertoire of group members over time, or even of the jointly negotiated enterprise, may therefore lead to mutations in authenticity values.

If the authenticity value of x is high in a given community, it is so from the point of view of the continually changing constellation of authentication practices in a continually mutating present. It is thus always at the mercy of change. As Taruskin says of 'historically authentic performances' in WAM, '. . . even at their best and most successful – or especially at their best and most successful – historical reconstructionist performances are in no sense re-creations of the past. They are quintessentially modern performances, modernist performances in fact, the product of an esthetic wholly of our own era, no less time-bound than the performance styles they would supplant' (Taruskin 1995: 60). What role, then, do the concepts of 'authenticity', 'authentication practices' and 'tradition' play in folk song performance in terms of the discourse archives governing the what-can-be-said and what-is-believed of the folk song world? We start by looking at how 'authenticity' is presented and discussed in Regina Bendix's groundbreaking book *In Search of Authenticity* (1997) and compare her ideas with those presented by Coupland and Eckert within the framework of sociolinguistics.

Authenticity as the Process of Searching for the 'Lost Other'

Bendix's book *In Search of Authenticity*, although it is mentioned briefly in Coupland (2003, 2010), is not dealt with in any detail and is entirely missing in Middleton's 2006 book *Voicing the Popular*. This latter omission is surprising when we consider that both Middleton and Bendix are deeply concerned with the state of cultural scholarship in the globalised world of late modernity. In her 'Introduction', Bendix reminds us of the Greek roots of the English adjective *authentic* in the noun *authentes*, 'one who acts with authority; one who makes with his/her hands', underlying which is the violent secondary meaning of 'murderer' (1997: 14). The 'authentic' is thus a quality pertaining to something made, said or performed by someone 'in authority', and that authority shifts to whoever is competent to guarantee, or authenticate, the 'real-ness', the 'genuine-ness' of the object. As Bendix says, '[o]ne definition of authenticity, used in the realm of art and antiques, refers to the clear identifiability of maker or authorship and uniqueness of an artifact, relying on the "made by one's own hand" etymology' (ibid.: 15). The maker of the 'object', the doer of the 'action', however, is no longer present and can only be assumed or believed to have acted from some kind of invested authority. Whatever is 'authentic' thus acquires a value from the *present* status of the originator's *past* authority, even though that authority was not necessarily there when the *authentes* did what s/he did.[18]

If we begin to ask what an authentic folk song, an authentic style of performance, or an authentic custom is, we enter a vague area in which authenticity resides in 'the anonymity of entire social groups, or the "folk"' (ibid.). From the nineteenth century on, 'the call for "authenticity" implied a critical stance against urban manners, artifice in language, behaviour, and art, and against aristocratic excesses; it promised the restoration of a pure, unaffected state of being' (ibid.: 16). In other words, it constituted part of an alternative discourse. It goes without saying that 'a pure, unaffected state of being' was not to be found, although it was often invented. It was, as Middleton (2006: 51) aptly puts it, 'a structure built around a lost object', an aspect of the 'forbidden Other', and '[i]t is not the object ... but the desire, the process of searching itself, that yields existential meaning' (Bendix 1997: 17). At the same time, Bendix warns us that the searching arises from 'a profound human longing' to 'be' the Other and that 'declaring the object of such longing non-existent may violate the very core around which people build meaningful lives' (ibid.). Thus, in late modernity, the 'authentic' still has some sense as a lay concept, and as Bendix points out, 'what is authenticity?' is probably the wrong question. We should be more interested in asking 'who needs authenticity and why?' and 'how has authenticity been used?' (ibid.: 21).

Coupland (2003: 417) also sees authenticity as something 'that we actively seek out, in most domains of life, material and social', and, like Bendix, it is the 'seeking out' that is significant rather than the subjective authenticity itself. If this is the case, sociolinguistics 'has a role to play in the analysis of how we engage with authenticity' (ibid.). Sociolinguistics has always 'invested very heavily' in forms of language and types of speakers in non-establishment social settings in an effort to determine degrees of authenticity beyond those of standard speakers, i.e. what Coupland calls 'vernacular authenticities'. In doing so, it has focused on giving a voice to various types of 'Other', e.g. women, youth gangs, non-indigenous ethnicities, working-class environments, migrants, etc., and has developed an ideology 'against *establishment authenticities*' (2003: 419; italics in the original). Variationist sociolinguistics, in other words, has already engaged in anti-hegemonic discourse. But Coupland criticises the assumption that the relationship between speech and speaker is 'non-complex'. Not enough work has been undertaken in investigating irony, playfulness, quotative language and other kinds of 'performance' that speakers

---

[18] For example, an authentic Van Gogh may be worth millions of dollars/pounds/euros, but Van Gogh himself died in poverty and his painting will only be accessible now to the general public when displayed in an art exhibition.

engage in, and Bakhtin's dictum that all speech is dialogic, even speech with oneself, needs to be placed on the research agenda of sociolinguistics more explicitly.

Coupland comes close to Bendix and Middleton in his concern that socio-linguists need to engage more seriously in the 'politics of modernity', in which the standard position is to use different forms of Other as a means of justifying modernist ideological discourses. This is particularly important in a globalised world in which old authenticities travel and take on shifting, subjective values (cf. Blommaert 2003). He goes so far as to state that '[l]ate-modern social arrangements are likely to make the quest for authenticity *more rather than less* necessary. The affective, subjective dimension of authenticity – the need to feel rooted through language to a community and even to a physical place, which has driven the sociolinguistics of vernacular communities – is not simply vanishing' (Coupland 2003: 427; italics in original). How do communities that for centuries had developed their own modes of authentic social, cultural and linguistic behaviour recover from socio-economic decline and collapse, in the face of globalisation? How do they begin to build new concepts of authen-ticity? The vital empirical question with which sociolinguists should engage is thus 'how do members of communities of practice create through new forms of emergent social interaction new identities and thus perpetuate their practices?' Coupland sees a gap here between 'traditionally-structured social meanings . . . and the outcomes of self-identification processes in social interaction', and he believes that we can see this gap 'as *a performance space*' (ibid.: 428; italics in original). We return, in the next subsection, to the period in which folk song suddenly became a gateway to building new forms of authenticity in the 1960s and the 1970s.

'The Good Ship Authenticity' and the Second Folk Revival

Middleton also insists on the need to investigate how authenticity is produced: 'Authenticity is a quality of selves and of cultures; and they construct each other: which is another way of saying that the question here is not so much what or where authenticity is, but how it is produced' (Middleton 2006: 206). To illustrate how the very opposite has been done in the popular music worlds of the latter half of the twentieth century, he presents the following evocative pastiche:

By the middle of the century, the good ship authenticity – under threat not only from philosophical critiques but also the baleful lessons of fascism and Stalinism – seemed definitely holed below the water, and yet so pressing, still, appeared its demands, as God, reason, progress lay dead or at least unconscious, that in another way it steamed ahead even faster, into the turbulence of the '60s, folk revivals, rock purism, punk nihilism, and world beat just some of its musical manifestations. (ibid.: 218)

In the resurgence of the folk music revival in Britain in the 1950s to the early 1970s,[19] two generations came into conflict: on the one hand, the war-weary opponents of fascism and Stalinism longing to return quietly to the 'authenticity' of a lost bourgeois world of imperial glory, isolated from Europe and its '-isms', the 'parent generation', and on the other hand, their children born during the Second World War or shortly after and growing up in the austerity and shabbiness of late 1940s and 1950s Britain, who began to construct their own alternative yet-to-be-discovered 'authenticities'. In the folk music world, however, there already existed an authenticity, an Other, 'invented' by Herder in the late eighteenth century called the 'Volk', referring to the peasantry (standing symbolically for the dream of a united German nation), but explicitly excluding the urban working classes ('*Volk* does not mean the rabble in the alleys; that group never sings or rhymes, it only screams and truncates' [Herder 1807 (1774): 69, quoted in Bendix 1997: 40]). Herder's view is typical of bourgeois ventriloquism aimed at giving the rural lower-class Other a voice. As we saw earlier in this chapter, this same authenticity was voiced at the end of the nineteenth and the beginning of the twentieth century by Cecil Sharp, i.e. again by a member of the middle classes.

In the late 1950s and 1960s, however, the three major figures in the revival movement were of the 'parent' group, Jimmy Miller (alias Ewan MacColl, born in 1915), A. L. 'Bert' Lloyd (born 1908) and Alan Lomax (born 1915). MacColl and Lloyd were members of the British Communist Party and, although the FBI found no substantial 'incriminating' evidence against him, Lomax had manifestly leftist sympathies. This led to a reclassification of the 'folk' in folk music circles as the labouring classes in general and those Others who were suffering under various forms of oppression from the establishment, e.g. Afro-Americans in the US (cf. Chapter 4) and migrants from the West Indies in Britain.

The pre-1968 generation – those born during or shortly after the war, who spent their teens in the late 1950s – revelled in 'all things American'. The late 1950s and early 1960s were the era of rebellion against the authenticities of the 'parent' generation, e.g. the British imperial dream, splendid isolation from Europe, the quiet 'English' countryside with its village greens and country pubs, with little thought given to Scotland, Wales, Northern Ireland or even the industrial North of England. But for the pre-1968 generation it was *rebellion*, not revolution.

---

[19] 'Resurgence' because, as we made clear earlier in this chapter, it never died but simply disappeared from the public eye. In her acceptance speech for the English Folk Dance and Song Society Gold Badge Award, Maddy Prior used the image of folk song being on an elliptical course around popular music, at times at the greatest distance from it and thus unfashionable, but at present rather closer to it.

At the Ballads and Blues club in the 1950s, then later at the Singers' Club in the 1960s, MacColl and Lloyd and others of the 'parent generation' who had no faith in the old authenticities began to discursively construct the 'authentic' folk singer as a member of the 'people', i.e. all the labouring classes, rural and urban, whose duty it was to seek out the 'authentic', orally transmitted 'heritage' of the people, 'the tradition' as they called it, and to use the burgeoning folk club scene to reinstate the values of this set of authenticities. They failed to realise that it was the music that fascinated the pre-1968 generation, not the responsibility to revive authenticities. In Coupland's words, a gap was thus created between 'traditionally-structured social meanings' of music 'and the outcomes of self-identification processes in social interaction' through music. It was, in other words, a perfect 'performance space', in which folk music and other forms of popular music could be experimented with *outside* the folk club circuit to provide new values and new authenticities.[20]

Instead, within the folk club circuit, as we learn from MacKinnon (1993), Brocken (2003) and Bean (2014), MacColl and Lloyd's insistence on 'the tradition', i.e. a body of 'traditional' folk songs and a postulated 'traditional' way of singing them, seriously insulated folk song from other musical influences and effectively isolated it from the late 1970s to the late 1990s from contact with other musicians and other musics – at least in the folk clubs. A 'traditional' singing style meant singing a cappella without accompaniment and singing in ways determined largely by MacColl with no reference to or concrete knowledge of how the songs might have been sung before the advent of recording technology. It also restricted singers to singing in their own dialects and even prohibited them from singing songs from outside the area in which they had been born and brought up.[21] Small wonder, then, that the 1950s baby-boomer generation that was in its teens around the year 1968 found it easier to relate to the Beatles, the Rolling Stones, Pink Floyd, the Who, etc. than to folk. As we have argued throughout this book, the essence of folk music and folk song is hybridity, not purity. Small wonder, too, that folk groups like Pentangle, Planxty, Fairport Convention, Steeleye Span, the Incredible String Band, the Bothy Band, Clannad and a host of others preferred to arrange concert tours, or have them arranged, and were happier at folk festivals than at folk clubs (cf. Sweers 2005; Young 2010). Sweers has a point when she argues that '[l]ooking back now, thirty years in retrospect, it seems obvious that

---

[20] It is interesting to draw parallels here between the folk circles in the US and in Britain. In both cases the younger performers acknowledged their debt to the parent figures (Pete Seeger or Guthrie and MacColl, Lloyd, Lomax; cf. Bean 2014), but at the same time started to assert themselves and their own approach to the music. So it is hardly surprising that both Pete Seeger and MacColl openly disapproved of Dylan going electric (and abandoning the stance of the protest singer).

[21] MacColl referred to these principles as 'the Policy'.

[MacColl's] ideas would lead to a musical blind alley, spurring many innovative musicians out of the clubs and in many cases into part of what is now known as electric folk' (2005: 219). That the search for authenticity and purism in the mid-1970s also led to an increased focus on entailed answering back (see Chapter 4) eventually prepared the ground for social comment and criticism to be taken over by punk, whose answering back was much more explicit.

A folk song, however, is not to be understood, in an essentialist manner, as a 'song of the people', nor even a 'song for the people', since however we understand the word 'people' – the nation, the working classes, the lower classes, the peasantry, etc. – different kinds of authenticity are built from these understandings that either are no longer valid in the period of globalised late modernity or were always simply phantom instantiations of a lost Other. A song is only a song when it is sung, and the performance of a folk song is a contribution towards the construction of a community. This means, of course, that many kinds of song can become folk songs in performance. But a folk song, however expertly and meticulously it is performed, also has to be performable by others, including, in many performance settings, by the audience. The singer must have the ability to move her/his audience and to allow members of the audience to construct their own authenticities as a community in the performance spaces s/he affords during a performance. To do this, s/he must have enough experience in performing individual songs in different performance contexts, thus authenticating her/himself as a singer. We take up this point in the final section of this chapter.

Adapting a Song to Different Performance Contexts: Authenticating the Singer

Apart from musical crossovers and the injection of new energies from other forms of music (see Chapter 12), the resilience of folk song is also the result of the emergent nature of folk song performance, the fact that a performer will adapt the material in response to the audience and the performance context. We illustrate this with a practical example, 'The Cruel Mother' (Child ballad 20, Roud 9) ☂87. According to Roud and Bishop (2012), this ballad has been 'widely collected in Britain and Ireland, and in North America' and has 'struck a chord with singers over a number of generations'. It is a classic ballad with a burden,[22] which can take a number of forms. In Scottish versions it is often 'hey wi' the rose and the lindie-o' and 'along the green burn sidie-o' (Purslow 1965: 105). In the Hammond MS. version, in the form in which Purslow (ibid.: 22) reprints it, it is 'all alone-y alone-y' and 'down by the greenwood side-y', as

---

[22] The repetition of lines 2 and 4 as, for example, 'parsley sage rosemary and thyme' and 'then s/he'll be a true love of mine' (cf. 'Scarborough Fair').

in Bronson version 4 (1959: 279). In version 1 (1959: 276), it is 'fine flowers in the valley' and 'and the green leaves they grow rarely'.[23]

The story is told in a number of couplets, corresponding to lines 1 and 3 in each stanza of a ballad. If a performer were to adopt this song, it is of course possible to take on any of the many versions. Bronson lists as many as fifty-seven with varying degrees of completeness in the song schema. The singer's choice may be based on which tunes are thought to be particularly appealing, with a large number of Aeolian, Dorian or Aeolian/Dorian mixed modes to choose from, whose haunting melodic quality underlines the effect of the lyrics (see Appendix). The tune may be chosen on its own merits, but another set of lyrics may be more appealing to the singer. Experienced singers may even opt for constructing their text out of the various versions they have access to, either to suit their singing style/language variant or to make the story more accessible in its narrative flow. At the same time, one burden may seem more attractive than another as the best means of offsetting the narrative couplets, which according to Roud and Bishop (2012) is part of the hypnotic quality of this ballad.

For the sake of the argument, we present a set of lyrics telling the entire story without any gaps in the narrative and complemented by a burden that seems to flow quite easily with the Aeolian (minor) tune given by Purslow (1965: 22) and Bronson No. 4 (1959: 279) but that falls more easily into the phrasing of this part of the verse. The full version with textual elements from a variety of versions, mainly based on Purslow's version, but complemented by several Bronson sources, is printed in Table 6.1 with variants.

We now discuss the experience of performing the ballad in three different performance contexts: firstly, as a relational performance in a song gathering, secondly, as a representational performance at a graduation ceremony and, finally, as a representational performance during a literary Halloween soirée to conclude a reading of ghost stories and Gothic poems.

Each of these performances was subject to different conditions. The *song gathering* comprised a seasoned folk audience but was rather large, which made it appropriate not to sing a version with the entire narrative. In keeping with many printed versions, it was necessary to leave out all but the elements that significantly make up the narrative. Since the audience, as part of the folk discourse community, could be assumed to know the story, they could also be expected to fill in the frequent gaps. The performance at the *graduation ceremony* had to be relatively concise for a non-specialist audience, but at the same time it had to be as comprehensive and comprehensible as possible from a narrative point of view. In the performance itself this did not result in fewer but in a different choice of stanzas. Finally, the performance for the audience at

---

[23] The list is by no means exhaustive.

Table 6.1. *Textual variants of 'The Cruel Mother'*

	Main version (mainly based on Hammond)	Alternative elements (mainly from Bronson)
1.	there was a lady lived in York *all alone-y alone-y* she was proved with child by her father's clerk *down by the greenwood/burn sidey-o*	there was a lady in yonder town *fine flowers in the valley* she was courted by her father's clerk *and the green leaves they grow rarely*
2.	she leaned her back against an oak but first it bent and then it broke	
3.	she leaned herself against a thorn and there she had two pretty babesborn	
4.	she had a penknife long and sharp and she pressed it through their tender hearts	
5.	she wiped the knife upon the grass the more she wiped it the blood ran fast	
6.	she washed her hands all in a spring thinking she would be a maiden again	
7.	a) and she was sat at her father's hall oh there she saw two pretty babes playing at ball	b) and as she was going to the church she saw two pretty babes playing in the porch
8.	oh babes sweet babes if you were mine I would dress you up in scarlet fine	
9.	oh mother oh mother we once were thine you did not dress us in scarlet fine	
10.	the coldest earth it was our bed and the green grass was our coverlet	
11.	babes sweet babes come tell me true what's the death I must die for you	
12.	a) seven long years a bird in the wood and seven long years a fish in the flood/brook	b) oh Mother oh Mother for your grave sin heaven's gate you shall not enter in
13.	a) seven long years a tongue in a bell and seven long years a porter in hell	b) there's a fire burning beyond hell's gate where you shall burn both early and late

the literary soirée was also aimed at a non-specialist audience, but as they were prepared to listen to unabridged literary texts, this allowed both a consistent, gapless narrative and a choice of stanzas that presented intriguing concepts and metaphors, especially when describing the mother's punishment. The choice of stanzas sung is represented in Figure 6.1 and is for the most part self-explanatory:

The main difference between the song gathering and the graduation ceremony was that the former audience was part of the discourse community.

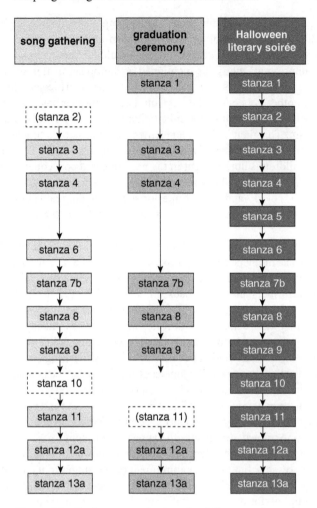

Figure 6.1. *Performance selections for different performance contexts*

In folk circles, the dialogic nature of ballad narrative is well established and expected. But for the non-initiated at a graduation ceremony some of this can be sacrificed to concision, hence the potential exclusion of stanza 11. In the song gathering, if the time factor and the related issue of hogging the floor were not a consideration, stanza 2 and stanza 10 might be sung as well, but stanza 1 might well be deemed unnecessary. For this reason, it does not occur in many versions since the narrative would be understood to refer to an unmarried mother.

All of these aspects – adapting tunes, exchanging elements like the burden/ chorus, adding stanzas from other versions, down-toning or heightening dialectal variants to suit personal singing styles – could be seen as tinkering with the aim of 'improving' the lyrics mentioned at the outset of this section, for which, as we have seen, some collectors have been criticised. Including elements from other versions makes it plain that the mother has given birth to children *out of wedlock* and that the infanticide is a desperate attempt to avoid social ostracism. This then includes an element of addressing a timeless social drama and constitutes a form of answering back to a situation in which the father of the children is non-existent in the narrative and consequently refuses responsibility for his part in the woman's pregnancy. Alternatively, the fact that he is 'her father's clerk' and thus of inferior social standing adds to the social issues underlying the narrative and creates the condition for the desperate situation.

The fact that this is a folk song of some antiquity addressing the discrimination of unmarried mothers could well be interpreted as a social comment on 'real folk' by 'unreal folk', of presumably unauthenticated middle-class singers and performers answering back on behalf of disenfranchised women. But the undoubted appeal of this haunting and hypnotic song successfully demonstrates that the fascination with it lies in its timeless tragedy as well as in the eerie beauty of its melody and lyrics. Hence, the question of expropriation in the face of this fascination becomes manifestly meaningless and irrelevant. A song like this, because of its timeless tragedy, transcends issues of class and 'ownership' as well as narrow-minded purist constructions of tradition and authenticity. In other words, the fact that it is re-entextualised and performed by a singer from outside the original labouring community (if it ever existed in this idealised form) in no way diminishes the appeal of the song.

The authenticity of a song depends not primarily on its longevity or the traditions it represents, but on the commitment of the singer to the creation of a fictive world in which s/he is perceived by the audience as socially involving the whole group, performer(s) and audience. This is as important in relational as in representational performance settings. Our conclusion is that songs are authenticated by and, in turn, authenticate singers in performance events. Although we may search for authenticity in the representation of past traditions, the performance is always in the here-and-now.

'Insects Caught in Amber': Preserving Songs
     in Print, Transcript and Recording

> Literacy and the invention of notation are clearly important factors that may
> generate extended musical structures, but they express differences of degree,
> and not the difference in kind that is implied by the distinction between 'art'
> and 'folk' music.   (Blacking 1973: 9)

Folk Song as a Process or a Product?

The basic idea behind Michael Crichton's novel *Jurassic Park* (1990) is that
scientists have succeeded in recreating long-extinct dinosaurs by extracting
their DNA from blood found in the digestive tract of bloodsucking insects
caught in amber. The notion of gaining access to an ephemeral creature through
a form of preservation is a metaphor that can also be applied to the ways in
which we gain access to songs that have often been in circulation for centuries,
or even of recreating them, like the creatures in Crichton's novel. The insects
caught in amber exemplify individual specimens of countless peers. Folk songs
fixed for posterity through print, musical transcription and recordings, both
sound and film, are, in a similar way, individual instances of potentially
countless performances. The representation of one specific performance may
not be the most typical, but it is nevertheless that on which we may base our
perception of the song in question. Roud makes this point in his Botkin
Lecture[1] (2011) when he talks about indexing a song: 'If a song hasn't been
written down or recorded or in some way *perpetuated* in stone, then I can't
index it. If I . . . hear somebody singing a song, as I walk past, I can't index that
performance . . . because nobody can go back to it. I can only index what's been
documented' (our emphasis).
    As a result, a song becomes accessible to others who need not have been
present at the performance. However, by being perpetuated, that version
achieves a status of 'definitiveness' and acquires the aura of an authoritative

---

[1] The Benjamin Botkin Lectures are held each year at the American Folk Life Center of the Library
    of Congress in Washington.

product, to which we can potentially return at any time and which can serve as a model, albeit a static one, for future adoption (see Chapter 5).

Preservation in Performance and the Perpetuation of Songs

Despite the fact that emergent as well as perpetuated songs available in different versions show variation, they are surprisingly stable when compared with early written records and recent recordings. Conservatism, or preservation, seems to be a characteristic of folk song, but considering a song to be an emergent social process is different from concluding from its preservation that it is a reified object. Songs as processes or songs as products are two very different things. In an idealised oral transmission with *in situ* adoption, the adopters need to rely on their memory for the lyrics and the tune, as these are usually embedded in a community of practice, or diachronically in a discourse community. 'Traditions' of embedding allow potential singers to construct, or reconstruct, the model that they are trying to adopt in a way that, diachronically, is often surprisingly consistent. As Roud (2011) puts it, 'folksong singers are basically conservative, in that they do, more or less, sing what they learned'. This not only applies to the songs themselves but also to folk singing practices in general, which are tacitly accepted among singers practising the craft, but are also explored in the scholarly literature (cf., e.g., Foley 1988; Lord [1960] 2000; Nettl [1983] 2005, etc. Cf. also the oral history as presented by Bean 2014: ch. 8) and pointed out or at least referred to in song collections (Vaughan Williams and Lloyd 1959; Buchan and Hall 1973; Kennedy 1975; Roud and Bishop 2012).

Such songs are emergent within the framework of the 'tradition' of the discourse community and are in keeping with the changing discourse archives of folk performance. Individualistic elements may be added by any one performer but may be lost at the adaptation stage of other singers (cf. Figure 5.1), who either find them difficult to remember or to reconstruct when similar, more current elements are generally available. They may consciously set out to expunge them because the elements in question may be considered inimical to the song – or to 'the tradition'. In language, innovation is likely to be successful if it is striking and meets a communicative need, or in performance if it is conceptually salient but needs to be balanced against the sensitivities of the community and, in folk performance practice, its understanding of tradition.

The conservatism that stems from a printed version, a transcription or recorded source is rather different. Because an individual effort to create a top-quality performance underlies the 'perpetuated' song, producing it reflects, retains and in the final instance potentially passes on individualistic traits to an adopter by virtue of the performance being considered 'authoritative'. As soon as a song is 'caught in amber', singers can return to it if and when the need arises. This also gives those responsible for the perpetuation – the collector, the transcriber, the recording or performing artist – considerable control over the product. They can select, shape and perpetuate conceptions of what they consider to be authentic and representative for the song, the schema or the macro-schema. This may result in a song performance being seen as representative, or even as the 'authentic' song, by potential adopters, rather than the instantiation it actually is. Because of its accessibility and its fixedness, textual variants are likely to be more restricted and to relate to the written or recorded version.

The situation is different with notated tunes as these do not always have precise indications as to phrasing or tempo. In some cases, this is part of the mission statement of a collection. Bishop and Thomson explain their approach to musical notation in Palmer (1972: ix) as follows: 'Our representation of the tunes is intended to help the singer to a deeper interpretation of the songs. We do not wish to impose any arbitrary interpretations and have therefore avoided all but the most essential directions as to tempo and expression.' Roud and Bishop (2012), in keeping with Vaughan Williams and Lloyd (1959), are even more restrained as they give neither 'directions as to tempo' nor indications of 'expression' and only provide the tune. We return to this issue below. Nevertheless, in any songbook the melody remains fixed even if phrasing, tempo and key are adapted by a singer adopting a song. Unless the singer makes a conscious decision to use the melody of another song,[2] variation is likely to be more restrained than it might be in oral transmission where imperfectly heard or remembered tunes may ultimately create distinctly different tunes.

Standardisation

The 'perpetuation' of songs can also be seen as an attempt, particularly with respect to the song collectors of the late Victorian age, to standardise them. This may not have been the collectors' overt intention, but simply what the hegemonic discourse archive of the time dictated to them as the only 'true' and acceptable set of procedures. In sociolinguistics, the nineteenth century in Europe is often seen as the age of language 'standardisation'. $Song_2$ combines the ability of music to generate intense emotional states in both performer and listener with the communicative purpose of languaging, defined in Chapter 1 as 'convey[ing] to the listener enough information with enough pragmatic and affective import to allow him/her to generate meanings and to activate some form of response'. So it is hardly surprising that folk songs also came under the purview of the urge to 'standardise' (cf. Watts 2010).

---

[2] Because of the textual nature of folk songs, setting the words of one to the tune of another is unproblematic, particularly if both melodies share the same basic time signature.

Deumert (2010) points out that 'standardisation' in relation to language has now become one of Ulrich Beck's (2002) 'zombie categories', by which he means 'sociological concepts' that are either empty or are full of outdated, bygone meanings. The fact that terms such as 'standard language', 'standardisation', 'non-standard', etc. are still with us two centuries after they first began to appear indicates that far from being empty, their meanings are still present like 'the living dead, soul-less shells which haunt those alive' (Deumert 2010: 259). The urge to elevate one variety of a 'language' above all others as the only legitimate form for writing, teaching, administrating, etc. was, throughout the nineteenth and far into the twentieth century, a fundamental pillar in constructing the nation-state with one territory, one people, one religion and one language. It is hardly surprising that the variety selected in every effort to standardise a language was that of the socially elite and politically powerful. To call that variety the 'standard', by which all other varieties were judged to be 'defective', was to elevate it as 'the teleological goal of any historical language development' (Mattheier 2010: 354) and to attempt to create a totally homogeneous, unchanging form of language. The history of a language then becomes the history of its standard variety. But we now know that standard varieties also change through time and that their users are not averse to introducing elements from other varieties. Heterogeneity has sociolinguistic precedence over homogeneity.

The early and late Victorian song hunters and collectors were steeped in the ideology of the 'standard' and in the discursive construction of middle-class Victorian social and moral values, both being integral parts of the hegemonic social discourse archive of the time. We might classify this discourse archive as a product of modernism in which the positively valued concept – the 'standard language' – was opposed to a negatively valued and yet always 'desired' Other – in this case, non-standard varieties of the language, dialects, vernacular speech and writing, colloquial speech, etc. Like nineteenth-century writers on the history of English, Victorian song hunters used the same kinds of metaphor. For example, Henry Welsford in his book *On the Origin and Ramifications of the English Language* (1845) expresses the emergence of standard English from 'other' forms of language in terms of an extended geographical/geological metaphor:

The Sanskrit may be regarded as the pure *fountainhead*: the *streams which flowed from it* remained long in a troubled state from the turbulence of the middle ages, till, having found a *more spacious and secure channel*, they have gradually *deposited the dregs* of the Frankish, the Anglo-Saxon, the Cimbric, and the Celtic and reappeared in the beautiful languages of Montesquieu and Racine, Goete [sic] and Schiller, of Byron and Scott. (1845: 259; our italics)

A similar metaphor is used by Sabine Baring-Gould in an introductory essay to one of the eight volumes of his *English Minstrelsie* (1895–97) and is quoted by Hitchcock (1974) in his posthumous selection of songs collected by Baring-Gould, entitled *Folk Songs of the West Country*:

Our folk music is *a veritable moraine of rolled and ground fragments from musical strata far away*. It contains songs of many centuries, *all thrown together in a confused heap*. What are the origins of these songs? It is impossible to say but some are ballads that have been handed down by minstrels and troubadours of many continents; archaic melodies from before the Golden Age of Elizabeth. (in Hitchcock 1974: 7; our italics)

Both folk songs and the standard language were conceptualised as important parts of the English (rather than British) national heritage. The major difference was, as we saw in Chapter 6, that collectors like Sharp, Baring-Gould and others perceived 'rural' folk song culture to be rapidly disappearing, if not already dead – a demonstrably false assumption. But in contrast to the 'struggle' to assert the standard language as superior to the linguistic Other, a struggle ultimately doomed to failure but still being played out today, the assumption that folk song culture was dead or dying enabled the collectors to 'save' the songs for a (middle-class) posterity and 'justified' their attempts to edit out 'unseemly' themes and language. Publishing edited folk song lyrics and musical arrangements suitable for WAM concert performances as a means of perpetuating the songs was an attempt to standardise them, i.e. to homogenise them as products. Folk song as process rather than product, however, is always open to change, heterogeneity and hybridity.

Further Ideologies

Any debate on standardisation can only be carried on with knowledge of the ideological sub-structures that justify the elevation of one variety of language above all others. We have argued that the same is true for folk song, where we are faced with a body of songs, some of them relatively widely known and frequently sung, constituting standardised material acceptable for inclusion in a song collection. The criteria for inclusion have varied over time, but their impact on what is included and what is deliberately excluded or consciously edited to attain 'standard' status should not be underestimated.

Harker's (1985) account of song collecting from the eighteenth century to the second half of the twentieth century shows this clearly, but his ideological stance is persistently Marxist. Every generation of song collectors has been subject to ideas concerning the value of, the need to preserve or the motivation for collecting folk songs, popular songs or songs of the (common) people. Their views have informed their activities, and they have had an impact on the rationale behind the songs being of interest in the first place, what or whom the song hunters sought out as their sources, what they deemed worthy of inclusion, what they thought needed to be done to the songs to standardise them and make them worthy of preservation.

Harker calls the collectors 'mediators' who, in publishing their works, had a vested interest in conveying their ideas to their middle-class readers. These ideas ranged from nationalistic motivations in some of the 'early mediators', i.e. the search for a nation's original lyrical soul (particularly in the case of Sir Walter Scott), the search for 'pure' folk poetry for Francis James Child (arguably influenced by German Romanticism), the longing for a pre-industrial arcadia among the late Victorians (cf. Chapter 6) and the left-of-centre bias of the latter half of the twentieth century, which tended to favour, though not exclusively, explicit modes of answering back.[3]

But apart from ideological considerations, in the eighteenth and nineteenth centuries an identifiable commercial interest played a role in the selection of material deemed fit for inclusion. Song publication aimed at a largely middle-class public that could afford and would buy music for pleasure and was financially rewarding, but it had to be tailored to suit the audience. Whether the target audience was all male, mainly female or mixed required different criteria for selection. Even Joseph Ritson (1752–1803), who, more than his contemporaries, was intent on presenting an accurate and honest picture of what the songs of the people were like,[4] has this to say in the introduction to the first volume of his *A Select Collection of English Songs*: 'Throughout the whole of the first volume, the utmost care, the most scrupulous anxiety has been shewn to exclude every composition, however celebrated, or however excellent, of which the slightest expression, or the most distant allusion could have tinged the cheek of Delicacy, or offended the purity of the chastest ear' (Ritson 1783: v).

Selection of material is one way of acting on an ideology underlying a given collection, as is the effort to represent the songs of a particular region or era. Another is editing and emendation. The motivations for these activities were often stated to be the improvement of the 'poor' quality of the material from incomplete or partially destroyed manuscripts. In other cases, the texts themselves were bowdlerised to remove erotic or otherwise non-suitable content and are thus striking examples of song standardisation. We discuss such practices in more detail in the following section.

---

[3] John Tams, for instance, preferred 'industrial songs [to] the elfin knights on milk-white steeds and the whack-fol-de-dols' (quoted in Bean 2014: 141).

[4] According to Harker, he was unusual among his competitors in pointing out what had been emended in his collections.

Types of Amber

For methodological reasons, we have decided to define three broad categories for the perpetuation of folk songs: (1) print with a focus on text reproduction including the simple musical notation of many songbooks; (2) transcription, mainly of music and lyrics; and (3) recordings, both audio and video. This simplifies the methodological intricacies in the history of song collection and reproduction, and it has the advantage that general tendencies can be more easily described.

Preservation in Print

There is a long history of collecting popular songs in print, not all of which were songs of the lower classes. At the outset, in the late sixteenth and seventeenth centuries, there was little interest in the antiquarian approach that characterised later collectors. Many of these collections were not meant to be scholarly works of folklore, as the title page of Thomas D'Urfey's *Wit and Mirth, or Pills to Purge Melancholy* (1698–1720) outlines:

Songs Compleat, / Pleasant and Divertive; / SET TO M U S I C K / By Dr. John Blow, Mr. Henry Purcell, / and other Excellent Masters of the Town. / Ending with some Orations, made and spoken by me several times upon the Publick Stage in the Theater. Together with some Copies of Verses, Prologues, and Epilogues, as well for my own Plays as those of other Poets, being all Humerous [sic] and Comical.

In fact, we would be hard pressed to find much in the way of traditional material in D'Urfey's collection although certain songs in later collections, e.g. Roud and Bishop (2012), are more obviously derived from folk songs that can be traced back to this collection.

Nevertheless, *Pills to Purge Melancholy* and other collections of this early period, in the seventeenth to the early nineteenth century, contained a mixture of material, some penned by the editors, as well as some traditional songs that were often edited and emendated by the collectors. As we have seen, Joseph Ritson, vociferous in his criticism of Bishop Percy's practice of adding and editing in his *Reliques of Ancient English Poetry*, was a notable exception here. Percy's approach to collecting and publishing songs is typical for the period, based, as he claims, on a manuscript found in the servants' quarters at his friend Humphrey Pitt's residence. However, the folio was incomplete and in a bad state as it had been partially used to light fires, and Percy's reliance on this 'authentic' source was limited. According to Harker (1985: 33), out of the 180 ballads that the *Reliques* contain, 'perhaps only thirty texts were genuinely "extracted" from the MS'. The rest came from other sources and from a variety of publications, some rather less 'ancient' than the title suggests.

Percy himself is known to have written or rewritten a substantial amount, partly because he was unconvinced by the quality of the source manuscript and partly because he felt the need to 'polish' the material to meet the social pretensions of the buying public.[5] The focus on the 'reader of taste and genius' indicates that the intended readership was middle-class and learned, in keeping with the social and moral principles of the dominant hegemonic discourse archive of the time (cf. the discussion in the subsection 'Further Ideologies' above). This was a collection not for singing but for reading, satisfying the widespread interest in such songs both in Scotland and England at the time as part of a national literary heritage. Percy never attended song performances in compiling his collection. But despite their concentration on text and their reliance on printed or written sources, Percy's *Reliques* were still considered a milestone in song collecting and proved an inspiration for a variety of young writers and poets including Sir Walter Scott, whose own collection of ballads, *Minstrelsy of the Scottish Border*, represented a further pivotal collection of folk song material.

Like Percy, Scott mentions tunes and singers, but he is principally focused on the words. His object was not so much to preserve the songs of the Border area as to see them embedded in a culture and a history, which he laid out in some detail in what he claims were 'hasty sketches of border history' on page xlv of his 'Introduction'. He, too, saw the ballads and songs he collected as textual artefacts rather than living and breathing songs. So it is no surprise that his *Minstrelsy* provides no music. He was also a keen editor of his material as Francis Child's introduction to 'Clerk Saunders'[6] attests:

Clerk Saunders was first given to the world in the *Minstrelsy of the Scottish Border*, and was there said to be 'taken from Herd's MS.[7] with several corrections from a shorter and more imperfect copy in the same volume, and one or two conjectural emendations in the arrangement of the stanzas.' Sir Walter arranged his ballad with much good taste, but this account of his dealing with Herd's copies is far from precisely accurate. (Child, in Sargent and Kittredge 1904: 142)

The quotation indicates that Scott, in keeping with the practice of the day, edited and emended his material and amalgamated versions if necessary, especially if this meant that the final product would be 'better' in terms of the narrative cohesion and story logic, but also in terms of standardised song and ballad poetics.

Child himself, although like Scott more interested in texts than songs, is meticulous about including ballad fragments, sometimes so minimal that we

---

[5] The 'Advertisement to the Fourth Edition' indicates that Percy was at pains to defend his work against critics as being 'a work which hath been admitted into the most elegant libraries; and with which the judicious antiquary hath just reason to be satisfied, while refined entertainment hath been provided for every reader of taste and genius' (Percy, as reprinted in Rhys 1906: 2).

[6] Child ballad 69.   [7] Another important collector and contemporary of Percy.

occasionally need to question the grounds on which they are attributed to a particular ballad. His interest is scholarly, literary and philological, and, as an American, he hardly shares Percy's or Scott's nationalist motivations. He did, however, have a mission. In the introduction to the first volume he writes: 'What was once the possession of the folk as a whole, becomes the heritage of the illiterate only, and soon, unless it is gathered up by the antiquary, vanishes altogether' (Child, in Sargent and Kittredge 1904: xii). This places him in the position of the scholarly antiquarian and preserver of something that seemed doomed to disappear. For him, balladry was a relic of a lost Other, a testimony of 'a time when there were no formal divisions of literate and illiterate; when the intellectual interests of all were substantially identical, from the king to the peasant' (ibid.), i.e. the relic of a lost golden era of classlessness. His collection is considered definitive to the point that ballads are still referred to by the number Child allocated to them. But, like Percy and Scott, he did not record any tunes.[8]

Because most early song collectors were not interested in the songs as performances (song as process) but as texts (song as product), they often refer to their sources, if not members of the polite middle classes, obliquely and generically, e.g. 'a woman from ... ' or 'a blacksmith' (Harker 1985: 66–67). Middle-class informants, however, were not singers but were in possession of a song in written form, heard from a servant, a nurse or a rustic contact, or from a manuscript. Many songs were consequently taken from a written source or someone else's collection. The typical mediators were not in the habit of observing song performances as this would have meant coming into direct social contact with members of the lower classes. But it would be unwise not to acknowledge the importance of these collections. Just as Child relied on earlier collections, later anthologies, e.g. the *Faber Book of Ballads* or anthologies of poetry that contain a section of anonymous poems (mostly traditional ballads), drew from these sources. But like their sources, they are not aimed at singers or intended for future performance; they are meant exclusively for literary study and scholarly scrutiny.

The situation is somewhat different for the vast stock of lyrics available on the internet. Unlike many of the printed sources discussed above, these are not aimed at a reading public but at potential adopters, especially websites with folk song lyrics. One example, Mudcat.org, online since 1996, is particularly interesting in this context. It grew out of an earlier initiative called Digital Tradition (dating back to pre-World Wide Web days in 1988) and was originally blues-focused as the term 'mudcat', the name for a Mississippi delta catfish, suggests. It is a repository of song lyrics as well as an online forum whose members can place requests for lyrics. There are often animated discussions about variants

---

[8] This deficit was rectified considerably later by Bronson (1959–72), who made the significant point that 'a ballad [is] not a ballad ... [w]hen it has no tune' (Bronson 1959: ix).

and meanings of songs or individual words. Such websites are also different from printed collections in that they may have the tunes as MIDI files, ranging from a simple melody line to quite sophisticated arrangements, which indicates that the sites themselves are meant for potential performers.

Despite their restrictions, however, older eighteenth- and nineteenth-century song collections still continue to be a source for singers and performers. Like the broadsides, which also used song lyrics that had already appeared in collections, they represented (and still represent) points of orientation, something to work from, particularly in the pre-internet days. Both Martin Carthy and Maddy Prior[9] have acknowledged their debt to them but are also quite prepared to construct their own versions of an old song by amalgamating versions from different sources and to edit the material, just as the older song collectors did (cf. our discussion of 'The Cruel Mother' in Chapter 6 and our argument in Chapter 12). The motivation, however, is different as the editing is always oriented towards performance. Two issues are usually addressed: firstly, the length of many printed texts makes them impracticable in a contemporary performance context; secondly, many of the songs contain elements that are not Standard English – unless the collectors changed their material with a view to a greater marketability. Both informants acknowledge that they edit the language in the printed sources to varying degrees to suit their own variant. Carthy, as a Londoner, goes so far as to say that before he sings a Child ballad, especially one of Scots origin, he 'completely dismantles' and then reassembles it because to sing it in fake Scots is not an option.[10]

Much of the printed material, especially where it appears without a melody, represents a form of perpetuation that suggests definitiveness thanks to antiquity. Many collectors edited and emendated with the aim of bringing out the literary merit of these 'rough diamonds' or 'poor remnants', often with the aim of presenting the definitive versions, restoring what they considered had been corrupted at the hands of the illiterate and standardising them by expunging the bawdy and low. But the ideological mindset of the collectors and the fact that they lacked faith in the aesthetic abilities of their lower-class sources (with the notable exception of Robert Burns) make it extremely unlikely that they ever had any social interaction with them. As a result, these song perpetuations are stylised and often overly polished chunks of amber whose insects, as a result, are difficult to discern.

Preservation in Notation

Collectors whose focus was on music needed to rely on their informants much more directly than the compilers of printed texts. Songs in pre-recording days

---

[9] In an interview with F.A.M.   [10] We shall return to this issue in Chapter 10.

could only be accessed in direct contact with the singers. But judging by what song collectors tell us, access did not normally take place in those environments in which the singers naturally performed the songs, i.e. in the context of singing within a community of practice or while working. They appear rather to have been taken down under artificial conditions on a one-to-one basis. Lord ([1960] 2000: 124–30) recounts some of the difficulties in noting down the words of his epic singers, in particular how the relatively slow process of notation (textual or musical) can be reconciled with the speed of the performance. Although Lord is referring here to taking down the words of his performers, the process for doing this with music is much the same. One way around the issue of divergent speed in performance and transcription is to ask a singer to sing the same song repeatedly and to compile the transcription during this serial performance. But the main stumbling block is that '[i]n a truly oral tradition of song there is no guarantee that even the apparently most stable "runs" will always be word-for-word the same in performance' (ibid.: 125). Obviously, the wording of a song influences the durations of the musical notes (cf. the discussion below).

The problem for the ethnomusicologist is familiar to the phonetician and conversation analyst: any attempt to translate sound into writing involves choices of what to include and what to leave out. This becomes obvious when we choose between phonemic and phonetic transcription, and in the latter a further choice between narrow and wide transcription. Theoretically, prac-tised phoneticians should be able to read a narrow transcription correctly even if they are not familiar with the language transcribed. But the more diacritics that are used in a transcription, the more demanding it will be to read. It remains doubtful whether even very narrow transcriptions can ever truly reflect the idiolectal peculiarities of an individual performance. By contrast, phonemic transcription presupposes that the basic phonemes of the language transcribed are familiar to a reader and ignores all allophonic/idiolectal details.

The dilemma in ethnomusicology is very similar. Unless we are looking at sheet music, the performance pre-dates the score. On the macro-level, this creates the problem that a transcriber needs to transfer a four-dimensional experience into a linear notation. On the micro-level of the song, how do we notate the differences between stanzas, when in performance the number of unstressed syllables between the stresses may vary and the main downbeats of a bar may require different note values from stanza to stanza? Sachs (1962: 31, as quoted in Nettl [1983] 2005: 76) sums the problem up succinctly: 'No musical script can ever be a faithful mirror of music.'

We illustrate this with the first eight bars of stanzas 1 and 3 of the Scottish song 'Johnny My Man' ☯88, which reveal a number of issues that arise in notating this song. The following transcript is based on the notation in *Tocher*

1.[11] Some assumptions on our part had to be made for the notation given here as the source gives a full transcript for stanza 3 but only isolated bars that differ from that stanza in the remaining stanzas.

1. Johnnie my man dae ye no think o risin

   the nicht it's weel spen(t) an the time's wearin on ...

3. Johnnie my man oor bairns is aa greetin

   nae meal in the barrel tae fill their wee wames ...

As far as prosody goes, there are relatively few differences between the excerpts: the second foot in line 1 of stanza 1 is dactylic and trochaic in stanza 3, whereas the second stressed syllable in the second line is monosyllabic (*spent*) in stanza 1 and disyllabic (*barrel*) in stanza 3. The musical notation, however, displays greater differences between the two stanza openings, apart from the fact that the first stanza starts with a somewhat different melody, whose higher notes may be there to heighten the drama:

Johnnie My Man
1st eight bars of verses 1 and 3

trad.

[11] The song is listed as having been recorded from Lizzie Higgins, Aberdeen, in January 1970.

1a consists of two syllables with relatively short vowels, whereas 1b has a long vowel followed by sonorant, which makes this a rather longer syllable that can easily be slurred.[12] In 2a there is a relatively short monophthong in Scottish pronunciation (*no*) followed by *think* with a short vowel and a nasal, allowing for the note on the vowel to be tied. By contrast, 2b has a long vowel in *bairns* and two sonorants /r/ and /n/, which provides leeway for ornamentation with grace notes before each slurred note that the vowel is sung over. Contrary to 2a, the main unstressed syllables that follow the stressed *bairns* are both short and should therefore be sung staccato, not slurred. 3a and 3b differ in terms of vowel quality: *nae* is clearly longer than *the*, which is why it can be sung over a triplet rather than two equal notes, highlighting the absence of food at home while the husband is drinking. In 4a and 4b there are two short vowels (*meal* likely to be short in Scots), but in 4a the stressed word *nicht* marks the end of a phrase, whereas *meal* in 4b is post-modified by a prepositional phrase and requires a different prosody reflected in the change from 3/4 to 2/4 time signature. Because of the syllabic regularity in the feet (both dactylic), it would seem that the missing beat of the 2/4 bar is then made up in the following bar, which is in 4/4 before the music returns to the original 3/4 time signature. 5a and 5b have already been discussed as they represent a difference in the metre (the monosyllabic *spent* vs a disyllabic *barrel*). The last elements to be compared are the words *and the* in 6a, both with reduced vowels and thus sung on a short note, with *tae* in 6b being potentially longer and thus sung over a triplet.

With such a detailed analysis we might assume that the musical notation would reflect Lizzie Higgins' singing fairly accurately, but it still cannot represent what the anonymous contributor notes about her performance: 'She sings it very slowly and lingers on the sung consonants, notably m, n and l, especially at the end of a word' (Munroe 1971: 17). It is perfectly possible, if somewhat idiosyncratic, to rely on sonorants (potential syllabic peaks in their own right) to carry the tune, but notation cannot represent this. It is also difficult to represent the changes in tempo and timing typical of unaccompanied singing, which the changes in the time signatures in the third stanza illustrate. The time signatures in line 3, which is not represented here, are even more complex with a 3/4 bar followed by a 4/4, then another 3/4, with the fourth bar in 5/4 time, which has the effect of heightening the drama as the last line of each stanza is crucial to the content of the song. Two of the four stanzas end in the words 'arise up my Johnnie an come awa hame' with the final variation in stanza 4 'fareweel tae ye whisky for I'll awa hame'. But even with these time signature changes to account for the variations in the performance of a folk singer, the notation is only an approximation as the editor's notes on lines 2 and

---

[12] Two different notes sung in succession without renewed attack are said to be *slurred*.

3 suggest: 'The high D in measure 1 of lines 2 and 3 is arrived at earlier, as a method of emphasising a word and heightening the emotion' (ibid.). The editors of *Tocher* are aware of such notational difficulties. Bruford and MacDonald preface the first issue with the information that '[t]he staff music notation . . . represents the tune of the first verse, which should indicate the *basic shape* of later verses' (*Tocher* 1971; emphasis added).[13]

This discussion illustrates some of the problems that a linguist may come across in a detailed transcription: the more meticulous the attention to intricacies in the performance, the more difficult it is to read the transcript.[14] This questions the function which musical notation needs to or can fulfil. While it might be desirable to capture the details of an individual song performance on paper, the difficulties of this highly descriptive approach remain. Charles Seeger (1958) 'identified two purposes of musical notation: one provides a blueprint for the performer, and the other records in writing what actually occurred in sound' (Nettl [1983] 2005: 77). Seeger uses the term 'prescriptive transcription' to designate a 'blueprint for the performer', whereas 'descriptive transcription' is meant to give the detailed analysis of what 'actually occurred in sound'. Here we have a parallel to phonemic and phonetic transcription, a point Nettl makes. A reader of phonemic transcription needs to know the phoneme repertoire of a given language; the reader of a 'prescriptive' notation has to be familiar with the performance practices of a given type of music or song; the readers of a 'descriptive' score or narrow phonetic transcription may receive more information about the 'sounds' produced, but they need to be aware of the limitations of each set of writing conventions and that both are the result of choices made by the transcribers.

For practical purposes, a highly 'descriptive' score *pace* Seeger may well create problems for an adopter as its complexity limits its usefulness to all but the initiated. In addition, many folk singers do not read music, or only rudimentarily, and even a relatively simple notation may be challenging. For this reason, most anthologies and songbooks contain little more than an elementary notation for one verse, and singers are expected to adapt the tune to the prosodic variations of the other verses. Learning a song from such minimal input may give an adopter little guidance, but it does provide considerable

---

[13] Lea Hagmann has attracted our attention to the following quotation from Ewan MacColl that aptly sums up singers' reactions to the need to retain variability from performance to performance: 'Folksingers tend to alter melodies at each performance with the result that the tunes are always in a state of flux. . . . A singer may, if he chooses, give more attention to the story than to the musical line; or he may concentrate on the tune, explore it, adding here and subtracting there as the mood takes him.' (*Travellers' Songs from England and Scotland*, p. 17).

[14] But it remains questionable to what degree the result can convey the sum of the performance. The same applies to the musicologist. Bartók, according to Nettl, provided 'incredibly detailed transcriptions of Eastern European folk songs . . . but even this master with the infallible ear didn't have symbols for many aspects of singing style' (Nettl 2005 [1983]: 78).

freedom to create a personalised version of the song in the process of singing. It represents Seeger's 'prescriptive' notation and thus requires adopters who are familiar with the practices of song performance, either to emulate them in their adaptation or to deviate deliberately from the tradition, an issue we discuss in more detail in the following subsection.

Preservation in Recordings

Returning to the metaphor of insects in amber, we can say that in most cases printed texts represent the least typical specimen of the actual insect, given the need to prepare it for inspection by a reading public. If there is one element that most of the printed sources share, it is the overt reliance on 'common folk' sources, tempered with a strong mistrust in their ability to do folk art justice. Musical notation, especially if it is 'descriptive', represents something closer to an actual performance, to *one* instantiation, although the outcome may well be a carefully edited product on the part of the transcriber based on several repetitions by the singer. The process of narrow transcription is, after all, very slow. More choices are required, and a greater abstraction results in the case of 'prescriptive' musical or in-song compilation that gives the tune a model for adaptation in all stanzas. Both forms of preservation (musical or in-song) are examples of medial transfer, from sung performance to paper, from oral to written, with all the implications inherent in this transfer.

The advent of the gramophone and radio, and then, at a later point in time, portable recording devices, especially tape recorders, marked a significant change in the perpetuation of songs by allowing a listener and/or adopter access to a performance without the need to be physically present. But recording and playback also paved the way for a shift from music production to music reception. Up to the early years of the twentieth century, if music was required, it had to be produced *in situ*. As a consequence, the First World War was the last to lead to bursts of musical production by the soldiers themselves (cf., e.g., Palmer 1990 and Pegler 2014; also Andres Morrissey in preparation).

When assessing the impact of recordings on song perpetuation, we need to be aware of the many different forms the recordings can take. In this subsection, we present a brief discussion of the various types, from simple field recordings via studio productions to audio-visual musical performances. They all share some features, but also differ from each other quite significantly. As far as pure audio recordings go, we can distinguish between simple field recordings with portable recording devices under relatively primitive conditions, which are primarily of interest to the ethnomusicologist or the folklorist, and potentially much more polished studio productions, with 'live' recordings somewhere between the two, both aimed at a record-buying public.[15] A similar situation exists with audio-visual material, although the complexity of recording performances requires more personnel to carry it out (at the very least a sound technician and a camera operator). At the end of the spectrum, we have the production of 'music videos', which typically mimic rather than represent the performance. However, in both fields, audio and audio-visual production, the arrival of computers and the internet have made a huge difference in three ways: (1) they have shifted control over musical output away from large production companies and their gatekeeping function and passed it on to the performers themselves; (2) they have allowed performers to become their own marketing managers (although big business, now in the shape of online distribution, still takes a large share of the market, e.g. iTunes[16]); and (3) they have provided platforms that bypass conventional sales channels (e.g. high-street shops), making the products available to a public that often expects them to be free.[17]

From the perspective of capturing music for posterity, *field recordings* are not subject to the concerns of 'printed' or 'transcribed' perpetuation. They appear to represent an actual performance in its most natural form, but there are two caveats here, one familiar to conversation analysts, the other inherent in the recording situation. How do we ensure that recorded data reliably represent natural linguistic behaviour, i.e. a performance that is not affected by the very fact that it is being recorded? This is the same problem we encounter in sociolinguistics when trying to find real, 'authentic' language data. It is also true of field recordings, particularly if they do not take place in a natural performance environment, but on a one-to-one basis. The unforced recall of song lyrics may be affected by the untypical recording situation.[18] The issue of *accommodation* or *audience design* may come into play when informants tailor their performance to suit what they think the collector expects. Recordings of Sam Larner's or Harry Cox's song performances reveal a much closer affinity to a regional form of standard English than the conversation recorded between the songs, when both singers' Norfolk dialect becomes very pronounced and difficult to understand for the uninitiated.

---

[15] We use the term 'record' to denote audio recordings including shellacs, vinyls, cassettes, CDs and, more recently, downloads, all of which are of commercial interest to a distributor and/or a performer.

[16] In this context, https://www.apple.com/itunes/working-itunes/sell-content/music-faq.html (accessed 5 April 2015) makes very instructive reading.

[17] The last point represents a diametrically different approach to marketing in popular music. Touring used to be one way of promoting an album, whereas now albums are a marketing tool for tours. According to a festival organiser of our acquaintance, this means that newcomers, whose debut album has been very successful, rarely have enough material for a concert of more than the duration of that album.

[18] F.A.M. recalls a conversation with a collector reporting an informant who claimed he would remember the missing lines of a song if he were working in a field at that point in time.

If the field recording takes place on a one-to-one basis, the performance becomes representational rather than relational, as there is no real community present to address. *Live recordings* are similar to field recordings in the sense that they also represent an instantiation caught on a recording device, obviously with a focus on representational performance, but with the relational aspect of interaction with an audience (cf. the videos of Maddy Prior's concert at Cecil Sharp House). However, perhaps the performance space is such that audience interaction is drastically reduced, and the *communitas* is played to rather than constituting an inherent part of the performance, thus minimising the difference between a folk song performance and any other popular music performance.

Live recordings, then, lie somewhere between a field recording made primarily for research purposes and the somewhat contrived *studio recording*. Here, too, there is a gradient of possibilities. The Beatles' first album *Please Please Me* with its fourteen songs was recorded in live performances over a mere twelve hours, whereas guitarist Tom Scholz (with producer John Boylan, singer Brad Delp, drummer Sib Hashian and a number of session musicians) spent from October 1974 until April 1975 on the eight songs of Boston's debut album *More than a Feeling*.[19] In live studio recording, the musicians can bounce their individual performances off their fellow musicians, thus creating a musical group performance, albeit one without an audience, but for the musician overdubbing track after track the feeling of communal music-making, let alone playing for an audience, is largely surrogate. In folk recordings a similar spectrum may obviously exist, but the fact that many of the early folk recordings required little more than a small studio and two microphones made them an interesting proposition for the record companies, Dylan and Columbia being a case in point. To give a further example, The Dubliners formed in the quartet line-up with lead vocalists Luke Kelly and Ronnie Drew in 1962 on the Dublin pub circuit, and they recorded their debut album in 1963, at the instigation of producer Bill Leader, in front of a live audience at the Livingstone Studios in London.[20] Once folk performers went for more complex arrangements, particularly involving electric instruments, the studio, with its production possibilities, gained in importance. But whether recorded 'live' or with modern studio technology, where recording can take less time than editing, recordings require a range of choices to be made by performers in the absence of an audience and without its feedback. Such choices effect style and stylisation in line with Bell's (1984) discussion of mass media. We discuss such issues in greater detail in Chapters 10 and 12.

---

[19] This has led to it being described as 'one of the most complex corporate capers in the history of the music business' (Daley 2000).

[20] For more information, in particular the liner notes of various issues of the first Dubliners album, see http://itsthedubliners.com/dubs_d21_with_Luke.htm, accessed 8 April 2015.

To conclude this subsection, we turn to the audio-visual perpetuation of folk songs. Filmed performances come in a variety of guises, including the highly stylised staging of chart shows like the British *Top of the Pops*, which has occasionally featured folk artists (Ralph McTell with 'Streets of London', or Fiddler's Dram's 'Daytrip to Bangor' ☉89). But the promotional video of Steeleye Span's 'All Around My Hat' ☉90 also looks as though it would fit into the mould of sleek staging mimed to a recording that the audience would be familiar with, i.e. the studio recordings played on the radio. The format of the music video or 'promotional clip' had been around for some time, but it became a welcome tool for the Beatles when their and George Martin's elaborate arrangements outgrew what they could credibly perform on stage and when they had grown tired of relentless touring. Rather than appearing live on *The Ed Sullivan Show* to promote their new singles, they had lavish promotion films produced, 'Paperback Writer' being the first,[21] featuring shots of them playing and singing but conspicuously without amplifiers and microphones. With the advent of MTV in 1981, playing music videos around the clock,[22] the genre moved into an ever more stylishly produced format where the visuals put musical performance into second place. But because of the soaring production costs, such promotional videos were clearly not for folk musicians. Offerings on film were VHS-cassettes and, later, DVDs of concerts, but, again because of production costs, they were mainly concert footage by electric folk acts or were otherwise taken from television specials, often before a live audience. In other words, unlike the highly stylised pseudo-performances typical of chart shows on TV or music videos, audio-visual perpetuation of folk songs was and is very much a case of representational performances caught on film. Traditionally they were marketed and on sale in shops or at concerts. Online video platforms such as YouTube and Vimeo have dramatically changed audio-visual perpetuation, since many of these filmed performances can now be watched, in varying degrees of quality, for free. Audio recordings are also available online, often with minimal animation, sometimes only a static image of the album cover, but it is possible to access many recorded songs on these channels and to convert them into MP3s for home use.

Parallel to the development of home-made audio recordings, YouTube and related video platforms also afford non-commercial artists and amateurs the opportunity to use their computer webcams to record audio-visual folk song performances. These are somewhat raw and often lack sophistication, but they are perhaps the most 'authentic' performances and thus prime examples of

---

[21] www.youtube.com/watch?v=qf5Eclt6, accessed 28 November 2017.

[22] Famously the first offering was the slickly produced 'Video Killed the Radio Star' by the Buggles (https://www.youtube.com/watch?v=W8r-tXRLazs, accessed 23 November 2017), a further refinement from their mimed 1978 appearance on *Top of the Pops* (https://www.youtube.com/watch?v=ngZ7F7isIZE, accessed 7 April 2015).

insects caught in amber. They also demonstrate, perhaps more honestly than other forms of electronic perpetuation, the multimedial nature of folk song performance comparable to 'floor singing', where virtuoso musical ability and a professional degree of competence in performance are of minor importance, with the consequence that there are some rather impressive achievements alongside rather less convincing ones. The main but crucial difference is the spatio-temporally removed audience and, as a result, the rather unnatural performance situation that we have observed in other instances of recordings, particularly studio recordings.

At the beginning of this section, we made the point that printed and transcribed sources, in contrast to recorded material, represented a medial transfer and an abstraction from the performance on which they were based. This is true to a certain extent for studio recordings and for the stylisation of the music video, a rare occurrence in folk music. Such instances of recording require a considerable degree of conscious and painstaking design, comparable to what would be required of the careful editing and the conscious choices made for print editions or sheet music compilations of folk songs. These choices reflect what the mediators intend to include but also what their work cannot disclose, i.e. all the elements that the medial transfer excludes from the medium of the printed page. This problem does not occur in recorded perpetuation. For the potential adopter, the lyrics of the songs as well as their lyrical and musical phrasing, ornamentation in singing, tempo, level, etc., are in evidence, which may create the impression that a recorded version of a performance is definitive in ways other forms of perpetuation are not. Subsequent performances may well be judged against the 'benchmark' of an iconic recorded version by a performer considered to be authoritative or particularly 'authentic' (cf. the discussion of Joan Baez's version of 'Geordie' in Chapter 5). In addition, the rendition of the lyrics may come to be regarded as definitive, and this may have an impact on the perception of the speech/singing style in which a particular song should be sung. Finally, depending on the clarity of the recording and/or the language competence of a prospective transcriber of the words, the lyrics may be rendered somewhat differently from the way they were sung by the performer. These and other aspects are discussed briefly in the following section, which looks at the impact these forms of perpetuation have on future performances.

Perpetuation and Transmission

The final question we need to address in this chapter is how perpetuation in print, transcription and recording affects the process of transmission. The discussion so far has indicated that all forms of perpetuation open up transmission to spheres beyond the original performance community. Local songs become interregional, if not – with the persistent popularity of all things Celtic – international.[23] This raises the issue of how the phonological elements of a local song translate into the variant of the receiving culture, an aspect we discuss in more detail in Chapter 9.

We can consider forms of perpetuation primarily as the cultural artefacts that they undoubtedly are and were seen to be by the collectors or mediators of songs as poetry or as pieces of music reproduced in print. But for us their role as a starting point for transmission, as indicated in Figure 5.1, is of greater interest. What do these various forms of perpetuation offer an adopter? Clearly, the trans-medial forms of print and musical transcription present greater freedom for adoption and, in the absence of a model of performance, greater leeway in how to adapt a song to a singer's repertoire. The printed source may invite an adopter to emulate the early collectors and produce a textual version from several sources, perhaps even to meet an ideological agenda that the adopter may have (cf. our discussion of 'The Cruel Mother' in Chapter 6). This pick-and-mix approach may also apply to the music. Often ballads, broadsides or songs by known or anonymous writers are indicated in collections as 'to the tune of . . .'. Many World War I soldiers' songs used hymn tunes, children's songs or the choruses of popular music hall songs for their new anti-authoritarian lyrics. But even if adopters use sheet music, or more recently its translation into a midi file, or if they seriously try to come to terms with the complicated nature of 'descriptive' notation (in Seeger's 1958 terminology), the medial transfer from page to stage is likely to result in a much freer adaptation than would be the case, for example, for a WAM score. This freedom may, of course, also lead to criticism from purist circles – defenders of what they take to be the sole authentic practice – that more daring adopters get 'the tradition' wrong. Interestingly, such discussions became quite heated in the pages of the Swiss *Folk Song Journal* in the 1970s (which R.J.W. edited and to which F.A.M. occasionally contributed), where neither adopters nor upholders of 'the tradition' were members of the original discourse community.

In contrast to the relative freedom that arises out of the medial transfer from print and musical notation, recordings, by their very nature, are multimedial and multidimensional. They are thus much more 'fixed' in perpetuation as no transfer from one form to another is needed. In that sense they represent models or standardisations, which are much harder to ignore in adoption, effectively requiring that adopters place their adaptation somewhere between a copy and an attempt at a radically new version. The dilemma can perhaps best be illustrated with versions that have acquired iconic status. The first song on

---

[23] That the kind of regionality advocated by the likes of Ewan MacColl (cf. Bean 2014) is a myth becomes obvious when we look at the American versions of 'Scottish and English' ballads (cf. Pound 1913 and Bronson 1959–72).

The Dubliners' 1964 album is 'The Wild Rover', which according to the liner notes was 'collected by Luke in England. There is also a Dublin version.'[24] This version has by now become nothing short of a standard. The same could be said of 'Scarborough Fair' ☺91 after Paul Simon acquired the song and the guitar accompaniment from Martin Carthy. Once folk songs become standardised in this fashion – something that happens very frequently on the basis of a recording – they are more likely to be used in relational performances as there is little interest on the part of a seasoned performer in reproducing someone else's version. As Martin Carthy states, in the early days of the folk scene in Britain, 'if someone sang an old song that was new to everybody . . . your duty was to go and find a new version of it . . . that was the duty'.[25]

The same would apply to Thin Lizzy's 1972 take on the popular drinking song 'Whiskey in the Jar' ☺92, a hard rock version that owes nothing save the tune and the words to the many folk recordings, but was in turn 'covered' by Metallica in 1998, complete with Thin Lizzy's opening guitar lick but in their typically heavier rock style. Whereas Thin Lizzy had recreated the song as a new representational performance piece, Metallica seemed to have been reverential enough to perpetuate the earlier rock version with relatively minor changes that might have been avoided by one representational folk performer taking over a song from another. In essence, a song recorded and/ or performed by one folk singer is seen as 'hers' or 'his' (in the same way as in a pub or club setting singer B will not sing singer A's song because 'that one's Sam's'). To adopt such a song, it would have to be adapted quite markedly, an act that could be described as the song being *claimed* by a new performer. On the other hand, well-known songs based on iconic performances tend to move towards the relational end of the spectrum and are likely to be sung along the lines of the recording in sing-song settings.

One area in which there is leeway for variation and change arising from recordings, more so in the case of audio than of video, results from misheard lyrics. In the days of internet sites devoted to song lyrics, song texts with the same misheard passage can be found in several places. The term for this is *mondegreen*, coined by Wright (1954) in her essay 'The Death of Lady Mondegreen'. The opening stanza of 'The Bonny Earl of Murray' (Child 181 A) ☺93 reads:

> ye Highlands and ye Lawlands
> oh where have you been
> they have slain the Earl of Murray
> and they layd him on the green   (Child, in Sargent and Kittredge 1904: 444)

---

[24] http://itsthedubliners.com/dubs_d21_with_Luke.htm, accessed 8 April 2015.
[25] www.bbc.co.uk/programmes/b05stg0l, 14:21, accessed 10 April 2015.

Most sources elide 'they', rendering the line as 'and laid 'im on the green' thus creating the potential mishearing 'and the Lady Mondegreen'.

There are several reasons why 'mondegreens' occur (cf. Konnikova 2014), but one that plays a role in song perpetuation can be explained by the *Cohort Model*: 'At all times, the system computes the *best interpretation* of currently available input combining information in the speech signal with prior semantic and syntactic context' (Davis 2013, emphasis added). The 'best interpretation' can be understood as requiring the least cognitive effort on the part of the hearer while at the same time reconciling what s/he has or thinks s/he has heard. In other words, when a concept or a term is not or no longer part of our shared knowledge, we try to make sense of what we hear as best we can.

How this mechanism contributes to the diffusion and adoption of a song can be illustrated with 'The Snows They Melt the Soonest' (Roud 3154) ♪94 as sung by the Furey Brothers and their spin-off the Buskers and printed on the lyrics sleeve of *The Second Irish Folk Festival on Tour*, a double album with live recordings from 1975 on the German label Intercord. One excerpt will have to suffice to make the point. The song was current from the singing of Scottish performer Dick Gaughan, who claims to have learnt it from another Scot, Archie Fisher, 'by osmosis' (according to the sleeve notes of *Handful of Earth*). The Irish adaptation is on the right in Table 7.1.

We have no space at this point for a detailed phonological analysis that would explain the Furey Brothers' version, but two elements stand out: the phonetic similarities in terms of syllabic peaks, especially if we consider the pronunciation of vowels in Scots and Irish, and in terms of manner although not place of articulation (plosives, nasals with the exception of the fricative /θ/ as opposed to the /p/ in *thing* vs *pain*). In addition, the phrases in question can be

Table 7.1. *Dick Gaughan's and the Fureys' version of 'The Snows They Melt the Soonest'*

Dick Gaughan, who claims to have learnt it from Archie Fisher 'by osmosis' (sleeve notes of *Handful of Earth*) from https://main lynorfolk.info/anne.briggs/songs/thesnowit meltsthesoonest.html (accessed 11 April 2015)	The Buskers (on The 2nd Irish Folk Festival on Tour) and the Furey Brothers https://www .youtube.com/watch?v=HZFXqplWcx4 (accessed 11 April 2015)
And I've seen a woman's anger melt between the night and the morn	And I've seen a woman's anger melt between the neck and arm [different from the Furey Brothers' recording, unique to Intercord LP]
So it's surely not a harder thing to melt a woman's scorn	So it's surely not a heart of pain to nod a woman's scorn

seen as loose oronyms: as they are a sung 'string of sounds', they can be parsed into different words depending on the interpretation and the least conceptual effort on the part of the hearer (or transcriber of lyrics) in accordance with the Cohort Model. With the Fureys' version printed on the sleeve of an album that seemed to sell quite well at the time, those misheard lyrics are likely, at least in Germany or continental Europe, to have been adopted by other singers.

One last thought: the collectors frequently viewed themselves as making a last-ditch effort to save the poetry and music of the common people, because the latter were felt to be unable or not sufficiently motivated to preserve their own culture. It is difficult to speculate on what would have happened if these efforts had not been undertaken, but the fact is that the music and songs had never died, nor had they ever completely gone away. They were in the process of changing, and they are still developing to this day. Some elements will disappear, and some references will become too obscure for the majority of singers and audiences over time and morph into something new that fits within the conceptual framework of the new singers. Bemoaning such changes is akin to what the irate writers of letters-to-the-editor vainly do, who see themselves as the guardians of language purity and civilisation-as-we-know-it. If songs are processes rather than products, they will, like language, change and live on.

Part III

Folk Song Performance and Linguistics

8 Voices in the Folk Song

> People's classifications of songs by form and by function may provide important evidence of musical and extramusical transformation processes that are acceptable in a culture. They may also be relevant in assessing the effects of music.
> (Blacking 1973: 43)

Voices in Performance

The following four chapters are devoted to the sociolinguistic analysis of folk songs in various performance contexts. The current chapter and Chapter 9 focus on decisions made by singers in delivering different entextualisations of the song 'text', or 'blueprint,' occasioned by different types of performance (relational or representational, staged or impromptu, rehearsed or unrehearsed). The sociolinguistic model of song performance in Chapter 2 presents it as a social process enacting a ritual occasion. As such, it is distinct in different degrees from everyday social interaction, first of all in being $song_2$[1] and secondly in being carried out primarily to create or strengthen relations between the participants (performers and audience) or to represent to an audience specific aspects of human social experience. Folk song has the function of bonding participants through performance into communities of practice, several instantiations of which help to create a historically durable discourse community.

In Chapter 2 we discussed the need to key into the performance mode (PM) and, once the performance is over, to key out of it again in order to return to everyday social interaction. The purpose of this and the following chapters is to discuss what goes on and why, in performances involving folk songs, between keying into the performance mode (PM) and keying out.

---

[1] See the distinction between $song_1$ and $song_2$ made in Chapter 1.

Frith's Voices

In Chapter 5, we introduced Frith's hypothesis that all songs are, at the very least, 'implied narratives', by which he means narratives that are only hinted at, are only partly narrated or that can be derived from the account given in the rest of the lyrics. The majority of folk songs are in fact explicitly narrative, giving the audience access to different kinds of story. Other songs appear to have very little to do with storytelling. But, as Frith says, the central character in any song is the singer with 'an attitude' and 'in a situation' (albeit a fictive situation), 'talking to someone'. In the context of an 'implied narrative', the listener needs to use her/his imagination to generate a story from what is heard. As Frith maintains, the lyrics of a song 'let us into songs as stories', and this is just as much the case with work songs like 'The Herrin's Heid' and 'Sally Brown' or cumulative drinking songs like 'The Barley Mow' or 'The Bargeman's Alphabet' ☺95 as it is with explicit stories like 'A Sailor's Life' or 'Geordie'. However, we disagree with Frith when he posits that the central character of a song is the singer her/himself. Singers ventriloquise[2] the voices of others, even when the story is a personal story, and we adopt this point of view on the grounds that a performance is primarily characterised by the feature of 'fictionality'.

To make such distinctions between different voices in a song, Frith (1996) suggests a set of levels, or layers, at which song performers function, which is reminiscent of the literary stylistic approach to 'voice levels'. It implies that the listener has to 'peel off' an upper voice layer to find deeper layers below. The theory we outline below allows for creative flexibility on the part of the singer to switch from one voice to another within a fictional world and to stylise the differences between voices in whatever way seems most appropriate. A singer always takes on the role of a performer, even in the work song settings discussed in Chapter 3. In the presence of an audience, in relational or representational performance, s/he sets her/himself up for evaluation. An evaluation of the singer is an evaluation of the singer *in that role* and *not* an evaluation of the singer as a person outside the performance mode. To use Schechner's definition (1985), the singer is not her/himself but is simultaneously not not her/himself in performance. Frith also contends that '[t]he voice ... may or may not be a key to someone's identity, but it is certainly a key to the ways in which we change identities, pretend to be something we're not, deceive people, lie' (1996: 197). In this sense, the real key to his concept of 'voice' is contained in the following quotation, in which he appears to contradict the assumption that the singer is the central character of the song:

---

[2] We defined 'ventriloquism' in Chapter 4, following Middleton (2006), as 'giving a voice to someone, the Other, who is otherwise silent'.

... a singer's act ... is complex. There is, first of all, the character presented as the protagonist of the song, its singer and narrator, the implied person controlling the plot, with an attitude and tone of voice; but there may also be a 'quoted' character, the person whom the song is about (and singers, like lecturers, have their own mannered ways of indicating quote marks). On top of this there is the character of the singer as star, what we know about them, or are led to believe about them through their packaging and publicity, and then, further, an understanding of the singer as a person, what we like to imagine they are really like, what is revealed, *in the end*, by their voice. (ibid.: 198; emphasis in the original)

There are at least five voice levels to be accounted for here: (1) the singer/ narrator = the implied person controlling the plot; (2) the character = the protagonist of the song; (3) a 'quoted' character = the person the song is about; (4) the character of the singer as a star; (5) the singer outside the performance situation as a person. Presenting voices as different layers of fictionality or reality, however, cannot account for the immensely more creative options offered by song lyrics in presenting different voices for the singer to ventriloquise. A socio-cognitive understanding of voice is superior to viewing it as a layer or lamination of analysis, and we argue in favour of voice conceptualised as *an instance of languaging adapted to a particular interactional context*, which a speaker (or in our case, singer) can internalise as a part of her/his 'self'.

Voice and Voicing

The terms 'voice' and 'voicing', defined in this subsection within a socio-cognitive theory of languaging and musicking such as that outlined in Chapter 1, are central to our discussion in this chapter. Psycholinguistic theories of language acquisition informed by the socio-cognitive orientation in much of present-day cognitive psychology posit that post-natal infants react to, among many other forms of contact with caregivers, instances of languaging[3] by significant individuals. For the pre-linguistic infants themselves, of course, instances of languaging are instances of voicing, and one of the central indices of personhood beyond the 'I' is the embodied voice that represents for the infant the Other (see Bertau 2007). Since different caregivers have physically distinct voices, infants learn to 'identify' members of the social group to which they belong through their voices. In addition, they quickly realise that acts of voicing involve themselves as well as the vocalisers, i.e. that voicing is a dialogic addressive activity demanding some form of response.

---

[3] This way of looking at 'voice' is directly traceable to the influence of Bakhtin (1981) and the group of Soviet researchers associated with Bakhtin (e.g., in particular, Voloshinov and Vygotsky). For Bakhtin, 'language' refers to the system of language, but the dialogic nature of using language can only be properly studied by means of what he calls 'speech', i.e. by what we refer to as 'languaging' in the present book.

It is, in other words, social. Whenever a caregiver vocalises with an infant (i.e. whenever s/he voices), the infant takes this as an index to engage socially with the vocaliser. Voice is therefore a physically embodied index of the need to engage in social interaction.

Pre-linguistic infants internalise as part of their cognition a range of different voices indexing different identifiable persons, and although, at the very early stage of their lives, they are not physically equipped to imitate the Other, they become aware that the Other imitates them and that they need to imitate the Other in order to be able to function adequately as social beings.[4] Internalised voices, the kinds of social practice engaged in with each voice and the identities constructed from voicing and then later languaging thus become an essential part of a notion of the 'self'. No 'self' is possible without the Other. Because identities and relationships between the internalised voices change through time, the 'self' can never be a consistent cognitive entity but is subject to constant shifts in changing interactional contexts.

Since the ontogenetic development of human language beyond roughly one year of age is dependent on a phylogenetically adaptive mutation in *Homo sapiens*, voicing mutates into, but still remains the basis of, languaging. The voice retains the ability to sing but gains the ability to construct, transform and transfer information. 'Voice' remains, in other words, crucially involved in forms of social interaction between the self and the Other.

In literary analysis, the term 'voice' implies different perspectives on the action represented in a text and can be used to index multiple levels of interaction. This is particularly the case in the analysis of the novel and likewise in texts that focus on narrative from various interpretative perspectives, such as different forms of folk song. In sociolinguistic research, voice quality is one focus of sociolinguistic research (e.g. Keating and Esposito 2007), but 'voice' is also used metaphorically as a concept. For example, the three first sentences of the introduction to a special issue of the journal *Anthropology and Education* run as follows: 'Voice refers to the capacity to make oneself heard. Someone who can speak has voice; someone who cannot lacks voice. Someone who can make him/herself heard may be said to have a voice; someone who is unable to make him/herself heard lacks or is denied a voice' (Juffermans and Van der Aa 2013: 112). We prefer to call this concept 'having a voice' rather than simply 'voice'.[5]

The closest we have come to work in sociolinguistics that views 'voice' in much the same way as we are viewing it here is Johnstone (2000). Johnstone challenges the understanding of voice as 'a strategically adopted way of sounding that a speaker designs and modifies as a result of analyzing the

---

[4] Middleton (2006) calls the use of one's own voice to imitate the voice of an Other 'ventriloquising', and the ability to ventriloquise will become an important factor in the PM.

[5] This understanding of 'voice' can also be found in Maybin 2001, Hornberger 2006, Heller 2007, Blommaert 2008, Creese and Blackledge 2012, etc.

rhetorical or aesthetic task at hand. In this conventional view, the issue of how speakers "project themselves into discourse" (Cherry 1998) arises only in the context of relatively overt strategic choices in relatively planned discourse' (Johnstone 2000: 405). She states that she is not interested 'in exploring differences in how speakers are connected to discourse and language in different ideological and material contexts (which can indeed vary widely, with diverse consequences), but in thinking about how speakers are always *necessarily* connected to discourse and language' (ibid.: 406–7; our emphasis). We therefore define our understanding of *voice* as, in Johnstone's words, the connection of 'particular individual human beings with particular utterances and ways of speaking and thinking' (ibid.: 407). We define voicing as *an instance of languaging adapted to a particular interactional context* and the self as *a continually changing indefinite number of distinct voices internalised by an individual*. This implies that the activity of voicing constantly involves potential changes in the ways in which 'individuals' are connected to 'particular utterances and ways of speaking and thinking' in emergent socio-communicative interaction.

Performance Voices

Within the performance mode in which languaging is a central mode of communication, the nature of the performer's voices changes in accordance with four features that distinguish performing from simply interacting.[6] The four features are as follows:

(1) *Fictionality*: Regardless of whether or not the performer sings about or tells about a personal experience, the performance mode is always governed by the assumption that the events have been fictionalised (i.e. that they do not conform to an exact representation of what happened factually).

(2) *Representation*: The PM is used by the performer to *re*present a story or state of affairs to an audience.

(3) *Ritualisation*: The PM always involves participants in an interaction that is characterised as a sequence of acts that are performed in the same way and set apart from everyday social interaction.

(4) *Uni-directionality*: During the period of time in which the PM is in force, performers have the right to address an audience, but the audience has waived its own right to address the performers.[7]

---

[6] We need to bear in mind at this point that because the performance mode requires the consent of the non-performers to waive their rights to contribute to the interaction (unless encouraged by the performers to participate), the potential performers need to key into the PM explicitly and to key out of it once the PM is concluded.

[7] This does not of course mean that audiences are always inactive. They may assist the performer in accomplishing the performance or they may heckle or vocally encourage a performer.

A performer's voices (as instances of languaging) must therefore be adapted to these features of the interactional context of social practice in the PM, which renders the voices heteroglossic, hybrid and largely ventriloquistic.

Song$_2$ entails a performance that releases the song from being caught in amber to becoming a social process. It uses instances of languaging, i.e. the use of heteroglossic, hybrid and ventriloquistic voices in a PM, and music, which has the function of evoking in the audience emotional states accompanying those instances of languaging. Performing a song thus opens a window onto a hybrid, multi-voiced, fictional world in which hybrid, fictional voices are ventriloquised by the performer with the intention of evoking emotional responses to the story, implied story, story protagonists or simply the social situation represented in the song.

In both relational and representational performances of folk song, however, we have a situation in which a performer shifts, within the fictional PM, from voices within the performance world of each song to voices outside that world. The performer, in other words, shifts from playing the role of a ventriloquist for the fictional voices of others to using her/his own voices, i.e. s/he shifts from representation to relation, and can invite the audience to participate in the singing. In relational performance types (cf. Figure 2.4), those shifts may be very marked, whereas in representational performance types the audience's ability to engage in addressivity with the performer decreases the further we move towards the apex of 'maximal audience affect' in Figure 2.4. Figure 8.1 indicates the relationship between the song performances (on the representational level) and interaction with the audience via languaging without song (on the relational level).

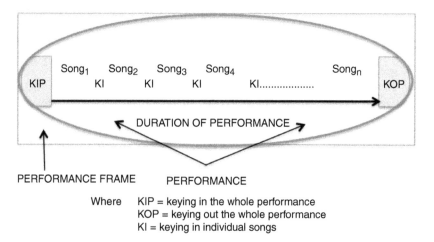

Figure 8.1 *The 'typical' structure of a folk performance*

Most of the time – but certainly not always – the shift from the representational to the relational level of communication with the audience entails the keying-in of the next song, and it may also contain a comment on the song that has just been or is about to be sung. For this reason, we have labelled each of these interpositions KI, i.e. 'keying-in'.

Exemplifying Performance Voices

We give a concrete example of a folk song performance here. F.A.M. agreed to participate in 2014 in a British Embassy event billed as a 'talk and performance' to commemorate the centenary of the beginning of the First World War in 1914 in a small theatre in Bern. The audience invited to the occasion was composed of diplomats, political and economic contacts, academics and British expatriates; it was, in other words, not strictly a public event but a hybrid performance consisting of lecture elements and concert elements. As a 'lecture', the performance raised a number of academic expectations, but as a concert it presupposed a relatively high level of musical and vocal proficiency on the part of the performer and a carefully devised selection of songs.

For the performer, F.A.M., this meant presenting the voice of an academic researcher, which was certainly one aspect of his own range of voices, i.e. it was not a ventriloquist's voice, but the audience was composed in such a way that the voice needed to be shaped so that both academics and non-academics could be addressed. It also meant adopting the role of the artist as a credible ventriloquist of the voices of the protagonists presented in the songs, as a director of the material and as a competent musician. Two further voices from beyond the PM were that of the activist protesting against the futility of the war and assessing its socio-political implications and that of the private person enjoying the activity of performing while worrying over the effect it was having on the audience. Switching between or combining these various voices, many of which composed valid aspects of F.A.M.'s sense of self and some of which, in particular in the song performance, were ventriloquised, is a first indication of the complexities of the social practices needed to carry out a successful performance.

The non-ventriloquised voices took on a different weight at different moments in the performance. In the design of the performance, the relational voices, e.g. those of the *academic*, the *activist* and the *private person*, were more detailed in view of the lecture character of the evening. They came to the fore in different forms and at different times, with the *artist* being on display as a ventriloquist's voice during the songs, but again intermingled with the *activist* and the *private person* whenever there were lapses in the *artist's* control. In the songs themselves, there were various fictional voices in evidence, e.g. in 'The Conscientious Objector's Lament' ♪96, a music hall song depicting its subject as a camp coward. This song suggested a very high degree of 'being camp' that had to be stylised by the *artist* as a representative of the genre in a first-person voice. At the same time, however, the desire of the activist and private person was to distance himself from the homophobic and generally unjustified stereotyping of conscientious objectors in World War I. This example indicates the complexity of the interaction between the various voices, but it also clearly demonstrates that these are not layered hierarchically. Rather they vie with each other for various degrees of prominence at different times in the performance.

Voices and Music in Narrative Songs

In this section we give an analysis of two songs about tailors using Labov and Waletzky's model but focusing explicitly on the evaluative elements in each story and how these correspond with the musical structure of the songs. We argue that before performing the songs, the performer considers how knowledge of the song voices, modes of ventriloquising them and the music might be used to gain the maximum effect on the audience.

Exemplifying Fictional Voices: Two Songs about a Tailor

When songs are performed, they are released from whatever amber they happen to have been perpetuated in to become processes within the performance mode. At the same time the complexity of voices that a performer can manipulate by ventriloquising them is also released. In this subsection, we discuss two songs about a tailor, 'The Unfortunate Tailor' (TUT) ♪97 and 'The Tailor's Breeches' (TTB) ♪98. Until the twentieth century a tailor's profession was felt to be much less 'manly' than that of, for example, a blacksmith, a ploughman, a factory worker, a sailor, a fisherman, etc., even though a tailor produces the clothes we wear. In the first half of the nineteenth century, the type of venue containing an audience listening to this kind of song might have been a raucous bar in the seedy red-light district of a port, say, London, Liverpool, Bristol, a gathering of musicians in one of a number of pubs, rural or urban, across the country, a gathering of neighbours enjoying this kind of musical entertainment at someone's house, a sing-song on board ship in the very rare moments in which sailors were able to relax, a family sing-song, etc.

The first song, TUT, is a story supposedly told by a tailor who has been jilted by his girl and, as a consequence, resolves to try his luck at sea:

The Unfortunate Tailor

1. oh list oh list to me sorrowful lay
   attention give to me song I pray
   you have heard it all you'll say
   that I'm an unfortunate tailor

2. oh once I was happy as a bird on a tree
   me Sarah was all in the world to me
   now I'm cut out by a son of the sea
   and she's left me here to bewail her

3. why did me Sarah serve me so
   no more will I stitch and no more will I sew
   me thimble and me needle to the winds I'll throw
   and I'll go and list as a sailor

4. now me days were honey and me nights were the same
   till a man called Cobb from the ocean came
   with his coal-black beard and his muscular frame
   a captain on board of a whaler

5. well he spent his money both frank and free
   with his tales of the land and his songs of the sea
   stole me Sarah's heart from me
   and blighted the hopes of a tailor

6. well once I was with her when in came Cobb
   avast he cried you blubbering swab
   if you don't knock off I'll stubble your knob
   and Sarah smiled at the sailor

7. so now I'll face the raging sea
   for Sarah's proved untrue to me
   me heart's locked up and she's the key
   of a very unfeeling jailer

8. so now kind friends I'll bid you adieu
   no more me woes will trouble you
   I'll travel the country through and through
   and I'll go and list as a sailor

No one in the audience would have been, or would now be, likely to equate the singer with a tailor. Nor would a tailor ever have been likely to sing in so public a fashion about his 'sorrowful' plight. The first stanza is a meta-discursive comment on keying into a performance situation. It lies outside the framework of the story proper and refers to the discursive context in which the 'tailor' needs to call the audience to order so that he can sing his song to them. But there is a significant difference from the usual utterances that commonly function as means of keying-in a performance. The keying-in in stanza 1 is not only part of the song itself. It also charac-terises a 'tailor' who wants to sing 'a sorrowful lay' and who feels that the audience will feel sorry for him when he has finished. From a narrative point of view, it thus includes an abstract (see the discussion of Labov and Waletzky's narrative categories in Chapter 5), a brief statement about the theme of the song. If we imagine someone singing the song in one of the disreputable taverns along the Ratcliffe Highway in London or in a pub near the Albert Dock in Liverpool in the early nineteenth century, the first thing the singer would have done is to call for the audience's attention, regardless of what s/he wanted to sing. However, there is one major difference here; the keying-in would not normally be part of the song.[8]

But why would anyone in such company be willing to listen to the story of a jilted tailor? The tone of the whole song is set in the first stanza, in which the singer places himself (or perhaps herself!) in the fictive tailor's shoes, in full knowledge of the fact that tailors were frequently despised by other members of the working classes. It can only function as a performance if it plays on the joke of a tailor publicly intoning a 'sorrowful lay' about losing his girl to the captain of a whaler – which is exactly what it does. In the second stanza the tailor 'bewails' his lost love. In stanzas 3 and 4, a contrast is set up (by the singer/narrator/tailor) between someone who uses thimbles and needles to make his living and the captain of a whaling ship who uses his muscles. In stanza 5, the 'tailor', wallowing in self-pity, complains that his hopes have been 'blighted', and the hiatus of the humour (unnoticed by the fictive tailor, but certainly noticed by the singer and the audience) is reached in stanza 6 in which Captain Cobb bursts in, physically removes the tailor, to be greeted by a smile from Sarah. The final two stanzas provide a coda in which the tailor expresses his intention to give up his profession and go to sea, and stanza 8 is an elaborate keying-out from the performance mode. From a modern-day perspective, TUT is a 'macho' song, but within the social context of female and male role models in the early nineteenth century, its greatest appeal has

---

[8] It is for this reason that we might call it a 'performance song', i.e. a song which makes explicit reference to the performance mode, e.g. by asking his audience to listen to his tale of woe and to commiserate with him afterwards.

always been the humorous way in which a bond is created between the performer and the audience during the performance itself. The orientation in TUT consists of the first two lines of stanza 2 and the first line of stanza 4.[9] The complication is that his true love's affections have shifted to Cobb.

TUT is tightly constructed in terms of lyrics and music, but judging by the fact that no broadsides are in evidence during the nineteenth century, it cannot have had much currency. The Roud Index lists just one song with the title we have used, Roud 1614, collected by Alfred Williams from John Webley of Arlington, Gloucestershire, and two with the title 'Oh List, oh List to my Sorrowful Lay', one collected from George Lovett in 1906 by Gardner and Gamblin and the other, also collected by Gardner and Gamblin, from Alfred Oliver near Basingstoke in 1907. As we would expect, all three versions are relatively similar, although adaptation has taken place in the course of time. Lovett's version omits the final stanza, Oliver's version has eight stanzas but adds a fourth stanza contravening what we take to be the point of the song, i.e. ridiculing tailors – 'Sarah was the daughter of a publican / a generous kind good sort of man / who spoke very plain what he thought of a man / but he never looked crow at the tailor'[10] – and omits our stanza 7. Webley's version has eleven stanzas, the eight that we sing, Oliver's fourth stanza and two further stanzas, in one of which Sarah's beauty is extolled and in the other of which the tailor explicitly proposes to Sarah and is turned down. Webley also uses stanza 3, as given above, as a chorus, which may account for the fact that it appears a little displaced as a stanza. We have eight stanzas, with lines 1 to 3 of each stanza rhyming together and the fourth line rhyming with the fourth line of every other stanza, leaving the following sequence of fourth lines that underscore the tailor's laughable lament at the loss of his love:

that I'm an unfortunate tailor > and she's left me here to bewail her > a captain on board of a whaler > and blighted the hopes of a tailor > and Sarah smiled at the sailor > of a very unfeeling jailer > and I'll go and list as a sailor > and I'll go and list as a sailor

The second song about a tailor, entitled 'The Tailor's Breeches' (TTB), ventriloquises an implicit third-person voice and also aims to generate humour at the expense of the fictive protagonist presented by the narrator:

---

[9] Which, as we argue in the next section, would incline us, in performing the song, to shift stanza 3 to just before present stanza 7.

[10] 'To look crow at' is an idiomatic expression meaning 'to exult gloatingly, especially at the distress of another' (Merriam-Webster; www.merriam-webster.com/dictionary/crow, accessed 12 February 2017).

The Tailor's Breeches

1. it's of a brisk young tailor this story I'll relate
    he lived at an inn called 'The Ram and the Gate'
    'The Ram and the Gate' was the place where he did dwell
    and wine and women's company he loved exceeding well

    Chorus: oh well oh well oh well me boys oh well
            and wine and women's company he loved exceeding well

2. now this tailor he'd been drinking a glass or two of wine
    and not bein' used to drink it caused his face to shine
    it caused his face to shine just like the rising sun
    and he swore he'd have a bonny lass before the night was done

    Chorus: was done was done was done me boys was done
            he swore he'd have a bonny lass before the night was done

3. he took her in his arms and he called her his dear honey
    and as they were a-talking she was fingering of his money
    she was fingering of his money when the tailor smiled and said
    if you'll lend me your petticoats I'll dance like a maid

    Chorus: a maid a maid a maid me boys a maid
            if you'll lend me your petticoats I'll dance like a maid

4. the tailor pulled his breeches off and the petticoat put on
    the tailor danced a dance and the lassie sang a song
    the tailor danced a dance and they played a merry tune
    they danced the tailor's breeches right out of the room

    Chorus: the room the room the room me boys the room
            they danced the tailor's breeches right out of the room

5. have you ever seen a tailor undone as I'm undone
    me watch and me money and me breeches are all gone
    I can't go out dressed up like this they'll call me 'garden flower'
    and if ever I get my breeches back I'll never dance no more

    Chorus: no more no more no more me boys no more
            and if ever I get my breeches back I'll never dance no more

The same effect is achieved if a first-person narrator is present (as in TUT), but in the case of a third-person narrator the protagonist is fully under the control, and therefore the implied criticism, of the ventriloquising singer/narrator. The first stanza is an abstract without the need to key into the performance mode, and the orientation is in the final line of this first stanza and the whole of stanza 2, in which the tailor gets drunk. It is also an evaluation of an aspect of the tailor's character that will ultimately lead to his 'downfall' in the song. The complication in TTB is that, in a state of drunkenness, the tailor makes a fool of himself by taking off his breeches, putting on the 'bonny lass's' petticoats and having his breeches (together with his watch and his money) stolen.

The whole of the final stanza, in which the third person narrator withdraws behind the first-person voice of the tailor himself, functions as a coda. There is no switch to a first-person narrator throughout the song until this final stanza is reached. In addition, the song is designed for audience participation with a chorus at the end of each stanza. The fictional third-person narrator, through his/her comments and through his/her incitement to the audience to join in, controls the way humour is generated at the expense of the tailor. The narrative voice assumed by the singer is in full control of manipulating the audience's reactions. Narratives often end without a positive resolution to the complication (cf. the analysis of 'A Sailor's Life' in Chapter 5), and that appears to be the case in both these songs. In each case the tailor decides to change his lifestyle, in TUT by giving up his profession and going to sea and in TTB by deciding never to dance again – although he says nothing about giving up drink.

Voicing and Ventriloquising

As a performer, a singer entextualises his/her song text/song-blueprint to achieve the maximum effect on his/her audience in a performance mode.[11] This involves recognising the voices that go to make up the 'self' of the narrator and the protagonists, while remaining aware of the feature of fictionality that characterises a stretch of verbal social practice as a performance and not simply as an instantiation of everyday interaction. Simultaneously, both singer and audience know that beyond the performance mode each performer and each audience member has internalised a wide range of voices that go to make up a person's fluid and

---

[11] In Chapter 9 this notion will be discussed theoretically in more detail.

changing conceptualisation of the 'self', as well as the ability to 'give a voice to the Other', to ventriloquise. In the fictional situation of folk song performance, that 'Other' will remain silent until a performer has given her/him a voice.

Earlier in this chapter we argued that folk song performances are unique in allowing the singer to introduce a selection of her/his own genuine voices in the presence of an audience as well as ventriloquising the voices of narrators and fictional participants in the (implied) narrative of the song. This is generally accomplished through a brief commentary on the song just sung, the keying-in of the next song, or both, but, as we see later in this chapter, the fictional narrative voices of the song itself may also provide access to one or more of the singer's own personal voices.

With respect to the fictional situation in TUT, the song can only be successful if the singer stylises her/his ventriloquism of the tailor's voice to represent a character unsure of himself and his standing in the eyes of the opposite sex. How this might be done convincingly is part of the performative art of singing the song. To sing it as if it were a sea shanty – which would be possible given the strong 2/4 time signature with a stress on the first beat of every bar typical of a sailor's hornpipe – would hardly achieve the kind of stylisation necessary to convey the ironic effect in the audience that a performance of TUT requires. The fictional third-person narrative voice telling the story in TTB is used to evaluate the tailor, cf. line 2 of stanza 2 ('and not bein' used to drink it caused his face to shine'), lines 2 and 3 of stanza 3 ('and as they were a-talking she was fingering of his money / she was fingering of his money when the tailor smiled and said'), and the singer's stylisation of a narrator poking fun at a tailor can be based precisely on these evaluations and in particular on the switch to the tailor's voice in the final stanza.

Looking for Voices in the Ballad

The type of song generally considered most closely related to storytelling is the ballad (cf. Scott, Child, etc.), but ballads are unusual in terms of the voices that they reveal. Storytelling involves the narrator in ventriloquising, even in the case of natural narratives, such that the narrator positions her/himself with respect to the events of the story and the protagonists involved in it. The positioning of a voice with respect to an event, state or character is equivalent to evaluating that event, state or character. When a third-person narrator controls the storytelling in a song, evaluations are assumed to be those of the narrator. Hence, when the narrator in 'The Tailor's Breeches' follows the comment that the tailor has drunk some wine with the remark 'and not being used to drink it made his face to shine', we can infer that s/he creates a bond of complicity with the audience. It is as if the audience were being invited to smile complacently at the tailor for not being able to hold his drink. As we have seen, the success of the complicity between narrator and audience in TTB is vital for generating the inference that tailors are somehow 'unmanly'. Labov and Waletzky's narrative category of evaluation is not therefore equivalent to the instantiation of an event within a narrative, as is a complication or a resolution. Evaluation permeates the whole narrative, revealing different stances assumed by a narrator towards events, states and characters in the song. In the ballad, however, narrative voices hardly evaluate and do not seem to ventriloquise – which does not of course mean that there is no evaluation.

Telling or implying a story in the ballad involves different degrees of interpretative work on the part of the audience. Information that links narrative clauses or those clauses implying a narrative often has to be inferred by the listener. For this reason, identifying the voices is one of the first steps in shaping the performance in such a way as to enable the audience to 'enter' the song. Ballads not only reveal high degrees of formulaic linguistic expression (cf. Chapter 9); they also reveal voices whose only apparent function is to carry the events forward, any evaluation generally being through formulaic linguistic expressions and quoted speech from protagonists in the story with either a minimum of tagging ('he said', 'she said') or no tagging at all. The singer's job in the ballad is to present to the audience a non-committal narrative voice and to allow the drama to arise through quoted speech.

In a very real sense, the withdrawal of the narrative voice links the ballad to other types of folk song – and indeed to other genres of song. Our analysis of 'A Sailor's Life' in Chapter 5 revealed that the most effective and moving versions of the song were those in which the audience needed to 'fill the informational gaps' in the story. Sandy Denny's version opens in stanza 1 with a third-person narrative voice openly assuming a negative evaluative stance towards the behaviour of sailors towards their 'young girls', after which the voice withdraws and leaves the floor open to a female first-person narrative voice openly praising her lover in stanza 2. In stanza 3, this voice opens the narrative events of the story by asking her father to build her a boat with which she can go to sea to search for her lover. The third-person narrative voice continues the story in lines 1 and 2 of stanza 4 but withdraws again in lines 3 and 4, in which the question–answer sequence between the first-person narrative voice and the sailors on the ship (stanza 5) reveals the complication, i.e. the fact of her lover's death. The final stanza, in which we assume that the girl commits suicide by smashing her boat against a rock, is taken up by the third-person narrator, who appears to be confirming, at the end of the song, her/his negative evaluation of what it means to fall in love with a sailor. Voice structure here is very similar to that in the ballad, as we see in the next subsection, and what is left unsaid but can be inferred by the audience from direct verbal interaction between protagonists and song characters is as

significant as what is explicitly told. The stanzaic structure of the song, however, is different from that of a ballad. Each line has four major beats, with
assonance or rhyme in lines 1 and 2 and lines 3 and 4.[12]

Voice Complexity in Ballads

Ballads form part of the discussion in Chapter 9, but we begin that discussion in
this section by presenting the complexity of voices in ballads with a song that is
not often performed, 'Brown Adam' ☉99.[13] There are a number of shifts from
an assumed third-person non-committal narrator to quoted speech from the
protagonists in the narrative. But things are not quite so simple in ballads. If we
take Labov and Waletzky's model, there appear to be two stories in BA, the
first – implicitly – the reason for the second, but there is no abstract to either
story at the beginning of the ballad.

Brown Adam

oh   who   would wish the   wind to blow   or the   green leaves fall   there - with

or   who   would wish   a   bet - ter love___ than   Brown Ad - am___ the   smith

1. oh who would wish the wind to blow
    or the green leaves fall therewith
    and who would wish a better love
    than Brown Adam the smith

2. his hammer's of the beaten gold
    his study's of the steel
    his fingers white are my delight
    he blows his bellows well

3. but they banished him Brown Adam
    from father and from mother
    they banished him Brown Adam
    from sister and from brother

9. when he came to his lady's bower
    he stood a little foreby
    and there he heard a full false knight
    a-tempting his lady gay

10. he's taken out a gay gold ring
    had cost him many a pound
    oh grant me love for love lady
    and this shall be your own

11. I love Brown Adam well she says
    I know that he does me
    I would not give Brown Adam's love
    for no false knight I see

---

[12] Comparing 'A Sailor's Life' with the ballad 'The Cruel Mother' in Chapter 6 is also instructive.
Just as much explicit information can be missed out of the more powerful versions of 'A Sailor's
Life', so too can much explicit information be omitted in performances of 'The Cruel Mother'
with an experienced 'folk' audience.

[13] We present our adaptation of the A version of this ballad below. The tune is Child 98, Number 2
in Bronson's tunes. Cf. also the analysis of 'Brown Adam' given in Buchan (1997: 107–8).

4. oh they have banished Brown Adam
    from the flower of all his kin
    but he's built a bower in good greenwood
    between his lady and him

5. as it fell out upon a day
    Brown Adam he thought long
    that he would to the greenwood go
    to hunt some venison

6. he's ta'en his bow all o'er his arm
    his sword unto his hand
    and he is to the greenwood gone
    as fast as he could gang

7. then he's shot up and he's shot down
    the bird upon the briar
    and he's sent it home to his lady
    bade her be of good cheer

8. then he's shot up and he's shot down
    the bird upon the thorn
    and he's sent it home to his lady
    that he'd be home the morn

12. and he's taken out a purse of gold
    was full right to the string
    grant me love for love lady
    and this shall be all thine

13. I love Brown Adam well she says
    and I know that he does me
    and I would not be your light leman
    for more than you'd give me

14. then he has drawn his long long sword
    and he's flashed it to and fro
    now grant me love for love lady
    or through you this shall go

15. then sighing said that lady gay
    Brown Adam tarries long
    and up then starts her Brown Adam says
    I'm just at your hand

16. he's made him leave his bow his bow
    he's made him leave his brand
    he's made him leave a better pledge
    four fingers from his right hand

The first story begins with a voice in stanza 1 putting two rhetorical questions, the first a metaphor for the second. But whose voice is this? There is no explicit statement of what the song is about, but we do have information that Brown Adam the smith is at the centre of the song – for the voice in stanza 1, that is.

The second stanza metaphorically extols the (sexual) virtues of Brown Adam ('his hammer is of the beaten gold / ... / he blows his bellows well'), and it locates for us a first-person narrator in the third line – 'his fingers white are my delight' – who, we can now infer, is a female first-person voice. Stanzas 3 and 4 tell us that Brown Adam has been 'banished' from his family by a group of people referred to as 'they', and that he has found refuge for 'his lady and him' in the greenwood. Are we to infer from 'his lady' in the fourth line of stanza 4 that the voice has now become a third-person narrative voice? Or could the lady be referring to herself in that line? Everything else that the audience can infer from the first four stanzas remains speculative. Was Brown Adam at the royal court with his family? Did he begin a sexual liaison with a lady of the court and was banished for that reason? And has his lady gone with him? The first story thus lacks an explicit complication and therefore gives no resolution. For this reason it can be taken to fulfil the function of an orientation for the whole ballad, which thus effectively begins in the middle of quoted speech by a female voice.

The second story begins in stanza 5 in typical formulaic fashion – 'as it fell out upon a day' – and introduces the narrative clauses representing Brown Adam's hunting expedition in the wood. Since the lady and Brown Adam are referred to by the use of third-person reference, we have a narrative persona from this point on, but not one who evaluates Brown Adam's actions. The complication begins in stanza 9 when Brown Adam arrives home to overhear a 'false knight' trying to seduce his lady. Is this false knight someone from the court who has found out where Brown Adam and the lady are hiding? The complication consists of two quoted offers to the lady to tempt her to have sex with him, but the lady refuses each offer. The third attempt is an overt threat to kill her, after which Brown Adam resolves the complication by appearing, disarming the false knight and hacking off four fingers from his right hand as a pledge (probably never to appear again, but also to render him incapable of wielding a brand or sword). We can conclude from this that the first four stanzas of the ballad are filtered through the female voice of Brown Adam's lady, and that the rest of the ballad is told by a third-person narrator with dramatic effect provided by the quoted direct speech of his lady and the false knight.

Voice complexity in 'Brown Adam' thus arises from the fact that the primary narrative is derived from a secondary, sketchily outlined narrative preceding and determining what follows in the ballad. But voice complexity is determined by switching between voices during the song rather than by embedding one narrative into another.

Voicing and Ventriloquising in Ballads

Our discussion of 'Brown Adam' reveals a third-person narrative voice whose major function is to unfold the thread of the narrative events. In taking on that voice, the ballad singer becomes a narrator, but unlike narrators in natural narratives or songs in which there is a regular abstract, that voice is not used to evaluate either the characters in the story or the events.[14] The singer ventriloquises only to the extent that s/he gives a voice to the ballad, i.e. becomes a non-committal narrator; the ventriloquised voice does not offer evaluations or opinions to the audience.

---

[14] This fact represents a clear distinction between the third-person narrative voice in 'Brown Adam' and that in 'A Sailor's Life'.

On the contrary, the audience is expected to infer from the events, the actions of the characters and their frequent dramatic speech exchanges some moral, cultural or social message. Whatever the mythical background might be to this ballad, two things are clear to the audience through its performance: (1) that Brown Adam has been banished from his family, a fact that is lamented by a female voice in the first four stanzas; and (2) that 'a false knight' takes advantage of the fact that Brown Adam has gone hunting to try and seduce his 'lady'. No explicit link is offered between these two situations, but it can be assumed that an audience steeped in the performance tradition would infer the explanations needed.

The discussion also reveals that, rather than the ballad beginning with the third-person non-committal narrator, it begins *in medias res*, offering a woman's voice lamenting the fact that Brown Adam, repre-sented by her, via metaphorical means, as her sexual partner, has been banished by an ambiguous 'they' from his family. The audience is thus encouraged to take this as the reason for his banishment and possibly also the reason for the false knight turning up to seduce his lady. The quoted altercation between the false knight and the lady offers the drama of the ballad, but this is presented in a thoroughly conventional way with two offers by the knight, two refusals by the lady, a threat from the knight followed by a third refusal by the lady, in other words the typical 'incremental repetition', whose last reiteration precipitates the event(s) that follow.

The Role of the First-person Narrator in Implied Narratives

The distinction between song schemata and macro song schemata made in Chapter 5 is significant in assessing the role of first-person narrative voices in folk song. We began our discussion of voices in songs with 'The Unfortunate Tailor', which is a first-person narrative relying on the ability of the audience to separate the voice of the singer ventriloquising a character and the character her/himself. TUT thus has a unique song schema allowing for such adaptations in added or deleted stanzas (cf. Chapter 5), different wording in the stanzas and variation in the melody, deriving from similar types of song blueprints for different sing-ers. In the case of a song such as 'The Four Loom Weaver' (sung by June Tabor and Maddy Prior at the Cecil Sharp House concert), which also has a first-person narrative voice, similar forms of adaptation are in evidence, although the story takes second place to a criticism of the social situation of Lancashire cotton weavers in the mid-nineteenth century.

In Chapter 5, we defined a macro-schema as a macro-narrative indexing social groups rather than individual characters (cf. the examples given there, 'The Shoals of Herring', 'Go, Move, Shift'), and the 'stories' of those social groups provide a platform for different forms of answering back. So it is hardly surprising that songs containing first-person voices lend themselves more readily to indexing the lifestyles of social groups than third-person voices (e.g. in 'Shoals of Herring' and 'The Four Loom Weaver').

When such songs are performed, the singer needs to empathise with the representative 'I' of those social groups in such a way that the audience can suspend its disbelief for the length of the song. We present two modern songs here, the first of which, 'I Just Can't Wait' ⨀100, contains the first-person voice of a worker, who, very early in his working life, is bored with his job but is unable because of social and socio-economic pressures to cut free until he is finally pensioned off, at which point he finds it difficult to imagine how he will spend the rest of his life. The singer's job in 'I Just Can't Wait' is to present that type of character as genuinely and effectively as possible. The second song ('No Man's Land' – NML ⨀101) simulates a person hiking through Flanders and visiting one of the huge cemeteries containing the graves of those killed in the First World War. He sits down by a graveside and imagines a 'you' to fit the name on the gravestone. As in the first song, the singer's job is to present a convincing narrator, but, in singing NML, we find that identification with the first-person narrator in performance is so natural that it is extraordinarily difficult to sing the song without becoming emotionally involved with the situation. In this kind of song, separating the two voices that make up the self of the singer from those of the fictive protagonist is imperative in opening up a fictional yet frighteningly realistic world for the audience.[15]

Presenting a Representative 'I'

The first song, 'I Just Can't Wait (to Collect My Cards)' (IJCW), was written by Ian Campbell and put to music by John Dunkerley.

---

[15] The song could be called a 'pin drop' song, in which the audience becomes so involved with the imaginary situation described that, as a singer, you could hear a pin drop.

I Just Can't Wait (to Collect My Cards)

Words: Ian Campbell   Music: John Dunkerley

1. I took this job when I left school
   and I thought it might be fun
   and I signed the papers binding me
   till I was twenty-one

   Chorus:
   but I just can't wait to collect my cards
   I just can't wait to go
   I can't get along with the people here
   and my work it bores me so

2. so I learnt the trade for what it's worth
   and the time has gone so slow
   but soon my birthday's coming up
   and I'll be free to go

3. well I think I'll wait till the wedding's over
   before I say goodbye
   for the girlfriend tells me we must save
   if a house we hope to buy

4. now I'll have to wait till the baby's born
   before I can be free
   for I understand a pregnant wife
   must have security

5. now I'll have to wait till the kids leave school
   before I break away
   for growing kids eat money
   and I need the steady pay

6. now I think I'll wait till the house is mine
   before I break the tie
   for the interest rates keep rising
   and the car it bleeds me dry

7. now I'll have to wait till retiring age
   before I risk the break
   for the pension scheme insures the wife
   and it's mainly for her sake

8. well thank you for the gold watch sir
   the silver collection too
   but are you sure I have to go
   I won't know what to do

   Chorus:
   for I just can't bear to collect my cards
   I just can't bear to go
   I'm sure I'll miss the people here
   and my life it bores me so

The major difference between IJCW and NML is that the addressee in the former appears to be the audience, whereas the addressee in NML is the narrator's imagined soldier, the audience being the witness of the narrator's imagination. The point in IJCW at which it becomes clear that the audience is not being addressed is stanza 3. The narrative past tense of the first two stanzas (*took, signed, learnt*) gives way completely to the present tense of verbs like *think* and *understand* and to ratiocination rather than narration for the rest of the song. The protagonist indulges in a series of decision-making processes at different stages through his adult life, all of which prevent him from doing what he really wants to do, i.e. give up his job and find something more interesting to do. But because these processes span the protagonist's working life up to retirement, we still have an implicit narrative. The audience can even imagine themselves to be the addressees of the protagonist's verbalised thoughts – until the final stanza, in which he addresses his employer on the occasion of his retirement. The first-person voice of the song is not a narrative voice despite the fact that we can infer a life narrative from it. The 'I' of the song represents a large number of real-life 'I's who have found themselves in a similar predicament. The singer ventriloquising the protagonist thus needs to embody himself as authentically as possible in the role of the protagonist, which in this case might tend to preclude a female singer.

Imagining a 'You'

The song 'No Man's Land', which also goes under the title 'The Green Fields of France' or 'The Flowers of the Forest', was written by the Scottish songwriter Eric Bogle, who emigrated to Australia in 1969. It appears to be adapted from the song schema of 'The Unfortunate Rake' ('The Young Sailor Cut Down in His Prime') ☘102 in which a sailor (or a cowboy in American versions, e.g. 'The Cowboy's Lament'/'The Streets of Laredo' ☘103) comes across a comrade on his deathbed lamenting his early death, presumably from syphilis, and instructs the narrator to prepare his funeral. Bogle's melody is similar to that of 'The Unfortunate Rake', but he has extended it quite considerably. The chorus shows a number of close affinities with the 'The Unfortunate Rake' song schema.

No Man's Land

Eric Bogle © Robertson Brown & Associated

1. well how do you do Private Willie McBride
    do you mind if I sit here down by your graveside
    and rest for a while in the warm summer sun
    I've been walking all day and I'm almost done
    I see by your gravestone you were only nineteen
    when you joined the Glorious Fallen in 1916
    oh I hope you died quick and I hope you died clean
    or Willie McBride was it slow and obscene

    Chorus: did they beat the drums slowly did they play the fife lowly
            did the rifles fire o'er ye as they lowered you down
            did the bugles play 'The Last Post' in chorus
            did the pipes play 'The Floo'ers o' the Forest'

2. did you leave a wife or a sweetheart behind
    in some faithful heart is your memory enshrined
    and though you died back in 1916
    to that loyal heart are you forever nineteen
    or are you a stranger without even a name
    forever enshrined behind some glass pane
    in an old photograph torn tattered and stained
    and fading to yellow in a brown leather frame

3. the sun's shining now on these green fields of France
    the warm wind blows gently and the red poppies dance
    the trenches have vanished long under the plough
    no gas and no barbed wire no guns firing now
    but here in this graveyard it's still No Man's Land
    the countless white crosses in mute witness stand
    to man's blind indifference to his fellow man
    and a whole generation who were butchered and damned

4. and I can't help but wonder Willie McBride
    do all those who lie here know why they died
    did you really believe them when they told you the cause
    did you really believe that this war would end wars
    well the suffering the sorrow the glory the shame
    the killing the dying it was all done in vain
    for Willie McBride it all happened again
    and again and again and again and again[16]

The first-person voice in NML addresses the dead soldier directly from the very beginning of the song and continues in that vein till the end, imagining how Willie McBride might have died (stanza 1) and whether he left a sweetheart behind or is just one of innumerable nameless young men caught in the sepia of a fading photograph before their deaths on the battlefields of France (stanza 2). In the third stanza, the voice muses on 'man's blind indifference to his fellow man' that led to the senseless butchering of 'a whole

[16] At this point we would like to thank Eric Bogle warmly for allowing us to use 'No Man's Land'. We are happy to print his 1975 version of the lyrics, as requested, although we have followed the conventions for representing lyrics as outlined in the Introduction.

generation' in World War I, and, in the final stanza, he addresses Willie McBride to ask him whether he, like others, felt that this war would end all wars. His conclusion is a damning evaluation of those who believe that war can solve deep-rooted problems.

As in IJCW, the audience becomes a witness to this process and, even more than in IJCW, is unable to provide any answers. But members of the audience have no difficulty in empathising with the voice, even if it has been 'fictionally' created to carry the song. Bogle's live performance of the song at the Stonyfell Winery outside Adelaide in 2009, which has now been produced as a DVD, is a study in how to sing a song with as much emotional impact as NML. Throughout most of the song Bogle keeps his eyes closed, as if imagining what he is singing about, and in the first half of the final stanza he opens them and moves into a set of stressed, almost non-sung questions to Willie McBride – although of course they are sung – and then closes his eyes to sing his final moving evaluation. Singing this song involves the singer in 'becoming' the fictional 'I'-voice, basically in becoming Bogle himself (cf. June Tabor's fine rendering of the song on her CD *Ashes and Diamonds* with piano accompaniment[17]). Songs involving first-person voices thus present difficulties in deciding the extent to which those voices are presenting a narrative – and if so, whether the narrative is about that person or someone else – or an implied narrative. The singer, who in cases such as NML is never the experiencer of what is sung,[18] nevertheless needs to evoke credibility in inducing the audience to suspend its disbelief.

Song Voices

The ontogenetic cognitive development of a human being from birth until adulthood is like a genetic blueprint, which every human being follows, given the appropriate social conditions and barring individual genetic defects that may hinder that development. It reflects hundreds of thousands of years of evolutionary adaptation in the species *Homo sapiens*. We argued in Chapter 1 that musical vocalisation precedes the acquisition of human language; $song_1$, in other words, must precede $song_2$. But $song_1$ was – and in the case of pre-linguistic infants still is – carried by different voices through which infants not only recognise caregivers and others as distinct individuals but also position and identify them as having distinct attributes with respect to the self.

---

[17] Tabor's solution in the final stanza is to sing the questions in the first half more quietly and then to raise the volume level and to stress the evaluation with more emphasis, particularly the final line 'and again and again and again and again'. She also uses the same strategy in the second half of the third stanza.

[18] Cf. the features set up in the first section of this chapter, which, we maintain, determine the voices used in the performance mode. A performance mode always implies fictionality.

In the first section of this chapter, we accepted Johnstone's interpretation of voice as an index of and connection to 'particular individual human beings with particular utterances and ways of speaking and thinking' (Johnstone 2000: 407). We hypothesised that even pre-linguistic infants develop a notion of voice regardless of the fact that at this stage in their development they are not yet able to recognise 'utterances' as indices of 'ways of speaking and thinking' but only of different ways of vocalising that signal various emotive contents. Once language begins to develop, even at the stage at which comprehension of what is spoken is present prior to speech production, those voices, already internalised in the infant's cognition, index different instances of languaging adapted to different interactional contexts. In this sense, children learn not just language but also the strategic use of different voices, and the ways in which they use those voices constitute a fluid notion of 'self', to which new voices may be added and from which redundant voices may be deleted.

Performance in the widest sense thus involves the use of different voices in the presentation of instances of $song_2$. Some of those voices may be those of the performer *qua* person, even when singing rather than simply keying-in to the singing, but many are likely to be fictional voices interpreted from the song blueprint and adapted to the audience on the occasion of performance and to the social conditions of the ongoing performance mode. Both singers and audiences are aware of these facts, although perhaps not on an overtly conscious level. Since folk performance is geared towards the construction, transformation or confirmation of a sense of *communitas*, it stands to reason that the evocation and recognition of voices is equivalent to the construction of identities that represent the values and aspirations of the community of practice under construction and, by projection, of the wider discourse community.

Singing 'The Unfortunate Tailor' is very different from singing 'No Man's Land'. In both songs we have a first-person voice, but whereas in TUT the singer needs to make a distinction between her/himself as an individual and the identity of a nineteenth-century tailor lamenting the fact that his girl has jilted him, in NML it is imperative that the singer's identity should be indistinguishable from the 'I' musing over the identity of Willie McBride.[19] It is not important that Eric Bogle wrote the song and might actually have gone on a hike in Flanders. In point of fact, Bogle could simply have used this fictional situation as a way of raising the issues in the song. So Bogle the songwriter, Bogle the performer and other performers of his song are all fictionalising, and the important point in performing the song is to create a community of practice that is, as the voice of

---

[19] In fact, it is precisely this that makes it so difficult to sing NML and still to retain enough distance from it to present the issues to an audience while not being swept away by the emotion the song raises.

the activist, united in its condemnation of war. But singing TUT is also different from singing 'The Tailor's Breeches'. The third-person narrator in TTB fulfils the same purpose as the first-person narrator of TUT, i.e. getting the audience to laugh at the tailor. The difference is that the voice is that of a fictional person singing about an incident that s/he claims to have witnessed, and the abstract in the first stanza begins with an address to the audience – 'it's of a brisk young tailor this story I'll relate'. Here at least the tailor is 'brisk' and 'young', and the story might easily have been told as a natural narrative, except that the final stanza is quoted speech by the tailor. The irony is far stronger in TUT than TTB, and the criticism, as a result, is more stringent.

Voices in the ballads appear to be used largely to carry the story forward, and the narrative personality of the voice is less significant than the drama enacted through the quoted speech of the characters. The general trend here is towards unevaluated story building in which the characters are presented almost as pawns in a wider social cosmos. This is not to say that issues are not raised for the audience to evaluate, but those issues are less commonly personal and more generally social and moral. In 'Brown Adam', the implicit issue appears to be one of the social inappropriateness of a sexual relationship between a smith and a noble lady set against the loyalty of the two lovers to one another.

Identifying voices in the folk song is thus a means of identifying characters and also indexing social and moral problems. Performing types of song as different from one another as 'No Man's Land' and 'I Just Can't Wait', on the one hand, and 'Brown Adam', on the other, requires the singer to use the songs to allow the audience to create its interpretations, and this primarily depends on distinguishing between different types of voice in performance.

9   The Song: Text and Entextualisation in Performance

> Even Venda children are able to set entirely new strings of words to an existing melody in a way that is recognized as characteristically Venda ... although they receive no formal instruction and the rules of the system can be derived only from a comparative analysis of many songs. (Blacking 1973: 98)

In Search of the Text

Our aim in this and the following chapter is to deal more explicitly with the way oral 'texts' are performed in ongoing instances of folk performance. In this chapter, we focus on the significance of the terms 'text', 'entextualisation', 'contextualisation' and 'recontextualisation' in assessing what role languaging plays in performance.

We first reconsider our analysis of song performance as presented in the Prologue of this book (Chapter 1). In Chapter 1, we reanalysed song$_2$ in the post-language phase of *Homo sapiens* as languaging presented in musical form and argued that this sets it apart, as a form of performance, from goal-oriented uses of language. We then argued that song is central in constructing and consolidating forms of social bonding in groups of human beings and thus has a crucial ritual function in achieving those ends. We defined a folk song as a song performance, or a singing, 'used to create, constitute and construct a group of people, to bond them together for a space of time and in a specific location, to allow individuals, however transiently, to construct identities with others' (p. 11).

In Chapter 2, we posited that song performances be placed on a continuum between relational and representational performances. Both types of perfor-mance are instantiations of Gamble's ritual 'oval of performance'. Even if, in the case of relational performances, there is no pre-determined stage or concert hall, a space is always created for singers and players to perform 'in'. But it goes without saying that the performers in strongly relational or in predomi-nantly representational performance settings, while possibly selecting the same song to perform, need to approach their performance differently. We revisit this notion and explore it further in Chapter 10, but in the present chapter we focus on the fact that in different performance situations we are likely to be confronted with differences in length due to divergent choices of stanzas (cf. the discussion of 'The Cruel Mother' in Chapter 6), more or less elaborate decoration in singing and intricacy in instrumental accompaniment, different pieces of information focused on keying-in a song (or even a complete absence of any keying-in) and different approaches to audience participation, all in relation to what we expect to be the same song.

Such variation between performances is explained by the fact that they take place in slightly or even very different situations and in front of a different audience each time. But they may also represent different degrees of relational or representational objectives, aspects that a good performer would be aware of and take into consideration in order to pitch the performance correctly. To do this, the singer needs to draw on an underlying cognitive 'competence' which, on the one hand, allows her/him sufficient 'room for manoeuvre' to accommodate to the demands of a performance situation but which, on the other hand, also offers a reliable and stable body of material to draw from in accordance with the performance situation. Given the cultural continuity of the folk song and its demands on performance optimality, one might expect there to be considerable changes over time, but as our discussion in Chapter 3 demonstrated, despite adaptations, e.g. in terms of repertoire and instrumentation, folk song is surprisingly stable in its discourse community.

This stability is also quite prominent in the language of folk song, even though one might expect a degree of linguistic 'updating'. However, updating applies to more recent singer-songwriter material, although there, too, we see language use that eschews the innovativeness of, say, rap, but retains more archaic forms of language use associated with the timelessness of the songs that were quite comfortably adapted by songwriters well into the 1970s. One factor that may contribute to the resilience of types of 'formulaic language' and the wide range of constructions that strike modern ears as 'archaic' is what Anne Lorne Gillies considers 'great literary themes' that 'leap across geographical, historical, cultural and linguistic barriers' (2010: ix) in the sense that they present human predicaments familiar to all of us, predicaments that are as alive today as they were hundreds, perhaps even thousands of years ago. There is thus no great need to update the language if what seems archaic or formulaic is perfectly comprehensible in modern terms, especially if it highlights the fact that the predicaments of the past are as alive as those of the present.

We explore the cognitive competence of singers and performers in the following sections, with a special focus on what a performance event requires of them but also on how it enables their languaging and musicking, i.e. the *use of language and music for a purpose in emergent situations*. This entails enquiring into notions of entextualisation, the nature of the 'text', the role and indexicality of formulaic language as well as formulaic elements in reentexualisation and, finally, the interrelation between formulae as a prosodic/ melodic convenience or even necessity.

Written Texts vs Performance Blueprints

When we attend a WAM concert, a poetry reading or go to see a play, we assume that what we are about to witness will be within clearly defined parameters given by the score or the written version of the poem or play. In the musical performance, the dynamics, speed, phrasing, etc., may vary, the reader will have his/her approach to presenting a poem, and the director of a play will have made some decisions about setting, costumes, focus of the performance and possibly cuts. But in all these cases, we can safely assume that the piece of music, the lines of the poem or play will largely conform to our expectations, because what the performance is based on is available in a 'canonical' *written* format, familiar to the audience, to which they can have access if they wish.

The situation is different in any artistic genre based on oral rather than written transmission, e.g. jokes, folk or popular tales or well-rehearsed personal narratives as well as popular songs and nursery rhymes. Although most of these are accessible in printed format, we do not anticipate the exact reproduction of a model such as in performances based on literary texts or musical scores. It is enough to have a narrative 'blueprint': when we tell a joke, we need to know the protagonists, the setting, what happens in what order and, of course, the punchline. Of these, only the punchline needs to be remembered word-for-word. What leads up to it, how much detail is included or left out, the sense of timing with an audience, etc., is up to the individual telling the joke, and it represents an informal basis on which an audience can evaluate the success of the performer. The teller of a folk tale is in a comparable situation in that s/he needs to be able to recall the protagonists and the direction of the story, but it is enough to be aware of the narrative modules that make up the tale and their sequence. Only relatively few elements need to be remembered word-for-word, mainly ritualised pronouncements or exchanges, e.g. the dialogues between the three Little Pigs and the Big Bad Wolf. Several other elements may also be predictable, keying-in phrases such as 'once upon a time', narrative orientations such as 'after three days' or 'no sooner had ... when ...' or formulaic endings like 'and they lived happily ever after'. How many such phrases and formulae are used is at the discretion of the storyteller, although their presence can index the genre and the social practices typical for storytelling situations.

Text and Entextualisation Revisited

In his analysis of storytelling in the Mexicano community of Córdova, Briggs (1988) uses the concept of 'text', which Hanks (1989: 95) defines as follows:

'When used as a mass noun . . . text can be taken (heuristically) to designate any configuration of signs that is coherently interpretable by some community of users.' As a non-mass, countable noun, its origins lie in the past participle *textus* of the Medieval Latin verb *texere* ('to weave, to join, fit together, braid, interweave, construct, fabricate, build'). Hence a 'text' is something that has been 'woven, fitted together, constructed or built'. This implies (a) that 'text' inherently signifies a configuration of written signs, (b) that the configuration of signs must be interpretable and (c) that there must be a community of users able to carry out the interpretation. If a configuration of signs exists that is not interpretable by any present community of users, it has lost its status as 'text'. Bauman and Briggs (1990) revisit the concept and discuss it in connection with five further concepts derived from the lexeme 'text': 'contextualisation', 'decontextualisation', 'recontextualisation', 'entextualisation' and 're-entextualisation' (see the discussion in Chapter 2). 'Text' itself is useful for our purposes if we see it as a mental blueprint in a singer's mind.

A singer's blueprint is derived from an encounter in an earlier context (a *contextualisation*), with that context stripped away and representing the material that can be assembled to suit the requirements of a future context (a *recontextualisation*). In that sense, like the joke or the folk tale, the musical score, the poem or the play have a 'text' that only comes to life and is made available for interpretation by a community of users when performed and thus realised as an *entextualisation*.

Clearly, the written 'text' for an entextualisation is much more fixed than a mental blueprint, and this accounts for its greater degree of conformity with audience expectations. In oral performance genres, the entextualised outcome is more likely to vary, not only between instantiations by the same performers, but also when a text in its typically generic format is entextualised by different performers. This is as much an outcome of potentially divergent takes on a given text by various performers as it is the result of different contexts in which the entextualisation takes place. In addition, audience expectations also differ. Unlike the case of a score, it is understood that reproducibility in an oral performance genre is not based on a fixed and generally obtainable source, even if the text in question is known or assumed to exist somewhere in printed format.

A distinction needs to be made at this point between the two terms 'entextualisation' and 'recontextualisation'. Leppänen *et al.*, who look at the terms from the point of view of discourse analysis, propose the following: 'Entextualization highlights how such recycling [of texts] involves two related processes: decontextualization – taking discourse material out of its context – and recontextualization – integrating and modifying this material so that it fits in a new context' (2013: 7). Barton and Hamilton (2005: 23), who take a literacy studies view of what a 'text' is, define 'recontextualisation' as 'moving texts across contexts'. We prefer 'entextualisation' throughout this book to highlight the fact that a text on its own and out of a context is a reified object, i.e. it is 'decontextualised', but that it always has the potential of being brought to life as a process in performance, in an 'entextualisation'. 'Text' can thus be seen as the decontextualised abstraction of a performance, a blueprint for future recontextualisations of, say, an oral narrative. Can we then apply the same criteria to songs embedded in and intended for a discourse community in the sense that we understand the term 'folk song', i.e. a song that creates and promotes a *communitas* and that 'answers back' in reaction to social friction in more or less direct ways?

A 'Flexible Schematic' for Performance

We posit that in the case outlined at the end of the previous section, there are parameters that go beyond the way in which 'text' has hitherto been understood. In a folk song performance, the performer also needs a performance blueprint and textual blueprint, a plan to help assemble the essential elements of a song as derived from earlier performances, or from some form of perpetuation. However, this blueprint is more complex, connecting aspects that go beyond those we need for an oral narrative, simply because the performance of a song is a multimodal process. Apart from the song lyrics, entextualisation needs to take the music – tunes, harmonies, keys and arrangements – into consideration. In addition, most folk singers have an 'agenda', to inform an audience and to preserve for them what they may, rightly or wrongly, perceive as a cultural artefact in danger of disappearing. It is also probable that they would like to share with their listeners their indignation about a social condition or a human predicament, in forms of 'explicit', but more often 'entailed' and 'encoded' answering back (as discussed in the third section of Chapter 4 and in Andres Morrissey in preparation). Such aspects are typically part of the keying-in of a song as established in Chapters 2, 7 and 8. Hence, the content of the keying-in needs to be considered as part of the performance. Finally, for the purposes of a representational performance a song is typically embedded in a series of other songs, all chosen with the purpose of creating a set. This must remain adaptable in performance to audience reaction and needs to be flexible and emergent.

The 'Flexible Schematic'

Because of the complexity of elements far beyond those required for a potential entextualisation, we also refer to our development of the Bauman and Briggs concept of 'text' as a *flexible song schematic*. A *schematic* represents a blueprint or plan for (re)assembly in electrical engineering showing the

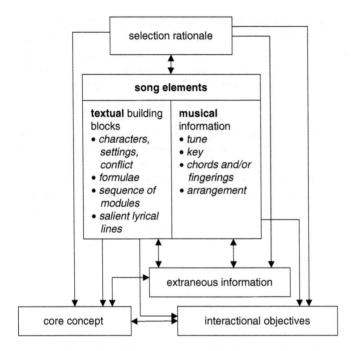

Figure 9.1. *'Components' of a flexible song schematic*

wiring in an appliance in the form of a plan of all the potential connections and switches that can be activated if and when the operation of the appliance requires it. For a flexible song schematic, the same applies in an actual performance where the potential connections between the various elements can be made if they are appropriate in the performance situation.

In Figure 9.1 we present a model of what a flexible song schematic might contain to ensure the singer's ability to achieve a successful re-entextualisation.

The 'Components'

A singer decides to adopt a song into her/his repertoire for a number of different reasons. The *selection rationale* for a song may arise from hearing a formative or iconic performance. It may be influenced by the way a concept is expressed in the song. It may be a consequence of the appeal of the melody. The song may address an issue to which it answers back that is close to the singer's heart, often once s/he has explored its historical or socio-political background. It may be perceived as lending itself to the successful promotion of a *communitas*, either by inviting audience participation or by presenting the singer with an opportunity to appeal emotionally to the audience (cf. our analysis of 'No Man's Land' in the previous chapter). Although such a rationale for the inclusion of a song in a repertoire may become less than overt over time, it still represents its *raison d'être* in the singer's material,[1] which may be expressed in some detail in a representational, but less so if at all in a mainly relational performance.

The *song elements* form the central component in the schematic. One focus of attention lies in the lyrical elements, the 'text' proper. For a song with a narrative (see our discussion of voices in Chapter 8), the singer needs to have cognitive access to characters, settings, conflicts or complications and the sequence of events. S/he further needs to be familiar with the language, the typical discourse used in folk songs, which is often highly formulaic, indexing the song type (e.g. ballad, lullaby, protest song). The song narratives are often in modular form and composed in song schemata. Alongside such formulaic elements, there might also be individual lines that have appealed to the singer, as heard in a specific performance or found in a printed source, lines that may constitute an innovation (see Chapter 5).

In addition to the textual elements, the singer also needs to have access to *musical elements*, in particular the melody of the song and the phrasing, i.e. where to slow down, where to pause for effect, which elements to highlight with voice level, etc. Directly linked to the melody is the question of the key in which to sing. In many cases this can be considered with a degree of sanguinity as many songs, especially traditional ones, use either the authentic range (from lower to upper tonic, e.g. in the key of G from G_0 to G_1), or the plagal range (from the fourth below to the fifth above the tonic; in the key of G from D below G to D above). In other words, they remain within an octave (see Figure 9.2). The so-called mixed range, from the lower fifth to the high tonic is obviously more demanding as it requires a reach over twelve notes, but it is not particularly widespread in traditional folk songs (cf. Bronson 1962 or Palmer 1972: 104). The key of the song is important, as it needs to fit the singer's range comfortably[2] and should not be beyond the audience's vocal range if they are to join in.

Unless a song is to be performed a cappella, a further consideration for the performer is the chords and chord changes and/or instrumental demands such as the fingering on the accompanying instrument. If it is to be performed in

---

[1] Significantly, such considerations are often verbalised in the keying-in sequences during performances, on sleeve notes or in CD booklets and in song collections by individual singers (e.g. Christy Moore in Connolly 1984).

[2] A case in point is 'The Flying Cloud' (Roud 1802) ♪104 which requires the singer to reach a small second below the root note and a fifth above the octave root note, i.e. F#-1 to D1. To sing the notes at the extreme ends of the spectrum the amateur singer must be aware of her/his vocal limitations.

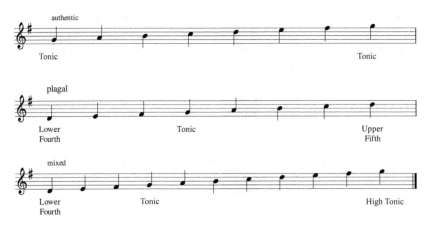

Figure 9.2. *Ranges of folk song tunes*

a group, the singer needs to have a clear idea about the arrangement of the song, e.g. preludes, intermezzi, instrumental passages and codas. These may vary or shift, depending on the context in which the song is played, but their potential places need to be stored in the schematic.

Most folk performers do not regard their craft as purely entertaining, even though entertainment is an important element. In contrast to many other forms of popular music, there is often a more or less overt component that focuses on educating or informing the audience. Singers therefore acquire extraneous information about the provenance of their material, the origins of the lyrics, their social and/or political significance and possibly traditional performance practices (e.g. in work songs; see Chapter 3) but, in addition, they often give the history that underlies the events presented, especially in the case of songs with entailed or encoded protest (see the discussion of Maddy Prior's concert at Cecil Sharp House in Chapter 11). Other items of extraneous information may be observations on the origins of the tunes since many songs, typically broadsides but also protest songs, are noted as being 'sung to the tune of . . .'. The aim in doing this was to aid their distribution since the tunes would have been widely known, and such information may also be provided for an audience.

The impetus for gathering extraneous information may also stem from a central element either influencing the selection rationale or derived from an analysis of its building blocks, viz. what we call the *core concept*. The core concept constitutes the central idea in the singer's mind about what the song might convey to different audiences in both relational and representational performance frames. In the first instance, a core concept may be relevant to a socio-political, socio-cultural or philosophical theme that an audience may (or are expected to) concern themselves with. It may also convey the emotions of the character ventriloquised in the song, narrator or protagonist, e.g. longing or regret in songs of unrequited love, affection for a loved one or relief at a happy ending when separated lovers are reunited.[3] A third type of core concept is simply to amuse the audience by the way in which characters or their conflicts are depicted.[4] Finally, in some cumulative songs, the core concept may be to show off the singer's verbal dexterity and control of the material, e.g. R.J.W.'s version of 'The Barley Mow' (Roud 944), in which the list of the objects and persons whose health should be drunk is usually delivered with increasing tempo as the song progresses, leaving the audience, who have been invited to join in, hopelessly behind.

In other words, the core concept, apart from conveying an idea, communicating emotions, creating amusement (e.g. inviting complicity between singer and audience in the case of encoded sexual references, e.g. 'The Trooper's Nag' as sung by Maddy Prior at the 'Back to the Tradition' concert) or allowing a performer to showcase virtuoso control, is also informed by the *interactional objectives* of a song. A central objective in many songs is the invitation to the audience to join in; in other songs, it is to engage an audience in an emotion. Interactional performance objectives in representational performance frames can also decide on the position a song occupies in a set, e.g. as an opening song or a closing number, as a rousing song to get an audience involved or as a calming influence at the close of possible encores before performers and audience leave the ritual oval of song performance. The core concept is just as much part of the song schematic as the selection rationale, the song elements and the extraneous information. The singer is aware of these, just as s/he is of the stanzas, potential additional narrative elements such as a further dramatic exchange between the protagonists, various intermezzi or instrumental passages in the music, etc., all of which can be (re)assembled into an actual performance or adapted during it, i.e. be re-entextualised.

The number of stanzas chosen for a performance may vary, depending on the situation (e.g. the length of the set) or on expectations concerning the composition of the audience. An audience of hard-core aficionados may be prepared to sit through all the ritual repetitions of a traditional ballad, whereas a less

---

[3] A classic example of this latter situation is the song 'The Plains of Waterloo' ☉105 (Roud 960), in which Annie welcomes her lover William returning from the final battle after not recognising him at first.

[4] The song 'An Old Man Once Courted Me' ☉106 (Roud 210), where the young female first-person narrator warns the audience not to wed an old man, or the song 'The Brisk Young Butcher' ☉107 (Roud 167), in which the young rake is repaid with his three-month-old baby being sat on his knee as the 'change' to 'a sovereign' with which he duped the chamber maid into spending the night with him.

seasoned, general audience might be better served by an edited version with cuts (cf. our discussion of 'The Cruel Mother' in Chapter 6). 'Tam Lin' ☺108 (Roud 35; Child 39) provides an interesting example of how this works in practice. The ballad is printed in Child (1965, vol. I: 340–58) with nine variants, the longest being variant G (fifty-nine stanzas) from Buchan's MSS and variant I (fifty-six stanzas) from the *Minstrelsy of the Scottish Border, II.* The A version is listed as having been 'communicated by Robert Burns' and has a total of forty-two stanzas. Interestingly enough, it contains a full account in three stanzas (by Tam Lin) of what the Queen of the Fairies will turn him into when his lover Janet pulls him off his horse while the fairy procession passes by. The actual rescue, however, is given laconically in two lines, 'sae weel she minded what he did say / and young Tam Lin did win' (ibid.: 342). The rescue could have been retold in a repetition of the warning, but we can only speculate. The informative website mainlynorfolk.info[5] not only furnishes a comprehensive recording history but also lists the lyrics of several seminal recordings. The forty-two stanzas of the A version are cut considerably, ranging from twenty-one (Fairport Convention) to thirty-seven stanzas (Mike Waterson). But only the Fairport Convention version on the 1969 LP *Liege and Lief* retains the shortened account of the transmutation. All other documented versions, Dave and Toni Arthur (1970), Anne Briggs (1971), Mike Waterson (1977), Steeleye Span (1991, live recording) and Jon Boden (2010 on *A Folk Song a Day*, www.afolksongaday.com) furnish the three transmutations both in the foretelling and in the narrative. In all likelihood, unlike Burns and the seminal Fairport Convention recording, these performers felt the need to conform to the expectations of the ballad text within the folk singing discourse community.

Such practice is evident in the treatment of the lyrics, i.e. the selection of textual building blocks to create a version for performance, but similar choices are made when deciding on musical arrangements, the greater or reduced complexity of an accompaniment, how to involve the audience in the song and how much background needs to be imparted during the keying-in of a song.

The Language of Folk Song

Folk songs, and in particular ballad lyrics, are conspicuous for the high degree of stability in the language they use. Many songs perpetuated in the early days of antiquarian endeavours have survived with relatively few changes to their language. One might assume that folk song lyrics, as they are passed on through the generations, would tend to update their phraseology, but this has not been

---

[5] https://mainlynorfolk.info/sandy.denny/songs/tamlin.html, accessed 21 April 2015.

the case. In general, the retention of formulaic and archaic language in no way hinders our present-day understanding of the texts, since the songs themselves often deal with timeless human and social predicaments that have always concerned us and are always likely to do so.

Retaining the language of a song is not a wilful exercise in harping on the past, as parodists of folk song like the Kipper Family or Kenneth Williams (in his character Rambling Sid Rumpo) appear to suggest. On the contrary, it indexes the timelessness of the problems dealt with and the answering back they provoke as a form of cultural memory. More modern songs do not use the same kinds of linguistic formulation, but they certainly deal with the same kinds of problem (see Bogle's 'No Man's Land' and Campbell and Dunkerley's 'I Just Can't Wait' in Chapter 8). As long as we have no difficulty in interpreting the lyrics, there is no call for any linguistic updating. In this section we describe the typical language of folk song lyrics to prepare the ground for a later section, in which we explore more reasons why we have this textual predictability and what it means for singers/performers.

Formulaic Lexis and Phrases

Formulaic nouns and adjectives are a characteristic of traditional folk songs and ballads: men are described as 'lively', 'brisk' – which is often collocated with 'young' – or 'bold', 'jolly' or 'merry', often with a reference to their occupation or rank as an indicator of their social status, with the adjectives suggesting that they are energetic and (sexually) proactive. Alternatively, they may be 'brave' or 'valiant', usually in descriptions of conflict. Apart from their occupation, they are represented as 'blades', 'lads' or 'coves'. Women are often 'maids', 'damsels', etc. and are usually generically described in terms of their looks – and possibly their disposition – as 'fair', a term also used for men as a love-interest, or 'sweet', again often collocated with 'young'. In terms of adjective/head noun word order, they can also be placed in post-nominal position, e.g. 'lady gay', the post-nominal adjective not only being easier to create a rhyme with, but also conforming to lyrical prosody (avoiding two adjacent stressed syllables) and the needs of the tune with its downbeats, corresponding to the structure of a typical folk song measure. 'Loves' of both sexes are 'true' to the point, even in some modern compositions in the folk idiom, e.g. Sting's 'You Will Be My Ain True Love' ♪109. This particular A+N construction is so fixed that a case might be made for the nominal compound 'true love' since a deceitful lover is described as a 'false true love' as in the song 'The False True Love' (Roud 419) ♪110. In addition, in some print versions we find the hyphenated spelling 'true-love'.

If there is a limit to the range of adjectives used, the same is true for descriptions in general. A 'fair maid(en)' is also of good character, whereas her evil counterpart is 'black as coal'. Women have 'lily-white hands' and 'yellow hair', and confronted with a catastrophe they grow 'pale and wan'. Penknives as murder weapons are often 'wee' and simultaneously 'three feet long', 'steeds' are 'milk-white', 'berry-brown' or 'dapple-grey', 'goshawks' are 'gay' and momentous communications are made in 'a broad letter'. Men sexually on the prowl 'have' or 'cast a roving eye', disapproving persons of authority are known to 'look a grim look' and in formal contexts they 'look over' their 'left shoulder' to make pronouncements. Sexual encounters are described in which the lover 'lay the lady on her back / and asked no man's leave'. Similes are equally formulaic, steeds or messengers 'run swifter than the wind', a dress is 'greener than the grass' or, indeed, the nearly homophonic 'glass' (a possible mondegreen); in riddle ballads, the riddles are usually quite predictable, with 'heaven' being 'higher than/nor the trees' and 'hell . . . deeper than the sea'.

Formulaic Lines, Stanzas and Episodes

Riddle songs and ballads (e.g. 'Riddles Wisely Expounded', Child 1; Roud 161 Ⓐ111; or 'Captain Wedderburn's Courtship', Child 46; Roud 36 Ⓐ112) are also interesting in that they tend to share not just formulaic images but formulaic lines or even formulaic stanzas. Some, e.g. 'The Two Sisters' Ⓐ113, have a chorus in the second and fourth lines. Apart from the questions about the height of trees and the depth of the sea, we often have riddles involving 'a cherry that has no stone' or 'a chicken that has no bone', the answers being 'a cherry when it's blooming' or 'a chicken in the egg', with both the questions and the answers formulated almost identically. Cumulative songs like 'The Maid Freed from the Gallows' (Child 95; Roud 144) Ⓐ114, 'Lord Randall' (Child 12; Roud 10) Ⓐ115 or 'Billy Boy' (Roud 326) Ⓐ116 take the formulaic elements one step further by repeating the same stanza or exchange with minimal changes. In 'The Maid Freed from the Gallows', none of the family members brings the gold to save the girl from being hanged, but the 'true love' does. In 'Lord Randall', the murder becomes obvious through the repetitions, but again it is the last one that clinches things. And in 'Billy Boy', it is the sexual intercourse indicated in the last-but-one stanza that makes the crucial difference, although the final stanza breaks the repetition and contains the almost biblical age of Billy's prospective lover as a form of coda. This way of presenting a conflict or the resolution of a complication through repetition is referred to as *incremental repetition* (Gummere 1907: 90), a device that is also widely used in ballads that have actual narrative passages unlike the three mentioned above, where the action is played out exclusively in a dramatic dialogue.

Formulaic elements are a mainstay of folk song narrative. They can be individual lines, e.g. in 'The Jolly Beggar' Ⓐ117 the curious and attractive daughter 'views' the handsome visitor, a beggar or a rambler of apparently lower class, 'cheek and chin', or where the messenger or the lover runs 'through the moss and the mire' (e.g. in 'The Hexhamshire Lass' ♫118).[6] They can cover two lines, e.g. 'out then spake the Queen o' Fairies / and an angry woman was she' in 'Tam Lin' and an almost identical wording in 'Bonnie Jean o' Bethelnie/Glenlogie', Child 238; Roud 101 ♫119) 'up spoke her faither / and a wae man was he'. A heroine getting ready to go to a place where the next complicating action occurs is often presented in an entire stanza, e.g. in 'Tam Lin', 'Janet kilted her green kirtle / a little aboon her knee / and she has snooded her yellow hair / a little aboon her bree'. The beauty and attraction of the main character can be presented in two formulaic stanzas, in 'Bonnie Jean o' Bethelnie/Glenlogie' with 'there were six and six horsemen / rode through Banchory fair / and bonnie Glenlogie / was the flower that was there // there were nine and nine nobles / sat at the king's hall / bonnie Glenlogie / was the flower of them all'. Essentially the same stanza with minor changes can also be found in 'Tam Lin' and 'Little Sir Hugh' (Child 155; Roud 73) ♫120. The formula could be schematised as follows: 'it's [any significant number] [males or females] / were doing x / and [hero or heroine] / was the y-est of them all'.

Finally, an entire episode can be told in a number of formulaic stanzas, notably the motif of the two lovers being buried in separate places and the plants that grow out of their graves (in a first stanza) entwining in a true lovers' knot (often in a second stanza). A third stanza may be added in which a villain or their adversary comes past and uproots the plants. This example illustrates that songs may use formulae beyond lines or stanzas, but that they can also occur as episodes told in several stanzas used across a number of ballads with the macro-schema of ill-matched or ill-fated lovers who lose their lives either for love or at the hand of disapproving family (cf. 'Earl Brand' Child 7; Roud 23 ♫121, or 'Sweet William and Fair Margaret' Child 74; Roud 253) ♫122.

Formulae for Structuring Narratives

The formulaic elements discussed so far refer to the content of the songs and ballads. However, other formulae may indicate a narrative 'abstract' or function as a narrative 'orientation' (cf. Labov and Waletzky 1967). They usually occur at the beginning of a song, but some may reoccur as the song progresses.

'It's/'Tis of a ...' or 'There was a ...' introduce the protagonist(s), often indicating the direction the narrative will take; they thus have the function of an

---

[6] Sound symbolism would merit a discussion in its own right, the alliterations in 'gay goshawk', 'berry brown' and here, but also in instances of vowel harmony, e.g. in 'lady gay'. For reasons of space, we can merely allude to such phonological phenomena here.

abstract. However, the type of protagonist introduced with formulae such as the 'fair young damsel', the 'bold highwayman', the 'brisk and lively blade', etc. indicates the content that audiences can expect if they are familiar with folk song discourse. The collocations conjure up the character and her/his personal features and are thus pivotal to the narrative, representing a reliable indication as to what subsequent action can be expected. The next line, often in the form of a non-finite verbal post-modifier, typically shows what the character is doing when the narrative opens, shifting from the abstract to the orientational function.

Other opening formulae have a more overtly orientational function in that they situate the narrative in time and/or space. Like the features of the protagonists and the circumstances described, these are generic rather than specific, as few if any of the typical characteristics of the time or place invoked are made use of in the narrative. The 'Geordie complex' (see Chapter 5) is a convincing example for this. The opening lines of different versions mention identifiable places, i.e. 'London Bridge' or 'Banstead Downs', but the lyrics in any of the versions make no further reference to either location, and they do not seem to be crucial to the story except possibly by implication.[7] The spatial orientation may appear to be of some importance to indicate whether the setting is urban, as in 'oh the highland lads are *come to town* / and landed in head quarters' ('The Rambling Siuler', Roud 7972 ☉123) or rural 'the pauky auld carle came *oer the lee*' ('The Gaberlunzie Man'/'The Beggar Man', Child 279, Roud 118 ☉124), but it is often vague, e.g. 'as I roved *out*'. However, as both the 'Rambling Siuler' and the 'Gaberlunzie Man' have a similar song schema,[8] a disguised guest with designs on the beautiful daughter of the house, in both cases successful in their endeavours, it can be argued that the rural or urban setting is not crucial for either narrative.

A similar phenomenon can be observed for openings that serve as a temporal orientation. Here, too, we get an apparently clear indication as to when the narrative is meant to take place, but, again, this reference is little more than generic. 'As it fell out on a midsummer morning' or ''twas in the merry month of May/June', but like the locations mentioned in opening formulae, there is typically little if any further reference to the time at which the events take place. It is possible that some of the budding relationships or the erotic encounters could be associated with the awakening of nature and fertility in May as symbolised by the maypole. So the connection could be as loose as with London Bridge and Banstead Downs in the Geordie complex, i.e.

---

[7] London as the capital city might be a place where a sufficiently powerful authority might pardon Geordie. The generic reference to 'the judge', who is reduced to the archetypal arbiter over life and death, however, seems to obviate the necessity for a supreme central authority.

[8] Cf. http://mudcat.org/thread.cfm?threadid=134274, post by Steve Gardham, accessed 23 April 2015.

plausible but not indispensable. This also applies when, less typically, the narrative is apparently set in winter as in 'Cold and Raw' (Roud 3007) ⓐ125, where nothing beyond the first stanza is made of the fact that 'winter has come severely'. It is much more likely that phonological considerations are the basis for some of these choices as 'severely' is made to assonate with 'morning early'. 'May' and 'June' are quite productive as rhyming words, and 'midsummer morning' with its two stressed syllables neatly fills a first line with its four stressed syllables and leads up to the second with three.

A final formulaic opening invites an implied, relatively specific audience with little or no relation to those actually present in a folk club, a concert hall or on a festival stage, with a phrase such as 'come all you ...'. This opening expression is even used to refer to so-called 'come-all-ye' ballads and broadsides. They are also widespread in songs by songwriters of the twentieth century, e.g. Ed Pickford in 'The Worker's Song' ⓐ126 or 'The Pound-a-Week Rise' ⓐ127, in Guthrie's 'Ranger's Command' ⓐ128,[9] and later in Dylan's work. In his 2015 MusiCares Person of the Year acceptance speech, Dylan gives an interesting account of precisely this phenomenon and how he adapted it in 'The Times They Are a-Changin'' ⓐ129 (in itself a non-standard and somewhat archaic usage):

If you sung all these 'come all ye' songs all the time like I did, you'd be writing, 'Come gather round people where ever you roam, admit that the waters around you have grown / (...)'

You'd have written that too. There's nothing secret about it. You just do it subliminally and unconsciously, because that's all enough, and that's all you know. That was all that was dear to me. They were the only kinds of songs that made sense.[10]

More generally, addressing the audience, as we saw in Chapter 8, is often a way to open a song and to key in the actual or implied narratives. As in these cases, they mostly have a coda, a moral or some advice for the group of individuals addressed, expressed at the end of the song (Labov and Waletzky 1967).

Our discussion in the previous chapter has demonstrated that there is often a switch in narrative perspective, in the 'voice', between the opening stanza with its typical formulae from first-person to third-person narration or vice versa. But opening stanzas also introduce the speaker to the rest of the song, i.e. they contain a switch from an initial to a second first-person narrator, a protagonist introduced in that first stanza. The first narrator is not gendered and the audience can thus understand that persona as the performer, but

---

[9] In this particular song Guthrie makes conspicuous use of formulaic language (including mention of a 'fair maiden') (www.letrasdemusicas.fm/woody-guthrie/ranger-s-command#saying-come-all-you-cowboys-and-fight-for-your-land, accessed 23 April 2015).

[10] www.rollingstone.com/music/news/read-bob-dylans-complete-riveting-musicares-speech-201 50209#ixzz3fPxKy0Jn, accessed 23 April 2015.

the second narrator invariably is. So the question arises as to whether such an 'orientation' (or possibly 'abstract') stanza has the function of a narrative frame which avoids the issue of gendering in the main body of the song by allowing a contrast between the gender of the performer and the main voice.

In the first section of this chapter, we established the notion of the 'song schematic' as the singer's equivalent of Bauman and Briggs' conceptualisation of 'text'. The second section explored the language-based components of the song schematic and its reliance on formulaic language, but it left open the question as to why this is of importance for our analysis. In the following section, we explore this question in some detail.

The 'Song Elements': Functions of Language and Form for Entextualisation

In the quotation above Dylan indicates that songwriters writing in the 'traditional idiom' seem to be adopting, selectively, and in some cases quite regularly, the language of that tradition.[11] That language, its formulae and its lexical and syntactic elements, is part of a folk discourse archive and also an expression of cultural memory, and as such it is indexical of folk song as a whole.

It is not our purpose to enter a debate on the application of oral-formulaic theory (see Lord 1960; Parry 1930, 1932) in this context. As Atkinson (1997: 261) puts it, there are 'undeniable differences between ballads and folk songs and their context and the vastly longer South Slavic (and also Homeric and Old English) epics'. Even a lengthy ballad is unlikely to be much more than ten minutes long.[12] In addition, folk songs – and ballads – have rhymes or assonances and appear in a clearly stanzaic form, which, while allowing for freedom in formulations, nevertheless provide a framework that accounts for the high degree of conformity between versions of the same song extant in earlier collections or in various recordings (cf. Andersen and Pettitt 1979 and Bronson 1945). This conformity is also a result of the way in which ballads, but also many less overtly narrative song stanzas are structured, overwhelmingly, in alternating lines of four and three stressed syllables with any number of unstressed syllables in between. This structure is further dependent on and supported by the tunes, whose importance should not be underestimated in terms of the prosody of the language, the poetic form of the songs and, of course, as an aid to the performer's recall.

---

[11] This can be understood in the popular sense, but also in the way we have defined it earlier, as being a recognisable reproduction of what a discourse community would consider long-term practice.

[12] 'Jack Orion' (♪)129 on Pentangle's 1970 album *Cruel Sister* with its 18 minutes 38 seconds covering an entire side of the vinyl, is an exception. Fairport Convention's 'Tam Lin' is the longest piece on the album, but only lasts 7 minutes 20 seconds.

Whereas it makes a lot of sense to assume a re-composition on the fly with the use of modular elements – not dissimilar from the ballad – in an epic performance, it is more sensible to presuppose that performers of lengthy traditional folk songs, especially those with a relatively overt narrative, rely on sequences of events, on formulaic elements (collocations, phrases, lines, stanzas and units of stanzas; see also Buchan 1997[1972]), but also on the tune that determines the form of the lyrics to a considerable degree. Most singers we have interviewed for this book categorically reject the notion of a re-composition in performance as suggested in oral-formulaic theory. However, they do concede the increased ease with which they are able to internalise such songs through their reliance on events, formulae and the interplay between tune and stanza, and this ties in with Atkinson's view 'that memorisation is the most important element in the transmission of the Child ballads' (see also Andersen 1985; Andersen and Pettitt 1979) and that

the formulas not only denote the same action or narrative idea in different ballad types, but that they also share a common range of supra-narrative functions whereby they establish the same connotations in different ballad types. The formulas are seen not as a mark of the oral-formulaic re-creation of the ballads but as an essential part of the grammar of balladry which has been generated as the result of many generations of singers facing the problem of finding appropriate expression for recurrent ideas. (Atkinson 1997: 261–2)

It thus makes sense to look at the way in which a narrative in a song is structured into individual steps and what role the formulae discussed in the third section play in the composition of these individual steps. In the next two subsections, we examine this from the practical perspective of a singer preparing for a performance.

Song Schemata

For a prospective performer, learning a song is easier if it contains recognisable components, which can be combined or recombined in performance, in other words, if s/he can rely on formulae. Formulae are present not only in ballads, as the examples above may suggest, but also in other kinds of song. A solid knowledge of these formulae obviates the need to learn a lengthy text word-for-word. But in order to be able to assemble the formulaic lexis, phrases, lines, stanzas and sequences of stanzas into a song for a performance, the singer also needs to recall the narrative. This is possible if a singer has access to a narrative structure into which the formulaic modules can be integrated. The fact that many oral narratives are composed of motifs, which, in the case of folk tales, can be categorised into catalogues of motifs (Aarne and Thompson's tale type index, cf. Uther 2004; see also

Dundes 1997), facilitates this process. A folk singer is not only able to draw on formulae, but s/he can equally rely on modular elements told in a sequence of events involving recognisable character types that are often, but not always, differentiated from one another socially.

In what follows, we focus once more on the two ballads 'Earl Richard' and 'The Knight and the Shepherd's Daughter'. Their song schema illustrates the cast and the sequence of events needed to reconstruct the song for performance, which we repeat here for the convenience of the reader:

(A) *Character types*: a shepherd's daughter (low social class); a knight or a nobleman (upper social class); a king or a queen (the apex of the secular social system)

(B) *Sequence of events*:

    (1) knight, while out riding, meets shepherd girl;

    (2) knight seduces or rapes shepherd girl;

    (3) girl asks after knight's identity;

    (4) knight does not give a clear answer;

    (5) girl follows knight to the king's/queen's court;

    (6) girl accuses one of the king's/queen's knights of having had sexual intercourse with her;

    (7) king/queen calls up his/her knights and the culprit is revealed;

    (8) king/queen 'gives the knight's body' to the girl, i.e. orders him to marry her;

    (9) knight agrees to marry girl, or marries her, but is not pleased at the match he has made.

In some versions or songs with the same or a similar structure, there is also an event (10), where the woman is revealed to be either of high social status or very wealthy.[13] This is the case in the sixty-stanza E version of 'Earl Richard' (which Child lists under his versions of 'The Knight and the Shepherd's Daughter'), in which the noble identity of the girl as the king of Scotland's daughter is finally revealed at the end of the song.

Both ballads present the same sequence of events, the same *song schema*, i.e. steps (1) to (9), or (10) if this step is included. From this point of view we are likely to classify 'Earl Richard' and 'The Knight and the Shepherd's Daughter' as the same song, as Bronson (1962) indeed does. However, at the prototypical level of performance, because other elements in the flexible song schematic differ, most notably the tune, they may be considered to be two different songs. Roud (2012)

---

[13] However, nothing in the narrative would give an indication of either the woman's elevated social status or her wealth. Whether such endings are the result of an innovation at some stage in the transmission process is an open question. Bronson documents cases where endings have been changed because the singer, in his case 'Mrs Brown of Falkland', an important source for a number of early collectors, 'rounds off an inconclusive or non-climatic ending with additional lines intended to give force or point' (Bronson 1945: 132–33).

discusses the problem that two apparently separate songs may be listed in the index as one despite different titles and small differences in the surface manifestations of the song (including variations of the tune). He concludes that in this instance the song exhibits identical ideas and linguistic constructions.[14]

A song schema is represented in just enough generalised terms, rather than in terms of detailed characters and events, to distinguish that song schema from other song schemata. For example, at step (7) above, the significant event is that the king/queen calls up all her/his knights to discover the culprit. But in both 'Earl Richard' and 'The Knight and the Shepherd's Daughter', we learn that the knight who had sexual intercourse with the shepherd girl was the last to turn up ('Earl Richard': 'Earl Richard used to lead them all / but far behind came he'; 'The Knight and the Shepherd's Daughter': 'young William he came last of all / when first he used to be'). In each song, then, we have two lines of a highly formulaic nature that appear almost identically in other songs in which someone with a guilty conscience is not willing to show her/himself immediately. The detail itself has no direct consequence on the overall schema of the song, which would be the socially superior violator being forced to marry his socially inferior victim. But in an instantiation of a performance the sequence of these narrative motifs, the song schema helps the singer to perform what may well be a rather long and wordy song.

Formulaic Song Motifs (FSMs)

Familiarity with schemata, on the one hand, and with the formulaic language as discussed in this subsection, on the other hand, is a great help for singers to retain and adapt a song without needing to remember the lyrics word-for-word. Such formulae and schemata are a form of linguistic conventionalisation typical of oral transmission (see Lord 1960) in which pre-formulated 'chunks' of text are transferred from one song to another. We call these textual 'chunks' *formulaic song motifs* (FSMs). Apart from being typical features of the oral transmission of songs, they also act as mnemonic devices to aid singers in performance.

We demonstrate the use of FSMs for a singer in the first stanzas of 'Earl Richard' and 'The Knight and the Shepherd's Daughter'. The opening line of 'Earl Richard', 'it's of a brisk young shepherd maid', contains two FSMs, 'it's of X' and 'a brisk young shepherd maid', the latter indicating a favourite lower-class rural character type. The 'it's of X' FSM, as we saw above, serves as a formulaic abstract to the story that will be unfolded through the song. The fact that a shepherdess is a central protagonist immediately triggers a further FSM

---

[14] Roud explicitly mentions alphabet songs ('The Sailor's Alphabet' ♪131, 'The Miner's Alphabet' ♪132 and presumably also Captain 'Bob' Roberts' 'The Bargeman's Alphabet' as performed by R.J.W.) as being given one and the same Roud number. We would agree with this approach as we regard these songs as having the same song schema.

as the second line, the final lexeme of which requires a rhyme or an assonance in the fourth line: 'kept sheep one summer's day'. The third line, 'and by there came a brisk young man', is again composed of two FSMs, 'by there came X' and 'a brisk young man', the first of which introduces the second protagonist and the second a characterisation of that person as an attractive male alert to the chance of a sexual adventure. The fourth line is again an FSM, which conveniently ends with the required rhyme: 'and stole her heart away' – a probable euphemism for 'and raped her'. These FSMs help the singer to assemble the first stanza, but the implications raised by them would be immediately accessible to a folk audience as being indexical of a traditional ballad and possibly the suggestion of a song schema. Stanza 1 thus not only represents the first two steps in the song schema of 'Earl Richard', (1) knight, while out riding, meets shepherd girl and (2) knight seduces or rapes shepherd girl, but it is composed entirely of FSMs, which introduce the two protagonists (1) and confront the audience with the complicating action of the socially superior taking advantage of the lower-class protagonist (2).

The first four lines of 'The Knight and the Shepherd's Daughter' (the version given in *The New Penguin Book of English Folk Songs* as in Chapter 5) also present the first two song steps in the song schema, and they use almost identical FSMs. In the first line the 'shepherd's daughter' is substituted by a 'shepherd maid', which triggers the same FSM in the second line, but again with a slight variation, i.e. 'keeping sheep upon a hill'. The third line is composed of similar FSMs as in 'Earl Richard', with the variation that 'a brisk young man' becomes 'a roving blade', the word 'blade' being more indicative of his sexual intentions, whereas 'by there came' is mutated into 'came riding by', which in itself is similarly formulaic. The only line in both openings which is a debatable FSM is 'and vowed he'd have his will', although the formula 'x had his will (with …)' appears in many songs in reference to unwanted pregnancies.

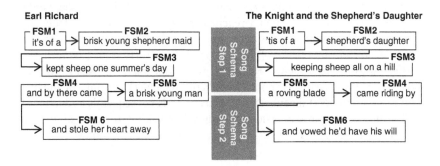

Figure 9.3. *FSMs and song schema steps 1 and 2 in the first stanza of two ballads*

In the first four lines of each song, the two main protagonists are presented and the complicating action, the 'rape', is hinted at, largely by using FSMs. Knowledge of these FSMs and of the song schema by a singer is an invaluable aid in committing the song to memory when one of the principal modes of transmission is through performance.

Stanza and Verse

Nevertheless, the tune also plays an important part here. Bronson lists a total of twenty-two, with one exception, whose inclusion is somewhat questionable, in either 2/4, 4/4 or 6/8 time.[15] Based on their rhythms, all of these measures have a regular downbeat. In the case of 4/4 and 6/8, the first would be prominent, the second somewhat less so. These downbeats correspond with stressed syllables, and unstressed syllables at the beginning of a line, especially lines 1 and 3, would fall on the anacrusis, usually maximally a quarter note/ crotchet, possibly split into two quavers in the case of two unstressed syllables or two slurred quavers if the vowel of the syllable allows (or demands) it. The anacrusis can vary from line to line or be absent completely if the first syllable of the line is stressed. The verse, i.e. the tune for one stanza, without the chorus, is typically eight bars long with two bars for each line. Because lines 2 and 4 only have three stressed syllables, the notes in bars 4 and 8 are held, emphasising the length of the vowel on rhyme or assonance. Some have a chorus, many simply a series of nonsense syllables, in the main composed of vowels, sonorants and voiced consonants, occasionally with unvoiced plosives to add a staccato element. Figure 9.4 illustrates this with No. 9 of Bronson's tunes (1962: 540).

Because of the rather rigid rhythmic structure, one tune can be exchanged for another for most folk songs that are based on the same prosody (cf. the discussion of the versions of 'A Sailor's Life' in Chapter 5) and that have male rhymes in lines 2 and 4 or generally a stressed syllable at the end of a line. This leads to the rather odd stress pattern in the line ''tis of a shepherd's daughter', where the tune with a wrenched stress effectively makes 'daughter' a spondee, which other versions avoid by substituting ''tis of a pretty shepherd maid'. A noteworthy feature of the first line is the stress on 'of', typically an unstressed word in a sentence. However, as the function of the first FSM is to indicate that the narrative is about a 'shepherd's daughter', 'of' falls on the first (and more prominent) downbeat, a crotchet, and is consequently pronounced with a full rather than the customary reduced vowel, i.e. /ɒv/, possibly even with a lengthening, instead of /əv/. The beginning of the following line is

The Knight and the Shepherd's Daughter

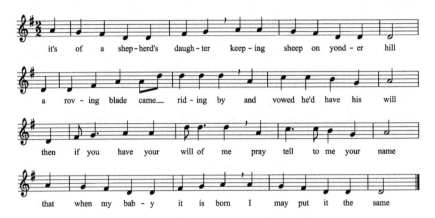

Figure 9.4. *F.A.M.'s arrangement of Bronson's version 9 of 'The Knight and the Shepherd's Daughter'*

'kept', an anacrusis with a crotchet although two quavers would also work if the word was 'keeping', with the stress on 'sheep' (main downbeat), followed by a lesser stressed 'on' and the third stressed word, 'hill', in the line being on the downbeat of the second bar of the line, which can be held despite the short vowel /ɪ/ because it is followed by the liquid /l/. This textual and rhythmic structure is supported by the harmonies, the first line ending on the dominant (Em) to the minor tonic (Am), the second in bar 4 on the minor tonic (Am). The third line in bar 6 ends on the parallel major C, as does line 4 in bar 8, which seems a little odd given that the tune is in Am (or Aeolian, according to Bronson). However, the chorus returns the mode back to minor (cf. Appendix).

What do these musical considerations tell us? Firstly, as with the song schemata and the FSMs, there is a certain amount of leeway in the composition or arrangement of a song of this kind. We can swap FSMs as well as tunes, we can combine quatrains into octets and adapt tunes from other versions or even completely different songs to accommodate this more complex structure and make it more varied for a contemporary audience.[16] But even if we do, the rigid rhythmic structure of folk songs in general and ballads in particular provides a lyrical and musical scaffolding for such practices. Secondly, it is the

---

[16] Harker (1985) disapproves of such meddling with lyrics – although he remains quiet on adaptations of the tunes. Bronson (1945) sees it as common practice at work in fabled 'Mrs Brown of Falkland', but most contemporary musicians freely admit that this is what they do to make a song performable for them, a point we return to in more detail in Chapter 10.

scaffolding that is, like the song schema and FSMs, an important mnemonic device for a performer, irrespective of whether s/he performs in a representational or in a more relational context: the stanzaic narrative style, the incremental repetitions, the fact that dialogues are presented dramatically with turns typically running over at least two lines, but often an entire stanza,[17] the fact that the narrative is driven not only by relatively sparse detail but at times also in a rather 'leisurely' way, the adjacent pairs of dialogues (the dialogue between the king and the shepherd's daughter being a case in point).[18] Nevertheless, all these elements can be combined quite freely. As long as they remain within the typical rhythmic parameters of the stanzas and the language of folk lyric discourse, they are a great help for a singer preparing a performance: they do not require a word-for-word internalisation but provide a clear enough structure for recall and even rearrangement in performance.

The last point raises an interesting question. Undoubtedly, the formulae discussed in the previous section are indexical of folk song. The fact that twentieth-century broadside and protest songwriters used such 'invitation' formulae as 'come all ye ... ' as well as some archaic phrases, e.g. ''twas', 'but' meaning 'only' or 'barely', and 'for' as a reason clause conjunction, etc., raises the chicken-and-egg question of whether FSMs are indexical of folk song per se as typical stretches of micro-discourse or whether they have become FSMs because they are such convenient textual or prosodic devices. After all, many FSMs are ideal for filling the musical phrases of the tunes, which we take to be an important aspect of the language of folk songs, since they fit into the tunes rhythmically and prosodically.

---

[17] Bronson states: 'It would be very hard to find an instance of a *single* musical phrase divided between speakers' (1959: x, emphasis in the original). The single musical phrase would typically be the four bars corresponding to two lines of text.

[18] As Leith puts it, 'ballad actants are shaped by, rather than shape, the words that they speak' (1988: 53).

There is a difference between music that is occasional and music that enhances human consciousness, music that is simply for having and music that is for being. I submit that the former may be good craftsmanship, but that the latter is art, no matter how simple or complex it sounds, and no matter under what circumstances it is produced.   (Blacking 1973: 50)

Performances in Relational and Representational Frames

The model of performance developed in Chapter 2 proposed two performance types, a more impromptu type whose function is primarily that of creating and consolidating relationships between the participants – *relational performance* – and a more formal type that needs definable performance spaces, e.g. a stage, a concert hall, a definable period of time within which the performance takes place, and whose primary function is that of representing forms of song to an audience for evaluation – *representational performance* (cf. Chapter 2). In this chapter we focus on instantiations of representational performance revolving around one song, Norman Blake's 'Billy Grey', but we start by examining the availability of data from both types of performance before beginning our analysis.

Performance Types

Relational performances are impromptu social events, in which song aimed at bonding groups of people together and/or simply enjoying the activity of singing per se also occurs. Such 'performances' tend to be loosely structured, often taking place concurrently with other types of social activity, and are always open to participation by any of those present. The number of participants varies and the duration of the 'performance' and venue are not always pre-determined. Those who sing are not expected to do so 'perfectly', although their level of musical accomplishment might still approach that of representational performance. Relational performances are not time-bound; they may be very short or go on for hours, but they are constitutive of the rituals of song and music. They are open to 'new' or 'unusual' types of song, so that any song in a 'relational performance' can become a folk song for that particular occasion. Performers do not need to pre-plan a set or to give a perfect rendition of a song. Songs, once begun, might be given up in favour of other songs during the course of events. Singers are free to experiment with harmonies, new text, new forms of instrumentation and accompaniment and sometimes even new melodies. 'Audiences' in such events are floating since members may not always be physically present for the whole performance occasion and may also be temporarily engaged in other forms of social interaction.

Representational performances are both time- and place-bound, i.e. they take place within a recognisable material oval of performance. They are expected to be as coordinated and 'professional' as possible and to be attuned to the audience's need, ability and willingness to participate, where this is required. A representational performance demonstrates a sense of community through song and music and aims to construct it where it is not expected beforehand. The performance is open to new and unexpected material in a restricted and pre-prepared way. The organisation of a representational performance is not loose, but pre-practised and rehearsed so as to gain the maximum effect from the audience and to exert the maximum effect on it. Performers therefore need to pre-plan and order the contents of a set and to decide on appropriate ways of keying-in individual items.

Representational folk performances are determined by the variety of songs presented for different social occasions and the degree to which a communal feeling is generated in the audience through the performance. This is important in creating a consensus for answering back whilst not compromising the artistic effect of the overall performance and in bonding with the singers.

A Focus on Representational Performance

Assuming that, at some point, folk songs were sung and passed on in a particular community and probably a confined area, local performers must have sung the songs in the linguistic variety familiar to the community. Cotterton (1989: 76) argues that 'in oral cultures most of the formal recognition [of cultural traditions] takes the form of performances repeatedly recited [in our case sung (R.J.W./ F.A.M.)] by the custodians of memory to those who hear of it. These large-scale performative utterances have to be cast in a standardised form if there is to be any chance of their being repeated by successive generations.' With the arrival of forms of perpetuation, the collectors and, later, the recorded performers needed to decide how to adapt the material to their medium and how to render, or to ignore, the 'standardised' vernacular of oral performances. Once recordings became available, listeners were able to hear what the performers sang without having to dislocate themselves physically to attend a concert. However, for the performers the problem arose as to whether they should copy the model of a printed text or a recording, thus potentially exposing themselves to criticism for 'not getting it right' by the community associated with the song, or whether to 'claim' a song for themselves. The latter decision involves adapting it to their own singing style, with textual changes potentially resulting in issues such as lost rhymes or changes in prosody.

One set of decisions is thus made at the level of sociolinguistic variation. On another level, however, decisions are only partially determined by the social criteria of song performance. For example, we need to make phonological decisions that have less to do with the expectations of the standard oral vernacular used for song performance and more to do with the musical structure of the songs themselves, e.g. questions of sonority. Many of the sociolinguistic inconsistencies in performance (Trudgill 1983; Bell 1984; Simpson 1999) can actually be explained more easily in terms of sonority, especially in pop and rock singing (Andres Morrissey 2008). In this chapter, we explore such issues in the context of folk performance.

Our discussion is skewed by the fact that we rely for our data on video recordings of exclusively representational performances. The loose structuring and unpredictability of relational performances make it extremely difficult to devise optimal empirical methods for recording such events. Consciousness of such recordings on the part of performers automatically triggers an awareness of an imaginary audience 'out there somewhere', thus compromising the initial *raison d'être* of relational performances, and shifts them towards the representational side of the performance spectrum (cf. Figure 2.4 in Chapter 2). Hence, because of the unavailability of recorded material from relational performances, we are constrained to focus on representational performances.[1]

'Billy Grey': A Case Study

To explore how various singers and musicians address the set of choices they have of basing their performance on a prototypical model, we take a close look at an American song in a variety of performances, both studio recordings and live videos in the New World and the Old. We have chosen to focus on just one song, Norman Blake's 'Billy Grey' (often spelt 'Gray') ☺133, and to analyse how Blake and other singers in other performance venues have chosen to perform it. One of the performances of 'Billy Grey' has also been retitled 'True Love Knows No Season' (Planxty on their 1980 album *The Woman*

---

[1] There are anecdotal reports of 'gatherings' and 'get-togethers' involving singing and musicking in some of the contributions to Rosenberg 1993, e.g. Posen's description of his visit to a Newfoundland fisherman's home on p. 133, or Burt Feintuch's vivid description of his first visit to the Bridge Club in Newcastle and his first encounter with the sound of the Northumbrian smallpipes (p. 184). Cf. also the lengthy descriptions of family singing sessions at a fisherman's house in Sidmouth in the first decade of the twentieth century in Reynolds 1909.

I Loved So Well). As we have seen, decisions on how to perform a particular song are partly sociolinguistic and partly phonological. When phonological problems arise, issues of sonority become a crucial factor.

Norman Blake's Song and First Recording

In 1975, American folk artist Norman Blake released 'Billy Grey' on his third album *Old and New*, a mix of traditional and self-penned material. It is an intriguing song for a number of reasons.[2]

Billy Grey
written by Norman Blake and reprinted with permission from the author

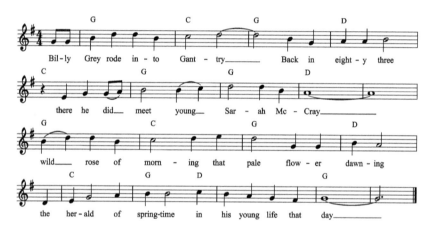

1. Billy Grey rode into Gantry back in eighty-three
   there he did meet young Sarah McCray
   wild rose of morning that pale flower dawning
   the herald of springtime in his young life that day

2. Sarah she could not see the daylight of reality
   in her young eyes Billy bore not a flaw
   knowing not her chosen one he was a hired gun
   wanted back in Kansas City by the law

---

[2] The notation has been adapted from that printed in *The Norman Blake Anthology: Transcribed by Steve Kaufman* (Pacific, MO: Melbay Publications). We have omitted the guitar tablature provided by Kaufman and, in the context of the lyrics provided in this book, taken out the punctuation and capitalisation, with the exception of names. Many thanks to Scott O'Malley for giving us permission to use this printed version.

3. then one day a tall man came riding o'er the bad lands
   lying to the north of New Mexico
   he was overheard to say he was looking for Billy Grey
   a ruthless man and a dangerous outlaw

4. and the deadly news came creeping to Billy fast sleeping
   there in the Clarendon Bar and Hotel
   he fled toward the old church there on the outskirts
   thinking that he would climb up to the old steeple bell

5. but a rifle ball came flying face down he lay dying
   there in the dust of the road where he fell
   Sarah she ran to him cursing the lawman
   accepting no reason knowing that he was killed

6. Sarah still lives in that same old white-frame house
   where she first met Billy some forty years ago
   and the wild rose of morning she's faded with the dawning
   of every day of sorrow the long years have sown

7. and written on a stone where the dusty winds have long blown
   eighteen words to a passing world say
   true love knows no season no rhyme nor no reason
   justice is cold as the Granger County clay
   yes true love knows no season no rhyme nor no reason
   justice is cold as the Granger County clay

The way the story is told, the song schema, brings together elements that would make a perfect script for a western movie:[3]

The lone rider, Billy Grey, arrives in a small town, meets the innocent local belle Sarah and the two fall in love; the idyll is threatened when 'the tall man', having crossed 'the badlands' in pursuit of Billy, who is revealed to be a 'hired gun / wanted back in Kansas City by the law', starts making enquiries after him; inevitably the shoot-out follows, ending in Billy's death 'face down . . . in the dust', and Sarah, heartbroken, lives out her life alone in an 'old white-frame house'.

Almost cinematically, the final focus is on Billy's gravestone with the lines (repeated in the song) 'true love knows no season / no rhyme nor no reason / justice is cold as / the Granger County clay'. If we trim away the trappings of the Western, the tale becomes an archetypical love story between a young woman, her lover and a mysterious stranger, which ends with Billy being killed in retribution for his crimes and Sarah being left to mourn for him. In that sense, it is reminiscent of Gillies' notion of 'literary themes' that cross 'geographical, historical, cultural and linguistic' boundaries (Gillies 2010: ix).

---

[3] We present it here as a story, rather than a song schema.

The song is also remarkable for reasons that are more closely linked to what we have identified as being typical of folk songs. Musically, it is in 4/4, and its stanzaic form corresponds to that discussed in Chapter 9. Each lyrical line corresponds to four bars – with an anacrusis where an unstressed syllable precedes the first stressed syllable – and each odd line has four main stresses, which fall on the first beat of the bar, in other words on the main downbeat. In the even lines, we usually have between three and four main stresses, alternating between the 'ballad' and the 'long metre'.The rhyming patterns are consistent with ballads in that lines 1 and 3 do not rhyme, in contrast to lines 2 and 4, where we usually have a rhyme or an assonance. Due to the longer note in bars 8 and 9 the final rest is on bars 17 and 18, but without these longer notes would actually be in bars 8 and 16 as usual. The norm of eight bars, also consistent with folk song practice, represents a single musical phrase (cf. Bronson 1959) that comes to a relative rest on bar 8, i.e. on the dominant, and to a final rest at the end of a stanza on the tonic (cf. Appendix).

The language is also consistent with what we have discussed in Chapter 9. Although there are spatial indications, 'Gantry', 'Granger County', 'bad-lands' ('north of New Mexico'), 'Kansas City' and the 'Clarendon Bar and Hotel', as well as dates and times (e.g. 1883) and the fact that Sarah still lives in the same place forty years later, i.e. in 1923, none of these details helps in tracing the protagonists or ascertaining whether the story can be related in any way to actual events, as is the case for most traditional ballads. The archetypal motif of blighted love, i.e. the story rather than history, is what matters here. This is borne out by phrases that have an archaic or at least an unusual ring to them but are useful for prosodic/rhythmical purposes, i.e. 'there he did meet with', 'Sarah she could not see' and 'Sarah she ran to him', but others appear to be more directly connected with standardised forms of folk song discourse and the way in which it often retains constructions that have long since fallen out of common usage, e.g. negation without periphrastic *do* as in 'Billy *bore not* a flaw' or the placement of a negative after instead of before a non-finite verb in '*knowing not* her chosen one, he was a hired gun'. One could argue that such forms index the narrative archetype, although it is unlikely that such a consideration would consciously enter a songwriter's mind.

Adopters and Adapters

It is impossible to look at more than a limited number of adaptations, but for the purpose of the present chapter we can safely reduce the scope to a few iconic or typical performances. Since its launch in 1975, the song has been adopted by a number of artists. Unsurprisingly, it is popular with Americana musicians and bluegrass performers, and the words in various versions feature on lyrics websites dedicated to these genres.[4] An informal trawl through online videos reveals a substantial body of performances indexing the genre, musically with guitars, mandolins, dobros, fiddles and five-string banjos and through the semiotics of clothing, with performers wearing ribbon ties and Stetsons. The singing, too, leaves a viewer or listener in no doubt as to the linguistic origins or orientation of the song. Alongside the instrumentation, the arrangements follow the practices of Americana and bluegrass performances in that various band members take instrumental 'breaks' between the verses;[5] the breaks are usually over the verse, with the following chorus either sung or, more rarely, played instrumentally. In bluegrass, as in jazz, it is the custom that all the musicians, typically with the exception of the rhythm section, have their break.

One such performance is by the Canadian band Hometown Bluegrass, recorded at the Tottenham Bluegrass Festival, Ontario, in June 2014. We chose it because it represents a North American model, on the one hand, but on the other hand, it obviously fits into the Americana and bluegrass tradition. The band consists of a classic bluegrass line-up: guitar, banjo, mandolin, fiddle and bass, and the arrangement is equally classic, starting with the tune played on guitar with mandolin, fiddle and guitar, though not the banjo, taking instrumental breaks over the verse. A further feature classical for bluegrass performance is the audience applause at the end of every break. The dress semiotics of Americana performance is realised by the appearance of two male members in suits and Stetsons, in particular the singer Don Couchie.

With its appearance as 'True Love Knows No Season', an alternative title, as the first song on the A-side of the 1980 Planxty album *The Woman I Loved So Well*, it can be said to have well and truly crossed the Atlantic. In the sleeve notes on the song, Christy Moore writes the following: 'In December 1979 I met Noel Shine (whistle) in the Phoenix Pub, Cork, where he sang this song for me. It was written by Norman Blake and it's special in that it's the first Cowboy song I've heard in a Cork City pub.'[6] So Christy is not just aware of the song's origin as a 'Cowboy song', he actually foregrounds this fact in the written form of keying-in. However, this does not stop him or the band from turning it into an unmistakable Planxty song with bouzouki/mandolin interplay in the introduction and Liam O'Flynn's uilleann pipes in an interlude. The interlude not only eschews the 'American' practice of being played over

---

[4] www.cowboylyrics.com/lyrics/keen-robert-earl/billy-gray-11785.html (based on Robert Earl Keen's rather more polished version), accessed 4 May 2015.
[5] We remind the reader of footnote 10 in the Introduction, where we refer to *verse* as a musical term, meaning the tune that is repeated over the *stanza*, which we understand to be a lyrical element of a song. *Chorus* would be used for both the repeated musical lyrical element that usually contains the lyrical focus of the song, in more traditional singing a repetition of nonsense syllables with, phonologically, a high level of sonority.
[6] www.taramusic.com/sleevenotes/cd3005.htm (accessed 21 July 2015)

the verse; the pipes are joined after sixteen bars by a harmonica, but in a different key. Whereas the verses are in C, the interlude changes to G before a G7 chord returns the key to C for the last two verses; the 'outro' is again the same interlude with the bouzouki/mandolin interplay and an added harmonica before a fade out.

In the live performance in 2004,[7] essentially the same arrangement is played, with the pipes substituted by a tin whistle and the harmonica absent. Both versions have an unmistakable 'Celtic' or Irish flavour to them, belying the cowboy song Christy Moore refers to. The same, interestingly enough, is true for the pronunciation. Christy Moore's Irish roots are unmistakable to the point that the lyricsfreaks.com website actually perpetuates a mondegreen in the Planxty version: where Moore, in opposition to Blake's 'the herald of spring-time in Billy's life that day', sings 'heralded springtime into Billy's life that day', and his pronunciation /hɜrldd/ is given on the site as the mondegreen 'hurled a springtime into Billy's life that day'.[8]

In 2012, the song was taken up by another band from the Old World, the young Scottish musicians of Barluath, on their debut album *Source*. They have also performed the song live as can be seen in an undated concert at the Victoria Hall, Helensburgh, Scotland. The six-piece band Barluath met as students at the Royal Conservatoire of Scotland, and they play a variety of traditional Scottish instruments (whistles, pipes and fiddle) alongside more modern folk instruments (bouzouki and guitar). But they also use keyboards and clarinet, thus broadening the spectrum of musical expression. Their website describes them as 'diverse and innovative' and their repertoire as 'embrac[ing] both the traditional and contemporary music of Scotland, Ireland and America'.[9] In their Helensburgh performance of 'Billy Grey', like Planxty's Christy Moore, singer Ainsley Hamill makes no attempt at 'Americanising' her singing. In fact, there is no difference between the language in which she keys in the song to an apparently 'home' audience, who clearly know the band and the song, and the way in which she pronounces the words during the stanzas, even though she introduces it explicitly as an 'American song'. Their rendition is faster than any of the other versions – including that of overt bluegrass acts like Hometown Bluegrass. It seems almost jaunty except where the tempo and the volume are noticeably reduced in the penultimate verse. Like Planxty, Barluath do not follow the Americana model with instrumental breaks over the verse. Their instrumental interlude is confined to one extended section before the two last verses; however, whereas Planxty play a tune in an Irish vein, Barluath's interlude is rather free over a rhythm strummed by bouzouki and guitar,

---

[7] *Planxty: Live 2004*, DVD.
[8] www.lyricsfreak.com/p/planxty/true+love+knows+no+season_21038703.html (accessed 21 July 2015).
[9] http://barluath.com/about, accessed 21 July 2015.

reminiscent of a bodhran 4/4 figure, and a melodic line taken up by clarinet and keyboard that varies the basic key of A into what could be described as a Dorian mode with G as the tonic (cf. Appendix). All this lends a much more contemporary feel to this part of the song. They also use the epitaph as a chorus, starting the song with it, repeating it after verse 4 and ending the song with a minimally played second line and a ritardando. This is still a folk arrangement, but it obviously demonstrates that this approach has evolved further from the folk music practices of the last century.

Lyrics and Pronunciation

Norman Blake's song has not changed fundamentally over its nearly forty-year history. The storyline remains unchanged, the song schema and the characters are the same, the lyrical line of the epitaph is as salient as in the original version, possibly even more so if Barluath are anything to go by. However, there is an evolution in evidence. There are changes that merit further discussion, as they are indicative of the considerations and decisions performers need to make. We now focus on lyrics and pronunciation.

The North American Instantiations

In terms of lyrics, ignoring the mondegreen mentioned above, the changes are largely superficial since they do not affect any of the song elements, but they still show that the adaptation stage of the *creation* (*innovation*), *adoption*, *adaptation*, *transmission* and *diffusion* process discussed in Chapter 5 is at work.

We focus first on the North American versions. As one might expect, there are a few lyrical differences between Norman Blake's studio recording and the live performance we have at our disposal.[10] Where they occur, they are minimal: 'there' dropped in the line 'he fled toward the old church (there) on the outskirts' and relative pronoun 'that' inserted in 'of every day of sorrow (that) the long years have sown'. In comparison to other performances, Blake's phrasing is striking. He is clearly freer in individual lines of the 1975 studio version than the adopters and is even freer in the live performance, perhaps because he sings the melody with more ornamentation.

There are also few differences in his pronunciation between the studio recording and the live version, as one might expect. In both versions, his Southern roots – he was born in Tennessee and raised in Georgia – are obvious, but not as obvious as when he speaks. In the documentary about his 2014 album *Wood, Wire and Words*, he speaks with the typical nasal 'twang' and

---

[10] A live recording uploaded on 15 July 2009. No indication of the venue.

consistently uses the Confederate vowel /aˑ/ for the PRICE vowel. Further features in evidence are the lowering of the /ɪ/ to something like /e/ in words like 'sit', 'thing' and 'singing' (/sẽŋẽŋ/) and the corresponding diphthong substitution in the mid-high vowel 'ten' and 'health' to /tẽən/ and /hẽəlθ/. In at least one instance, in 'entertainment', he substitutes the FACE vowel with something closer to /æɪ/. However, he hardly ever replaces alveolar with velar nasals in -ing verb forms, is consistently rhotic and realises intervocalic /t/ just as consistently as /ɾ/. In his singing, a slightly different picture emerges. There is alveolarisation of some but not all -ing forms ('the deadly news came creepin' to Billy fast sleepin'' but 'cursing the lawman / accepting no reason knowing that he was killed'), and he is less consistently rhotic, in particular in the assonance of 'morning' and 'dawning'. He also realises the intervocalic /t/ in 'reality' as such, not as one might expect as a /ɾ/, but this could be explained by the prosody of the lyric at that point, as the word-final /i/ or /ɪ/ is not as short and potentially lowered as it would be in speech. It represents rather a so-called 'wrenched' stress to rhyme with 'see' and would thus be [ɹiˈælɪtʰiː].

His vowels are also less typically 'Southern' as there is really only one instance when he uses the Confederate vowel in other contexts than in unstressed syllables: the word 'rhyme' in the epitaph in both repetitions is [ɹaˑm] in the studio as well as in the live recording. In other ways, his pronunciation is closer to General American, notably in his avoidance of the THOUGHT–LOT merger (Wells 1984), but there is a possible influence from Southern pronunciation of a slightly retracted and lowered initial vowel in the diphthong 'clay', which, however, does not quite match his pronunciation of the FACE vowel in 'entertainment' mentioned earlier. The picture that emerges is that Blake's singing is not as markedly Southern as his speech, which corresponds to performances by traditional English singers like Harry Cox and Sam Larner (cf. Chapter 7).

For the other North American instantiation of the song, Hometown Bluegrass's 'Billy Grey', we need to bear in mind that the band is from Ontario, Canada, but that the genre of music they play is bluegrass and Old Time Music, which is commonly associated with the Appalachians. Unsurprisingly, lead singer Don Couchie avoids the vowels associated with Canadian pronunciation, in particular the MOUTH and PRICE raising (Wells 1984: 494–95), which is seen as a salient Canadian feature. Another similarly salient Canadian feature, aspiration in 'wh', is nowhere in evidence. On the other hand, the THOUGHT–LOT merger, which Blake does not use, typically for both Southern or General American models, is in evidence in Couchie's pronunciation, e.g. for 'law' he sings /ɬɑː/ rather than /lɔː/, a feature that is associated with the northern Midwest and Canada (ibid.: 473–76). Like Blake, he weakens or avoids rhoticity altogether in 'morning' to rhyme with 'dawning' – although here the THOUGHT–LOT merger is not realised – but is otherwise fully rhotic. Three things are striking: firstly, that there is no alveo-larisation of -*ing* throughout; secondly, that the intervocalic /t/ in 'reality' is retained, probably for the same reason; but thirdly, at the end of the song Couchie seems to 'go more Southern' and in both instances of 'rhyme' in the epitaph uses the Confederate vowel /aˑ/.

There are some more marked lyrical changes in Couchie's performance compared to Blake's versions, some probably due to the heat of the perfor-mance ('he lay dying / there in the road by the dust'), but others indicate that he has adapted and internalised Blake's lyrics. Most notably, he changes Blake's 'knowing not her chosen one he was ...' to 'not knowing that her chosen one was ...'. Smaller changes are as follows: the law man is described as a 'strange' rather than a 'tall man', which in view of the archetypal Western narrative seems to make more sense; substitution of the demonstrative for definite determiners ('that' for 'the lawman'); some conjunctions ('then' for 'but', 'where' replaced with the adverb 'there'); and the insertion of discourse markers like 'well'. All in all, Hometown Bluegrass are not just faithful to the practice and semiotics of Americana performances; their handling of the song lyrics and their pronunciation is, too.

The Old World Adaptations

Although the lyrics and the tune are still Norman Blake's, the overall impression in both the Irish and Scottish versions is that of clear departures from the Americana genre from which 'Billy Grey' originated. In terms of lyrics, the setting remains entirely unchanged, and one character is only superficially differ-ent from Blake's original song, Sarah McRae (originally spelt 'McCray') becom-ing Sarah McLean. But perhaps the most obvious change is in Planxty's title, 'True Love Knows No Season', which shifts the focus from Blake's 'Billy Grey' to the catalyst of the tragedy. Although Barluath revert to Blake's title, they at least seem influenced by that shift in focus as they use the epitaph as a refrain starting the song with it and inserting it before the stanza describing Billy's death.

In chronological terms, it makes sense to examine the Planxty version first. There is a range of innovations in the adapted lyrics that merit attention. Some of the differences between Christy Moore's versions and Norman Blake's (studio) recording are, like the adaptations by Hometown Bluegrass, mostly structural – 'lying' to 'that lie', 'and' for 'but' – and lexical – 'o'er' becomes 'from the badlands'. Others remove some archaic features, e.g. 'there he did meet' becoming 'there he first met' and 'Sarah ran to him / *she was* cursing the lawman' in contrast to Blake's 'Sarah she ran to him / cursing the lawman'. However, the phrases 'Billy bore not a flaw' and 'knowing not her chosen one' are retained, perhaps because they represent 'salient lyrical lines' in the song schematic (Figure 9.1-in Chapter 9). There are also several changes that have a mainly prosodic function: 'he ran to the old church / *that lies* on the outskirts', in the relative clause, scans better than Blake's prepositional phrase 'on the outskirts'. The same can be said for Moore's 'Sarah *still* lives in that old white-frame house', which he sings more rhythmically than Blake's rather free phrasing in both studio and live versions where Blake sings 'house' in bar 3 rather than 4.

There are several changes that make a subtle difference to the meaning of the lyrics. With the replacement of Blake's 'the herald of springtime' with the verbal construction 'heralded springtime', an enjambement is created making the last two lines of the first stanza into a complete sentence rather than a series of appositions, thus creating more of a narrative flow. A similar effect is created in the escape sequence: where in Blake's version Billy Grey is said to want to 'climb up to the old steeple bell', the motivation is clearer with the fugitive aiming to '*hide* in the old steeple bell'. Another change describing Sarah's reaction to Billy's death substitutes Blake's non-finite subordinate clauses 'accepting no reason / knowing that he was killed' with the sentence 'poor girl knew no reason / except that he'd been killed', which, apart from being rhythmically easier to phrase also seems more logical in terms of the narrative. One final change that helps in telling the story is contained in the last two lines of stanza 6. Blake's original lyrics run '*and* the wild rose of morning / *she's* faded with the dawning / of *every* day of sorrow (that) / the long years have *sown*'. Moore changes this to the smoother syntax of '*but* the wild rose of morning / has faded with the dawning / of each day of sorrow that / the long years have *grown*'. Puzzling in both versions is the inherent logic of 'sorrow' as the object of sowing and growing. Given the phonetic dissimilarity of /gr/ and /s/, this change cannot be interpreted as a misheard lyric, but the rewrite makes a little more sense than the original version.

One of the most salient changes is in stanza 5. Blake has the assonance 'fell' (line 2) and 'killed' (line 4), which for a writer with a Southern-coloured American English is relatively close to a rhyme (/fẽəl/ and /kẽld/), also taking into consideration that word-final consonant clusters are often strongly reduced in sustained notes at the end of a musical phrase. Why Moore makes no attempt at rhyming, using 'lay' instead of 'fell', can only be explained by the fact that he sings a long monophthong [leː], making it easier to hold the note than the relative closure of the lateral approximant in /fɛl/.

Christy Moore's pronunciation, as this last point indicates, is typically Irish, which together with the instrumentation and its clearly Celtic flavour, espe-cially in the pipes (or, in the live version, tin whistle) interlude, creates a mismatch with the lyrics of the 'cowboy' song. The fact that the frequency with which the velar nasal in the suffix -*ing* is alveolarised surpasses that of Blake as well as that of Couchie (Hometown Bluegrass) does not represent a concession to an American model but is an Irish feature (Wells 1984: 427). Other typical features include a relatively consistent merger of the

FOOT–STRUT vowels, as well as a tendency to realise at least some inter-dental fricatives as dental plosives while dental plosives are frequently affri-cated. Many of these features can be observed, admittedly not always consistently, in the opening lines 'Billy Grey rode into Gantry (['gæntɹɪ]) way ([weː]) back in eighty-three (['æːtɪθɹiː] there [ðɛ] he first met (/t/ not or only minimally affricated) with ([wɪd] young ([jʊŋ]) Sarah McLean [with the short vowel, the note is actually held on the alveolar nasal]'.

A comparison of Barluath's lyrics with those of Blake and Moore reveals that they follow the Irish rather than the American model. There are very minor changes, e.g. 'and' added at the beginning of a few lines, 'dangerous man' and, somewhat tautologically, 'wanted outlaw', instead of Moore's 'wanted man' and 'dangerous outlaw', and the doubling of the subject 'Sarah she' is reintroduced. The most striking change, which makes sense lyrically in terms of folk song in that it harks back to the formulaic language of traditional music, occurs where Planxty change Blake's 'where he fell' to 'where he lay'; Barluath substitute 'killed' in the Blake and the Planxty versions with 'slain', a near rhyme with 'lay' ([ɫeː]),[11] which works particu-larly well because of the long vowel ([sɫeːn]), held dramatically by Hamill before the audience is allowed to contemplate this tragic outcome in the thirty-five-second interlude.

As with Planxty in the sleeve notes, Barluath's Hamill explicitly keys-in the song as being from outside the Celtic repertoire by saying 'we're gonna continue on [sic] with an American song now' and in the brief summary mentioning that 'it's about a cowboy named Billy Grey'. In this spoken sequence, she leaves the audience in no doubt about her roots; in fact, she is from Cardross, northwest of Glasgow, and speaks very noticeable Glaswegian, referring to Sarah as [seːrə] in keeping with Aitken's law (Aitken 1962, as discussed in Wells 1984: 400), according to which Scottish full vowels are short except at the end of a syllable/word (as well as preceding a voiced fricative or an /r/). She uses the same pronunciation in the song and even substitutes the Scottish 'tae' for 'to' on the slightly lengthened note in the phrase 'Sarah ran to him' when Billy is killed. We would be going too far at this point to discuss the intricacies of Scottish pronunciation in more detail, so a few pointers will have to suffice. Generally, we find the entire range of Scottish, or more accurately Glaswegian, vowels, e.g. the lowering and centring of the KIT vowel as in Billy ['bʌɫə].[12] The characteristic change to [æ] for the long and [ʌɪ] for short PRICE vowel in [ɫæz] for 'lies' and [rʌɪm] 'rhyme' are also in evidence, as well as the realisation of the MOUTH vowel as [ʌu] in 'framed

---

[11] Needless to say, Christy Moore uses a light /l/ here.
[12] For a more detailed discussion cf. Wells 1984.

[sic] house' [hʌus]. A little less clear is the realisation of *wh-*, which would be the aspirated semivowel that Wells (ibid.: 408–9) transcribes as /hw/ but also as /ʍ/, which we do not have in 'where he first met' and barely perceptibly in 'where she first met Billy some forty years ago'.

Preliminary Conclusions

These examples of adoption and adaptation demonstrate two very different strategies. On the one hand, Hometown Bluegrass, although, of course, closer to Blake's model to start with, obviously focus on representing and reproducing the Americana style. Given their Canadian roots, this is not problematic. It can at least be posited that artists without an American background may well choose to do the same, which would make them tailor both their musical endeavours and their singing style to suit the Americana model. Planxty and Barluath demonstrate an entirely different approach. Undaunted by the mismatch between the provenance of the song and their musical and vocal style, they treat it as if it belonged to their own tradition and make no attempt to make it sound otherwise. We could argue that we are looking at two different prototypical treatments here, one focusing on the genre of the model and the other on the archetypal nature of the narrative. This is borne out by the fact that both Old World artists evidently place more emphasis on the notion of tragic love, Planxty with the changed title and Barluath by foregrounding the epitaph as a chorus of sorts.

We argued above that folk songs are, at an early stage in their history, confined to a particular region and its local discourse community. If they move beyond that locality, it is because their singers do, but this is no longer the case once they have been perpetuated in one medium or another. 'Billy Grey' can be used to exemplify this. Many adopters are likely to have come across a recording and learnt their version from it. However, adopters, as we have demonstrated, can come from very different speech and/or discourse communities, and this opens up questions as to how to bridge the resulting disparities or whether to try to do so at all. Even for the older forms of perpetuation, a songbook or a collection of lyrics, the same issues arise: what does an adopter do to adapt the song, or to 'claim' it? In terms of 'Billy Grey', all performances arising from the record, including Blake's own – with the, for Americana, highly unusual inclusion of a cello rather than two guitars as on the album – represent a means of claiming the song. Claiming a song, then, requires a range of decisions that can be seen in terms of the song schematic discussed in the previous chapter. We focus on two of these decisions in the following two sections, the adaptation of the lyrics and the way in which the song is to be delivered, i.e. the 'singing style'.

From Perpetuation to Performance

An alternative term for folk song is 'vernacular song',[13] reflecting a belief that a song's provenance is linked to a language variety used in a specific region, the 'vernacular' of that region, which has consequences, phonologically, lexically and possibly even morpho-syntactically. In 'Billy Grey', we have demonstrated that the impact on the lexical level for adaptations outside North America is minimal and possibly confined to one aspect, the relative clause 'the dust where he fell' vs 'where he lay', with Barluath restoring the rhyme that Planxty lose with the more formulaic 'slain'. However, more tellingly, Barluath substitute 'to' with 'tae', which represents a more drastic change than might at first appear to be the case, suggesting, as it does, a change to a different linguistic variety. Other changes are related to the level of pronunciation, where both Blake and Moore show a use – albeit not always consistent – of alveolar instead of velar nasals in *-ing* verb forms, which Barluath do not have at all.

Two Types of Language 'Standardisation'

What is at issue here is the difference between the pronunciation practices in four varieties of English (Southern American, Canadian, Irish and Scottish), but that explanation does not hold up when we consider that Blake himself is not entirely consistent with his pronunciation in the recorded version of 'Billy Grey' and in the video clips of his various performances of the song. We are thus confronted with the following question: To what extent is a vernacular feature occasionally, or in some cases frequently, substituted with a more 'standard' form during the performance of a song?

We submit that there are two different interpretations of the term 'standard' at issue here. The first is a sociolinguistically canonical definition such as that given by James Milroy:

... standard languages are fixed and uniform-state idealisations – not empirically verifiable realities. That is to say, if we study the speech of people who are said to be speaking a standard language, it will never conform exactly to the idealisation. It is also true that any variety delimited and described by the linguist is an idealisation, and that the usage of an individual speaker will not conform exactly to that idealisation. However, a standard language has properties over and above those of non-standardised varieties, the chief one of which is existence in a widely used written form. (Milroy 1999: 18)

---

[13] Cf. Gammon 2008: 3: '"Vernacular song" is, ... as I use the term, a complex ragbag, a layered and porous repertory where the ancient and the ephemeral, the pious and the bawdy, the traditional and commercial all rub shoulders. It is the songs people have chosen to perform, whatever those songs' genres or origins.'

The second definition refers to the result of any kind of standardisation process, i.e. not necessarily of language, in which practitioners, in our case singers, informally follow the conventions of dominant usage. Cotterton's point in an earlier section of this chapter is that the custodians of cultural memory, in this instance, folk singers, would hardly have been able to transfer their songs across numerous generations and to diffuse them over great distances unless they were couched 'in a standardised form' (1989: 76), i.e. the informal conventions of dominant usage. Several of those informal conventions of song lyrics transferred from singer to singer and from generation to generation were dealt with in Chapter 9. Hence, we are now in a position to state that one important informal convention is the 'toning down' of heavily vernacular constructions, phonological, lexical and morpho-syntactic. Singers are not therefore 'singing in standard English'; they are merely singing to be understood beyond the confines of their own local dialect area.

An example of this tendency can be observed in recordings made by Alan Lomax and Peter Kennedy in 1953 of Norfolk folk singer Harry Cox, in which Cox displays a much stronger use of his local Norfolk dialect in conversation with Lomax than when he sings his songs.[14] Indeed, recordings of older singers from the 1940s to the 1960s follow the same strategy, even Scottish traditional singers like Jeannie Robertson. The phenomenon is not restricted to the English-speaking world. For example, in the traditional Swiss song ''S Brombeeri Lied' ('The Blackberrying Song') ⊕133 from von Greyerz's ([1908–25] 2008: 194) collection of Swiss folk songs *Im Röseligarte*, the same phenomenon can be illustrated in a manner that would not work in normally spoken language. In most contexts, speakers can place themselves on a cline between vernacular and standard, e.g. in Scotland between Scots/Lallans and RP.[15] In conversational use, this is not possible in Swiss German, where speakers must make an either/or decision. Yet the first two lines of the 'Brombeeri Lied' demonstrate the working of informal singing conventions in a folk song. We have neither Swiss German nor Standard German here; the distinction is much less rigid (the 'toning down' of the dialect is printed in italics): '*es wollt* es mägetli früeh ufstaa / drüü stündeli *vor dem tag*' ('it's of a maid who wanted to rise / three hours before it was day'). For a singer of a Scottish song, there is considerable

---

[14] Cf. the Portraits series of CDs produced in 2000, made from Lomax and Kennedy's recordings entitled *Harry Cox: What Will Become of England?*, Rounder 11661–1839–2.

[15] Scots and Swiss German dialects are both described by Kloss (1967) as 'Abstandsprachen' in the sense that they are far enough removed from Standard British English and Standard German to warrant being considered separate languages although they both lack that official recognition.

leeway between singing a song in Scots and replacing lexical items like 'kirk' or 'nicht' with 'church' or 'night', indexing Scottishness merely with pronunciation. The same freedom exists for a Swiss folk singer, who might adapt the words to her/his own variety (e.g. Bernese 'es wott es meiteli früeh ufstaa / drüü stündeli vor em tag', or for a German to sing it in Standard German ('es wollt ein Mägdelein früh aufsteh'n / drei Stündelein vor dem Tag'). We submit that although folk songs are associated with the vernacular, they need not be, and are often not, an expression of everyday non-standard language, but rather an expression of the 'informal conventions of a dominant folk usage'. They are rooted in people's every-day lives (at least historically), but are different enough in their diction and in their subject matter to stand the test of time. We may even be confronted here with the phenomenon of 'destandardisation', which Deumert (2010: 244) defines as 'a weakening of the norm, a centrifugal movement which increases linguistic heterogeneity', although any weakening of the 'norm' in folk song diction does not appear to be made consciously by the singers themselves. We return to the standardisation vs destandardisation question in Chapter 12.

Dealing with Differences

But how does an adopter, who is also an adapter, deal with differences between her/his style and her/his material? Although we pointed out that surprisingly little updating is evident in the formulaic (and archaic) language conventions of folk song, some will become necessary. Bronson discusses the interesting case of '[o]ne of Child's esteemed sources ... Mrs. Brown of Falkland, in Fife', each of whose ballads was reprinted in Child's collection, in some cases as the only version and often as the A text (Bronson 1945: 129). Bronson discusses three manuscripts, the first two in the 1780s referred to as the Jamieson-Brown and the William Tytler-Brown manuscripts and a third from 1800 called the A. F. Tytler-Brown MS. There are some reworkings in these collections, and Bronson argues that as Mrs Brown had the first copy (Jamieson-Brown) in hand when she reworked her material (in William Tytler-Brown), 'any changes must have been deliberately intro-duced' (ibid.: 131). He identifies five reasons for amendments in the later copies: '(1) corrections of memory; (2) rationalizing; (3) metrical considera-tions; (4) *regularizing and reducing dialectal features*; (5) considerations that may loosely be called aesthetic' (ibid.; emphasis added). Most, if not all, of these five features, perhaps least of all (1), are also in evidence, it could be argued, in some of the versions of 'Billy Grey', but they are certainly present in reworkings of traditional material of twentieth- and twenty-first-century adapters. Apart from the length and in some cases the tune of a song that needed to be adapted, many of the songs in collections, written or recorded, exhibit dialect features, but to what degree an English adapter might attempt what Ewan MacColl did with his Scottish material is an open question. In a conversation in Stones Barn, Cumbria, during a workshop on Child ballads in 2014, Rick Kemp (bass player in Steeleye Span), Maddy Prior and Martin Carthy discuss this issue (transcript: 'Martin Carthy and Rick Kemp on adapting Child ballads.mp3'):

```
Martin:  obviously\ (...) an important thing is not to be precious\[ (...)  at it\ whereas/
Rick:                                                                [right\
         I think\[ (...)  whereas you can u- use :aagh: even go to/ I- I- I think that you can go in-
Rick:        [mm
         into the :er: almost into your own vernacular (...) [        ]:erm: and still be true to it\
Rick:                                                         [yeah]
Rick:                                                                                           oh\
         all right\[ okay\
Martin:       [ I think so\ (....) but I've just/ I've sung[ (??????) quite a few (????)—
Maddy:                                       [ it's better not to be arch isn't it\[ (???)
Rick:                                                                            [ that's
         the difficulty for me is that it get/ that it tends to get kind[ of arch and arcadian [
Maddy:                                                               [ yeah\              [ you sort of
         think it's[ (???)
Rick:           [like I'm trying to (.) imitate [ (..) something that (..) patently I know nothing about\ or
Martin:                                        [ yeah\
Rick:    have never experienced\ you see\ you're trying to imitate (.) that style\ and what Kittredge is
         saying in the foreword there\ is that Child had a- a- an absolute handle on it\ he really knew ( )
         what- what is was doing\ and I just wondered if you'd (.) kind of encountered any difficulties in
         that direction\ cos you've moved a lot of bits around\ (...) and they always work\
Maddy:   what—
         (...)
Rick:    well the one that I heard\[
Maddy:                            [ well [ (????)
all:                                     [ <@general laughter@>
```

The consensus is that a singer needs to avoid sounding 'precious' or, in Kemp's words, 'arcadian', in referring to both vernacular features and the retention of archaic language. Carthy goes even further when he says that 'you can go into almost your own vernacular and still be true to' the material. In practice, this would mean reconstructing the material considerably, removing or downtoning vernacular language that does not come naturally to the performer.

How consistently this is done may be a matter of debate or taste, but Bronson points out that there is a tradition to this: Mrs Brown's 'treatment of dialect is not consistent ..., but generally dialect is muffled in revision, unless *rhyme requires its emphasis*' (ibid.: 132, emphasis added). Rhythm, particularly, and rhyme are an important feature of songs, but rhymes may not translate into other spellings of the lyrics or into words other than vernacular expressions. Thus, in the Scottish ballad 'Twa Corbies' ⓐ135, rhymes in Scots like 'mate' (spouse/lover) and 'swate' (sweet), 'bare' and 'ever mair' or near rhymes like 'bane' (bone) and 'een' (eyes) work without any difficulty, but they obviously do not work in most south-of-the-border varieties of English.[16] In comparison, vernacular expressions in the same song like 'hause-bane' could more easily be substituted with 'neck bone' although the problem with the rhyme would persist. In the same way, the opening line of 'The Gaberlunzie Man' (Child 279; Roud 119) 'the pauky auld carle came oer the lee', can be and is successfully replaced with 'an old beggar man come over the lea' in 'The Beggar Man' ⊕136 as sung by Lal and Norma Waterson (cf. track 15 on *Watersons, The Definitive Collection*).

It is probably fruitless to try and determine which version represents an adaptation of the other, but whichever way adaptation took place, the lyrics had to be changed to fit in with the style of the adopter, thus resulting in some updating. But if performers can retain archaic formulae without too much difficulty, why should lexis from a different vernacular or discourse community create a problem? The answer is that this is not solely a lexical issue, but that pronunciation also plays an important part. According to Andres Morrissey (2011), much of the comical effect of the Bonzo Dog Doo-Dah Band's song 'Can Blue Men Sing the Whites' arises from the mismatch between genre, i.e. blues, and singer Vivian Stanshall's delivery of the lyrics in over-the-top RP. To avoid creating inadvertent comic effects, it makes much more sense to bring lyrics and their delivery into line. In the following section, we examine the issue of 'delivery' further.

Style and Stylisation

Folk-linguistic concepts of 'accent' or 'dialect' are not adequate to describe how performers sing their songs. Some do not differ markedly in the way they speak and the way they sing, as we observed above, but folk performance can show varying degrees of departure from everyday language and everyday delivery. It may not show the same degree of divergence between singing and speaking as we note in rock singing (e.g. the Stones' Jagger's and Richards' African-American-influenced singing and their Dartford-originated English speaking accent), but the following transcript from a discussion at Stones Barn in 2013 shows how amateur folk singers are aware of what they (attempt to) do with their pronunciation when they sing:

---

[16] There often are lines in (written) folk song lyrics that may well be attributable to such reworkings where the word used is no longer a rhyme or even an assonance.

Franz: cos I've noticed on that recording there\ that was- that was fairly bluesy\ and/ it sounded
        very (.) American\[(..) and yet when you sang the song about/ you know\ the fishing
Lynn: [:erm:
        industry\ that was[(..)   Geord[—
Lynn: [Geordie\   [you mean the (???) song last night\
Franz: yeah\[yeah\
Lynn: [very[—
Ken: [why\
Lynn: :er: :er: I think partly with the (???) song/ because it's a funny song\ I sort of lay::: into it even
        more\ I think if I'm aware that people just really haven't got a clue what I'm talking about\ (..)
        you know\ I'd probably sort of deliberately turn it back a bit\
Franz: right\
Lynn: <not usually consciously> but always sort of naturally <just try and turn it [back a bit>\
Chris: [but some [of that
Franz: [say if
Chris: comes from the outside\ [somehow\ I don't know why\ I don't know why it is (???)\[but it
Franz: you—   [yeah\ yeah\ that's probably   [
Chris: does\   [
Lynn: [because
        it seems like in 'The Lampton Worm' (..) :er:: you- you know\ when you have to rhy/ when you-
        when you get to the end of the line\ and it doesn't really rhyme\ unless you actually really lean
        into it\ and make it rhyme\ sort [of thing\ you kind of force a rhyme\ and you do that (..) by
Franz: [mmhmm\
Lynn: using/ you know\ put an extra syllable in\ [(..) a- a single syllable word\ [(??) but you/ if you
Chris: [yeah\   [
Franz: [mmhmm\
        lean into that\ I think that[(?????)
Franz: [but would you say that say if you recorded/ if you- you/ no\ would/ if
        you sing in/ obviously if you sing in Newcastle\ you would (…) sort of pitch it differently than if
        you sort of sang in a folk club in (..) I dunno\ London\
        (…)
Chris: would you\ deliberately\
        (..)
Lynn: I don't know if I'd do it deliberately\ I- I- I- I- :erm: [—
Chris: [I know I would\ but it wouldn't be
        deliberate\ I'd hear myself [doing it\ (????) have a word with meself\ Chris\[
Lynn: [yes\ yes\ yes\   [
all: [<@general
        laughter@>
Lynn: :er: :er: I dunno\ I suppose I feel to some extent/ I think I kind of tune in to (???) you know
        who's out there\ it's really difficult if you don't\
Ken: everybody does\ because the- the vocabulary that you look/ use changes significantly\

Opting for a song associated with a language variety different from one's own
may represent a problem. Lynn indicates that the type of song plays an
important role in determining the degree to which a singer orients towards non-
native pronunciation, but others, e.g. Chris, make it clear that they feel uneasy
about doing so. In another passage, Chris openly voices his concern about
singing an Irish song 'with an Irish accent'.

The potential pitfall is that English, particularly southern English, singers are
wary of being perceived as patronising, as attempting to create a comical effect,
or, perhaps more obviously, as 'not getting it right'. We are confronted in this
instance with the sociolinguistic notions of *style and stylisation*, on the one
hand, and *audience design* on the other.

Style as a Sociolinguistic Dimension

We prefer the term *style* to *accent* or *dialect* because we more readily associate style with a form of presentation in performance that a speaker can adopt to varying degrees and in varying contexts.[17] We understand *style* as referring to those choices made by speakers in their speech, not necessarily consciously, to position themselves in an interactive context to the best effect and with the intention of projecting themselves most appropriately in the ongoing situation. Style is thus an important element in identity formation, is negotiable and emergent and may take place without the speakers' awareness of making those choices. It might thus be compared to Bourdieu's (1979 [1984]) notions of surface correlates and habitus (cf. Higgins 2015: 141; Auer 2007).

A speaker can choose either to converge with or to diverge from her/his interactants if the situation requires this and in so doing may index membership of a specific group or discourse community, present or absent. To achieve this, s/he may emphasise certain elements in her/his speech that might result 'in a mannered adoption of another's voice' (Bell and Gibson 2011: 560), a process that can be referred to as *stylisation*. As Higgins (ibid.) puts it, '[s]tylization is powerful because it allows speakers to position themselves in strategic ways in reference to the speech they are performing'. Stylisation, then, goes beyond the notion of style by highlighting those features that the speaker characterises as typical in positioning Bell and Gibson's 'Other'. The more aware a speaker is of the audience and of the effect her/his language use is meant to have, the more highly stylised the delivery becomes.

What might impact on the choices made when performers embark on stylisation? Bell's (1984, 2001) notion of *audience design* is useful in assessing how folk performers position themselves in relation to their audiences, i.e. to the *referee design* of the performance. Referee design 'involves the initiative use of linguistic features to index a targeted reference group' (Bell and Gibson 2011: 560), but referee design in relation to different performance contexts is a little more complex than this, as we see in Figure 10.1.

In the centre circle of Figure 10.1 is the performer (referred to here as the 'artist'), the 'I' of the referential pair 'I'–'you', but the 'I' may in fact be an internally inclusive 'we' if two (or even more) singers are performing together, and with the co-musicians and supplementary singers in the second circle they form an exclusive 'we' with respect to the referee(s), the audience. In a folk performance, however, the audience may join the 'we' by displaying an openly affective reaction to the songs and by participating in them when possible. This, as we know, is the major point of folk performance, viz. to create a 'folk', and it is characteristic of all relational performances and a very large number of

---

[17] For a more detailed discussion see Andres Morrissey (2008).

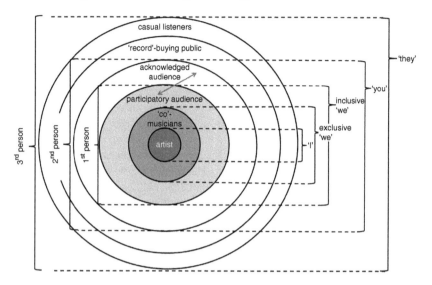

Figure 10.1. *Referee design in relation to different performance contexts*

representational performances. The aim of the performers is to create an inclusive 'we' that embraces the audience, and the aim of a folk audience is to become part of that inclusive 'we', the community of practice.

On the left-hand side of the diagram we have given these central levels of folk performance the label 'first-person' level of communication. As the performance context begins to involve a greater degree of distance between artist(s) and referents (audience), there is a shift towards a more distant 'you' rather than an inclusive 'we', indicated by the double-headed arrow, and it is precisely to overcome the referential gap created in this way that folk performers typically indulge in stylisation and in keying-in the songs and thereby communicating with the audience (see the analysis of the keyings-in in the Maddy Prior concert given in Chapter 11). This performance context is the 'second-person' level of communication although everything is done to stay at the 'first-person' level in folk performance. The 'third-person' performance context is reached when there is no direct face-to-face contact with the live performers, i.e. in the recording situation (cf. Chapter 7) or in relational contexts when there are bystanders who overhear the singing but do not participate in the performance oval.

A practical example from folk performances is Ewan MacColl's use of Scottish singing styles or those in northeastern England, even though he was born and raised in Salford and was adamant about the need to perform material from one's own culture. The speaker – or singer – may or may not be part of the reference group to which the audience belongs, or vice versa. Given that performers are granted a performance space, but in return open themselves to evaluation by those granting the space, this entails an evaluation of how acceptable stylisation in a performance is to the audience. The question of whether the audience is or is not part of the reference group plays an important role here. For example, a non-Irish performer may be seen as delivering a creditable performance of an Irish song anywhere other than in front of an Irish audience. Out-group referee design, i.e. performing a stylisation, can be a risky business, especially in folk circles, whereas it is taken as a matter of course in pop and rock performances, where style choices usually involving American features are taken for granted.

Style, stylisation and audience design are important factors in folk song performance for the simple reason that several songs are popularly associated with specific geographical locations.[18] Nevertheless, the vernacular lyrical elements discussed in Chapter 9 and in the previous section touch on a perceived need to adapt parallel vernacular features in one's singing. The long history of folk performance encourages the need to project assumed tradition and authenticity in singing folk songs (cf. Chapter 6), which manifests itself in varying degrees in individual singing styles. Ralph McTell's 1995 album *Sand in Your Shoes* is a good example of a performer accepting the risk of being accused of 'mannered adoptions' of others' voices (see Andres Morrissey 2008: 203). In the song 'The Enemy Within' ⊕137 – a song about the miners' strike of 1984 and the demise of a colliery band together with its mining community – he adopts a style similar to that of Tim Hart with a slightly lowered /æ/ and /ɛ/ in 'band' and 'felt'. In his Americana-influenced songs, he follows an American model with GenAm 5 (cf. Simpson 1999), and in other songs he mixes styles, e.g. in 'Peppers and Tomatoes' ⊕138. McTell thus reflects what Lynn says in the transcript above, i.e. that the song to a certain extent determines the style and the degree of stylisation.

The discourse community of folk song audiences can therefore be seen as a trigger for certain stylisations being in line with what an individual community might consider 'authentic' and 'traditional'. In singing 'Billy Grey', Canadian Don Couchie's use of the Confederate vowel in 'rhyme' is precisely such an instance of indexing the 'authentic' and 'traditional' style of the Appalachian origins of bluegrass. In this sense, we could say that the use of indexical, i.e. salient, features represents what Blom and Gumperz (1972) have described as 'metaphorical dialect switching' and that they require an 'awareness that a certain stylistic variant [i.e. such a salient feature] operates as an

---

[18] This is still the case even though research has shown that the same song may have been collected in very different parts of the country or even the world (e.g. Pound 1913; Bronson 1959–72).

index for a certain social meaning' (Bell and Gibson 2011: 559), a requirement that the discourse community is likely to meet.

Perhaps it is not surprising that, unlike the men, most of the first generation of British women folk singers (e.g. Shirley Collins, Jacqui McShee of Pentangle, Maddy Prior, June Tabor, Sandy Denny of Fairport Convention, Linda Thompson, etc.) followed and continue to follow a largely RP-oriented model in their singing but that later generations adopt a more or less markedly local colouring in their singing style (e.g. Eliza Carthy, Fay Hield, the Unthank sisters Rachel and Becky, Heidi Tidow, Belinda O'Hooley, Fran Smith, etc.). Such local colouring may well be an expression of indexical folk performance, a stylisation of tradition and authenticity and thus iconic for folk song, in much the same way as most of the collectors up to and including the Edwardian song hunters Sharp, Baring-Gould, Broadwood, etc., considered rurality as emblematic of folk music and song. In fact, the singing style, either directly attributable to a singer's background or as 'required' by the material may also be a remnant of that 'amalgamated reality' of rurality and folk, a 'reality' that ignored the rich urban folk tradition.

Phonological Constraints

One of the main problems identified by Trudgill (1983) was inconsistencies in the performers' style choices. Many of these can be explained by the fact that musical performers are not always thoroughly familiar with their reference style to the degree that they perform according to their model in all respects. Other inconsistencies, however, are due to phonological considerations. Many can be explained in terms of sonority. If singers have a choice between a realisation that corresponds to the referee style and a more sonorous feature which does not, or not necessarily, correspond, unless they overtly intend to stylise a reference group they will opt for the more sonorous segment, irrespective of whether it is part of the reference style or not. In general terms, intervocalic /t/ is dispreferred to dentalised /d/ or to an alveolar flap; unrounded, particularly low back vowels are preferred to rounded ones (which may reinforce Couchie's use of the unrounded back vowel in 'law'); and avoidance of closure in diphthongs or in post-vocalic /r/ may lead to the use of the Confederate vowel or a lengthened first segment with a minimal or absent realisation of the second segment in the former and diminished or absent rhoticity in the latter (Andres Morrissey 2008, 2011). Such choices make it easier for singers to perform their material, especially when competing with a musical accompaniment at an elevated volume level.

A related consideration is hyper-rhoticity as demonstrated in Cliff Richard's 'Bachelor Boy', where instead of 'a bachelor boy' Richard seems to sing /ɜɹ ˈbætʃələ bɔɪ/. However, a variation of this phenomenon was observed in a relational performance at a song gathering where a singer realised the /ʌ/ in the closing line of each stanza of Utah Phillips' song 'All Used Up', 'I'm all used up', not as /ʌp/ but as something akin to [ɜːɹp]. The reason for these realisations could be attributed to the American style model, but what is striking is that in both cases the short – and in Richard's case, an actually unstressed, reduced – vowel falls on a note that is held. The singers are therefore faced with a mismatch of note value and vowel length that can only be resolved by a form of epenthesis. In other words, to resolve this mismatch a segment has to be added, but it is vital that this does not create a potential mishearing. In both cases the simplest solution is a sonorant that requires little added articulatory effort. Most other possibilities may well create a difference in meaning or would sound incorrect. In Richard's case, a diphthong like /eɪ/ to lengthen the vowel would change the meaning to stressed indefinite determiner and would therefore suggest 'one of several' bachelor boys; 'an' is reserved for hiatus resolution; /l/ would change the meaning completely so the only close sonorant in articulatory terms is a the alveolar approximant /ɹ/. The same applies to 'up' in Utah Phillips' song, also because /r/ is in close proximity to the unrounded central vowel /ɜ/ and no confusion with mishearings can ensue.[19]

Another case of what we choose to call 'singer's epenthesis' can be observed in Christy Moore's 'As I Roved Out' ☺138, when he lengthens the /ʌ/ in *mother* in the line 'and will you come to me Mother's house' from [ˈmʌðəɹz] as one would expect, to [ˈmʌnðəɹz], inserting after the short/lax vowel /ʌ/ (possibly dentalised) /n/, which is close to the articulatory region of the following interdental fricative and thus fits with the phrasing requirement of the melody, the slightly lengthened note. The strategy is unproblematic in this context, as the modified pronunciation, if it is perceived at all, does not result in or is not suggestive of another lexeme. In other words, this does not affect the meaning of what is being sung.

This brief discussion indicates that not all pronunciation choices need be dictated by sociolinguistic considerations of style and stylisation. There are also decisions, as in other song genres such as pop and rock, which are the result of phonological factors. However, these are also subject to what works and what does not work in performance. The central issue in this context is the question of how feasible some lines or words are to sing.

---

[19] The other strategy is normally what is called an 'intrusive h', but this results in a staccato phrasing, which in these cases would make the words almost unsingable.

Rounding Off: The Impact of and on Performance

The discussion in this chapter has shown how a song, perpetuated as a recording and in all likelihood initially transmitted by the audio recording, becomes part, on the one hand, of the repertoire of one genre, Americana and bluegrass, and on the other hand, is adapted to a different musical tradition, Irish and contemporary Scottish folk. It has also demonstrated that there are changes, not so much in the tune, but in the instrumentation, on a small scale in the lyrics and in the singing style in which it is delivered. We can say that the live versions by the Blakes and Bryan, another one, not discussed here, with guitarist Tony Ricci, Blake's long-time associate, and the performance by Hometown Bluegrass represent re-entextualisations, with the musical accompaniment informed by the genre but also by the musicians performing the song. The same can be said of the singing style, although it is fair to postulate that what we are faced with, particularly in Blake's case, are stylisations that veer towards an informal performance standard rather than the more pronounced vernacular that characterises the singer's speaking style.

Planxty's and Barluath's versions, on the other hand, need to be seen as re-contextualisations, as they depart from the musical as well as the style model. Even though it is likely that Barluath, steeped in the Celtic music tradition, knew Planxty's version, their take on the song would constitute their own recontextualisation as evidenced by their title ('Billy Grey' rather than 'True Love Knows No Season') and their creation of a 'chorus'.

In terms of textual adaptations, all the versions show changes, but they are minimal, as one would expect with a relatively recent and relatively fixed perpetuation in the form of recordings (and videos). The changes are mostly performance-driven, rendering the words more acceptable to the singers' personal performance, both musically and in terms of style. They are indicative, however, of the processes at work in adoption and adaptation because the same questions need to be answered: how far should the expressions of a different vernacular be taken over vs how far should they be adapted to one's own vernacular? At the same time, should one adapt one's singing style or stylise oneself to adapt to the model of the 'text'?

This has probably been an issue for performers at any stage in singing history, and 'Billy Grey' illustrates this rather graphically. With improved technology for perpetuation and its more global spread, the connection between song and space, probably tenuous to a degree at any stage, has clearly been discontinued. Just as the English language is no longer the 'property' of the English or even of English-speakers, English language folk songs are no longer the 'property' of the people whose regions they evolved in, English, Welsh, Scottish, Irish, American, Canadian, Australian, etc., and not even of the English language speech community. They can be and are adopted and adapted by anyone with access to instances of perpetuation and an interest in Anglophone folk song. Their provenance may be passed on with the song, however, and new adopters may want to signal this in their stylisations. This creates the phenomenon of enregisterment, which we will discuss in the following chapter.

11 Enregisterment through Song: The Performer's Credibility

> ... the rules of Venda music are not arbitrary, like the rules of a game. In order to create new Venda music, you must be a Venda, sharing Venda social and cultural life from early childhood.... But I am convinced that a trained musician could not compose music that was absolutely new and specifically Venda, and acceptable to Venda audiences, unless he had been brought up in Venda society.
>
> (Blacking 1973: 98)

Enregistering Social Practices and Beliefs through Song

We have consistently argued that the main function of folk song is to bond people into communities, and one of the principal reasons for doing so in the modern world is to answer back to those in power (see Chapter 4). When a singer performs in a representational performance frame, her/his central questions must be: 'How do I perform the material I have selected as a means of answering back credibly and creditably? And in doing so how do I bond this audience into a community?' Selecting what songs to present depends on a number of criteria that we have discussed in Chapters 8 to 10. In the course of the performance, singers then need to display credibility to the audience, i.e. to show that they can serve as genuine voices for those on behalf of whom they answer back.

Constructing credibility is thus a reciprocal process involving both the singers and their selection criteria, on the one hand, and the audience, on the other. This is not always easy to achieve since political and social sensitivities are likely to have changed between the time when the song was first conceived and the emergent instantiation of the performance. For example, attitudes towards women, ethnic minorities, sexuality, social class, social beliefs and social practices, etc., fluctuate considerably through the course of time.

Credibility thus also depends on how the performer presents the songs through forms of keying-in and keying-out and on the way the material is sung. It is also reciprocally constructed during the performance. The degree to and the manner in which answering back is accomplished in a song or a set, i.e.

276

whether it is explicit, entailed or encoded, is thus determined by performance decisions. In addition, decisions also need to be made about how the song will be presented, e.g. a cappella, with instrumental accompaniment, influenced by other musical trends and styles, etc. A representational performer needs to make a specific piece of music sufficiently different from well-known versions, a process we have described as claiming a song in Chapters 3 and 10, and, finally, s/he needs to perform in a technically satisfactory way for the audience, i.e. the performance must be *creditable*.

To achieve all this, singers must be able to evoke the social meanings (practices, beliefs, configurations) that are potentially inferable from a song by enregistering these in a performance. The current chapter is thus concerned with the sociolinguistic concept of 'enregisterment' and the role it plays in folk performance. We begin in the following section by explicitly defining the term and adapting it to suit our purposes. This is followed by a section in which we consider implicit, entailed or encoded enregisterment in America and Britain. We then ask the crucial question of whether there is a recognisable 'folk singing' register in the discourse community of folk song. If so, what signs might there be that it has undergone or is currently undergoing forms of enregisterment, de-enregisterment and re-enregisterment (see the following sections)? To do this we have chosen to examine in a little more detail our iconic example of a representational folk performance, Maddy Prior's concert 'Back to the Tradition' at Cecil Sharp House on 23 October, 2008. In the final section, we discuss how folk song itself has helped to enregister the Geordie dialect and whether there are signs in songs from that area of Britain of de-enregisterment and re-enregisterment.

Registers and Enregisterment

Following Johnstone (2000), we defined the term 'voice' in Chapter 8 as '*an instance of languaging adapted to a particular interactional context*' (Chapter 8, p. 202). Adaptation to emergent instances of languaging is a social process entailing other forms of social knowledge than language itself and other forms of semiosis in addition to language. Social knowledge of various kinds can therefore be indexed in emergent interaction by what Agha (2005: 38) calls 'distinct forms of speech ... socially recognized (or enregistered) as indexical of speaker attributes by a population of users'. Language registers for Agha are not merely linguistic systems for use in specifiable social situations but rather '*reflexive models of language use* ... disseminated along identifiable trajectories in social space through communicative processes' (our italics). Registers are acquired gradually, and each has a developmental history of its own with the constant potentiality of change and transformation.

Voices, Indexicality, Styles and Enregisterment

Voices index what Agha calls 'figures of personhood' that can only be revealed and acted on in instantiations of entextualisation (ibid.: 39). Once voices are perceived to be in contrast with one another in entextualisation, they are seen as individual voices of characterological stereotypes, or styles, typifying different social configurations and attributes. They become *enregistered voices* when they are perceived as indexing social configurations, practices and beliefs, i.e. ideologies, beyond the forms of speech in which they are framed. These configurations, practices and beliefs are created through meta-semiotic processes of inferencing in instances of entextualisation, such that 'voices are not attributes of persons but entextualized figures of personhood' (ibid.: 43).

Registers are constructed through time and in forms of interaction (written, printed or oral) as 'repertoire[s] of speech forms' (ibid.: 45) which, as Agha points out, are 'widely recognized as indexing the same "social voice" by many language users' (ibid.). Registers may involve recognisable morpho-syntactic constructions not typical of everyday language usage, e.g. in legal language, or lexically complex constructions to avoid indexing problematic issues, e.g. in the language of the military when an expression such as 'collateral damage' avoids having to refer to 'civilian deaths'. But registers may also be constructed around specific types of accent, e.g. the RP pronunciation of 'Standard English'[1] – an enregistered accent – or around specific dialectal varieties of a language – an enregistered dialect. Agha also notes that 'registers have a dynamic social life ... mediated by metadiscursive practices of speech typification, reception, and response' (ibid.: 56), which amounts to saying that a major form of mediation is through the performance mode.

Enregisterment, De-enregisterment and Re-enregisterment

As we have seen, Agha considers registers to be 'reflexive models of language use' rather than specialised linguistic varieties that we use in specific social contexts. We suggest that there are two ways in which registers can develop:
1. Enregisterment$_1$: specialised forms of social activity lead to the creation and adaptation of linguistic expressions that suit the needs of the social activity in question. While enregisterment is taking place, meta-pragmatic processes are applied to generate social, characterological and local stereotypes that become part of the overall meanings triggered by the use of the register.

---

[1] Cf. Agha's discussion of the development of different forms of RP from the end of the seventeenth century to the present, in which talking in certain marked forms of RP has come to invoke inferences of authority, educatedness, sophistication, wealth, power, etc. (Agha 2003).

2. Enregisterment$_2$: already existent language varieties (accents, dialects, regional standards) become associated through time and through expansion in the use of the relevant variety with specific social activities or evolve in or through them to become stylised to the point at which they assume features that are no longer or not prevalent in those language varieties. As in the process of enregisterment$_1$, enregisterment$_2$ leads to the generation of social, characterological and local stereotypes that become part of the overall meanings triggered by use of the register.

Thus, if we were to trace the historical development of the accent of English known as RP, as Agha (2003) does, we would be dealing with a case of enregisterment$_2$, in which such social attributes as 'wealthy', 'well educated', 'raised in polite society', 'authoritative', 'knowledgeable', possibly also 'honest', 'trustworthy', 'reliable', local attributes such as 'British and not American, Australian, etc.' and such character types as 'member of the upper middle to upper classes', 'British Army officer', 'public school boy', etc. might be inferred. If, on the other hand, we were to trace the historical development of legal English, we would be dealing with a case of enregisterment$_1$, in which character types such as 'lawyers', 'defendants', 'bureaucrats' and social attributes such as 'stuffy', 'boring', 'nit-picking', 'devious', 'smart', etc. might be inferred.

We submit that the larger, or more powerful, the discourse community of the register, the greater will be the diffusion of the meta-pragmatically generated social stereotypes. At the same time, the more vulnerable the stereotypes will be to historical change with the concomitant result that the language variety might also change as a response to changes in the stereotypes. To return briefly to Agha's example of RP, there is evidence that its influence is on the wane due to changes in stereotypes, e.g. new associations with super-rich City of London bankers and financiers and new social attributes such as 'perfidious', 'greedy', 'double-dealing', etc. The following two processes are the consequence of changes in register: (1) de-enregisterment, in which a register loses its positive values and becomes moribund and (2) re-enregisterment, in which a register begins to generate new and possibly very different social stereotypes.

Features of Enregisterment

A song has the potential to invoke the meta-pragmatic enregisterment of social and characterological stereotypes, but that potential can only be fully realised if the singer is aware of which features can be credibly and creditably enregistered. The question as to how creditably these non-linguistic features can be invoked in a performance so as not to affect credibility adversely thus becomes crucial. To explore the features of enregisterment, we examine the song 'Take This Hammer' ☺144 (TTH) as notated in Lomax and Lomax (1947 [1975]: 404–5) and in Lomax (1964: 92).

Enregisterment in America

Both anthologies emphasise that TTH is a work song used for wielding 'axes, picks or sledge hammers' (Lomax 1964: 92) and that the song is sung at a slow tempo. In the notes, Lomax and Lomax (1947 [1975]) refer to a 'work grunt' as 'a regular and important part of the song', and this is also included in their notation (1947: 404). Lomax (1964) further notes that the song has been reported from 'Virginia, the Carolinas, and Georgia', but also that 'its cadences are commonplace in American Negro [sic] folksong' and that his version came from the 'Virginia State penitentiary, ... the fantasy of a Negro [sic] convict brooding about an escape from the "burning hell" of the prison farm' (ibid.: 92). The convict was none other than Huddie Leadbetter, better known as 'Leadbelly'. Although Lomax gives it the title 'The Hammer Song'/'Take this Hammer', he represents the African American non-rhoticity in the first line as 'take this *hammo* / carry it to the captain'. There are other linguistic style features, e.g. 'runnin'' and 'flyin'', the absence of third person -*s* as in if 'he ask you' (but 'they hurts') and 'Ize' for 'I am', as well as references to 'cornbread and molasses' and the term 'shooter' for the guards.

These linguistic elements illustrate how the song is enregistered as an African American prison work song. There are *phonological* indicators, e.g. non-rhoticity, there are *morpho-syntactic* constructions, e.g. the presence or absence of the inflectional verb suffix -*s*, and *lexical* elements, e.g. the reference to 'shooter' for 'guard'.[2] Non-linguistic, meta-pragmatically generated features of enregisterment include *social* and *historical* inferences (work song in a prison farm), *cultural* inferences ('cornbread and molasses' in Leadbelly's version) and *spatial/geographical* inferences (Lomax's information that the song was recorded in Virginia) either in the text or in the commentary on the printed versions. In addition, the music also helps the audience to infer the stereotypes, e.g. the minor third in bar 14 (Lomax 1964: 92), which realises an instance of what is known as the 'blue note' typical for blues and jazz (cf. Appendix), as does the *stance* adopted by the singer, i.e. defiance of the system in the last stanza: 'I'm gonna bust right past that shooter ... I'm goin' home, I'm goin' home.'

In its many recordings, the song has surfaced in a variety of different forms. Odetta's 1957 version is non-rhotic on 'hammer' but, unlike Leadbelly, rhotic on 'cornbread', but varies between standard and African American morpho-syntactic elements ('he ask' but 'I'm' rather than 'Ize'). The picture that emerges if we look at other, white American artists shows that the morpho-syntactic features are reduced although double negation ('I don't want no ...') is retained. Rhoticity is inconsistent with some; Willie Watson in his recording

---

[2] Many of these are missing in Leadbelly's recording.

for WFPK Radio Louisville (9 May 2014) varies this on 'hammer' and 'cornbread', possibly to avoid articulatory closure of the alveolar approximant (cf. Andres Morrissey 2008: 211). His version does not feature the grunt, but it is otherwise quite faithful to an African American model.

By contrast, the New York group the Tarriers on their 1959 album *Tell the World About This*, have slight *r*-colouring, are otherwise relatively standard American in their pronunciation and in their morpho-syntax, but by starting the song with the verse taken from 'John Henry', they change it into a song about railway workers. The tempo remains relatively slow, but the arrangement is typical for an Americana/Old Time production of the period, quite polished with elegant harmonies. Another departure, representative for the many bluegrass versions, is the cover version by the Osborne Brothers released in 1995, which has no references to railroads, but is too fast for a work song, as are all bluegrass versions. It is also typical of bluegrass singing in other elements, e.g. the falsetto harmonies and the instrumental breaks as well as rhoticity in all instances and Confederate vowels in 'pride' / praˑd/ or 'cold iron' /koʊld aˑrn/. In the American versions, then, there is a wide spectrum of enregistered features with few of them enregistering those implied by a song about an African American serving time on a prison farm, i.e. a heavy manual labour work song. They do not include the 'work grunt'.

De- and Re-enregisterment in British and 'New Folk' Versions

In Britain, a similar picture emerges in that only selective elements are enregistered. To begin with, the three early versions discussed here make no mention of guards or of cornbread and other prison diet. In other words, they do not enregister the convict but, at least to a certain extent, they attempt to enregister the African American. Lonnie Donegan, in a 1960 TV recording, shows some elements of African American linguistic stylisations, e.g. he is non-rhotic, uses the Confederate vowel and alveolarised -*ing* in 'flyin'' and 'ass' instead of 'asks', but as he varies the repetitions of the first lines, his morpho-syntax ends up being fairly standard for much of the time. African American enregisterment is also, at least tokenistically, present in the musical arrangement, which emphasises the backbeat and features a jazz guitar with a rather jazzier instrumental break than the more simple harmonies of the verses. But there is no hint of this being a prison or a work song, and the tempo is faster than in the versions by Leadbelly or Odetta.

The same applies for three sixties pop/rock versions. Two were recorded by the Beatles with Lennon on vocals, in all likelihood not meant for publication as they sound more like band jams.[3] In the version by the Spencer Davis Group,

---

[3] https://www.youtube.com/watch?v=qHeq MEubDmg, accessed 13 August 2015.

the musical arrangement is closer to the 'Brit Blues' of the mid- and late sixties epitomised by the Rolling Stones, the Yardbirds, the Small Faces, John Mayall and the Bluesbreakers, etc. Entitled 'This Hammer', its rhythm is dominated by a guitar shuffle lick, it features an instrumental break on the blues harmonica, and the harmonies include the minor to the tonic (cf. Appendix). The first stanza is 'Workin' on the railroad for a dollar a day/ *(three times)* / gotta earn my money boys gotta earn my pay'. Thus, like the Tarriers, they transform it into a song about the toil of railroad workers rather than members of a chain gang. With the introduction of such variation it is not surprising that on the single as well as on the *Second Album* (1966), it is credited to the band members Muff and Steve Winwood, Pete York and Spencer Davis, which is rectified on the 1967 *The Best of the Spencer Davis Group*, where 'This Hammer' is described as traditional, arranged by Steve Winwood.

A more contemporary take on the song[4] is by the self-styled '"mysticippi" blues man' Harry Manx (born on the Isle of Man, raised in Ontario and resident in British Columbia), which takes up the Spencer Davis Group version, including their first stanza and the harmonies, but is more consistent with a General American rather than with an African American model: among other things his rendition is fully rhotic. Nevertheless, it could be argued that he stylises the blues by dropping the inflectional -*s* suffix in 'ask'. Interestingly enough, in the Sydney performance his use of the Ellis Stompbox, a simple rhythm device that can be activated by foot-tapping, creates a slow steady beat that is reminiscent of a work song, albeit too frequent for axe or sledge hammer work.[5] It thus remains a forceful reminder of the toil of labourers and retains little of the defiance against the working conditions and power asymmetries inherent in them.

Shifts in Enregisterment and 'Answering Back'

Our discussion shows that from the full enregisterment of 'Take This Hammer', which covers (socio)linguistic, social, cultural, historical elements and musical features as well as the stance of the 'voice', a specific explicit and direct 'answering back' results. The song is a powerful protest against white hegemony and a senseless penitentiary system that is still in existence today. It bears testimony to the back-breaking drudgery that characterises it and to the role of the guards as enforcers of the system. However, with the decision to de-enregister certain features, e.g. the comment on the life of the convict, the anti-hegemonic discourse shifts, in our case, from convict to railroad navvy, from stone-breaking to the laying of rails. In the same way, the focus shifts from senseless toil to badly paid work paired with

---

[4] With various performances and a promotional video on YouTube.
[5] https://www.youtube.com/watch?v=Q8eA4Js7gdw,, accessed 13 August 2015.

having to eke out a living with meagre wages. As the days of railway work are largely over, such protest, explicit in Leadbelly's recording, has become 'entailed' (cf. Chapter 4) or may even become 'encoded' if it is seen as a pop/rock piece, played in a concert in which there is little or no overt answering back of any kind. A full enregisterment in a song of this nature is likely to represent an instance of explicit anti-hegemonic discourse. The greater the number of features that are absent or re-enregistered differently, the more the original protest becomes entailed or even encoded.

Enregistering 'Folk Talk' in Performance: Enregisterment₁

Our discussion shows that enregisterment₁ relies on features that are predictably present in the discourse – and in related domains – of a specific community or a particular characterological figure. As Agha maintains, registers are 'reflexive models of language use' rather than specialised linguistic varieties. In addition they are created and recreated in interaction within a discourse community and are thus emergent, but they are also perceived in less differentiated ways by a wider public outside the community, where certain iconic elements of such perceptions are likely to form part of an enregisterment, even if they are no longer prevalent or have fallen into disuse in that community.

To put it differently, the social and characterological stereotypes are generated not only by those actively engaged or passively interested in the production and performance of such discourse communities but equally, and often in a more negative, critical sense, by those outside them. Interestingly, it is often those iconic, widely recognised features of characterological figures that form part of the image of the discourse community's practices, and if they are sufficiently current in public perception, considerable mileage can be gained for the creation of comedy.

Characterological Figures and Distinctive Features

Striking examples of this phenomenon are the military figures, politicians, TV presenters, etc., in many Monty Python sketches, Wolfie Smith, bungling English urban guerrilla in the 1970s BBC comedy series *Citizen Smith*, or the alternately rude and fawning hotel manager Basil Fawlty in *Fawlty Towers*. Essentially, most parodists make use of the same strategy; they take one or several enregistered features of a characterological figure and exaggerate them into caricatures. For our present purposes the musical portraits by Christopher Guest, Michael McKean and Harry Shearer in the two 'mockumentaries' *This is Spinal Tap* (1984) and *A Mighty Wind* (2003) are striking examples. In the former, they portray English hard and prog rock 'dinosaurs' Spinal Tap, on a chaotic American tour to promote their latest album, which leaves out hardly any rock cliché, from the loudness of their equipment, machismo, overblown but mal-functioning stage shows, the hardships of touring to tragic deaths of band members, in particular their string of dead drummers. In *A Mighty Wind*, they feature as the Folksmen in a memorial performance for fictitious 1960s New York folk promoter Irving Steinbloom. There are two episodes that we consider striking: (1) the Folksmen's consternation about the need to scrap their opening song as the act before them, their saccharine but fierce competitors The New Main Street Singers have just performed it in their set; and (2) the scene when Harry Shearer as Mark Shubb, bass player and 'historian of the band', has to spin out a keying-in for a final, unplanned number for several minutes, because Mitch, the disturbed half of the last act Mitch and Mickey, has disappeared into the New York night. When he is finally found and ready to come on stage, compere John Steinbloom (played by Bob Balaban) highlights this verb-osity by suggesting the band should rename itself the Spokesmen.

Another parodist, who focused on keyings-in, but also on more linguistically oriented forms of enregisterment through the use of obscure words suggesting dialect or archaic folk-cultural terms, was Rambling Sid Rumpo, alias Kenneth Williams, whose sketches were originally part of the 1960s radio comedy programme *Round the Horne*. He typically started his performances with 'Hullo, me dearios', which could be seen as the enregisterment of a 'folksy' interaction with a club audience, through the substitution of 'me' for the possessive determiner 'my' and the use of *-o* at the end of a word, a frequent feature in folk songs to flesh out a lyrical line and render a masculine rhyme feminine to meet the requirements of a tune. Another form of caricature, this time a cartoon (Image 11.1); shown as Image 11.1, plays on the assumption that many folk singers are informal, or give themselves an air of informality and eschew what could be seen as the slick professionalism of show business. It unites a large number of characterological features of (more relational) folk performances. It is set in a pub (cf. the reference to real ale and the question on the left put by someone clearing away the empty beer glasses, 'Are these all dead?', which is also interpretable as a question concerning the singers them-selves). It contains assumed semiotic characteristics of the folk scene, such as the singer's sandals, duffle coat and beard, and displays the typical self-deprecation and/or lack of professionalism in the floor singer's keying-in as well as his suggestion that the audience can participate in the singing, viz. 'it's got a chorus'.

These examples illustrate a number of features associated with folk perfor-mances that are so salient that they are recognisable as parody aimed at a larger audience outside the discourse community. The members of the discourse community themselves would probably appreciate the details more than the general public, being familiar with them, even though the features themselves

Image 11.1. *Great floor singers*

would hardly ever occur in such a concentration of stereotypes at any one given time. In addition, most of them are unlikely to be associated with current 'folk talk' in the current discourse community. Nevertheless, they are typically manifested implicitly in the selection criteria (see the first section of this chapter). In addition, performers have a considerable amount of information beyond and concerning the song lyrics at their disposal, as we saw in our discussion of the text (Chapter 9), with only a selection of these entextualised in a given performance. Song selection bears testimony to some features of enregisterment, but the latter can be more easily expressed explicitly in key-ings-in to the individual songs. For this reason, we explore a practical example in more detail in the following subsection.

Enregisterment₁ in Maddy Prior's Performance 'Back to the Tradition'

Given our understanding of the principal function of the performance of folk song as the bonding of an audience into a social community and the indisputable fact that we can define a discourse community of folk music distributed across the English-speaking world and displaying a long historical continuity (see Finnegan 1989 and Chapters 3, 4 and 6), it is reasonable to argue for the existence of a linguistic register that suits the needs of the social activity of folk performance. Any instance of folk perfor-mance, whether relational or representational, should thus display forms of enregisterment₁ that go beyond linguistic expressions and include social and characterological stereotypes that become part of the overall meanings triggered by the register.

We have called this register 'folk talk', and keying-in practices in folk performances fulfil essentially three functions:
1. they help to create and maintain the performance oval and the community;
2. in relation to the performance context, they entextualise the selection criteria of the material, its core concepts and extraneous information (see Chapter 9);
3. they provide the singer with an opportunity to authenticate him/herself through enregisterment and by establishing credibility and creditability.

They typically carry out these functions through personal anecdotes and the use of humour. They may provide an 'abstract' of the material, not least with the purpose of making social references in songs explicit and/or highlighting – subtly or explicitly – their continued relevance. In the same way and potentially for the same purpose, they give historical and cultural background information to a song. They situate a song in terms of its provenance. They may also indicate or explicitly enregister a personal stance or 'political' position.

To explore a practical instance of folk talk, therefore, we turn to our example of a representational folk performance, Maddy Prior's concert 'Back to the Tradition' at Cecil Sharp House in October 2008.[6] We do not focus on the lyrics of the songs performed, but on the ways in which Prior, her band members and her guests key in their songs and communicate with the

[6] The entire transcript of the performance in the form in which it is now is on the website.

audience. The amount of keying-in is extensive, in keeping with what we established as a characterological feature in the previous subsection. In effect, this is how folk performance differs markedly from that of other types of musical performance that show no or only exceptional keying-in in WAM or typically elicit audience response ('are you having a good time?' or 'put your hands together') and acknowledge applause in pop and rock.[7] The more detailed keying-in in folk performance reveals a fundamental difference between it and other performance types. In the case of non-folk performances, especially since the 1950s, when the division of labour between composers and lyricists, on the one hand, and performers, on the other, disappeared in favour of performers mostly writing their own material, there has been an implicit performers' ownership/authorship of and thus a relationship with the material performed. By contrast, in folk music, in particular in traditional folk, such ownership/authorship is inherently non-existent or often largely ignored although reference concerning adoption (and also adaptation in liner notes) can be and is made. But the relationship to the material needs to be established, and appropriation of the songs is made or substantiated in a performance through keying-in and in recordings and songbooks, forms of perpetuation, through (liner) notes, etc. (cf., e.g., Connolly 1989).

To begin with, we focus on function 1, keying-in as a means for *creating and maintaining community* and in order to *reference the performance frame*. An obviously effective strategy for a performer is to address the audience directly. Prior does not resort to this very often but does so when greeting the audience and when acknowledging applause. Tim Hart also acknowledges applause, but he also actively encourages the audience to sing along when he says in keying-in 'Who's the Fool Now?' 'you can join in', thus indicating what we referred to in Chapter 9 as an interactional objective in the selection of a song for performance. Fiddler and oud player Giles Lewin most frequently addresses the audience directly, keying in his oud songs with 'some of you might be wondering what an Arabic oud is doing in a programme which is called "Back to the Tradition"' or two fiddle tunes with a reference to barley wine, saying 'd'you remember that, (...) very tasty. and highly effective'. This can also be seen as an instance of humour as the audience responds to 'highly effective' with laughter, an element of folk talk we return to below.

Prior nevertheless frequently establishes a personal rapport with the audience in several ways. She relates to the performance space, Cecil Sharp House, and to Cecil Sharp, 'who/:er: after this building is named', but she also allows

---

[7] The characterological 'check it out' at times lampooned in rap is probably not so much an attempt to establish communication with the audience but a strategy to buy time in order to compose (improvised) lines.

the audience glimpses into her personal views and emotional responses, when she refers to a song or someone else's performance as 'lovely', but most touchingly in her comments on 'I Heard the Banns', where she relates to the spurned lover with considerable empathy, highlighting the pain of the voice in the song, on the one hand, hearing about her man marrying another woman, but also not being able to leave the church where the marriage banns are being read because of the stir this would cause in the congregation. To similar effect, she uses personal narratives, in particular in keying in 'Magpie', a song she wrote herself. The following excerpt is an illustration of such narrative, which contains two instances of another strategy, the use of humour, underlined:

I wrote it back in sixty-six, in the/:er: in Tim's dad's vicarage, actually. and :er: it was/oh it was a nice song. but then the television programme came along, with the wrong rhyme. cos the right rhyme I got is one for sorrow, two for joy, three for a wedding, and four for a boy, five for fiddler, six for a dance, seven for Old England, and eight for France. so that was my version, and they came on with this totally wrong (..) rhyme. <@@@@> everybody's gone off somewhere. completely different now. and erm:/and I thought/:er: when we were making the album I saw seven magpies. and I thought 'oh seven for Old England. oh title for the album'. the song. I could do the song, you see, nothing wasted. <@@@@@>

However, the largest number of utterances that relate to the audience concern references to the material and to performers taking a solo spot. Such utterances frequently refer to the titles of songs, for instance, 'and this is :er: :er: a piece/ another piece from Scotland [...] and it's called "Jock of Hazeldean"'. They may include pointers to general themes, e.g. in introducing 'Bitter Withy' after singing 'Dives and Lazarus': 'and we're going to stay in a sort semi-Biblical theme'. They also inform the audience about the structure of the set ('*another* piece', emphasis added) or more directly 'well we're going to finish with a piece'. And, finally, they are used to introduce additional performers, e.g. her first musical partner Tim Hart, whose appearance on stage is announced with 'and now we've got our last (..) very special guest'.[8]

References to Cecil Sharp House are used to relate to the venue and its audience, but folk talk in this performance also includes comments on facts that are linked with the discourse community and are assumed to be shared knowledge or might be of interest if they were a little less arcane. Interestingly enough, Giles Lewin, in his keying-in of both fiddle tunes and pieces he performs on the oud, most frequently resorts to this thematic category by making reference to the origins of his material. One significant instance is his explanation of a tune called 'Of Noble Race was Shenkin', which he relates to two iconic sources:

---

[8] In hindsight, this was a very emotional moment as Tim Hart was diagnosed with lung cancer in December 2008 and died a year later in his home in La Gomera, Spain.

it appears in *The Beggars' Opera*. :er: this piece, and I think it's originally from D'Urfey's *Pills to Purge Melancholy*. a big collection of ballads, witty and (. . .) often slightly rude ballads.

Lewin also tells the tale of how he came to learn the content of the Arabic songs he performs in some detail. His attempt to place the performance of those songs within the 'shared tradition' can be explained with the less obvious need that Prior, as the Grande Dame of Folk, has to position herself. We return to the point of a tradition and of community a little later. At this juncture it is significant to emphasise that some of the categories under discussion seem to relate primarily to one function whereas others play a role in two or even all three.

The second function, *entextualisation of 'text' beside the 'Song Elements'* (Figure 9.1), gives clues and indications of the performers' selection criteria for their material, its core concepts and the extraneous information considered necessary to appreciate the songs as well as, in this case, the tunes. High on the list is imparting cultural and historical background information and the provenance of the song. There are several instances of this function in the performance under discussion. Prior's comment on 'Bitter Withy', which depicts Jesus as a child quite vindictively causing the death by drowning of 'three rich young lords' because they will not 'play at the ball' with someone who is 'nothing but a poor maid's child', gives the audience cultural information: 'it's what you call an apocryphal story'. Historical, social and geographical information is given in Prior's and June Tabor's keying-in of 'The Doffin' Mistress':

MADDY: well we're going to do a piece now, which is about spinning. :erm: er: little
           doffers, they're called. who put on the/take off the full :er: spindles and put on
           the empty ones. and apparently it's not/I thought it was from Lancashire. but
           apparently it's—[looks at June]
JUNE: it's from Belfast. the national anthem of the Belfast mills.

Such information entextualises a much more detailed set of points that form part of the 'text' outside the actual song 'text' itself. It also includes references to sources, to songwriters whose material is performed or information about musical aspects of the songs. Once again it is Giles Lewin who is most detailed here, both in terms of reference to sources and with comments about the music, e.g. when he talks about John Playford as a source for his tunes:

his *Dancing Master*'s :er: probably the earli/:erm: the- the biggest collection of :er: early tunes from the mid-seventeenth century. and it was tremendously popular. ran to eighteen editions I think, :erm: but it seems that- that the tunes that appear in the early editions, seem to be a bit/little bit fresher than the later ones. it's as if they came from a kind of a (. . .) popular tradition already existing, and then kind of subsequently the popularity of the piece/maybe they had to get all these hacks in, to write :erm: tunes to keep up with the- the demand.

Such information is also part of keying-out, e.g. when Prior comments on 'The Collier Lad', attributing the song to 'the singing of :er: Harry Boardman's mum. and :er: Harry Boardman was a seminal figure in the Lancashire folk scene'. Her detailed account of northeastern songwriter Tommy Armstrong (1848–1920) in her introduction to his 'Trimdon Grange Explosion' is another good example of this.

A final aspect of this second function is the abstract of the song content. Before singing 'Martinmas Time', Prior summarises the content of the song as follows: 'it's a story of a young girl, who gets :er: inveigled into making a solemn vow, :er: that she will meet a troop of soldiers at a particular time and place. and she realises that she/because it's such a solemn vow, she has to : er: stick to the letter of the :er: vow. but not necessarily the spirit. so this is the story of "Martinmas Time".' However, she highlights the plot without actually giving away the details, which allows the audience to concentrate not so much on what happens in the narrative, but on how it happens, i.e. the details of how the girl preserves her virginity without breaking her vows.

Many of the points made above cannot be separated completely from and will play into the third function of keying-in, the performer authenticating her/himself as a singer and establishing credibility and creditability through the song material. Creditability will largely need to be established in performance and through the evaluation by the audience, but if the performer is well known, her/his creditability is probably established by reputation, although iconic performers sometimes fail to live up to what is expected of them. In such authentification, a performer also establishes and launches the voices (cf. Chapter 8) and recreates her/his identity as a performer. In the context of folk performance, this includes the position from which s/he 'answers back'. It may be done stridently, particularly by performers with an overtly anti-hegemonic discourse stance, e.g. Billy Bragg, who routinely makes no bones about his politics, either in his songs or in how he keys them in. In 'Back to the Tradition' performance, anti-hegemonic discourse, answering back, is mainly entailed and only occasionally comes to the fore, e.g. when, before giving the title of the song 'The Doffin' Mistress', June Tabor gives the social and geographic information about the song, i.e. that it was 'the national anthem of the Belfast mills', and then adds the caustic comment 'when Belfast still had mills.' A similar aside indicating her anti-hegemonic discourse stance can be observed in the introduction to 'The Four Loom Weaver', where she combines historical information indicating an entailed protest and then makes this protest more explicit by adding: 'it concerns the plight of skilled workers, after the end of the Napoleonic Wars, when wages fell by nearly two thirds. this seems to be another one that's coming round again, isn't it.'

Function 3 also helps the singer to situate her/himself and the song material in the tradition of the discourse community. It can be accomplished by references to transmission, i.e. highlighting the singers from whom the material was learnt or who wrote a particular song, by connecting the song with external information relating to the second function of achieving a continuity of transmission as well as enhancing the credibility of the performer as a collector of and researcher into songs and tunes. Related to this element are references to continuity in the discourse community, in our case across the generations of folk performers. One instance of this is that Prior's daughter Rose Kemp is a guest, and that they perform one of her songs, 'Nature's Hymn'. It also includes references to musicians who are not present, e.g. when Prior talks about musicians on her latest album, two of whom are performing with her, and mentions 'Benji in fact, who's not with us tonight. but :er: Benji is John Kirkpatrick's (.) son. [...] strange how things come round, isn't it.' Given that 'continuity' is a salient characteristic of folk song and folk music, it is not surprising that the authentification of performers and material goes beyond highlighting the antiquity of the material and includes generational continuity. This was also in evidence in Pete Seeger's performance of 'This Land Is Your Land' with his grandson Tao Rodriguez-Seeger at Barack Obama's inauguration on 18 January 2009.

To sum up how enregisterment$_1$ works in folk performance and the connection between its various features and the three functions of keying-in, consider Table 11.1:

Table 11.1. *Folk performance and keying-in/out*

Community bonding and performance frame	Entextualisation outside the 'Song Elements' (see Fig. 9.1)	Performers' authentication
• *directly addressing the audience* • *humour* • *references to the performance space* • *inviting audience participation*	• *cultural/historical background information* • *song narrative or song abstract*	• *personal stance: answering back* • *references to the continuity of the tradition through the generations*
	• *information about sources* • *reference to songwriters and other artists* • *musical information*	
• *personal/emotional response* • *personal narratives* • *insider (shared?) information pertinent to the discourse community* • *reference to co-performers and material performed*		

As the discussion and Table 11.1 show, there are certain categories that can be linked to one, others to two and some to all three of the functions of 'folk talk'. As such they represent different elements of the enregisterment$_1$ of 'folk talk', which may be selected for the keying-in of a particular song in a set as is appropriate and deemed necessary by the performers. It is fair to assume that most, if not all, of them are present in a set of more than two or three songs, but that their prominence differs depending on whether the performer aims primarily to entertain or to engage the audience ideologically or, in the widest sense, to educate them.

Enregistering Geordie through Song: Enregisterment$_2$

We now turn our attention to an instance of enregisterment$_2$, in which 'already existent language varieties (accents, dialects, regional standards) become associated through time and through expansion in the use of the relevant variety with specific social activities'. We focus specifically on the enregisterment of the Geordie dialect through song. Like other varieties of English such as Scouse or Cockney, Geordie – the dialect of Newcastle-upon-Tyne and the old coal-mining areas of County Durham, or the dialect of the three present counties of Durham, Northumbria and Tyne and Wear – has acquired its own 'name', which is an indication of its enregisterment. Geordie also enregisters social values and coal-mining character stereotypes that exist elsewhere within Britain, but in the course of time it became at least iconic for other industrial areas of the north of England, yielding a discourse community large enough to enregister such social attributes as 'hard work', 'humour', 'working-class solidarity', 'toughness', etc. It has also been extended to include a vibrant local culture of song, music hall (in the nineteenth century), storytelling, dancing, Northumbrian piping and fiddling, etc. Beal (2009) argues that the Geordie dialect has been successfully commodified in dialect dictionaries, phrase books and commercial souvenirs and that visual icons such as the Tyne Bridge and characterological stereotypes such as the collier and the keelman (see also Wales 2006: 235) have played their part in enregistering Geordie.

Enregisterment took place in a flourishing local culture of dance, song and oral recitation in performance venues like pubs, dance halls and, most significantly, from the second third of the nineteenth century on, music halls. It was also strongly supported by a vibrant and long-lasting tradition of broadsheet and chapbook production and distribution, and, in the form of songwriting, i.e. by modes of answering back, by working-class opposition to industrial oppression.

Songs from Bell's Rhymes of Northern Bards *(1812)*

The songs in this section are taken from John Bell's *Rhymes of Northern Bards* (1812), a compilation of songs popular at the turn of the nineteenth century – many of them from the song collections of Joseph Ritson and

intimately connected to the tradition of Northumbrian smallpipes playing –
rhymes, 'ballads' and songs by contemporary songwriters. The connection
with the piping tradition indicates that those songs to which no author is
attributed were popularly in use throughout the eighteenth century, possibly
longer, and that the gradual enregisterment of Geordie may have begun before
that of RP. We begin with 'The Hexhamshire Lass' (THL), a song that
appeared in print in 1812. The version that Bell prints omits three stanzas
that are still sung today.[9]

Hexhamshire Lass   trad.

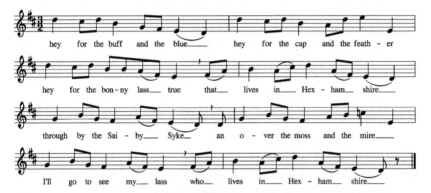

hey   for the buff   and the blue____   hey   for the cap   and the feath - er

hey   for the bon - ny lass____ true   that____ lives in____ Hex - ham__ shire____

through   by the Sai - by____ Syke__   an   o - ver the moss   and the mire____

I'll   go to see   my____ lass   who____ lives   in____ Hex - ham__ shire____

1. hey for the buff and the blue
   hey for the cap and the feather
   hey for the bonnie lassie true
   that lives in Hexhamshire

   chorus: thro' by the Saiby Syke
   and o'er the moss and the mire
   I'll go to see my lass
   that lives in Hexhamshire

2. her father loved her well
   her mother loved her better
   I I love the lass mysel'
   but alas I cannot get her

5. her petticoat is silk
   and plaited round with siller
   her shoes are tied with tape
   she'll wait 'til I go till her

---

[9] In the other songs in this section, we indicate Geordie constructions in boldface type. As an
impassioned antiquarian, it is probable that even Bell was prone to leaving out stanzas for reasons
of propriety (cf. the second of the missing stanzas) and to tone down the amount of dialect in the
lyrics. The three 'missing' stanzas in Bell are as follows: 'if only I could be / lying there aside
her / while I watched my dear / my arms would be denied her'; 'her skin is like the silk / and her
hair is like the silver / her breasts are deep but full / they'll warm when I get near her'; 'away with
the parson's shilling / and away with the cap and feather / I want to see my lass / who lives in
Hexhamshire'.

3. oh this love this love
of this love I am weary
sleep I can get none
for thinking on my deary

4. my heart is like to break
my bosom is on fire
so well I love the lass
that lives in Hexhamshire

6. were I where I would be
I would be beside her
but here a while I must be
whatever may betide her

7. hey for the thick and the thin
hey for the mud and the mire
and hey for the bonny lass
that lives in Hexhamshire

Adding the three missing stanzas to the version in Bell (1812) turns THL into an unmistakable night-visiting song, in which a lover visits his beloved without the knowledge of her parents.[10]

The only traces of Geordie to be found in Bell's version of THL are *bonny lassie*, which might equally well be Lowland Scots, in stanza 1, *mysel'* in stanza 2 in which the final /f/ is dropped and where the 'my' would be pronounced [mɪ] in Geordie, *think on* in stanza 3, *lass* in stanzas 4 and 7 (again possibly also Lowland Scots), the lexeme *siller* for 'silver' and the preposition *till* for 'to' in stanza 5. This does not, of course, prevent local singers, when extextualising the song, from producing *weel* for 'well' in stanzas 1 and 4, *bryek* [bʁjɛˑk] for 'break' [bɹeɪk] in stanza 4 and *tyep* [tjɛˑp] for 'tape' [teɪp], monophthongising the 'I' to [ɑː]/[ɔː] or producing further pronunciations to make the song 'sound' Geordie. In addition, THL contains formulaic and archaic expressions that index 'folk song standard' (see the discussion in Chapter 10), e.g. 'hey for the X', 'alas', 'sleep I can get none / for Xing … ', 'my heart is like to break / my bosom is on fire', 'whatever may betide her', thus rendering it even more accessible to singers outside the Geordie area.

Another song from Bell (1812), firmly rooted in the Northumbrian piping tradition, is 'Elsie Marley' (EM) ⊛140, which is so widespread as a dance tune that whole stanzas have been transferred from it to other songs. The lyrics do not easily allow us to discover a song schema, but like Scots Gaelic *puirt à beul*,[11] or vocal dance music, it has extemporised lyrics revolving around both the character of Elsie Marley and the dance tune of that name:

[10] Fairport Convention's various performances of THL, which are all at breakneck speed and thus – in our critical opinion – destroy the sly, ironic undertones of the night-visiting song and most certainly any interpretation as a love song, have become iconic, with singer after singer trying to emulate Fairport Convention's speed. There is almost no way in which this song from Northumbria can now be said to enregister Geordie.

[11] Cf. Anne Lorne Gillies' discussion of *puirt à beul* in Gillies (2010: xxv).

Elsie Marley

trad.

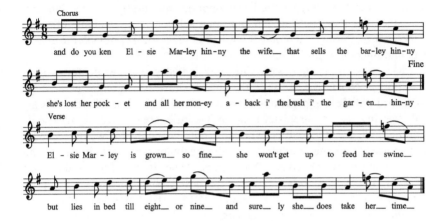

Chorus: and do you ken Elsie Marley hinny
the wife that sells the barley hinny
she's lost her pocket and all her money
a' back o' the bush i' the garden hinny

1. Elsie Marley is grown so fine
    she won't get up to serve her swine
    but lies in bed till eight or nine
    and surely she does take her time

2. Elsie Marley is so neat
    it's hard for one to walk the street
    but every lad and lass they meet
    cries do you ken Elsie Marley hinny

3. Elsie Marley wore a straw hat
    now she's got a velvet cap
    she may thank Lambton men for that
    do you ken Elsie Marley hinny

4. Elsie keeps wine gin and ale
    in her house below the dale
    where every tradesman up and down
    does call and spend his half a crown

5. the farmers as they come that way
    they drink with Elsie every day
    they call the fiddler for to play
    the tune of 'Elsie Marley' hinny

6. the pitmen and the keelmen trim
    they drink bumbo made of gin
    and for to dance they do begin
    the tune of Elsie Marley hinny

7. the sailors they will call for flip
    as soon as they come from the ship
    and then begin to dance and skip
    to the tune of 'Elsie Marley' hinny

8. so to conclude these lines I've penned
    hoping there's none I do offend
    and thus my merry joke doth end
    concerning Elsie Marley hinny

The only constructions typical of Geordie in Bell's version of EM are the ubiquitous *hinny*, the lexical item *ken* for 'know' and the prepositions *i'* for 'in' and *a' back o'* for 'behind' and possibly the occurrence of *lass* in stanza 2. As in the case of THL, local singers are still free to introduce further Geordie pronunciations, e.g. [ɛɪ] for [aɪ] in *fine, swine, nine* and *time*, [uː] for [au] in *down* and *crown* or [e:] for [eɪ] in *ale, dale, way, day, play.* And yet both the pipe tune and the song are emblematic of Geordie. Why is this so? The enregistered dialect known as Geordie indexes as part of its macro-semiotic social stereotypes the Northumbrian smallpipes and folk dancing, and since the song, with its tenuous song schema, is an example of vocal dance music, to sing it and play it without being a speaker of Geordie entails a commitment to Geordie culture.

Characters associated with the coal industry and its centuries-long tradition in Newcastle, on the other hand, show a far greater percentage of Geordie dialect expressions in Bell's texts. Significant characterological stereotypes of enregisterment in Geordie are related to the coal-mining industry, the collier who dug out the coal, the waggoner who transported it to the staithes[12] and the keelman who took it out to the ships waiting in the river. Two songs, 'The Bonny Pit Laddie' and 'The Bonny Keel Laddie' (BKL), are based on a seven-part 6/8 pipe tune called 'The Bonny Pit Laddie' ♫142. The tune is included in a collection made by John Peacock and published by Thomas Wright as a *Favourite Collection of Tunes with Variations Adapted for the Northumberland Small Pipes, Violin or Flute* in the first decade of the nineteenth century. Here is the second of the two songs, which is based on the A part of the tune:

Bonny Keel Laddie

trad.

my bon-ny keel lad-die my bon-ny keel lad-die for me oh_____

he sits in his keel__ as black as the deil__ and he brings the white money to me oh

> 1. my **bonny** keel **laddie** my **canny** keel **laddie**
>   my **bonny** keel **laddie** for me oh
>   he sits in his keel as black as the **deil**
>   and he brings the white money to me oh

> 2. **ha'** ye seen **owt** o' my **canny** man
>   **an'** are **ye** shure he's **weel** oh
>   he's **geane o'er** land **wiv** a stick in his hand
>   **t'** help to moor the keel oh

> 3. the **canny** keel **laddie** the **bonny** keel **laddie**
>   the **canny** keel **laddie** for me oh
>   he sits in his **huddock** and claws his bare buttock
>   and brings the white money to me oh

---

[12] A dialect word for the wharves for the trans-shipment from wagons (in the nineteenth century from coal trains) to the keelboats.

The lexemes *canny, hinny, bonny* and *laddie* are plentiful in Geordie songs, so stanzas 1 and 3 are no surprise, but stanza 2 makes no doubt about enregistering the stereotypical character of the keelman as an integral part of Geordie dialect enregisterment.

The classic example of the collier in Bell is 'The Collier's Rant' (TCR) ☮32:

The Collier's Rant

trad.

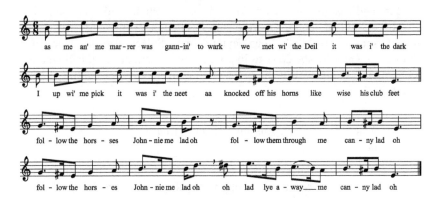

1. as **me** and **me marrow** was **ganning** to **wark**
    we met **wi'** the **deil** it was in the dark
    I up with me pick it being **i'** the **neet**
    I knocked off his horns likewise his club feet

chorus: follow the horses Johnnie me laddie
    follow them through me **canny lad** oh
    follow the horses Johnnie me laddie
    o lad **lye away** me **canny lad** oh

2. as **me** and **me marrow** was **puttin'** the tram
    the **lowe** it went out and me **marrow** went **wrang**
    you would have laughed had you seen the **gam**
    the **deil gat** me **marrow** but I **gat** the tram

3. oh **marrow** oh **marrow** what **dost thou** think
    I've broken me bottle and spilt all my drink
    I lost **a'** my **shin-splints** among the great **stanes**
    draw me **t'** the shaft it's time to **gan** hyem

5. oh **marrow** oh **marrow** this is **wor** pay week
    we'll get plenty loaves and drink to our **beek**
    an we'll fill up our bumper and round it shall go
    follow the horses Johnnie lad oh

6. there is me horse and there is me tram
    twee horns full of greese will make her to **gang**
    there is my **hoggars** likewise my half **shoon**
    an' smash me heart **marrow** me **putting's a'** done

4. oh **marrow** oh **marrow** where **hast thou**
     been
   driving the **drift** from the **low seam**
   driving the **drift** from the **low seam**
   had up the **lowe** lad **deil stop oot** thy **een**

In both cases, Bell has given enough Geordie features to indicate
that singers are free to expand on these and to sing the songs totally
in Geordie. For example, in TCR, Bell could have consistently written
an' for 'and', *myek* for 'make', *thu* and *ut* for 'thou' and 'out', etc., but
a restricted set of iconic Geordieisms is enough to indicate to a native
dialect speaker that s/he can extend the dialect features and also
allows non-Geordie speakers to index the enregisterment of the characters
concerned as being part of the meta-pragmatic stereotypes that the dialect
represents.

Nineteenth-century Enregisterment of Geordie in Song

Songs that contain dialect but do not, or only obliquely, refer to colliers
and that have no ascription to a songwriter also abound in Bell's *Rhymes*,
and all of these enregister different characters and social situations in
working-class life by using the dialect. But there are also songs, in the
oral tradition of transmission, containing virtually no dialect and thus
representing more universal issues. A large number of these songs also
appeared in Thomas Allan's *Tyneside Songs* in 1862, those that did not
appear (e.g. 'Footy Again' the Wall') being considered morally unsuita-
ble. Five further editions of *Tyneside Songs* were published between 1862
and the final edition in 1891, entitled *Allan's Illustrated Edition of
Tyneside Songs and Readings: With Lives, Portraits, and Autographs of
the Writers, and Notes on the Songs*. Songs by well-known Tyneside
songwriters like Thomas Wilson, Joseph Watson, George Ridley, Ned
Corvan, Joe Wilson and many others were also included, though they
were largely written for the music halls. As a general principle, if the
songs concerned Tyneside dignitaries, national issues and comments on
Tyneside institutions, the dialect was not used. However, when stereotypical characters and social situations were dealt with, Geordie dialect
was used to enregister them in song.
    The example we give here is George Ridley's 'Cushie Butterfield' ♫142, to
the tune of a London music hall song by Harry Clifton, 'Pretty Polly Perkins of
Paddington Green':

Cushie Butterfield

1. aa's a broken **hairted** keel man
   an' aa's ower **heed** in **luv**
   wiv a young lass in **Gyetsid**
   an' aa caall **hor** me **duv**
   hor nyem's Cushie Butterfield
   an' she sells **yalla** clay
   an' her cousin is a **muckman**
   an' they **caall** 'im Tom Gray

Chorus: she's a big lass **an'** a **bonny** lass
   an' she likes **hor** beer
   an' they **caall hor** Cushie Butterfield
   an' aa wish she **war heor**

2. her eyes are like two holes
   in a blanket **bornt throo**
   an' her brows in the morning
   wad spyen a young **coo**
   an' when **aw heer** her **shootin'**
   will **ye** buy **ony** clay
   like a candy man's trumpet
   it steals **ma** young heart away

3. ye'll oft see **hor doon** at **Sangit**
   when the fresh **harrin cims** in
   she's like a bagful **o' saa**dust
   tied **roond wiv** a string
   she **weers** big galoshes **tee**
   an' **hor stockins** once was white
   an' **hor bedgoon** it's **laelock**
   but **hor** hat's **nivver strite**

5. she **sez** the **chep** that gets me
   'll **heh** to work **ivry** day
   an' when he **cums hyem** at **neets**
   he'll **heh te gan** an' seek clay
   an' when he's away **seekin't**
   aal myek balls an' sing
   weel may the keel row
   that my **laddie**'s in

6. **noo aw heer** she **hes anuther chep**
   an' he hews at Shipcote
   if **aw thowt** she **wad** deceive me
   ah'd sure cut me throat
   aal doon the river **sailin'**
   an' **singin' aam** afloat
   biddin' addo te Cushy Butterfield
   an' the **chep** at Shipcote

4. **whan aa axed hor te** marry **us**
    she started te **laff**
    noo nyen o' yor munkey tricks
    for **aa** like **nee** such **chaff**
    then she started **a' blubblin'**
    an' roared like a bull
    an' the **cheps** on the keel
    sez aa's nowt but a **fyeul**

The version presented here is one recorded by Sting in 1999 on an album entitled *For Our Children*. In this instance, virtually the whole song is transcribed in dialect with all the typical Geordie pronunciations given. Ridley's original text does not go quite so far as Sting, but almost, and it reveals that by around the 1860s Geordie had become thoroughly enregistered. Why, then, does Sting, himself a Geordie, decide to go one step further and sing the whole song in dialect? We pick up this thread in the following subsection.

The final step – writing the whole song in dialect and displaying the full enregisterment of Geordie – was reached in many but not all of Tommy Armstrong's songs in the 1890s. Armstrong was a prolific and well-loved miners' songwriter, and the following song was written after he had spent some time in Durham jail ('Dorham Jail'. This time the whole song is in dialect (with the regional accent represented) with one or two minimal concessions to the standard in such words as 'but', 'get', 'for', 'is' and the occasional 'your' in place of dialect *yor*.

Dorham Jail

Words by Tommy Armstrong   trad. ('There's Nae Gud Luck aboot th' Hoose')

1. **yil awl hev ard o' Dorham** Jail
   but it **wad** ye much surprise
   to see **th'** prisoners in **th'** yard
   wen thay'r on **exorcise**
   this yard is **bilt eroond** we walls
   se noabil en see **strang**
   we ivor gans thae heh te bide
   thor time be it short or **lang**

Chorus: **thare's nee gud** luck in **Dorham** Jail
   thare's nee gud luck **it awl**
   wat is **breed en skilly** for
   but just **te muaik ye smaul**

2. **wen ye gan** to **Dorham Jail**
   thae'll find **ye wiv emploi**
   thae'll dress **ye** up se **dandy**
   in a **suite e cordy-roy**
   thae'll fetch e cap **wivout e** peek
   en nivor axe yor size
   en like **yor suite** it's **cordy-roy**
   en cums doon ower yor ies

3. **th' forst munth** is **th' warst iv awl**
   i your **feelin's thae** will try
   thare's nowt but two **greet** lumps e wood
   on which ye **heh** to lie
   then **eftor** that **ye** get a bed
   but it is **ard is stuains**
   it **neet ye dorsint muaik e torn**
   for **feer ye brick sum buains**

4. **awl kines e wark thare's ganen** on
   upon **thyese noable** flats
   teesin oakem **muaiken'** balls
   en weeven coco mats
   wen ye gan in ye **mae** be thin
   but **thae cin muaik ye thinnor**
   if your oakem is not **teesed**
   thae'r shoor to stop **yor dinnor**

5. **th' shoos ye** get is **oftin** tens
   th'smaulist size is nine
   th'or big **eneuf te muaik** a skiff
   for Boyd **ipon** the Tyne
   en if ye **shud** be **caud** at **neets**
   just **muaik yorsels** at **yem**
   lap yor clais eroond yor shoos
   en get inside e them

6. **yi'l get yor meet en clais** for **nowt**
   yor hoose en firin' free
   awl yor meet's brought **te th' dor**
   hoo happy ye **shud be**
   thor's soap en too'l
   en wooden speun
   en e little **bairne's** pot
   thae fetch **yor** papers **ivory** week
   week for ye to clean your **bot**

Can non-Geordies credibly and creditably sing a song like 'Cushie Butterfield' or 'Dorham Jail' that display such a thorough-going dialect enregisterment in song? And what are contemporary Geordie singers doing when they decide to sing either of these two songs? These questions raise problems of de-enregisterment and re-enregisterment.

De-enregistering and Re-enregistering Geordie: 'Byker Hill'

One of the currently most popular Tyneside songs, judging by the large number of representational performances, recordings and videos of it, is 'Byker Hill' (BH) ☻143, which, like 'Billy Grey', appears to have broken out of its socio-cultural enregisterment. It is printed in Bell (1812) under the title 'Walker Pits' and reappears with the same title and in the same form in *Allan's Illustrated Edition of Tyneside Songs* with the instruction to sing it to the tune of 'Off She Goes'.[13] We have presented the lyrics of this version on the left below. The version on the right is from Bladey's website *Beuk of Newcassel Sangs*, and the tune is given by Bladey (almost) as we have it here.

Byker Hill

trad.

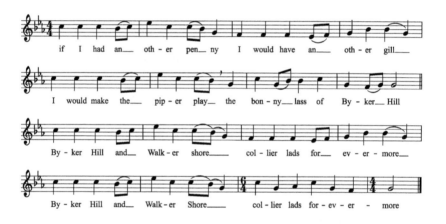

if I had an___ oth - er pen___ ny I would have an___ oth - er gill___

I would make the___ pip - er play___ the bon - ny___ lass of By - ker___ Hill

By - ker Hill and___ Walk - er shore____ col - lier lads for___ ev - er - more___

By - ker Hill and___ Walk - er Shore____ col - lier lads for - ev - er - more

The version given in Bell:

1. **wen forst aa** came down to Walker's work
    I haad nae pit trousers and **nae** pitshirt
    now **aa've getten** two or three
    the Walker's pit's done well for me

The version on Conrad Bladey's website[14]

2. **an' if aa haad** another penny
    aa would have another gill
    an' aa would make the piper play
    'The Bonny Lass of Byker Hill'

chorus: Byker Hill and Walker Shore
           collier lads for ever more

[13] If the tune 'Off She Goes' is the Irish fiddle tune by that name, then this is definitely not the tune given here, which is certainly the one most commonly used for the overwhelming majority of the performances we have studied.

[14] http://cbladey.com/sang/priests2.html#BYKER%20HILL, accessed 28 November 2017.

Byker Hill and Walker Shore
collier lads for ever more

repeat of chorus: Byker Hill and Walker Shore
collier lads for ever more
Byker Hill and Walker Shore
collier lads for ever more

3. now Byker pit is forty fathoms
on **wi' me duds an'** there **aa'm gannin'**
the biggest steeple in the land
an' it brings the silver to **wor** hands

4. Geordie Johnson he had a **peg**
hit with a shovel and it danced a **jeg**
aal the way to Walker Shore
to the tune of 'Elsie Marley'

chorus: Byker Hill and Walker Shore
collier lads for ever more
Byker Hill and Walker Shore
collier lads for ever more

repeat of chorus: Byker Hill and Walker Shore
collier lads for ever more
Byker Hill and Walker Shore
collier lads for ever more

5. the old coal cutter he gets eight **shillin'**
the deputy he gets a half a crown
my **ol'** man gets five an' a tanner
that's just for **ridin'** up and down

6. **an'** if **aa haad** another penny
aa would have another gill
an' aa would make the piper play
'The Bonny Lass of Byker Hill'

chorus: Byker Hill and Walker Shore
collier lads for ever more
Byker Hill and Walker Shore
collier lads for ever more

repeat of chorus: Byker Hill and Walker Shore
collier lads for ever more
Byker Hill and Walker Shore
collier lads for ever more

Bell's version, recorded and performed exactly as given here by the High Level Ranters, has a second stanza full of Geordie constructions (*wark, ne … ne, aw, getten, twe, deun, weel*). We have argued that elements of Geordie are evidence of the discursive construction of the coal-miner stereotype through song as an integral part of the Geordie dialect register, and this interpretation is supported by the reality of the place name (Byker Hill in the eastern part of Newcastle) and the colliery (Walker Shore). Songs written about collieries, pitmen, strikes and lock-outs in the nineteenth century retain these Geordie dialect features. Bladey's version on the right, however, contains not one single Geordie construction but takes over stanza 6 from EM and deletes *hinny* at the end!

The first known recorded performance of BH was by A. L. Lloyd in 1966 on his album *The Best of A. L. Lloyd*, although Lloyd had included a copy of it in his 1952 book *Come All Ye Bold Miners*. Lloyd sang it to the tune of 'My Dearie Sits Ower Late Up' (MDSOLU), and his version appears to be a mixture of stanzas from Bell and the vocal song associated with MDSOLU. As we saw with 'Elsie Marley', stanzas from vocalised versions of dance tunes can be borrowed indiscriminately into other songs, so it does not surprise us that Lloyd had a rather hybrid version of what he called 'Walker Hill and Byker Shore' (sic).

A second recording of 'Byker Hill' was also made in 1966 by The Young Tradition on their first album, which was exactly the tune and the lyrics given by Conrad Bladey, and it appears to have become the canonical version copied by singer after singer, choir after choir and group after group. The Young Tradition do not use Geordie to invoke the enregisterment of the collier and the dance traditions of Tyneside and Northumbria, and this can perhaps be taken as a first step in de-enregistering Geordie as a dialect indexical of the industrial of north of England.

Judging by the large number of performances, good, bad and indifferent, that have been made from the song as it appeared on the Young Tradition's album, it has now been claimed by Irish, English, Canadian, American and even Polish groups with little or no connection to the northeast of England. The dialect is no longer a significant aspect of the song. Does this indicate a process of de-enregisterment? If so, what do singers wish to express by singing it and what messages do audiences infer from it? Whatever these may be, they surely have little or nothing to do with Tyneside, either in the nineteenth century or in the present.

However, Agha suggests that registers are open to change and transformation by acquiring other meta-pragmatic stereotypes. If this is the case with the enregistered dialect of Geordie, are there versions of 'Byker Hill' that reflect those changes? One version of the song appeared on an album entitled *Backbone* by Pete Coe in 2010. It takes the canonical lyrics of the song and adds a final stanza to it, indicating that the collier stereotype, almost the object of encomium in the Young Tradition's version in 1966, is now no longer existent:

> there's no Byker hill no Walker Shore
> the collier lads they are no more
> it's been that way since eighty-four
> so farewell Elsie Marley

Could this be an attempt to re-enregister Geordie as symbolising a community victimised by the callousness of present-day southern England? If so, is Pete Coe's version an example of answering back? After all, Coe is from Northwich in Cheshire, and the stanza is a clear reference to the miners' strike in 1984. Looked at in this way, Geordie, by acting as a surrogate for the whole of the depressed north, could acquire the social value of answering back to the south. The tune that Coe uses (see below) is not the 'standard' tune sung by the High Level Ranters.

It appears to be the same tune as that used by Jeb Grimes on an album entitled *Heart & Hand* in 2013, and like Coe, Grimes adds new elements to the song and sings in broad Geordie. This is surely not just a coincidence.

Byker Hill

Peter Coe's version

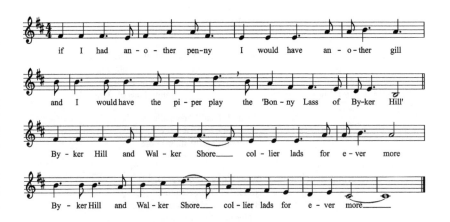

1. wen forst aa came down to Walker's work
    I haad nae pit trousers and nae pitshirt
    now aa've getten two or three
    the Walker's pit's done well for me

2. an' if aa haad another penny
    aa would have another gill
    an aa would make the piper play
    'The Bonny Lass of Byker Hill'

chorus: Byker Hill and Walker Shore
          collier lads for evermore
          Byker Hill and Walker Shore
          collier lads for evermore

repeat of chorus: Byker Hill and Walker Shore
                    collier lads for evermore

Byker Hill and Walker Shore
collier lads for evermore

3.   now Byker pit is forty fathoms
on wi' me duds an' there aa'm gannin'
the biggest steeple in the land
an' it brings the silver to wor hands

4.   Geordie Johnson he had a peg
hit with a shovel and it danced a jeg
aal the way to Walker Shore
to the tune of 'Elsie Marley'

chorus: Byker Hill and Walker Shore
collier lads for evermore
Byker Hill and Walker Shore
collier lads for evermore

repeat of chorus: Byker Hill and Walker Shore
collier lads for evermore
Byker Hill and Walker Shore
collier lads for evermore

5.   the old coal cutter he gets eight shillin'
the deputy he gets a half a crown
my ol' man gets five an' a tanner
that's just for ridin' up and down

6.   an' if aa haad another penny
aa would have another gill
an aa would make the piper play
'The Bonny Lass of Byker Hill'

chorus: Byker Hill and Walker Shore
collier lads for evermore
Byker Hill and Walker Shore
collier lads for evermore

repeat of chorus: Byker Hill and Walker Shore
collier lads for evermore
Byker Hill and Walker Shore
collier lads for evermore

Stanza 3 appears in no other version of the song. If Grimes has inserted it, he has introduced a narrative clause in the present tense, one that voices the collier stereotype's intention to go to work in the pit in the fictional present of the song and not as a collier looking back on his previous experiences (cf. Grimes' stanza 1). In stanza 5, he changes 'the overseer gets five and sixpence' into 'my ol' man gets five and a tanner', which fictionally relocates the singer as the son of the overseer. In this performance, there are efforts to call up a past experience in the present, to re-invoke the positive social values and characterological stereotypes of the enregistered dialect of Geordie. Is this a re-enregisterment of those values through the song, or is it simply a reminder to the audience that the meta-pragmatic social values and stereotypes of those bygone days were positive? Is this an inherent form of answering back? We are unable to give adequate answers to these questions at this point, but Coe's and Grimes' versions extend the song in interesting ways, which confirms the analysis given in this chapter of the rich possibilities of looking at folk performance with new theoretical concepts from sociolinguistics such as enregisterment.

Epilogue

12   Whither Folk Song, whither Sociolinguistics?

> The Venda taught me that music can never be a thing in itself, and that *all* music is folk music, in the sense that music cannot be transmitted or have meaning without associations between people.   (Blacking 1973: x)

Tying the Ends Together

In this final chapter we have two major aims: (1) in particular, to gather together the major 'threads' of argumentation presented in the book and to demonstrate the significance of focusing on the notion of performance for the analysis of folk song; and (2) in general, to project a socio-linguistics of performance into the future by showing how a more diversified understanding of variation and change may help to strengthen other central issues in sociolinguistic research. Third Wave Variation Studies have focused their attention more sharply on studying emergent social practice from the social individual's point of view, but there needs to be a stronger focus on the multimodality of socio-communicative interaction (van Leeuwen 2005; Kress and van Leeuwen 2001; Machin 2007) that enables us to move away from sedentary ways of looking at the data. The danger of sedentarism (cf. Cresswell 2006; Britain 2016) is that researchers consistently find themselves caught in the trap of imagining static and homogeneous speech communities, discourse communities and communities of practice that no longer reflect, if in fact they ever did, the continually changing hybrid nature of contact between human beings and the forms of social semiosis that they evolve in constructing interpersonal meanings.

We have set up a 'mind map' (see below) to help orient the reader to the complexity of ideas involved in accounting for folk performance within the framework of sociolinguistic research, and we elucidate the details of Figure 12.1 in the remainder of this section.

The centre of the mind map is the connection between the social practice of folk song and the approach to it from the perspective of Third Wave Variation

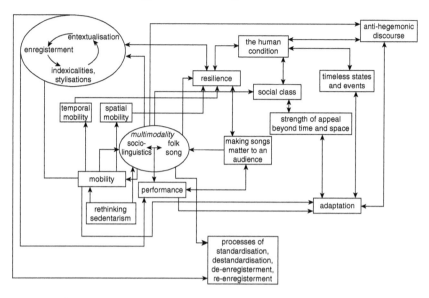

Figure 12.1. *Mind map of sociolinguistics and folk song from the perspective of performance*

Studies in sociolinguistics.[1] This approach leads logically to the social process of singing folk song, i.e. to *performance*.[2] Although sociolinguistics is usually conceptualised as centred on emergent *language* use, all language use naturally brings into play other forms of social semiosis such as – in the present case – music, but also gesture, movement, dress, pictorial images of various kinds (drawing, painting, photography, film, etc.), dance, mimicry and so on. Our mind map in Figure 12.1 documents the need to take a multimodal view of communication, and for this reason we have given the central oval the label *multimodality*.

As Britain (2016) argues, sociolinguistics can only move out into the component of mobility if it first rethinks the sedentary nature of research on social language use. Research in sociolinguistics is – or should be – concerned with mobility of all kinds, e.g. the degrees of fluidity in various population groups (migration, ageing, lifestyle changes, natural catastrophes such as earthquakes, floods, pandemics, etc.), the effects of this fluidity on structural variation in individual speakers' language use and the effects of contact between people speaking different languages or linguistic varieties.

---

[1] See the double-headed arrow running horizontally between sociolinguistics and folk song.
[2] See the double-headed arrow running vertically from the central oval to performance.

Studying folk song, however, leads us directly to considering the *mobility* of singers and songs, since there is nothing stable and homogeneous about the singing of songs that are rooted in the need to construct communities of practice. If the study of verbal social practice in sociolinguistics bypasses a rethinking of sedentarism, there will be a tendency to think of standardisation in linguistic varieties as a means of stabilising, homogenising and legitimising one variety over all others. Note, however, that a move to mobility after rethinking issues of sedentarism shifts both folk song and other forms of semiotic verbal practice into a number of different components, viz. spatial mobility, temporal mobility, thence into the component of resilience and, most importantly, into the area of indexicality/stylisation, entextualisation and enregisterment processes. From there, both singing and other varieties of languaging can be fed back into performance (and thence into the central oval; cf. our revised discussion of performance in languaging in the following section) or into the standardisation/enregisterment component where it then becomes possible to think of historical processes of destandardisation, de-enregisterment and re-enregisterment.

Other forms of languaging than singing may move directly into a consideration of indexicality/stylisation, entextualisation and enregisterment processes or to considerations of social class and to the study of anti-hegemonic discourses. In the latter two cases, there is still a way into the consideration of indexicality/stylisation, entextualisation and enregisterment processes via a consideration of what we have called 'the human condition' and resilience. From mobility and performance we can move, in the case of both singing and other forms of languaging, to the study of adaptation and innovation processes. Folk song itself has mutually strengthening links between adaptation and strength of appeal beyond time and space, adaptation and timeless states and events, and adaptation and anti-hegemonic discourse. From performance there are mutually strengthening links in folk song with the component of making songs matter to audiences, thence to resilience and thence again to indexicality/stylisation, entextualisation and enregisterment processes. In the hope that the mind map, enriched as it is through the component of mobility, at least helps us to envisage the immense complexity of singing and languaging processes and the centrality of a multimodal theory of sociolinguistics, we move to a discussion of languaging as performance in the following section.

Performance in Languaging

In Chapter 2, we proposed that performance, understood as the public presentation of an activity involving language such as singing, consists of the following five features: (1) human agency (i.e. an action [or set of actions] initiated consciously by a human being or a group of human beings); (2) goal direction-ality (i.e. the action [or set of actions] must be intended and directed by those involved towards the achievement of a goal); (3) human beneficiary (i.e. the goal is oriented towards the benefit of those who are co-interactants in the social practice but have willingly, temporarily and partially waived their own rights to perform);[3] (4) temporality (i.e. the actions carried out by a speaker take up a period of time which may have been agreed upon by the other participants prior to the performance or which may remain undefined); and (5) process (i.e. the actions carried out in social practice constitute a process, and since the process involves other co-participants, that process is always a *social process*).

Throughout the book we have distinguished between representational and relational forms of song performance on the basis of a distinction made between the public presentation of and private participation in singing events. Both types of performance have as their aim the bonding together of a social group (performers and audience, and performers and participants) in the creation of a community of practice. However, whereas representational performances are imbued with the communal fulfilment of different kinds of ritual, relational performances are an aspect of everyday life in which people sing together as a means of confirming – or even as a means of creating – interpersonal relationships.

Chapter 3 dealt with work songs of different kinds, in which we assumed that, while the lead singer might be considered as having her/his co-workers as an audience, her/his major social function was to lead the other workers in partici-pating in the singing as a means of easing the burden and increasing the efficiency of the work. The workers are in *the social mode* just as performers and audience are in representational performances. Song is used to execute an action or set of actions and to accomplish something, to react to the exigencies of the work situation and to bond the group of workers together in concerted effort. But there are also situations in which individuals may sing with no obvious audience or co-workers present, e.g. in the shower, while working at something else on their own or just walking down the street. As Russell ([1987] 1997: 182) suggests, impromptu solo singing is still performance and may be carried out with the idea of a possible audience in mind. He maintains that '[s]inging in the street seems to have been relatively common, at least by the Edwardian period, and could assume surprisingly high standards. "Even at the corner of the street, someone would start humming a popular tune, and soon everybody would be singing the song in real harmony", a Yorkshire miner recalled.'

It is time now to change the focus from singing as performance to languaging as performance. In this case, it might seem more difficult to differentiate

---

[3] Even in conversation, not everyone can talk at the same time, e.g. if a participant asks a question of the group, the others are constrained to listen, i.e. to waive their 'right to the floor'.

stretches of verbal social practice in the languaging mode as performances from stretches of what appear to be non-performance. If storytelling or joke-telling is arranged as a form of representational performance within a performance oval before an audience, the performance itself is shifted from the context of every-day languaging and takes on a ritual nature. A speech event such as narration or joke-telling may occur within ongoing verbal interaction, but it needs to be keyed in as a performance and keyed out to indicate that the floor is again open for general use. In addition, an instance of storytelling or joke-telling may generate other stories or jokes from other co-participants such that the perfor-mance mode becomes dominant throughout an emergent stretch of social interaction. Because performance is inherently fictional, those who tell the stories or jokes are held responsible for making them relevant to the topic of the social interaction and thus to the audience. For example, in the short anecdote of the fish and chip shop in Spain told by R and analysed in Chapter 2, the conversation prior to R's anecdote circled round the topic of English navy personnel in Gibraltar not having access to typical British food, so R's anecdote was relevant to that topic. In the narrative, the only two 'true' facts were that R had seen a fish and chip shop in Nerja and that it was called 'Chish 'n' Fips'. Everything beyond this was fiction.

Keying-in and keying-out are also properties of representational perfor-mances (see Chapter 2), particularly important between individual songs in folk performances (see Chapter 11). So we contend that the presence of these two features in a stretch of verbal social practice temporarily transforms it into a representational performance. An audience (albeit often an active audience) is constructed from the co-participants, the location in which the anecdote is told becomes a symbolic performance oval, and the ritualistic use of fictionality (see Chapter 8) is condoned. In languaging, therefore, it is possible to entex-tualise a performance on the spot, i.e. without having a prior text. This is not the case in performing song. In all cases, songs are retained in the singer's memory once acquired, but may be performed in slightly different versions on the occasion of each performance. Does this therefore mean that singing a song is always a representational performance, or can the distinction between representational and relational performances be maintained and carried across to instances of languaging?

All instances of languaging are social processes involving two or more individuals, so that, in order to language at all, we must be in the social mode.[4] When participating in an instance of languaging, we are establishing social contact with an Other/Others, projecting our 'selves' into what we say and encroaching on the Other's cognitive territory. If two speakers have already

---

[4] When individuals verbalise alone or do so only in their heads, they are still in the social mode. They are still 'talking to *themselves*' or they are imagining a potential audience.

established a relationship, we argue that the activity of languaging proceeds normally – which does not always mean smoothly – as a *relational performance*. It is, as Locher and Watts (2005) have argued, *relational work*. If the encroachment on Other's territory is problematic, the speaker may need to produce specific formulaic expressions as part of that relational work in accordance with the type of relational performance concerned. For example, if the speaker requires directions on the street as to how to find her/his goal, the territorial encroachment is attenuated by adding a formulaic apology, e.g. '*Excuse me*. Can you tell me the way to the station?' Such utterances are examples of relational work since they aim at achieving whatever goal is set by the relational performance. From this we can conclude that all instances of languaging are in effect relational performances that may also require various forms of relational work. When stretches of verbal social practice contain explicit keyings-in and keyings-out, the would-be performer attempts to construct an audience out of the other co-participants and is not always successful (cf. Watts 1991). In representational performances of song, keyings-in and keyings-out recognise the significance of an audience rather than a set of co-interactants, and performers expect evaluation from that audience. In relational performances of song, there is no need to key in or out (cf. the discussion of 'Who's the Fool Now?' in Chapter 2).

Folk Song as Song that Bonds Communities

Our purpose in refusing to define 'folk song' as a *genre of song* throughout this book derives from Blacking's assessment that all music is folk music since it 'cannot be transmitted or have meaning without associations between people' (see above). The sentence immediately preceding this in Blacking's Preface runs as follows: 'I can see no useful distinction between the terms "folk" and "art" music, except as commercial labels' (1973: x). All attempts to define folk music (hence, for our purposes, folk song) as a unique genre, or style, or form of music have failed to make any reasonable distinction not only between the labels 'folk' and 'art', but also between 'folk' and 'pop', or 'folk' and 'rock', or 'folk' and 'country and western', or 'folk' and any other label applied to a musical style. But if 'folk song' is not to be (adequately) defined as a genre of song, we need to see it as any style or type of song that is aimed at constructing the 'associations between people' that were so justifiably important to Blacking. We also need, in other words, to consider the social functions that song achieves in constructing a 'folk' through performance. As we outlined in Chapter 1, we take this to be the fundamental significance of song (and, extrapolating from song, music) for groups of hominids, whether now or before *Homo sapiens* even developed the language faculty.

In Figure 1.2, which illustrates the various forms of ritual function achieved by performing songs, some functions can be considered more significant than others. For example, entertaining, flyting or criticising others is arguably less significant than remembering the past or protesting against injustice, and celebrating seasonal activities is arguably less significant than healing others or lamenting. It is precisely for this reason that we have suggested the need to include in the mind map songs that refer to timeless states and events that concern any social group, songs which protest against social injustice or songs that appeal most strongly to the 'human condition'. Such songs are more likely to be considered 'folk songs' than those that simply entertain.

Singing *for* a group of people should, ideally, also entail singing *with* that group, so that song used as 'folk song' can create ties that bind and bond a group into a community with the ultimate aim of making it stronger in resisting adverse pressure from outside the group. The best way of achieving those ends is to keep the group together in one place, ideally in a place that the members of the community can recognise as the place for the performance of a large number of ritualistic functions (cf. Figure 1.2, Chapter 1).

We can exemplify the stronger or weaker significance of songs in bonding a group in performance by choosing six songs ('Yellow Submarine' ☺145, 'The Wild Rover', 'The Bargeman's Alphabet', 'No Man's Land', 'A Sailor's Life' and 'The Unquiet Grave')[5] and locating them on a diagram (see Figure 12.2) representing different degrees of appropriateness in the oval of performance and different degrees of ritual depth. The 'appropriateness' of a song in bonding a group is measured by the following factors: (1) its playability/singability or the degree to which audiences are able to participate in the singing, i.e. whether a song has a refrain or chorus that allows the audience to co-participate; (2) the degree to which a song lends itself to oral uptake and adaptability (cf. Chapter 4 on folk song and protest); (3) the degree to which the lyrics are memorisable enough for oral uptake; (4) the degree to and the manner in which a song answers back; (5) the degree to which a song, with or without a refrain/chorus, engages the audience as a social group. The ritual depth of a song is determined by whether the members of an audience are able to evaluate its historical longevity and its significance in the world of the present by their familiarity with the singing conventions, music and lyrics of the folk song register (cf. Chapters 9, 10 and 11) or by their ability to relate the significance of events and problems of past songs to events and problems in the contemporary world.

If we sang 'Yellow Submarine' around a campfire – using it, according to our definition, as a 'folk song' to help bond the group – its text (the lyrics) could hardly be said to 'answer back' or to contain diction that appears to characterise

---

[5] The tune and the lyrics of all six songs may be found on the website.

traditional folk songs. And yet, around the campfire, it is a 'folk song'. Similarly, if we sang 'The Unquiet Grave', it would be somewhat unusual for any audience who also knew the song to sing it along with us – although it is unlikely that anyone would object to this. Those who know 'The Unquiet Grave' also know that it is 'a song to listen to', 'a song with a social message' for the group, viz. that it is unwise to compromise one's own life by mourning too long for the death of a loved one. And even if the group members around the campfire do not know the song, the diction of the first stanza – 'how pleasant is the wind tonight / I feel some drops of rain /*I never had but one true love/and in greenwood he lies slain*'[6] – couched as it is in the ballad idiom, a recognisably archaic, formulaic style of 'standard English', alerts them to these two facts and also to the fact that the song has a longer historical tradition that any of the others. If we began singing 'A Sailor's Life', now relatively well known through Sandy Denny's version of it on the Fairport Convention album *Unhalfbricking*, the melody, the fact that it might easily be rendered a cappella and, as in 'The Unquiet Grave', the diction of the first stanza – 'a sailor's life is a merry life / they rob young girls of their hearts' delight / leaving them alone to sorrow and mourn / they never know when they will return' – would immediately signal a greater ritual depth than 'Bob' Roberts' 'The Bargeman's Alphabet' or 'The Wild Rover'. It is thus a 'song to listen to' with a complex nexus of social meanings.

In the case of 'No Man's Land', a song with a very powerful anti-war message, the quiet melancholic strains of the music and the diction of the first half of the first stanza – 'well how do you do Private William McBride / do you mind if I sit here down by your graveside / and rest for a while in the warm summer sun / I've been walking all day and I'm nearly done' – again signal that this is 'a song to listen to', 'a song with a message', although it is not couched in the ballad idiom but in a familiar form of colloquial standard English with a first-person narrator talking to (the ghost of) Willie McBride. It is thus interpretable as a song with as much ritual depth as 'The Unquiet Grave' or 'A Sailor's Life', i.e. reiterating a universal human problem, but because of its reference to World War I it has less 'traditional' depth, i.e. it is a song that can be located more precisely along a historical timeline.

Singing 'The Wild Rover' around a campfire is almost bound to involve the other members of the group in an enthusiastic rendering of the chorus. 'The Wild Rover' is well known as a pub song, a song that everyone can sing along with in a relational performance whether or not they sing in tune, but it would hardly be offered in a representational performance, even though it has a chorus – and even though it contains a significant message, 'beware of drink!'

[6] The lyrics in italics represent archaic construction ('I never had but x' vs 'I only had x') and the parts of the lyrics underlined highlight formulaic song motifs (FSMs).

It is, in other words, an iconic song for relational performance purposes, and to sing it in a representational performance framework would require the performer to claim the song for her/himself in some way or another. 'Bob' Roberts' 'The Bargeman's Alphabet' also has a chorus, but, as a song, it is not as well known as 'The Wild Rover'. It hardly presents anything interpretable as answering back, but it certainly is a celebration in song of a way of life and work on the old Thames barges plying between London and the east coast port of Yarmouth, a lifestyle and form of work that no longer exist today. For this reason, it has a greater historical depth than 'Yellow Submarine' or 'The Wild Rover', and we have placed it closer to the centre of our diagram in Figure 12.2.

The diagram is an attempt to indicate how certain songs may be drawn into a performance oval in which the performers are concerned to construct, affirm or reaffirm a 'folk', however transitory that folk may be, and thereby to contribute to a folk music discourse community. It also shows the degree to which the songs already situated within the oval are somewhat unlikely to be found in other musical performance frameworks (e.g. WAM, rock, pop, country and western, etc.), although adaptations are possible and have taken place. The darker the shading in the diagram, the greater is the perceived historical and ritual depth of the song.

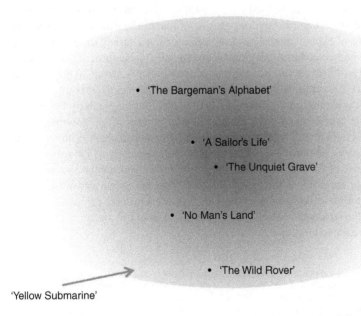

Figure 12.2. *The historical and ritual depth of songs within folk performance*

New Approaches in Sociolinguistic Research

The discussion of the mind map in the first section of this final chapter touched on three areas of sociolinguistic research where there is still a great deal of room for innovative, new approaches. The first of these, the multimodal approach to forms of social interaction and discourse (Machin 2007; Kress and van Leeuwen 2001), has already firmly established itself over the past twenty to thirty years, yielding a wealth of significant research into the inter-relation between language and other semiotic systems, including music (van Leeuwen 1999), in analysing how meaning is constructed and contested in a wide range of social settings. The first major impulse was in the area of media research, where seminal work by Bell (1991), Fairclough (1995) and Bell and Garrett (eds. 1998) has opened the way to considering the interplay between language and pictorial images (van Leeuwen 2006), the interplay between these two and sound in the new media[7] (Martinec and van Leeuwen 2009), visual journalism (Machin and Polzer 2015) and language and film (Machin and Jaworski 2006; Buckland 2007). Much of this work has also been related to a renewed interest in the contextual functions of space in the multimodal media (Jaworski and Thurlow 2010).

The second important area of research in sociolinguistics in which new approaches are necessary, language standardisation, has also been around for some time (see Milroy and Milroy [1985] 2012; Joseph 1987; Bex and Watts 1999), and we have mentioned it in a number of chapters. From a historical perspective, sociolinguists have, we feel, insufficiently considered the discursive implications of explicit moves towards standardising a variety of Language A in an effort to construct the only legitimate and socially viable form of that language (with the possible exception of contributions to Rindler Schjerve 2003 in the case of German). As James Milroy points out, a standard language is a 'fixed and uniform-state idealisation' (1999: 18). It is an idealisation precisely because no language can ever be fixed and in a 'uniform-state' except within its written form, and even then there will be a tendency for variation and change. With respect to European states, standard languages are part of the ideology of the nation-state, but in the case of Britain and France, standard English and standard French were certainly not the result of the nation-state ideology, but rather part of the reason for it. The tentative beginnings of the standardisation process for English can be located in the sixteenth century, and the process was in full swing by the second half of the eighteenth century.

---

[7] 'New media' are defined in the introduction by the authors as 'multimodal, combining language with visual communication and sound. They are non-linear, combining spatial and temporal patterns. And they are new, lacking the long history and the many years of systematic thought that have made language what it is ... It stands to reason that new media designers might have something to learn from the study of language ...' (Martinec and van Leeuwen 2009: 1).

Deciding on what variety of a language will become the standard is a socio-political act, since it demotes other varieties to an inferior status. Those with political and economic power naturally determine that their own variety must be raised to standard status, such that non-standard varieties take on the role of Others – a typical modernist move. Developing a standard language is thus a double-pronged process. On the one hand, it enforces the linguistic domination of standard users over 'inferior' speakers, and on the other hand, it enforces sedentism (the practice of living in one place only) as a means of fixing the geographical whereabouts of a population. In nineteenth-century Britain, the irony of this enforcement was that it was preceded by a massive migration of large numbers of the rural population caused by the enclosure system into sites of industrialisation, i.e. towns and cities. In a wider sense, standardising the English language became a potent move in constructing a global empire; it became part of the dominant discourse of imperialism (see Said 1993).

It is at the point where language standardisation can be seen as a significant move in imperialist discourse that it intersects with a new sociolinguistic interest in mobility and sedentism. Cresswell's book *On the Move* (2006) looks at how mobility, which has become a significant feature of modern lifestyles, has been consistently opposed in the discourse of modernity, since sedentism, i.e. staying in one place and not moving around, provides a means of exercising social control over the members of a population. The interest in mobility has inspired an approach in sociolinguistic research that places mobility at the focus of research into language variation and change. Britain (2016) argues that most approaches to language variation – First, Second or Third Wave Studies – appear to take it for granted that the speakers in a speech community or a community of practice are sedentary, while speakers themselves can be shown to be surprisingly mobile. It is this mobility that creates situations of language contact between speakers of different language varieties, and it is in those contact situations that variation occurs and innovations can be observed that may lead to language change. We can take this line of thinking even further and argue that it is mobility, not 'sedentarism',[8] that represents the usual state of affairs in the contemporary globalised world. If this is so, being a human, as Blacking states, really does mean being 'human + human'. It entails the need that every individual has for other people, and it recognises and encourages hybridity. This is a big step forward from the modernist notion of 'us' vs 'them', the superior vs the inferior, the white man's burden to enlighten the rest of the world. We argue in Chapter 4 (as does Middleton 2006) against this approach on the grounds that it only leads to sets of opposing Others rather than to an affirmation of hybridity.

In the final section of this final chapter we return to the core of our interest, folk song, to assess where it may be moving in the future.

---

[8] The term is used in place of 'sedentism' by both Cresswell and Britain.

In Defence of Appropriation and Authenticity:
The Resilience of Folk Song

We return here to questions of authenticity and appropriation, and in doing so we touch on issues in the top right section of the mind map in Figure 12.1 such as social class and answering back by framing folk songs as a part of an anti-hegemonic discourse. Since the Second Folk Revival beginning in the 1950s, one persistent question has been whether or not middle-class singers have a right to act as voices of the folk. In what sense are their renderings of folk song 'authentic'? Before we begin this discussion, however, we stress the central point that the modern English lexeme <folk> does not and never has referred to either a nation or any social class within a population. It is a term that refers in a local fashion to any group of people regardless of social class that bond together as a group. We can talk of 'intellectual folk' and 'rich folk' just as easily as we can talk of 'working folk' and 'poor folk'. 'The folk', as a coherent social class, is simply non-existent.

Marxist scholars of folk song like Harker (1985) and other critical observers[9] question whether performers, certainly since the mid-1950s if not earlier in the twentieth century, are in a position to perform folk songs with any degree of credibility if they are not from the social class in which the songs originated or in which they had their rightful place in some alleged golden era. Harker sees the way in which collectors and singers engage with folk songs as an imposition. Antiquarians 'improve' what they find, singers tinker with the material to make it fit their (ideological) purposes, and most of these 'adapters' are considered to be from middle- rather than working-class origins. In Harker's eyes, what they do is nothing short of appropriation, if not expropriation, of the lore of an underclass. Such 'appropriation'/'expropriation' is often considered typical for well-meaning busybody aficionados. On the one hand, we have collectors who, driven by the belief that they can or need to improve what the underclasses cannot be trusted to maintain or have already corrupted in their ignorant practice,[10] see themselves as the last bastion in preventing the songs from disappearing (cf. also Pettitt 1984 and similar ideas voiced in Bronson 1945). On the other hand, twentieth-century performers have been criticised for their presumption that the same underclasses need them to answer back on their behalf (see the discussion in Chapter 4).

This attitude is one that underlies the very question raised above: who can credibly engage with folk songs as a collector or as a performer? The position is based on two premises; (1) a labouring-class-based 'ownership' of folk song, which clearly does not apply in this day and age (if ever it did with

---

[9] For example, the poet who suggests in the list of impossible situations in his poem 'Tonight at Noon' that 'folk songs are sung by real folk'.

[10] This is a stance that Harker, not unjustifiably, takes strong issue with.

anything like such idealised neatness in the past); and (2) the element of anti-hegemonic discourse or the expression of socio-cultural friction so often present in this material. The central issue revolves around who is entitled to take part in the anti-hegemonic discourse or whose lives are sufficiently adversely affected by the socio-cultural friction thematised by the songs that they have a right to express it. The questions and the premises on which they are based, however, are not just flawed by the false assumption that folk songs are songs of 'the folk'; they are also irrelevant, if not absurd. The final consequence of this line of argument would be as follows: if it were the case that only a member of the community from where a song originated (or is assumed to have originated) were entitled to edit and/or perform it,[11] a whole range of songs referring to a lifestyle that has disappeared or changed out of all recognition would be forced into oblivion. Even more ridiculously, any encoded or entailed protest against underlying social injustices still present in other current social contexts would have to be deemed inadmissible. It is patently absurd to argue that only those directly affected by an adverse social state or development are entitled to speak out about it because only they have the credibility to do so.

Let us consider a practical example: with the successful campaign in the Great Britain of the 1980s to deprive organised labour of the strong voice it had, by closing mines and forcing the mining communities during an unsustainably long period of industrial action into a position in which they had no other choice than to accept the loss of their communities' occupational mainstay, we can justifiably argue that an entire way of life as well as the voice it had to answer back has effectively disappeared.[12] If the positions discussed above had any validity, this would also mean that songs about the mining communities would no longer have any genuine carriers of the tradition or any authentic performers. The spectre of 'appropriation'/'expropriation' thus haunts the discourse on folk music and folk song. Part of this discourse is a certain ideology of purism concerning what constitutes the 'real thing' and how it can, if at all, be best (pre)served, and a cultural pessimism linked with a discourse of decline. Such a discourse presupposes a period in the imagined but unattainable past when the conditions of the carriers of the tradition were ideal[13] and the material was as yet 'uncorrupted' or unsullied by careless adopters/adapters/performers.

This hypothesised 'golden age of folk song' fails to take into account two aspects that we have explored in the previous chapters: firstly, the emergent nature of social interaction and thus by extension of folk song performance over time, and secondly, the fact that far from being impermeable, songs which

---

[11] And this would constitute a ludicrous act of cultural censorship.

[12] Note that there are several labour-related songs about strikes and lockouts.

[13] These conditions are often associated with an Arcadia of rustic swains and wenches who were wont to burst spontaneously into rural ditties.

create or foster community need to be considered as folk songs (see above). Singers have always shaped 'texts' by taking into account what their audiences expected, by working with the sources, e.g. perpetuations of material they had an interest in and access to,[14] but also issues such as their own credibility, which might well result in certain re-workings that, for example, avoid performing variant or dialect features of a reference group. Generally speaking, a performer cannot *not* adapt the material if s/he is to perform it credibly and creditably in a performance space, and this means 'tampering' with the textual sources and often working on the tunes.[15] We can, of course, adopt Harker's stance and say that this constitutes a case of appropriation, but perpetuation of songs all the way back to first known collections has been invaluable for giving these songs life. They might otherwise have been unrecorded in writing and only performed in a small social circle, thus remaining unperpetuated and unavailable outside the performance context.

Similarly, a new breed of performers in the twentieth century whose emphasis was placed heavily on social comment took up this interest. One of their concerns in the final third of the twentieth century was to fill Coupland's gap between traditionally-structured social meanings ... and the outcomes of self-identification processes in social interaction (Coupland 2003: 417) by using folk songs as significant performance spaces in which audiences have an opportunity to create their own authenticities (see Chapter 11). Until the arrival of punk with a more topical comment on social issues, social comment was largely the domain of the folk movement, resulting in a tendency to favour songs with entailed and encoded anti-hegemonic discourse for inclusion in books and recordings. Performers in the late 1960s raised the issue of developing new ways into old songs with a new urgency concerning 'the right way' to perform them. While the jazz influences of Pentangle fused with traditional material, the rock consciousness of bands like Fairport Convention, Steeleye Span and Horslips in Ireland – and, of course, Thin Lizzy with their blues- and rock-influenced reinterpretation of 'Whisky in the Jar' – explored new avenues, other musicians remained staunchly traditionalist, and purism provided a strong antithesis to innovation. It could be argued that the obsession with purism, the focus on what was considered authentic and 'ethnic' (cf. the discussion of these questions in Chapter 6) was what cleared the stage for punk displacing folk in its role as a means to articulate social friction musically and to answer back more effectively.

---

[14] Which contradicts Lord's pessimistic view that 'one of the most common ways in which an oral tradition may die [is] not when writing is introduced, but when published songs are spread among singers' (Lord [1960] 2000: 130).

[15] This is particularly the case if the sources suggest that they are not very inspiring, a condition that is perhaps more of a consideration in a modern performance context where musical originality plays more of a role.

Folk music and song, however, have shown themselves to be much more resilient and much less in danger of disappearing than collectors and traditionalist performers have assumed (cf. the discussion of 'The Cruel Mother' in Chapter 6). Moreover, this resilience is a result of its adaptability and the fact that new generations have taken it on and developed it in new directions, taking current audience attitudes on board and adding contemporary performance practices to the mix. The 'mix' includes influences from other forms of music, the introduction of new musical instruments such as guitars, at first acoustic and later electric, bass guitars and other rock and jazz instruments such as keyboards and synthesisers, the popularity of (originally Greek) bouzoukis in Irish and Scottish music, the use of percussion, from the drum kits of the sixties and seventies to bhangra drums on the album *The Imagined Village* or the increasingly popular cajón, the inclusion of brass instruments in the case of Bellowhead and saxophones by the Mighty Doonans.

In her acceptance speech for the Gold Badge of the English Folk Dance and Song Society, Maddy Prior made the following points:

I think of traditional music as an ellipse around popular music in the middle, and the ellipse has been (.) a ride out there and come/ it comes back quite close to tradition/ to popular music for a while, and then it suddenly goes out, and it becomes the most unfashionable music in the world, and then it suddenly comes back again, and it's just/ it's on a real swing back again at the moment with all the young players so I've been on a <???> half curve, which is really fantastic. (February 2015)[16]

The image is a compelling one, and one that we would like to develop further here. If we accept the concept of an elliptical orbit that folk music, traditional and otherwise, is on, we can imagine that it courses around two foci. In analogy to Prior's point above, one of these represents what she calls 'popular music', or music that enjoys widespread public attention. Needless to say, this is not a homogeneous musical genre but consists of a variety of popular types of music including the (relatively) cutting edges of any given period, e.g. pop, R&B, rock, but also rap and electronic music, etc. The other focus represents music with a more limited popular appeal, niche forms such as experimental jazz, some forms of classical music (including renaissance and medieval music), but also ethnic musics, etc.

To remain with the astronomically inspired image, these foci do not represent points but they rather include these types of music in a kind of cosmic cloud – one which changes its composition depending on which happen to be 'popular' at any given period. Folk music then travels on its elliptical orbit, finding itself closer to or further away from broader public interest as Prior suggests. However, while passing through these clouds, exchanges take place:

---

[16] https://www.youtube.com/watch?v=x2fs6ouyz3A, accessed 15 September 2015.

rock and electronica acquire elements of folk, and vice versa; jazz may inspire new interpretations of existing folk music and song; medieval, renaissance or 'exotic' instruments and percussion may become incorporated in the music of some acts or be used to add new textures to recordings of artists on a quest for elements to 'claim a song'. Such crossovers are what open up folk song and folk music to new and, in some cases, unexpected audiences, but they also result in the core audiences being put into contact with different approaches to interpreting traditional music and songs or new versions of authored music in the folk idiom.

As Prior rightly points out, at the time of writing there is a renewed interest in traditional music but also in music performed on acoustic instruments, a trend quite probably initiated by the *Unplugged* series on MTV in the 1990s. This 'back-to-real-instruments' approach may well account for the popularity of many contemporary acts, often singer-songwriters, who favour acoustic instruments, former busker and pub performer Ed Sheeran being perhaps the most successful act at present, with three sell-out solo gigs in Wembley Stadium in July 2015 (cf. Petridis 2015).[17] The simplicity in the arrangements and the portability of the equipment of many such acts clearly appeals to the 'democratic' nature and the logistics of the folk circuit, and it is no surprise that the currently popular singer-songwriter scene inspires folk performers and vice versa. On the other hand, the 'Gothic' themes of many folk ballads have long appealed to Gothic rock and metal musicians and continue to do so. It is an appeal that owes a considerable debt to the modal tunes typical of folk music, Dorian, Mixolydian, Aeolian and even Phrygian, which work well with genre-typical power chords (cf. Appendix).[18] In sum, through such crossovers folk music revitalises itself, but also contributes to other types of music and helps to create new and interesting hybrid forms, both in music with a popular appeal and in music that has a more restricted but consistent following. It is this kind of revitalisation that is a central element to the resilience of folk music and song – but also the reason why fears concerning its imminent demise are misplaced. The resilience of folk song is not only the result of crossovers and the injection of new energies from other forms of music. It is also dependent on the very wide range of performance contexts in which the performers sing, and the degree to which performers are able to adapt what they sing to those contexts. As Maddy Prior says in her acceptance speech: 'it is for the music [...] 'cos that's what it is about, the music, not us [as singers]'. A song may have an enduring appeal in itself, but it is resilient because it continues to be made accessible to contemporary audiences.

---

[17] He was joined on a few songs by Elton John but otherwise performed solely with an acoustic guitar and an effect pedal.

[18] Power chords avoid the third, thus eliminating the note in the triad that indicates major or minor key, but notoriously create problems at distorted amp settings.

And So to Conclude

Our study has demonstrated not only that the field of sociolinguistics and research into folk song practice have parallel interests, but also that the exploration of the one yields valuable insights to the other. An awareness of what happens in languaging helps us understand phenomena in musicking and vice versa. Both sociolinguistics and the study of folk song practice address issues of group and community membership; both provide an understanding of how such memberships are constructed, maintained and perpetuated; and both inherently need to concern themselves with hegemonic discourses. Sociolinguistics engages those discourses by revealing that there is essentially no social interaction without asymmetries in the distribution of power. Folk song practice engages those discourses by addressing a variety of social frictions and creating communities of practice through anti-hegemonic discourse. Both address the status quo; both 'answer back'.

It is probably over-optimistic to assume that an area of academic humanistic enquiry can overturn social and political realities. It is equally over-optimistic, if not naïve, to assume that a cultural practice can make the world a better place. Yet both sociolinguistics and folk singing at the very least focus our attention on the issues they answer back to, i.e. the preservation of inequalities and injustice that are cemented through hegemonic discourse. Focusing attention on these issues, even if it is originally confined to a small but committed group or community, is a first step on a long journey, but without these first small steps, no journey is ever completed.

As a campaigner for civil liberties, Martin Luther King was as deeply aware of this as he was of the hegemonic discourse of his day, which he challenged unforgettably with his 'I have a dream' speech. The marches he led in favour of civil liberty testified to the need to confront the powers-that-be with an anti-hegemonic discourse against discrimination and segregation. The power of communal singing also came through on those marches. They were a demonstration that folk song has always been with us, is always with us and will always be with us to help us work together, live together and, importantly, to struggle together. It is therefore fitting to end this book by pointing out that Martin Luther King's final sermon, the day before his assassination, uses the lyrics of probably the greatest protest song of all time, effective in the simplicity of its lyrics and tune, but also as a rallying cry for the disenfranchised:

> we shall overcome
> we shall overcome
> deep in my heart
> I do believe
> we shall overcome

Martin Luther King concludes, and we with him, ' ... and I believe it because somehow the arc of the moral universe is long, but it bends towards justice'.

Appendix: Overview of Musical Concepts

This appendix addresses significant musical concepts that have been referred to but not explained earlier in the book. They were compiled with the layperson in mind and only cover aspects that are relevant to musical discussions presented, i.e. they are related to folk song performance practices. General musical theory is considerably more complex, but such complexities are not relevant here for our purposes.

Modes and Scales

To understand modes, we can imagine that all the notes of a modal scale are played on the white keys of a keyboard only, i.e. in the key of C. This means that for every octave (eight notes ending on the same note as the starting note but an octave higher) there are two locations where the notes are only a half tone apart, indicated with the symbol ∧. The position of these two half-tone steps, so-called semitones, defines the various modes. In Figure Appendix 1, the modes or modal scales most frequently used in folk song are given.

Many folk songs avoid the use of semitones, which results in a scale that does not have seven notes before returning to the root an octave higher, but six or – if all semitones are avoided – five steps. These scales are called 'heptatonic' and 'pentatonic' respectively. In a pentatonic scale it is impossible to differentiate between the Ionian and Mixolydian modes, which both have a 'major' feel to them, or between the Dorian and Aeolian, which both have a 'minor' feel to them (cf. Bronson 1962: xii).

The 'blues' scale, used mainly in African-American-influenced folk music and blues songs, is an exception to these modes. Here the characteristic note in the scale is the so-called 'blue note', the small third (from C to Eb instead of E). The notes in parenthesis in Figure Appendix 2 are usually not played in simple blues songs.

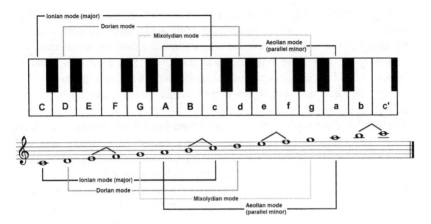

Figure Appendix 1. *Musical modes*

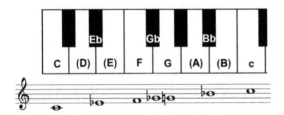

Figure Appendix 2. *The blues scale with the 'blue note'*

Basic Chords and Keys

Generally, we distinguish between major and minor keys. Major keys usually have a more cheerful quality to them, whereas minor keys tend to sound relatively melancholy. Blues scales will also create a slightly sorrowful feel, the minor blues scale potentially more so.

Folk songs in major or minor keys generally use three chords:

- The *tonic* represents the tonal centre of the tune and the final resolution of a song, i.e. the verse usually ends in the tonic. In major chords, it forms the 'root' note, the first and eighth note in the scale. C major thus has the 'root' note of C.

- The *dominant* represents the fifth note in the scale and is the second most important note (and chord). It represents the point in a tune that has a certain quality of 'rest', especially when it occurs about halfway through a verse. However, it calls for a resolution, i.e. we expect it at some point to return to the tonic. Some folk songs have all verses end in the dominant in order to draw the listener into the flow of the stanzas, but generally the last verse will return to the tonic. To add a little tension, instead of ending in the octave, the highest note is the seventh rather than the eighth, i.e. a note below the octave, which strictly speaking does not belong to the scale.

• The *subdominant* represents the fourth note (and third chord). The chord starts with the fourth note. "It can act as a correction between tonic and dominant in a typical folk chord progression." Verses may have a subdominant at the 'halfway point', but rarely end on it.

Major and related minor keys are focused around the same tonal centre, the major key being named after it, the 'parallel' minor key three semi-tones below it, but using the same notes (see Ionian and Aeolian modes) and being named after it. Hence, the major key of C is played with the same notes as the minor key of A. The table only indicates a few of the possible keys but illustrates the relationships between major and minor chords in those keys, i.e. the parallel chords in minor being three semi-tones below the major chords.

Table Appendix 1. *Major and related minor keys*

Notation		Tonic	Dominant	Subdominant
	C major	C	G(7)	F
	A minor	Am	E(7 or m)	Dm
	G major	G	D(7)	C
	E minor	Em	B(7 or m)	Am
	F major	F	C(7)	Bb
	D minor	Dm	A(7 or m)	Gm
	D major	D	A(7)	G
	B minor	Bm	F#(7 or m)	Em
	Bb major	Bb	F(7)	Eb
	G minor	Gm	D(7 or m)	Cm

Harmonies/Chords for the Modal Scales

The following diagram shows some relationships between the notes in a modal scale and the chords that are likely to be played by folk musicians. We need to remember that in most cases folk musicians (unlike jazz players) will opt for relatively simple harmonies, focusing mainly on major and minor chords and rarely using anything more complex than seventh chords. The examples are based on the overview of the modal scales above. Chords in brackets also contain the notes of the scale and may be chosen by players if they wish to add more tension or 'colour' to the accompaniment.

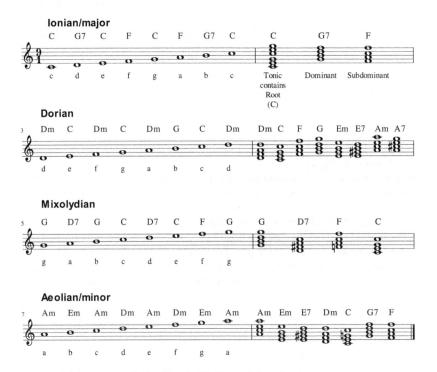

Figure Appendix 3. *Chords for the modal scales*

References

Aarne, A. and Thompson, S. 1961. *The Types of the Folk Tale: A Classification and Biography* (2nd revised edn), trans. T. Stith, Helsinki: Academia Scientiarium Fennica.

Adorno, T. W. 1973. *Negative Dialectics*, trans. E. B. Ashton, London: Routledge.

Agha, A. 2003. 'The social life of a cultural value', *Language and Communication* 23: 231–73.

Agha, A. 2005. 'Voice, footing, enregisterment', *Journal of Linguistic Anthropology* 15(1): 38–59.

Agha, A. 2007. *Language and Social Relations*, Cambridge: Cambridge University Press.

Aitken, A. J. 1962. 'Vowel length in modern Scots', Mimeo, University of Edinburgh.

Allan, T. 1972 [1891]. *Allan's Illustrated Edition of Tyneside Songs*, Menston, Yorkshire: The Scolar Press.

Andersen, F. G. 1985. *Commonplace and Creativity: The Role of Formulaic Diction in Anglo-Scottish Traditional Balladry*, Odense University Studies from the Medieval Centre, Vol. 1, Odense: Odense University Press.

Andersen, F. G. and Pettitt, T. 1979. 'Mrs. Brown of Falkland: a singer of tales', *The Journal of American Folklore* 92(363): 1–21.

Andres Morrissey, F. 2008. 'Liverpool to Lousiana in one lyrical line: style choice in rock, pop and folk singing', in Locher, M. and Strässler, J. (eds.), *Standards and Norms in the English Language*, Berlin and New York: Mouton de Gruyter, pp. 195–218.

Andres Morrissey, F. 2011. 'From Dartford to Detroit: transatlantic style choice in rock and pop music'. Unpublished paper presented at the SAUTE (Swiss Association of University Teachers of English) Conference, 6 May 2011.

Andres Morrissey, F. In preparation. 'Plucky tommies, angelic nurses and the others: identity constructions in hegemonic and antihegemonic discourse of First World War songs'.

Archer, R. 2012. 'Assessing turbofolk controversies: popular music between the nation and the Balkans', *Southeastern Europe* 36: 178–207.

Armstrong, T. 1971. *Tommy Armstrong Sings*, Newcastle-upon-Tyne: Frank Graham.

Atkinson, D. 1997. 'A Child ballad study guide with select bibliography and discography', in Cheeseman, T. and Rieuwerts, S. (eds.), *Ballads into Books: The Legacy of Francis James Child*, Bern: Peter Lang, pp. 259–80.

Auer, P. 2007. 'Introduction', in Auer, P. (ed.), *Style and Social Identities: Alternative Approaches to Linguistic Heterogeneity*, Berlin and New York: Mouton de Gruyter, pp. 1–21.

Bakhtin, M. M. 1981. *The Dialogic Imagination: Four Essays*, ed. M. Holquist, trans. C. Emerson and M. Holquist, Austin and London: University of Texas Press.

Bakhtin, M. M. 1986. *Speech Genres and Other Late Essays*, ed. C. Emerson and M. Holquist, trans. V. W. McGee, Austin and London: University of Texas Press.

Baring-Gould, S. 1895–96. *English Minstrelsie: A National Monument of English Song with Notes and Historical Introductions*, 8 vols., Cambridge, MA: Harvard University Press.

Barrow, J. D. 1995. *The Artful Universe*, Oxford: Clarendon Press.

Barton. D. and Hamilton, M. 2005. 'Literacy, reification and the dynamics of social interaction', in Barton, D. and Tusting, K. (eds.), *Beyond Communities of Practice: Language, Power and Social Practice*, Cambridge: Cambridge University Press, pp. 14–35.

Bateson, G. 1972. *Steps to an Ecology of Mind: Collected Essays in Anthropology, Psychiatry, Evolution, and Epistemology*, Chicago: University of Chicago Press.

Bateson, G. 1979. *Mind and Nature: A Necessary Unity*, New York: Bantam Books.

Bauman, R. 1975. 'Verbal art as performance', *American Anthropologist* 77(2): 290–311.

Bauman, R. 1977. 'Verbal art as performance', in Bauman, R. (ed.), *Verbal Art as Performance*, Prospect Heights, IL.: Waveland Press.

Bauman, R. 1986. *Stories, Performance, and Event: Contextual Studies of Oral Narrative*, New York: Cambridge University Press.

Bauman, R. and Briggs, C. 1990. 'Poetics and performance as critical perspectives on language and social life', *Annual Review of Anthropology* 19: 59–88.

Beal, J. 2009. 'Enregisterment, commodification, and historical context: "Geordie" versus "Sheffieldish"', *American Speech* 84(2): 138–56.

Bean, J. P. 2014. *Singing from the Floor: A History of British Folk Clubs*, London: Faber and Faber.

Beck, U. 2002. 'The cosmopolitan society and its enemies', *Theory, Culture and Society* 19(1/2), 17–44.

Bell, A. 1984. 'Language style as audience design', *Language in Society* 13(2): 145–204.

Bell, A. 1991. *The Language of News Media*, Oxford: Blackwell.

Bell, A. 2001. 'Back in style: reworking audience design', in Eckert, P. and Rickford, J. R. (eds.), *Style and Sociolinguistic Variation*, Cambridge: Cambridge University Press, pp. 139–69.

Bell, A. and Garrett, P. (eds.). 1998. *Approaches to Media Discourse*, Oxford: Blackwell.

Bell, A. and Gibson, A. 2011. 'Staging language: an introduction to the sociolinguistics of performance', *Journal of Sociolinguistics* 15(5): 555–72.

Bell, J. 1971 [1812]. *Rhymes of Northern Bards*, Newcastle-upon-Tyne: Frank Graham.

Bell, M. J. 1988. '"No borders to the ballad maker's art": Francis James Child and the politics of the people', *Western Folklore* 47: 285–307.

Ben-Amos, D. and Goldstein, K. S. (eds.). 1975. *Folklore: Performance and Communication*, The Hague: Mouton and Co.

Bendix, R. 1997. *In Search of Authenticity: The Formation of Folklore Studies*, Madison, WI: The University of Wisconsin Press.

Benveniste, E. 1974. *Problèmes de linguistique générale*, Paris: Gallimard.

Bergs, A. 2005. *Social Networks and Historical Sociolinguistics: Studies in Morphosyntactic Variation in the Paston Letters (1421–1503)*, Berlin and New York: Mouton de Gruyter.

Bertau, M.-C. 2007. 'On the notion of voice: an exploration from a psycholinguistic perspective with developmental implications', *International Journal for Dialogical Science* 2(1): 133–61.

Bex, T. and Watts, R. J. (eds.). 1999. *Standard English: The Widening Debate*, London: Routledge.

Bishop, P. and Thomson, K. 1972. 'Notes to music', in Palmer, R. (ed.), *Songs of the Midlands*, Wakefield: EP Publishing, p. ix.

Blacking, J. 1973. *How Musical Is Man?* Seattle, WA: University of Washington Press.

Blacking, J. 1987. *'A Commonsense View of All Music': Reflections on Percy Grainger's Contribution to Ethnomusicology and Music Education*, Cambridge: Cambridge University Press.

Bladey, C. *Beuk of Newcassel Songs*, http://cbladey.com/sang/alsang.html#Directory.

Blom, J. P. and Gumperz, J. 1972. 'Social meaning in linguistic structure: code-switching in Norway', in Gumperz, J. and Hymes, D. (eds.), *Directions in Sociolinguistics*, New York: Holt, Rinehart and Winston, pp. 407–34.

Blommaert, J. 2003. 'A sociolinguistics of globalization', *Journal of Sociolinguistics* 7(4): 607–23.

Blommaert, J. 2005. *Discourse*, Cambridge: Cambridge University Press.

Blommaert, J. 2008. *Grassroots Literacy: Writing, Identity and Voice in Central Africa*, London: Routledge.

Bourdieu, P. 1979 [1984]. *La Distinction: critique sociale du jugement*, Paris: Editions de Minuit. English translation, Nice, R. *Distinction: A Social Critique of the Judgement of Taste*, London: Routledge.

Boyes, G. 1993. *The Imagined Village: Culture, Ideology and the English Folk Revival*, Manchester: Manchester University Press.

Breuer, H. 1913. *Der Zupfgeigenhansl – das Liederbuch der Wandervögel*, Mainz: Schott.

Briggs, C. 1988. *Competence in Performance: The Creativity of Tradition in Mexicano Verbal Art*, Philadelphia: University of Pennsylvania Press.

Britain, D. 2016. 'Sedentarism, nomadism and the sociolinguistics of dialect', in Coupland, N. (ed.), *Sociolinguistics: Theoretical Debates*, Cambridge: Cambridge University Press.

Brocken, M. 2003. *The British Folk Revival 1944–2002*, Farnham: Ashgate.

Bronson, B. H. 1945. 'Mrs. Brown and the ballad', *California Folklore Quarterly* 1(2): 129–40.

Bronson, C. 1959–72. *The Traditional Tunes of Child Ballads: With Their Texts according to the Extant Records of Great Britain and America*, Vols. 1–4. Reprinted by permission of Princeton University Press. East Windsor, NJ: CAMSCO Music.

Brown, S. 2000. 'Evolutionary models of music: from sexual selection to group selection', in Tonneau, F. and Thompson, N. S. (eds.), *Perspectives in Ethnology*, New York: Plenum Publishers, pp. 231–81.

Bruford, A., MacDonald, M. and MacDonald, D. A. 1994. *Scottish Traditional Tales*, Edinburgh: Polygon.

Buchan, D. 1997 [1972]. *The Ballad and the Folk*, East Linton, Lothian: Tuckwell Press.

Buchan, N. and Hall, P. 1973. *Scottish Folk Singer*, London: Collins.

Buchan, P. 2009 [1828]. *Ancient Ballads and Songs of the North of Scotland*, Charleston, SC: BiblioLife.

Bucholtz, M. 1999. '"Why be normal?": language and identity practices in a community of nerd girls', *Language in Society* 28(2): 203–23.

Bucholtz, M. 2004. 'Styles and stereotypes: the linguistic negotiation of identity among Laotian American youth', *Pragmatics* 14(2/3): 127–47.

Bucholtz, M. and Hall, K. 2005. 'Intertextual sexuality: parodies of class, identity, and desire in liminal Delhi', *Journal of Linguistic Anthropology* 15(1): 125–44.

Bucholtz, M. and Lopez, Q. 2011. 'Performing blackness, forming whiteness: linguistic minstrelsy in Hollywood film', *Journal of Sociolinguistics* 15(5): 680–706.

Buckland, W. 2007. *The Cognitive Semiotics of Film*, Cambridge: Cambridge University Press.

Campbell, J. L. 1990. *Songs Remembered in Exile*, Aberdeen: Aberdeen University Press.

Carlson, M. 1994. 'Invisible presences – performance, intertextuality', *Theatre Research International* 19(2): 111–17.

Carlson, M. 1996. *Performance: A Critical Introduction*, New York and London: Routledge.

Cherry, R. D. 1998 [1988]. 'Ethos versus persona: self-representation in written discourse', *Written Composition* 15: 384–410.

Child, F. J. 1965. *The English and Scottish Popular Ballads*, 5 vols., New York: Dover Publications Inc.

Clark, G. E. 1867. *Seven Years of a Sailor's Life*, Boston, MA: Adams and Co.

Connolly, F. (ed.). 1984. *The Christy Moore Songbook*, Dover, NH: Brandon.

Cook, N. 2007. *Music, Performance, Meaning: Selected Essays*, Aldershot/Burlington, VT: Ashgate Publishing.

Cotterton, P. 1989. *How Societies Remember*, Cambridge: Cambridge University Press.

Coupland, N. 2001. 'Language, situation, and the relational self: theorizing dialect-style in sociolinguistics', in Eckert, P. and Rickford, J. (eds.), *Style and Sociolinguistic Variation*, Cambridge: Cambridge University Press, pp. 185–210.

Coupland, N. 2003. 'Sociolinguistic authenticities', *Journal of Sociolinguistics* 7(3): 417–31.

Coupland, N. 2007. *Style: Language Variation and Identity*, Cambridge: Cambridge University Press.

Coupland, N. 2010. 'The authentic speaker and the speech community', in Llamas, C. and Watt, D. (eds.), *Language and Identities*, Edinburgh: Edinburgh University Press, pp. 99–112.

Cox, J. H. 2013 [1925] *Folk-Songs of the South*, Morgantown WV: West Virginia University Press, p. 224.

Creese, A. and Blackledge A. 2012. 'Voice and meaning-making in team ethnography', *Anthropology & Education Quarterly*, 43(3): 306–24.

Cresswell, T. 2006. *On the Move: Mobility in the Modern Western World*, London and New York: Routledge.

Crichton, M. 1990. *Jurassic Park*, New York: Knopf.

Cross, I. 2001. 'Music, cognition, culture and evolution', *Annals of the New York Academy of Sciences* 930: 28–42.

Cross, I. 2003a. 'Music and biocultural evolution', in Clayton, M., Herbert, T. and Middleton, R. (eds.), *The Cultural Study of Music: A Critical Introduction*, London: Routledge, pp. 17–27.

Cross, I. 2003b. 'Music and evolution: causes and consequences', *Contemporary Music Review* 22(3): 79–89.

Cross, I. 2012. 'Music as an emergent exaptation', in Bannan, N. (ed.), *Music, Language and Human Evolution*, Oxford: Oxford University Press, pp.263–76.

Cross, I. and Movley, I. 2008. 'The evolution of music: theories definitions and the nature of the evidence', in Malloch, S. and Trevarthen, C. (eds.), *Communication Musicality: Exploring the Basis of Human Companionship*, Oxford: Oxford University Press, pp. 61–81.

Čvoro, U. 2014. *Turbo-folk Music and Cultural Representations of National Identity in Former Yugoslavia*, Farnham: Ashgate.

Daley, D. 2000. 1 September. 'Classic Tracks: Boston's "More Than a Feeling"'. Retrieved 10 May 2015, from Mix: Professional Audio and Music Production: www.mixonline.com/news/profiles/classic-tracks-bostons-more-feeling/374326.

Davis, M. H. 2013. 'The Cohort Model of auditory word recognition', in Pashler, H. (ed.), *The Encyclopedia of the Mind*, Los Angeles: Sage.

Deliège, I. and Sloboda, J. (eds.). 1996. *Musical Beginnings: Origins and Development of Musical Competence*, Oxford: Oxford University Press.

Deumert, A. 2010. '*Imbodela zamakhumsha* – Reflections on standardization and destandardization', *Multilingua* 29(3/4): 243–64.

Diamond, E. (ed.). 1996. *Performance and Cultural Politics*, London: Routledge.

Donald, M. 1991. *Origins of the Modern Mind*, Cambridge, MA: Harvard University Press.

Dunbar, R. 2012a. 'On the evolutionary function of song and dance', in Bannan, N. (ed.), *Music, Language and Human Evolution*, Oxford: Oxford University Press, pp. 201–14.

Dunbar, R. 2012b. 'Bridging the bonding gap: the transition from primates to humans', *Philosophical Transactions B* 367: 1837–46.

Dundes, A. 1997. 'The motif-index and the tale-type index: a critique', *Journal of Folklore Research* 34(3): 195–202.

D'Urfey, T. 1719. *Wit and Mirth: or, Pills to Purge Melancholy, 6 vols.*, London: W. Pearson, for J. Tonson.

Eckert, P. 2000. *Linguistic Variation as Social Practice*, Oxford: Blackwell.

Eckert, P. 2001. 'Style and social meaning', in Eckert, P. and Rickford, J. (eds.), *Style and Sociolinguistic Variation*, Cambridge: Cambridge University Press, pp. 119–26.

Eckert, P. 2004. 'Elephants in the room', *Journal of Sociolinguistics* 7(3): 392–97.

Eckert, P. 2008. 'Variation and the indexical field', *Journal of Sociolinguistics* 12(4): 453–76.

Eckert, P. and McConnell-Ginet, S. 1992. 'Think practically and look locally: language and gender as community-based practice', *Annual Review of Anthropology* 21: 461–90.

Eckert, P. and Rickford, J. (eds.). 2001. *Style and Sociolinguistic Variation*, Cambridge: Cambridge University Press.

Evans, C. 1903–59. *The American Bibliography*, 14 vols., digitised by the University of Michigan.

Fairclough, N. 1995. *Media Discourse*, London: Hodder Arnold.

Feintuch, B. 1993. 'Musical revival as musical transformation', in Rosenberg, N. V. (ed.), *Transforming Tradition: Folk Music Revivals Examined*, pp. 183–93.

Feld, S. and Fox, A. A. 1994. 'Music and language', *Annual Review of Anthropology* 23: 25–53.

Fernald, A. 1991. 'Prosody in speech to children: prelinguistic and linguistic functions', *Annals of Child Development* 8: 43–80.

Fernald, A. 1992. 'Meaningful melodies in mothers' speech', in Papousek, H., Jürgens, U. and Papousek, M. (eds.), *Nonverbal Vocal Communication: Comparative and Developmental Perspectives*, Cambridge: Cambridge University Press, pp. 262–82.

Finnegan, R. 2007 [1989]. *The Hidden Musicians: Music-making in an English Town*, Middletown, CO: Wesleyan University Press [first printing Cambridge University Press].

Firth, R. 1975. 'Appraisal of modern social anthropology', *Annual Review of Anthropology* 4: 1–26.

Fitch, W. T. 2005. 'The evolution of music in comparative perspective', *Annals of the New York Academy of Sciences* 1060: 1–21.

Fitch, W. T. 2006. 'The biology and evolution of music: a comparative perspective', *Cognition* 100: 173–215.

Foley, J. M. 1988. *The Theory of Oral Composition*, Bloomington: University of Indiana Press.

Foley, R. A. 2012. 'Music and mosaics: the evolution of human abilities', in Bannan, N. (ed.), *Music, Language and Human Evolution*, Oxford: Oxford University Press, pp. 31–57.

Foucault, M. [1969] 1972. *The Archaeology of Knowledge*, trans. A. M. Sheridan Smith. New York: Vintage Books.

Frith, S. 1996. *Performing Rites: On the Value of Popular Music*, Cambridge, MA: Harvard University Press.

Gamble, C. 2012. 'When the words dry up: music and material metaphors half a million years ago', in Bannan, N. (ed.), *Music, Language and Human Evolution*, Oxford: Oxford University Press, pp. 81–106.

Gammon, V. 2008. *Desire, Drink and Death in English Folk and Vernacular Song, 1600–1900*, Farnham: Ashgate.

Gaskell, E. 1849. *Mary Barton: A Tale of Manchester Life*, Leipzig: Tauchnitz.

Giddens, A. 1998. *Conversations with Anthony Giddens: Making Sense of Modernity*, Stanford, CA: Stanford University Press.

Gillies, A. L. 2010. *Songs of Gaelic Scotland*, Edinburgh: Birlinn Limited.

Gilroy, P. 1993. *The Black Atlantic: Modernity and Double Consciousness*, London and New York: Verso.

Glassie, H. 1982. *Passing Time in Ballymenone: Culture and History of an Ulster Community*, Philadelphia: University of Pennsylvania Press.

Gluckmann, M. 1977. *Politics, Law and Ritual in Tribal Society*, Oxford: Blackwell.

Goffman, E. 1959. *The Presentation of Self in Everyday Life*, Garden City: Doubleday Anchor Books.

Goffman, E. 1974. *Frame Analysis: An Essay on the Organization of Experience*, London: Harper and Row.

Goldberg, R. 1988. *Performance Art*, London: Thames and Hudson.

Gramsci, A. 1971. *Selections from the Prison Notebooks*, New York: International Publishers.

Gregory, E. D. 2010. *The Late Victorian Folksong Revival: The Persistence of English Melody, 1878–1903*, Lanham, MD: Scarecrow Press.

Grujić, M. 2009. Community and the Popular: Women, Nation and Turbo-Folk in Post-Yugoslav Serbia, PhD dissertation, Central European University, Budapest.

Gummere, F. B. 1907. *The Popular Ballad*, Boston, MA: Houghton, Mifflin and Co.

Gummere, F. B. 1961 [1897]. 'The ballad and communal poetry', in Leach, M. and Coffin, T. P. (eds.), *The Critics and the Ballad*, Carbondale: Southern Illinois University Press, pp. 20–29.

Hanks, W. F. 1989. 'Texts and textuality', *Annual Review of Anthropology* 18: 95–127.

Harker, B. 2007. *Class Act: The Cultural and Political Life of Ewan MacColl*, London and Ann Arbor, MI: Pluto Press.

Harker, D. 1985. *Fakesong: The Manufacture of British 'Folksong' 1799 to the Present Day*, Milton Keynes and Philadelphia: Open University Press.

Harper, L. 2006. Style-shifting by African American Actors in Hollywood Films. Unpublished master's thesis. Santa Barbara: University of California.

Heller, M. 2007. 'Distributed knowledge, distributed power: a sociolinguistics of structuration', *Text and Talk* 27: 633–53.

Herder, J. G. 1807 [1774]. *Stimmen der Völker in Liedern*, ed. von Müller, Tübingen.

Higgins, C. 2015. 'Insults or acts of identity? The role of stylization in multilingual discourse', *Multilingua* 34(2), 135–58.

Hitchcock, G. (ed.). 1974. *Folk Songs of the West Country: Collected by Sabine Baring-Gould*, Newton Abbot: David and Charles.

Hobsbawm, E. and Ranger, T. (eds.). 1983 [2003]. *The Invention of Tradition*, Cambridge: Cambridge University Press.

Hofgart, M. (ed.). 1971. *The Faber Book of Ballads*, London: Faber.

Hornberger, N. H. 2006. 'Voice and biliteracy in indigenous language revitalization: contentious educational practices in Quechua, Guarani, and Maori contexts', *Journal of Language, Identity and Education* 5(4):277–92.

Hugill, S. 1961. *Shanties from the Seven Seas: Shipboard Work-songs and Songs Used as Work-songs from the Great Days of Sail*, London: Routledge and Kegan Paul.

Hymes, D. 1964. *Language in Culture and Society*, New York: Harper and Row.

Hymes, D. 1966. 'Two types of linguistic relativity', in Bright, W. (ed.), *Sociolinguistics: Proceedings of the UCLA Sociolinguistics Conference, 1964*, The Hague: Mouton, pp. 114–58.

Hymes, D. 1971. 'On communicative competence', in Pride, J. B. and Holmes, J. (eds.), *Sociolinguistics: Selected Readings*, Harmondsworth: Penguin, pp. 114–58.

Hymes, D. 1974. *Foundations in Sociolinguistics: An Ethnographic Approach*, Philadelphia: University of Pennsylvania Press.

Hymes, D. 1981. *'In Vain I Tried to Tell You': Essays in Native American Ethnopoetics*, Philadelphia: University of Pennsylvania Press.

Jaworski, A. and Thurlow, C. (eds.). 2010. *Semiotic Landscapes: Language, Image, Space*, London: Continuum.

Johnstone, B. 2000. 'The individual voice in language', *Annual Review of Anthropology* 29: 405–24.

Johnstone, B. 2011. 'Dialect enregisterment in performance', *Journal of Sociolinguistics* 15(5): 657–79.

Johnstone, B., Andrus, J. and Danielson, A. E. 2006. 'Mobility, indexicality, and the enregisterment of "Pittsburghese"', *Journal of English Linguistics* 34: 77–101.

Joseph, J. 1987. *Eloquence and Power: The Rise of Language Standards and Standard Languages*, London: Francis Pinter.

Juffermans, K. and Van der Aa, J. 2013. 'Analyzing voice in educational discourses', *Anthropology and Education Quarterly* 44(2): 112–23.

Kallberg, J. 1996. *Chopin at the Boundaries: Sex, History, and Musical Genre*, Cambridge, MA: Harvard University Press.

Kaufman, W. 2015. *Woody Guthrie, American Radical*, Champaign: University of Illinois Press.

Keating, P. and Esposito, C. 2007. 'Linguistic voice quality', *UCLA Working Papers in Phonetics* 105: 85–91.

Kennedy, P. 1975. *Folksongs of Britain and Ireland*, New York: Schirmer Books.

Kirby, S. 2000. 'Syntax without natural selection: how compositionality emerges from vocabulary in a population of learners', in Knight, C., Studdert-Kennedy, M. and Hurford, J. R. (eds.), *The Evolutionary Emergence of Language: Social Function and the Origins of Linguistic Form*, Cambridge: Cambridge University Press, pp. 303–23.

Kirby, S. 2001. 'Spontaneous evolution of linguistic structure: an iterated learning model of the emergence of regularity and irregularity', *IEEE Journal of Evolutionary Computation* 5: 101–10.

Kirby, S. 2002a. 'Learning, bottlenecks and the evolution of recursive syntax', in Briscoe, E. (ed.), *Linguistic Evolution through Language Acquisition: Formal and Computational Models*, Cambridge: Cambridge University Press, pp. 173–204.

Kirby, S. 2002b. 'The emergence of linguistic structure: an overview of the iterated learning model', in Cangelosi, A. and Parisi, D. (eds.), *Simulating the Evolution of Language*, London: Springer, pp. 121–47.

Kittredge, G. L. 1897. 'Francis James Child', in *The English and Scottish Popular Ballads*, Vol. 1. Boston: Houghton Mifflin, pp. xxiii–xxxi.

Kloss, H. 1967. 'Abstand languages and Ausbau language', *Anthropological Linguistics* 9(7): 29–41.

Kogan, N. 1997. 'Reflections on aesthetics and evolution', *Critical Review* 11: 193–210.

Konnikova, M. 2014. 'Oronyms lead to mondegreens (how we mis-hear song lyrics)', *Artsjournal* 10 December .

Kress, G. and Van Leeuwen, T. 2001. *Multimodal Discourse: The Modes and Media of Contemporary Communication*, London: Arnold.

Krumhansl, C. 1997. 'An exploratory study of musical emotions and psychophysiology', *Canadian Journal of Experimental Psychology* 51(4): 336–52.

Labov, W. 1994. *Principles of Linguistic Change: Internal Factors*, Oxford: Blackwell.

Labov, W. 1997. 'Some further steps in narrative analysis', *Journal of Narrative and Life History* 7(1–4): 395–415.

Labov, W. 2001. *Principles of Linguistic Change: Social Factors*, Malden, MA: Blackwell.

Labov, W. 2010. 'Where should I begin?', in Schiffrin, D., De Fina, A. and Anastasia, N. (eds.), *Telling Stories: Language, Narrative and Social Life*, Washington, DC: Georgetown University Press, 7–22.

Labov, W. and Waletzky, J. 1967. 'Narrative analysis: oral versions of personal history', in Helm, J. (ed.), *Essays on the Verbal and Visual Arts*, Seattle: University of Washington Press, pp. 12–44.

Lakoff, G. 2010. 'Why it matters how we frame the environment', *Environmental Communication: A Journal of Nature and Culture* 4(1): 70–81.

Lakoff, G. and Johnson, M. 1980. *Metaphors We Live By*, Chicago: University of Chicago Press.

Lakoff, G. and Johnson, M. 1999. *Philosophy in the Flesh: The Embodied Mind and Its Challenge to Western Thought*, New York: Basic Books.

Lampell, M. 1972. *A Tribute to Woody Guthrie*, New York: Ludlow Music.

Leith, D. 1988. 'A pragmatic approach to ballad dialogue', in van Peer, W. (ed.), *The Taming of the Text: Explorations in Language, Literature and Culture*, New York: Routledge, pp. 35–60.

Leppänen, S., Kytölä, S., Jousmäki, H., Peuronen, S. and Westinen, E. 2013. 'Entextualization and resemiotization as resources for identification in social media', in Seargeant, P. and Tagg, C. (eds.), *The Language of Social Media: Communication and Community on the Internet*, Basingstoke: Palgrave, pp. 112–36.

Levitin, D. J. 2008 [2006]. *This Is Your Brain on Music: Understanding a Human Obsession*, London: Atlantic Books.

Lloyd, A. L. 1952. *Come All Ye Bold Miners*, London: Lawrence and Wishart.

Lloyd, A. L. 1967. *Folk Song in England*, London: Lawrence and Wishart.

Locher, M. and Watts, R. J. 2005. 'Politeness theory and relational work', *Journal of Politeness Research* 1(1): 9–33.

Lomax, A. 1964 [1974]. *The Penguin Book of American Folk Songs*, Baltimore: Penguin.

Lomax, J. A. and Lomax, A. 1975 [1940]. *Folk Song U.S.A: The 111 Best American Ballads*, New York: Signet.

Lord, A. B. 2000 [1960]. *The Singer of Tales*, second edition ed. by Stephen Mitchell and Gregory Nagy, Cambridge, MA: Harvard University Press.

MacColl, E. and Seeger, P. 1977. *Travellers' Songs from England and Scotland*, Knoxville: University of Tennessee Press.

Machin, D. 2007. *Introduction to Multimodal Analysis*, London: Hodder Education.

Machin, D. and Jaworski, A. 2006. 'The use of film archive footage to symbolise news events', *Visual Communication* 5(3): 345–66.

Machin, D. and Polzer, L. 2015. *Visual Journalism*, Basingstoke: Palgrave Macmillan.

MacKinnon, N. 1993. *The British Folk Scene: Musical Performance and Social Identity*, Buckingham: Open University Press.

Martinec, R. and van Leeuwen, T. 2009. *The Language of New Media Design: Theory and Practice*, Abingdon: Routledge.

Mattheier, K. 2010. 'Is there a European language history?', *Multilingua* 29(3/4): 353–60.

Maybin, J. 2001. 'Language, struggle and voice: the Bakhtin/Volsinov writings', in Wetherell, M., Taylor, S. and Yates, S. (eds.), *Discourse Theory and Practice: A Reader*, London: Sage, pp. 64–71.

McNeill, W. H. 1995. *Keeping Together in Time: Dance and Drill in Human History*, Cambridge, MA: Harvard University Press.

Merker, B. 2012. 'The vocal learning constellation: imitation, ritual culture, encephalization', in Bannan, N. (ed.), *Music, Language and Human Evolution*, Oxford: Oxford University Press, pp. 215–60.

Middleton, R. 2006. *Voicing the Popular: On the Subjects of Popular Music*, London: Routledge.

Miller, G. 1997. 'How mate choice shaped human nature: a review of sexual selection and human evolution', in Crawford, C. and Krebs, D. L. (eds.), *Handbook of Evolutionary Psychology: Ideas, Issues and Applications*, Mahwah, NJ: Lawrence Erlbaum Associates, pp. 329–60.

Miller, L. 1989. *Musical Savants: Exceptional Skill in the Mentally Retarded*, Hillsdale, NJ: Lawrence Erlbaum.

Milroy, J. 1999. 'The consequences of standardisation in descriptive linguistics', in Bex, A. and Watts, R. J. (eds.), *Standard English: The Widening Debate*, London: Routledge, pp. 16–39.

Milroy, J. and Milroy, L. 2012 [1985]. *Authority in Language: Investigating Standard English*, fourth edition, Abingdon: Routledge.

Mitford, M. R. 1824–32. *Sketches of English Life and Character*, Edinburgh and London: T. N. Foulis.

Mithen, S. 2006 [2005]. *The Singing Neanderthals: The Origins of Music, Language, Mind, and Body*, Cambridge, MA.: Harvard University Press.

Morley, I. 2012. 'Hominin physiological evolution and the emergence of musical capacities', in Bannan, N. (ed.), *Music, Language and Human Evolution*, Oxford: Oxford University Press, pp. 109–41.

Morris, W. 2004 [1890]. *News from Nowhere*, North Chelmsford: Courier Corporation.

Munroe, A. 1971. 'Johnny, my man', *Tocher* 1: 16–17.

Naumann, H. 1922. *Grundzüge der deutschen Volkskunde*, Leipzig: Quelle und Meyer.

Nettl, B. 2005 [1983]. *The Study of Ethnomusicology: Thirty-one Issues and Concepts*, new edition, Urbana and Chicago: University of Illinois Press.

Nystrand, M. 1982. *What Writers Know: The Language, Process, and Structure of Written Discourse*, New York: Academic Press.

Palmer, R. (ed.). 1972. *Songs of the Midlands*, Wakefield: EP Publishing.

Palmer, R. 1990. *'What a Lovely War!' British Soldiers' Songs from the Boer War to the Present Day*, London: Michael Joseph.

Parry, M. 1930. 'Studies in the epic technique of oral verse-making. I. Homer and Homeric style', *Harvard Studies in Classical Philology* 41: 73–147.

Parry, M. 1932. 'Studies in the epic technique of oral verse-making. II. The Homeric language and the language of oral poetry', *Harvard Studies in Classical Philology* 43: 1–50.

Partington, J. S. (ed.). 2011. *Life, Music and Thought of Woody Guthrie*, Farnham: Ashgate.

Patel, A. D. 2008. *Music, Language, and the Brain*, New York: Oxford University Press.

Peacock, J. 2009 [1805]. *A Favourite Collection of Tunes with Variations: Adapted for the Northumberland Small Pipes, Violin or Flute*, Fornovo: Pelliccioni.

Pegg, R. 1976. *Folk: A Portrait of English Traditional Music, Musicians and Customs*, London: Wildwood House Ltd.

Pegler, M. 2014. *Soldiers' Songs and Slang of the Great War*, Oxford: Osprey Publishing.

Pelucchi, B., Hay, J. F. and Saffran, J. R. 2009. 'Statistical learning in a natural language by 8-month-old infants', *Child Development* 80(3): 674–85.

Percy, T. 1765. *Reliques of Ancient English Poetry*, London: J. Dodsley.

Peretz, I. 1993. 'Auditory atonalia for melodies', *Cognitive Neuropsychology* 10(1): 21–56.

Peretz, I. 2003. 'Brain specialization for music: new evidence from congenital amusia', in Peretz, I. and Zatorre, R. (eds.), *The Cognitive Neuroscience of Music*, Oxford: Oxford University Press: pp. 247–68.

Peretz, I., Ayotte, J., Zatorre, R. J., Mehler, J., Ahad, P. Penhune, B. and Jutras, B. 2002. 'Congenital amusia: a disorder of fine-grained pitch discrimination', *Neuron* 33: 185–91.

Peterson, C. and McCabe, A. 1983. *Developmental Psycholinguistics: Three Ways of Looking at a Child's Narrative*, New York: Plenum Press.

Petridis, A. 2015. 'Ed Sheeran review: a singer, an acoustic guitar, an effects pedal – a triumph', www.theguardian.com/music/2015/jul/12/ed-sheeran-singer-acoustic-guitar-effects-pedal-complete-triumph, accessed 15 September 2015.

Pietsch, M. 2015. 'Archaism and dialect in Irish emigrant letters', in Auer, A., Schreier, D. and Watts, R. J. (eds.), *Letter Writing and Language Change*, Cambridge: Cambridge University Press.

Pinker, S. 1997. *How the Mind Works*, New York: W. W. Norton & Company.

Posen, I. S. 1993. 'On folk festivals and kitchens: questions of authenticity in the folksong revival', in Rosenberg, N. V. (ed.), *Transforming Tradition: Folk Music Revivals Examined*, pp. 127–36.

Pound, L. 1913. 'The southwestern cowboy songs and the English and Scottish popular ballads', *Modern Philology* 11(2): 195–207.

Pound, L. 1916. 'New World analogues of the English and Scottish popular ballads', *The Midwest Quarterly* III(3): 171–87.

Purslow, F. (ed.). 1965. *Marrow Bones: English Folk Songs from the Hammond and Gardiner MSS*, London: EFDSS Publications.

Rampton, B. 1998. 'Speech community', in Verschueren, J., Östman, J.-O., Blommaert, J. and Bulcaen, C. (eds.), *Handbook of Pragmatics Online*, www.benjamins.com /online.

Rampton, B. 2003. 'Hegemony, social class and stylisation', *Pragmatics* 13(1): 49–83.

Ravenscroft, T. 1609. *Deuteromelia: or the Second part of Musicks melodie, etc.*, London: Printed for Thomas Adams.

Reynolds, S. 1909. *A Poor Man's House*, London: Bodley Head.

Rhys, E. 1906. *Ernest Rhys Manuscript Material*, ed. H. Buxton Forman, in Carl H. Pforzheimer Collection of Shelley and His Circle: Manuscripts, 1772–1925.

Rindler Schjerve, R. (ed.). 2003. *Diglossia and Power*, Berlin: Mouton de Gruyter.

Ritson, J. 1783. *A Select Collection of English Songs*, London: J. Johnson.

Rosenberg, N. V. (ed.). 1993. *Transforming Tradition: Folk Music Revivals Examined*, Urbana and Chicago: University of Illinois Press.

Rosselson, L. 1974. *That's Not the Way It's Got To Be: Fifty More Songs By Leon Rosselson*, London: Sing Publications.

Roud, S. 2011. *Chorus and Verse: The Challenges of Designing the Roud Folk Song Index*, Washington, DC: The American Folklife Center at the Library of Congress.

Roud, S. and Bishop, J. 2012. *The New Penguin Book of English Folk Songs*, London: Penguin.

Rousseau, J.-J. 1781. *Essai sur l'origine des langues*.

Royce, A. P. 1984. *Movement and Meaning: Creativity and Interpretation in Ballet and Mime*, Bloomington: Indiana University Press.

Royce, A. P. 2004. *Anthropology of the Performing Arts: Artistry, Virtuosity, and Interpretation*, Walnut Creek, CA: AltaMira Press.

Russell, D. 1997 [1987]. *Popular Music in England, 1840–1914: A Social History*, Manchester: Manchester University Press.

Sachs, C. 1962. *The Wellsprings of Music*, The Hague: Nijhoff.

Sacks, O. 2007. *Musicophilia: Tales of Music and the Brain*, New York: Vintage Books.

Saffran, J. R. 2003. 'Absolute pitch in infancy and adulthood: the role of tonal structure', *Developmental Science* 6: 35–47.

Saffran, J. R., Johnson, E. K., Aslin, R. N. and Newport, E. L. 1999. 'Statistical learning of tone sequences by human infants and adults', *Cognition* 70: 27–52.

Saffran, J. R., Werker, J. F and Werner, L. A. 2006. 'The infant's auditory world: hearing, speech, and the beginnings of language', in Siegler, R. and Kuhn, D. (eds.), *Handbook of Child Development*, New York: Wiley, pp. 58–108.

Said, E. 1993. *Culture and Imperialism*, London: Chatto and Windus.

Sargent, H. C. and Kittredge, G. L. (eds.). 1904. *English and Scottish Popular Ballads, the Cambridge Edition*, London: David Nutt.

Scannell, P. [1998] 2002. 'Media–language–world', in Bell, A. and Garrett, P. (eds.), *Approaches to Media Discourse*, Oxford: Blackwell, pp. 251–67.

Schechner, R. 1977. *Essays on Performance Theory 1970–1976*, New York: Drama Book Specialists.

Schechner, R. 1985. *Between Theater and Anthropology*, Philadelphia: University of Pennsylvania Press.

Schechner, R. and Appel, W. (eds.). 1990. *By Means of Performance: Intercultural Studies of Theatre and Ritual*, Cambridge: Cambridge University Press.

Scherer, K. R. and Zentner, M. R. 2001. 'Emotional effects of music: production rules', in Juslin, P. N. and Sloboda, J. A. (eds.), *Music and Emotion: Theory and Research*, Oxford: Oxford University Press, pp. 361–92.

Scott, W. 1802–3. *The Minstrelsy of the Scottish Border*, 2 vols., Edinburgh: J. Ballantine.

Seeger, C. 1958. 'Prescriptive and descriptive music-writing', *The Musical Quarterly* 44(2): 1845–95.

Seeger, P. and Reiser, R. 1985. *Carry It On!: The Story of America's Working People in Song and Picture*, Bethlehem, PA: Sing Out Corp.

Sharp, C. 1907. *English Folk Song, Some Conclusions*, London: Simpkin and Co.

Shepard, L. 1962. *The Broadside Ballad: The Development of the Street Ballad from the Traditional Song to Popular Newspaper*, London: Herbert Jenkins Ltd.

Shepard, L. 1973. *The History of Street Literature*, Newton Abbot: David and Charles.

Silber, I., Nelson, P., Raim, E., Seeger, P., Silverman, J. and Traum, H. (eds.). 1992. *The Collected Reprints from Sing Out! The Folk Song Magazine, Vols. 7–12, 1964–1973*, Bethlehem PA: Sing Out Corporation.

Silverstein, M. 2003. 'Indexical order and the dialectics of sociolinguistic life', *Language and Communication* 23: 193–229.

Simpson, C. M. 1966. *The British Broadside Ballad and Its Music*, New Brunswick, NJ: Rutgers University Press.

Simpson, P. 1999. 'Language, culture and identity: with (another) look at accents in pop and rock singing', *Multilingua* 18(4): 343–67.

Small, C. 1998. *Musicking: The Meanings of Performing and Listening*, Middletown, CT: Wesleyan University Press.

Sperber, D. 1996. *Explaining Culture: A Naturalistic Approach*, Oxford: Blackwell.

Swales, J. 1990. *Genre Analysis: English in Academic and Research Settings*, Cambridge: Cambridge University Press.

Sweers, B. 2005. *Electric Folk: The Changing Face of English Traditional Music*, Oxford and New York: Oxford University Press.

Synge, J. M. 1997 [1907]. *The Playboy of the Western World*, London: Nick Hern Books.

Taruskin, R. 1995. *Text and Act: Essays on Music and Performance*, New York: Oxford University Press.

Thomas, D. 1995. *Music and the Origins of Language: Theories from the French Enlightenment*, Cambridge: Cambridge University Press.

Tocher. 1971. Vol. 1, 'Miscellany, from Shetland to Galloway: with ballads, tales and anecdotes of pipers etc. and Gaelic songs, four from Mrs Annie Arnott, Skye', University of Edinburgh, School of Scottish Studies.

Trehub, S. E. 2001. 'Musical predispositions in infancy', *Annals of the New York Academy of Sciences* 930(1): 1–16.

Trehub, S. E. and Schellenberg, E. G. 1995. 'Music: its relevance to infants', *Annals of Child Development* 11: 1–24.

Trehub, S. E. and Trainor, L. J. 1998. 'Singing to infants: lullabies and playsongs', *Advances in Infancy Research* 12: 43–77.

Trudgill, P. 1983. 'Acts of conflicting identity: the sociolinguistics of British pop-song pronunciation', in Trudgill, P. (ed.), *On Dialect: Social and Geographical Perspectives*, Oxford: Blackwell, pp. 141–60.

Turner, V. 1969. *The Ritual Practice*, London: Aldine.

Turner, V. 1982. *From Ritual to Theater: The Human Seriousness of Play*, North Boston, NY: PAJ Books.

Turner, V. 1987. *The Anthropology of Performance*, New York: PAJ Publications.

Uther, H.-J. 2004. *The Types of International Folk Tales: A Classification and Bibliography: Based on the System of Antti Aarne and Stith Thompson*, Helsinki: Suomalainen Tiedeakatemia.

van Gennep, A. 1960 [1909]. *The Rites of Passage*, ed. Vizedom, M. B. and Caffee, G. L.,London: Routledge.

van Leeuwen, T. 1999. *Speech, Music, Sound*, London: Macmillan.

van Leeuwen, T. 2005. *Introducing Social Semiotics*, New York: Routledge.

van Leeuwen, T. 2006. *Reading Images: The Grammar of Visual Design*, Abingdon: Routledge.

Vanghan Williams, R. and Lloyd, A. L. (eds.) 1959. *The Penguin Book of English Folk Songs*, Harmondsworth: Penguin.

Vicinus, M. 1974. *The Industrial Muse*, London: Croom Helm.

von Greyerz, O. (ed.) 2008 [1908–25]. *Im Röseligarte: Schweizer Volkslieder*, Bern: Zytglogge.

Wales, K. 2006. *Northern English: A Social and Cultural History*, Cambridge: Cambridge University Press.

Watts, R. J. 1982. *The Pragmalinguistic Analysis of Narrative Texts: Narrative Co-operation in Charles Dickens' Hard Times*, Tübingen: Gunter Narr.

Watts, R. J. 1991. *Power in Family Discourse*, Berlin: Mouton de Gruyter.

Watts, R. J. 2010. 'Using folk songs as a source of dialect change? The perrasire effect of attitudes', *Multilingua* 29: 307–35.

Watts, R. J. 2011. *Language Myths and the History of English*, New York: Oxford University Press.

Watts, R. J. 2012a. 'A socio-cognitive approach to historical politeness', in Bax, M. and Kádár, D. (eds.), *Understanding Historical (Im)Politeness*, Amsterdam. Benjamins, pp. 103–30.

Watts, R. J. 2012b. 'The actuation problem revisited', in Bergs, A. and Brinton, L. (eds.), *English Historical Linguistics: An International Handbook*, Berlin and New York: Mouton de Gruyter.

Weiss, M. W., Trehub, S. E. and Schellenberg, E. G. 2012. '"Something in the way she sings": Enhanced memory for vocal melodies', *Psychological Science* 23: 1074–78.

Wells, J. C. 1984. *Accents of English, Vols. 1–3*, Cambridge: Cambridge University Press.

Welsford, H. 1845. *On the Origin and Ramifications of the English Language*, London: Longman, Brown, Green and Longmans.

Wenger, E. 1998. *Communities of Practice: Learning, Meaning, and Identity*, Cambridge: Cambridge University Press.

Wier, E. 1913. *The Ideal Home Music Library. Vol. IX, Sentimental Songs*, New York: C. Scribner's Sons, pp. 152–53.

Williamson, V. 2014. *You Are the Music: How Music Reveals What It Means to Be Human*. London: Icon Books.

Winkler, A. M. 2009. *To Everything There Is a Season: Pete Seeger and the Power of Song*, New York: Oxford University Press.

Wray, A. 1998. 'Protolanguage as a holistic system for social interaction', *Language and Communication* 18: 47–67.

Wray, A. 2000. 'Holistic utterances in protolanguage: the link from primates to humans', in Knight, C., Studdert-Kennedy, M. and Hurf, J. R. (eds.), *The Evolutionary Emergence of Language: Social Function and the Origins of Linguistic Form*, Cambridge: Cambridge University Press, pp. 285–302.

Wray, A. 2002a. *Formulaic Language and the Lexicon*, Cambridge: Cambridge University Press.

Wray, A. 2002b. *The Transition to Language*, Oxford: Oxford University Press.

Wright, S. 1954. 'The death of Lady Mondegreen', *Harper's*, November.

Young, R. 2010. *Electric Eden: Unearthing Britain's Visionary Music*, New York: Faber and Faber, Inc.

Zentner, M. and Kagan, J. 1998. 'Infants' perception of consonance and dissonance in music', *Infant Behavior and Development* 21: 483–92.

Zimmermann, G. D. 1967. *Songs of Irish Rebellion: Political Street Ballads and Rebel Songs, 1780–1900*, Hatboro, PA: Folklore Associates.

Index

Lightning Source UK Ltd.
Milton Keynes UK
UKHW020913050722
405333UK00017B/253